Origami Dinosaurs of the Ancient World

35 Majestic Creatures from Deep Time

Books by John Montroll
www.johnmontroll.com
Instagram: @montrollorigami

Origami Symphonies

Origami Symphony No. 1: The Elephant's Trumpet Call
Origami Symphony No. 2: Trio of Sharks & Playful Prehistoric Mammals
Origami Symphony No. 3: Duet of Majestic Dragons & Dinosaurs
Origami Symphony No. 4: Capturing Vibrant Coral Reef Fish
Origami Symphony No. 5: Woodwinds, Horns, and a Moose
Origami Symphony No. 6: Striped Snakes Changing Scales
Origami Symphony No. 7: Musical Monkeys
Origami Symphony No. 8: An Octet of Cats
Origami Symphony No. 9: Ode to Australia
Origami Symphony No. 10: Lucky & Dangerous Sides of Origami
Origami Symphony No. 11: Folding on Land, Air and Sea
Origami Symphony No. 12: Where are the Gnomes?

Animal Origami

Jungle Origami
Arctic Animals in Origami
Origami Aquarium
Dogs in Origami
Perfect Pets Origami
Dragons and Other Fantastic Creatures in Origami
Bugs in Origami
Horses in Origami: Second Edition
Origami Birds: Second Edition
Origami Gone Wild
Mythological Creatures and the Chinese Zodiac Origami
Origami Sea Life: Third Edition
Bringing Origami to Life: Second Edition
Origami Sculptures: Fourth Edition
African Animals in Origami: Third Edition
North American Animals in Origami: Third Edition
Origami for the Enthusiast: Second Edition
Animal Origami for the Enthusiast: Second Edition

Geometric Origami

The Magic of Origami Polyhedra
Origami Stars: Second Edition
Galaxy of Origami Stars: Second Edition
Origami and Math: Simple to Complex: Second Edition
Origami & Geometry
3D Origami Platonic Solids & More: Second Edition
3D Origami Diamonds
3D Origami Antidiamonds
3D Origami Pyramids
A Plethora of Polyhedra in Origami: Third Edition
Classic Polyhedra Origami
A Constellation of Origami Polyhedra
Origami Polyhedra Design

General Origami

Magical Origami Gnomes: 38 Gnomes. Infinite Fun.
Origami Gnomes of the Forest Wonderland: Crafting 41 Gnomes, Mushrooms, & Forest Creatures
Origami Fold-by-Fold
DC Super Heroes Origami
Origami Worldwide
Teach Yourself Origami: Third Edition
Christmas Origami: Second Edition
Storytime Origami
Origami Inside-Out: Third Edition

Dinosaurs in Origami

Origami Dinosaurs of the Ancient World:35 Majestic Creatures from Deep Time
Dinosaur Origami
Origami Dinosaurs for Beginners
Prehistoric Origami: Dinosaurs and other Creatures: Third Edition

Dollar Bill Origami

Dollar Origami Treasures: Second Edition
Dollar Bill Animals in Origami: Second Revised Edition
Dollar Bill Origami
Easy Dollar Bill Origami

Simple Origami

Fun and Simple Origami: 101 Easy-to-Fold Projects: Second Edition
Origami Twelve Days of Christmas: And Santa, Too!
Super Simple Origami
Easy Dollar Bill Origami
Easy Origami
Easy Origami 2
Easy Origami 3
Easy Origami Coloring Book
Easy Origami Animals
Easy Origami Polar Animals
Easy Origami Ocean Animals
Easy Origami Woodland Animals
Easy Origami Jungle Animals
Meditative Origami

Origami Dinosaurs of the Ancient World

35 Majestic Creatures from Deep Time

John Montroll

Antroll Publishing Company

To Josh and Melanie

Origami Dinosaurs of the Ancient World: *35 Majesctic Creatures from Deep Time*

ISBN-10: 1-877656-77-1
ISBN-13: 978-1-877656-77-4

Antroll Publishing Company

Introduction

This book invites you to fold the giants of the ancient world.

Within these pages, you will learn to fold 35 dinosaurs, each formed from a single square sheet of paper. Every design captures a unique personality—gentle giants, fearsome hunters, and steadfast defenders—brought to life through thoughtful folds and careful shaping. While the models range from simple to complex, most are designed at an intermediate level. Curious beginners will find much to enjoy, and experienced folders will appreciate the creativity and challenge throughout.

All of the models are original designs by origami master John Montroll. Each dinosaur begins with a photograph and a brief introduction to set the stage. Clear, step-by-step illustrations guide you through every fold. Great care has been taken to keep each model as simple as possible while preserving the details that give it character and presence.

Your journey through deep time unfolds across five chapters:

Welcome to the Ancient World — From a baby dinosaur to a young Stegosaurus, these simpler models introduce key techniques and prepare you for the adventure ahead.

Long-Necked Titans — A procession of mighty sauropods leads you deeper into prehistoric lands, where balance, proportion, and sweeping forms take center stage.

The Great Two-Legged Walkers — Powerful theropods stride forward with energy and authority, challenging the folder to capture motion, strength, and presence.

Wings Over the Ancient World — Take to the skies with four pterosaurs and explore the ancient shores and forests.

Crests, Plates, and Horned Legends — Meet some of the most celebrated dinosaurs, adorned with dramatic ornaments that challenge your precision and reward careful shaping.

Most of the models can be folded from 6- or 7-inch origami paper, though 10-inch paper beautifully captures their scale and presence. The more complex designs are especially well-suited to larger paper, allowing their details to emerge more clearly.

The diagrams are drawn in the internationally approved Randlett-Yoshizawa style. Origami supplies can be found in arts and craft shops, or at Dover Publications online: www.doverpublications.com. You can also visit OrigamiUSA at www.origamiusa.org for origami supplies and other related information including an extensive list of local, national, and international origami groups.

Please follow me on Instagram @montrollorigami to see posts of my origami.

Enter the ancient world.

John Montroll
www.johnmontroll.com

Contents

Welcoming the Young Giants

The Long-Necked Titans

The Great Two-Legged Walkers

More ➡

Wings Over the Ancient World

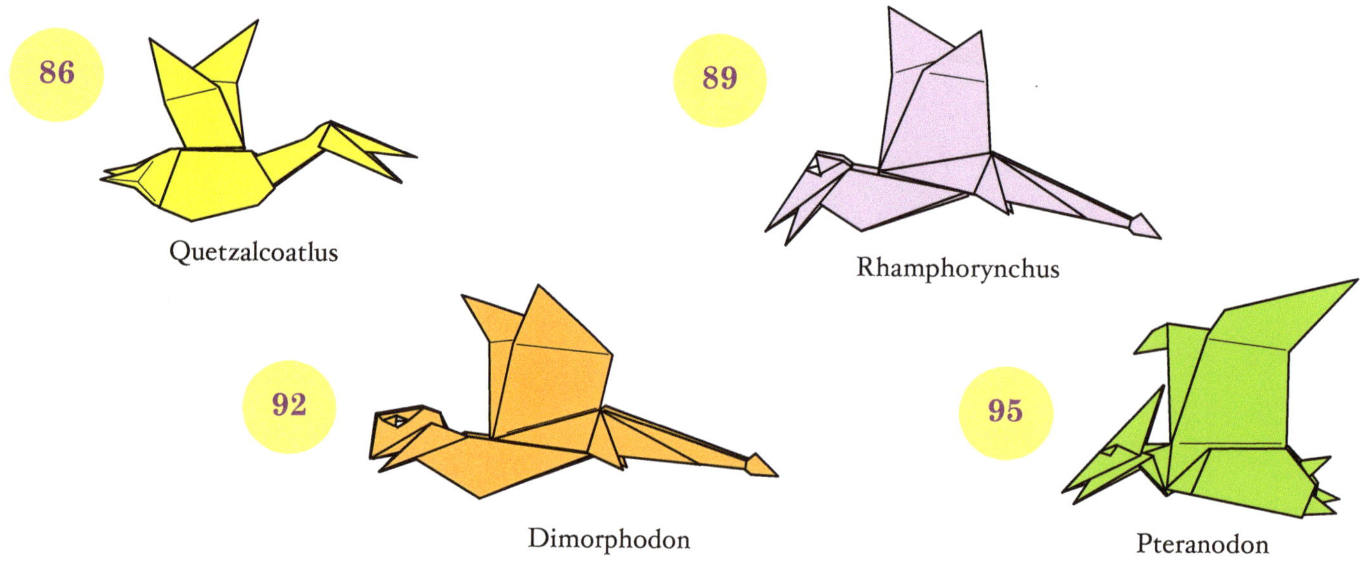

86 Quetzalcoatlus

89 Rhamphorynchus

92 Dimorphodon

95 Pteranodon

Crests, Plates, & Horned Legends

99 Protoceratops

102 Monoclonius

105 Triceratops

108 Styracosaurus

111 Graciliceratops

114 Tianchisaurus

117 Anoplosaurus

122 Stegosaurus

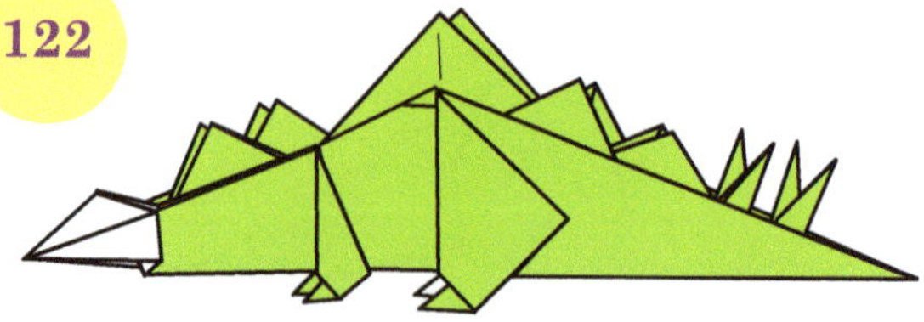

Symbols

Lines

Valley fold, fold in front.

Mountain fold, fold behind.

Crease line.

X-ray or guide line.

Arrows

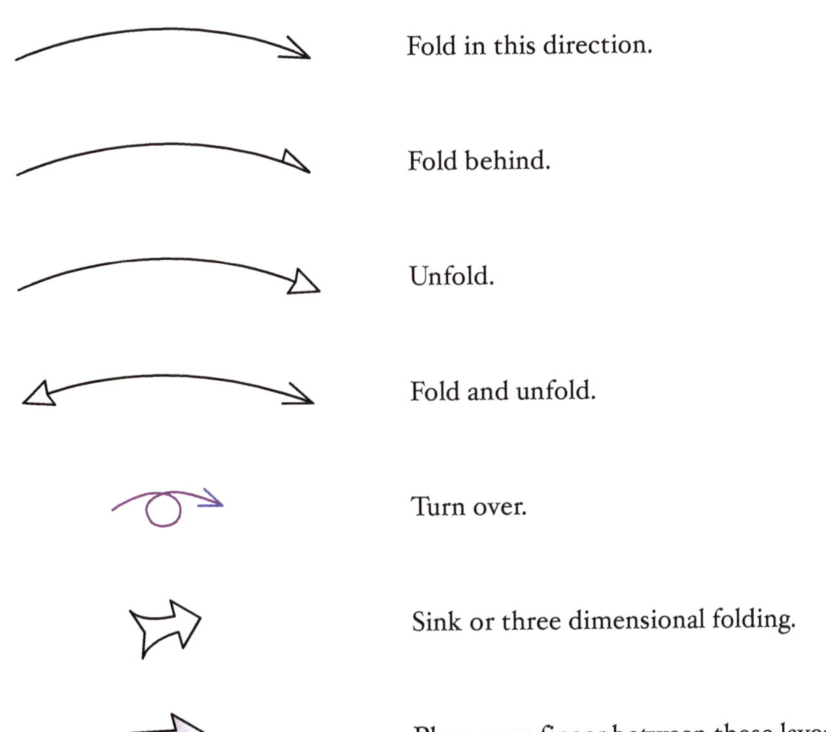

Fold in this direction.

Fold behind.

Unfold.

Fold and unfold.

Turn over.

Sink or three dimensional folding.

Place your finger between these layers.

Basic Folds

Pleat Fold.

Fold back and forth. Each pleat is composed of one valley and mountain fold. Here are two examples.

1

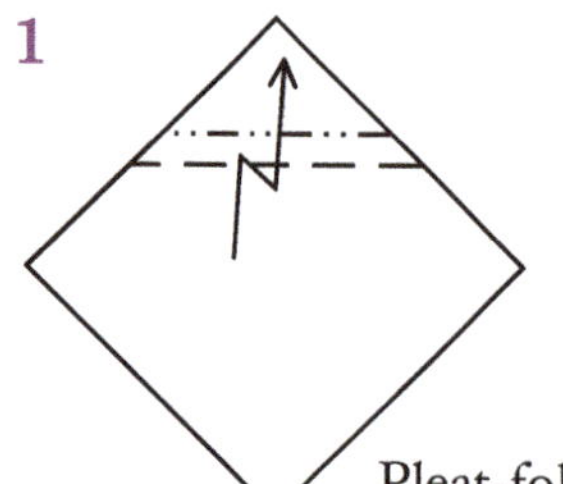

Pleat-fold.

2

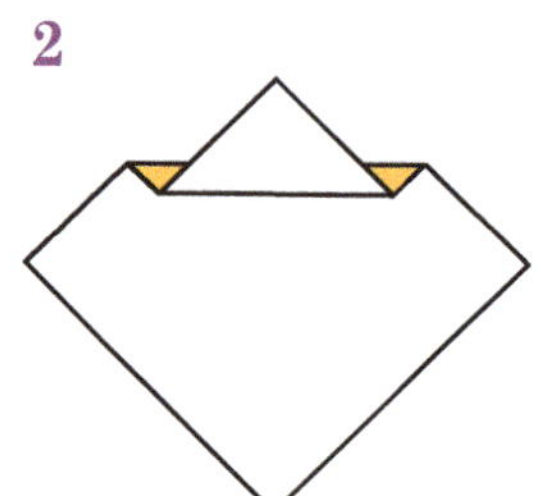

1

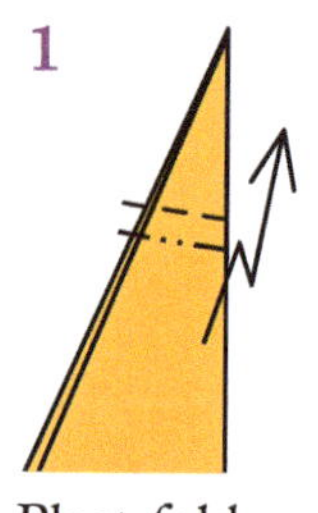

Pleat-fold.

2

Squash Fold.

In a squash fold, some paper is opened and then made flat. The shaded arrow shows where to place your finger.

1

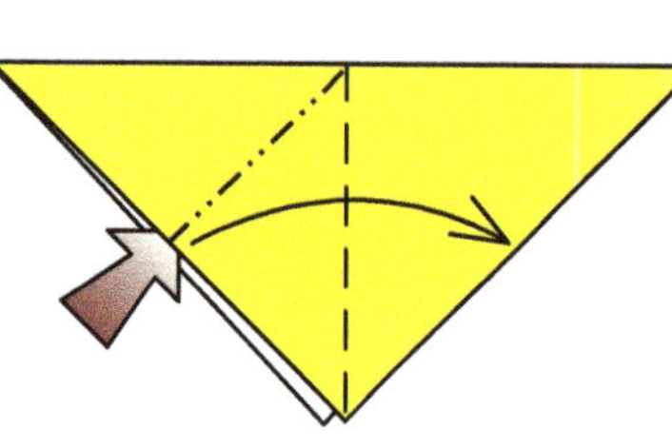

Squash-fold.

2

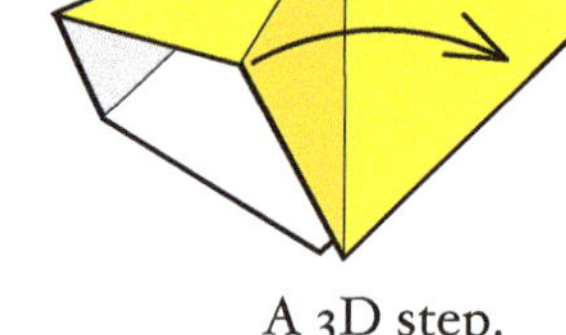

A 3D step.

3

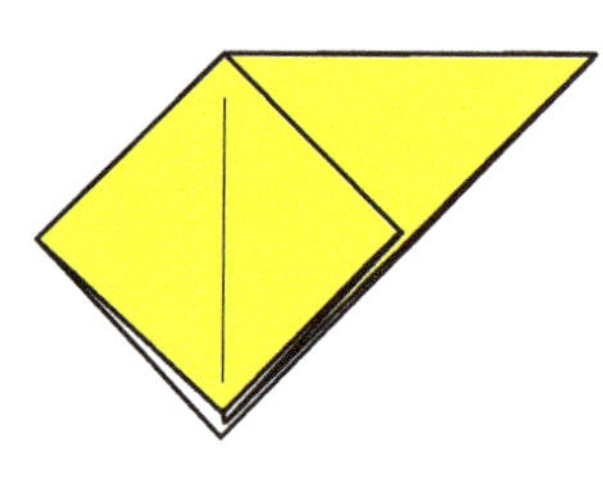

Petal Fold.

In a petal fold, one point is folded up while two opposite sides meet each other.

1

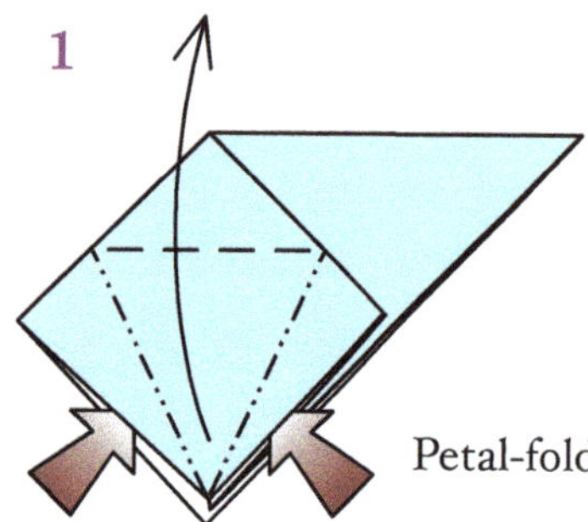

Petal-fold.

2

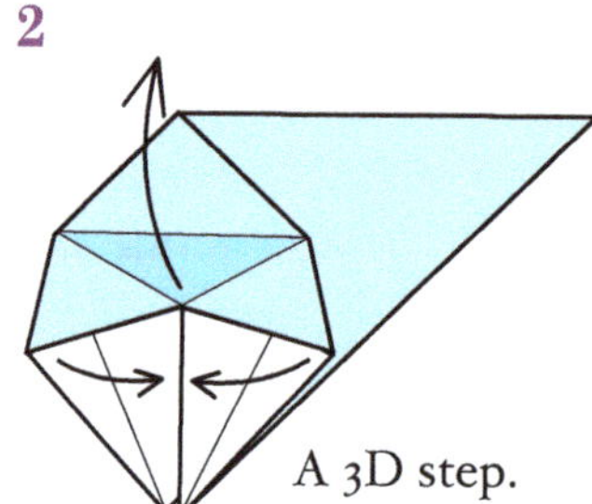

A 3D step.

3

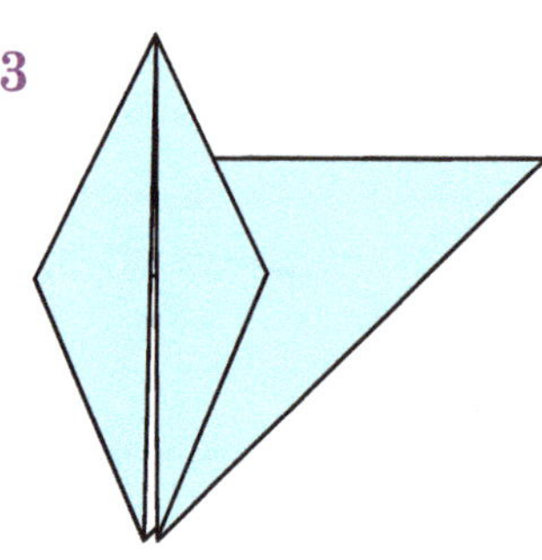

Rabbit Ear.

To fold a rabbit ear, one corner is folded in half and laid down to a side.

1

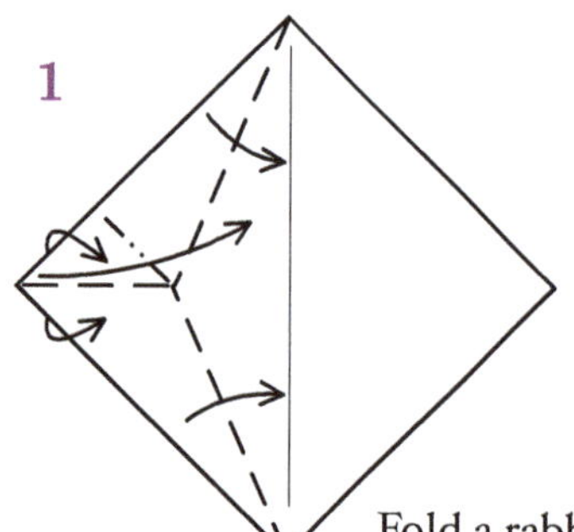

Fold a rabbit ear.

2

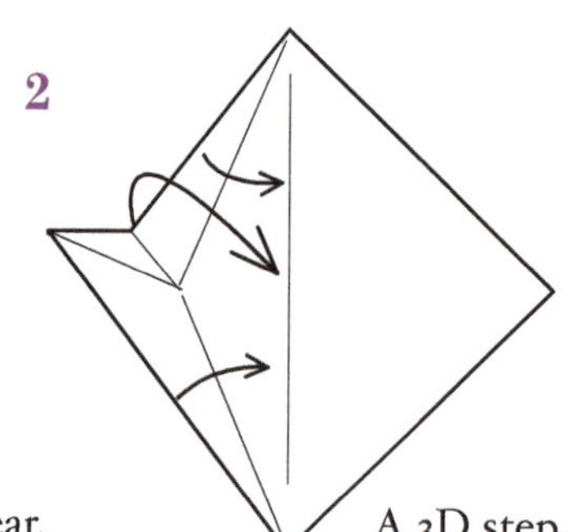

A 3D step.

3

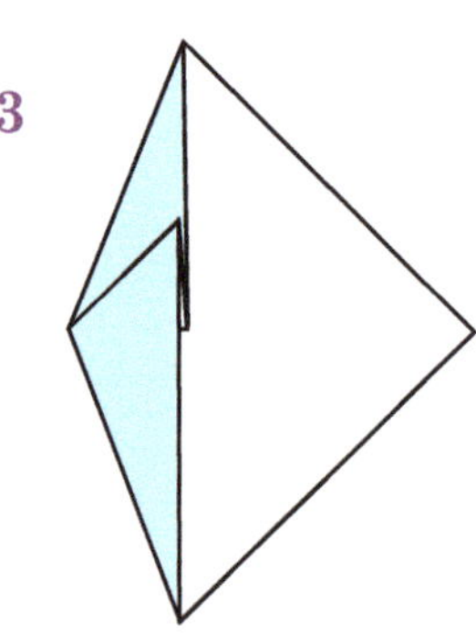

Double Rabbit Ear.

If you were to bend a straw you would be folding the double rabbit ear.

1

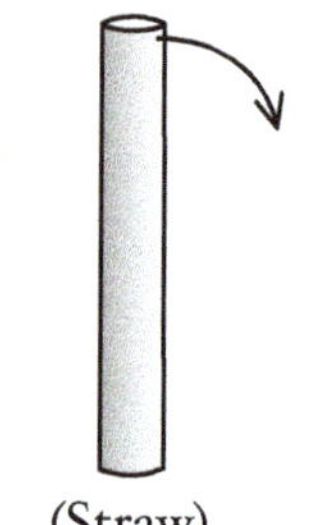

(Straw)

2

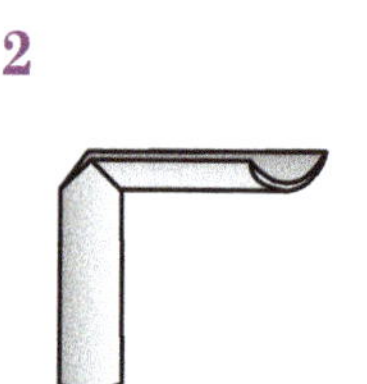

1

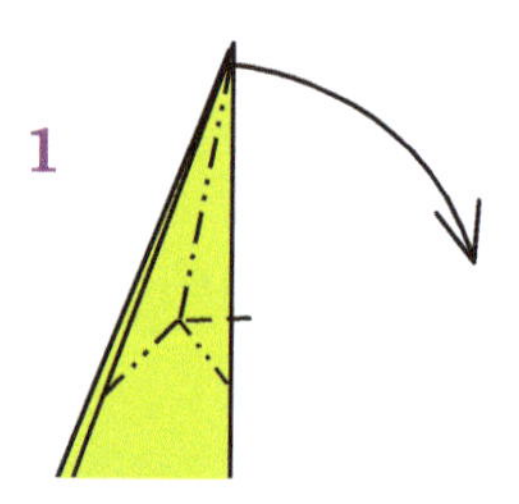

Double-rabbit-ear.

2

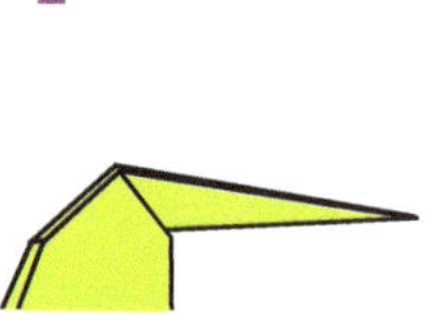

Inside Reverse Fold.

In an inside reverse fold, some paper is folded between layers. Here are two examples.

1

Reverse-fold.

2

1

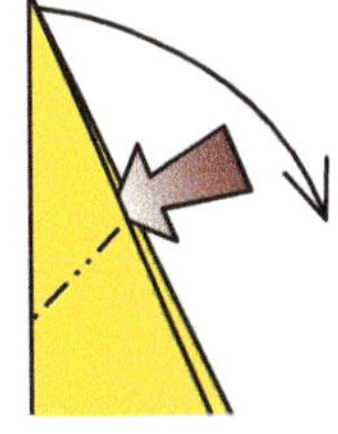

Reverse-fold.

2

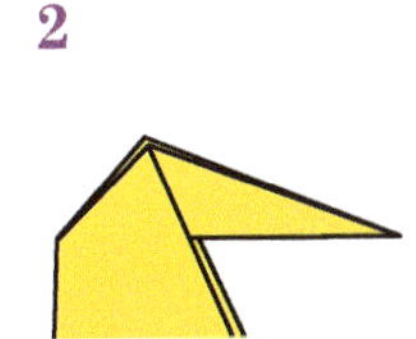

Outside Reverse Fold.

Much of the paper must be unfolded to make an outside reverse fold.

1

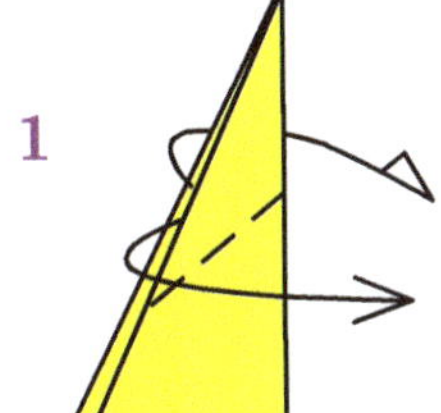

Outside-reverse-fold.

2

Crimp Fold.

A crimp fold is a combination of two reverse folds. Open the model slightly to form the crimp evenly on each side. Here are two examples.

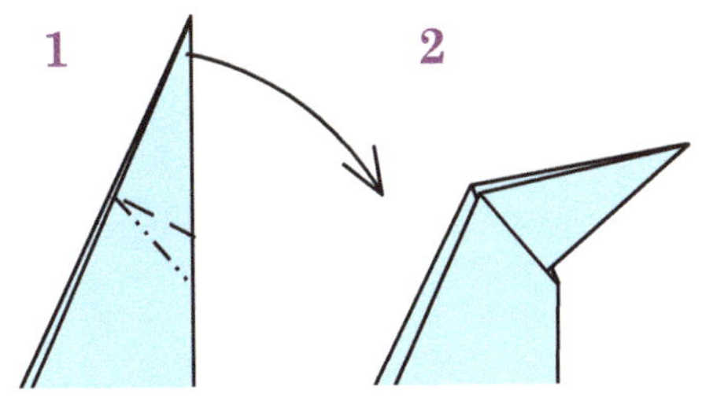

Crimp-fold.

1

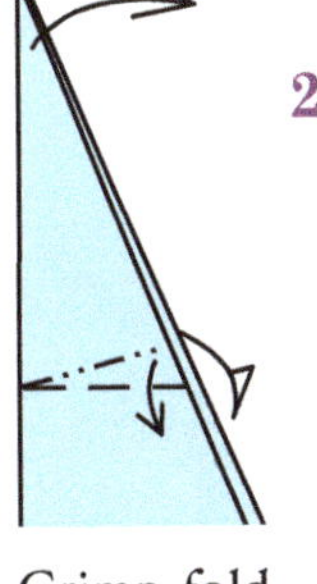

Crimp-fold.

2

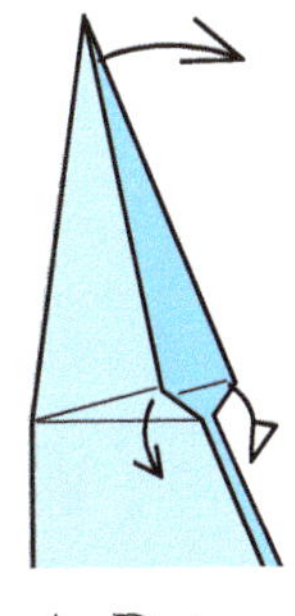

A 3D step.

3

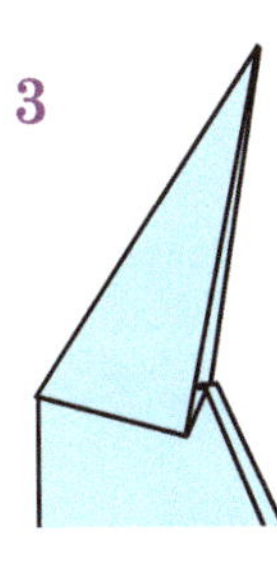

Sink.

For a sink, some of the paper without edges is folded inside. To do this fold, much of the model must be unfolded.

1

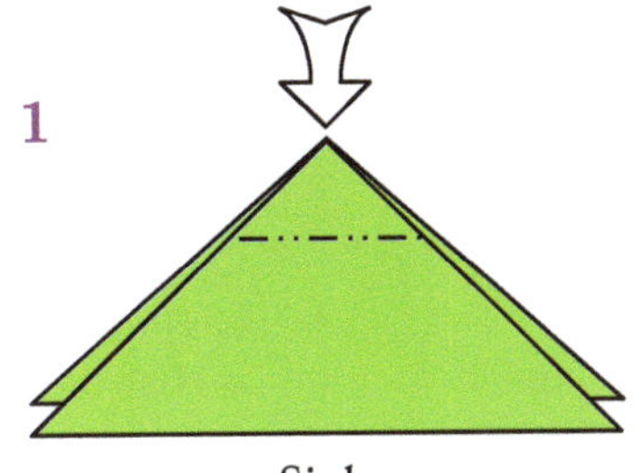

Sink.

2

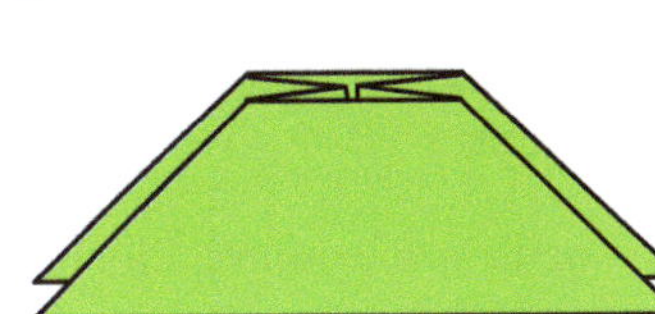

Spread Squash Fold.

A cross between a squash fold and sink fold, some paper in the center is spread apart and then made flat.

1

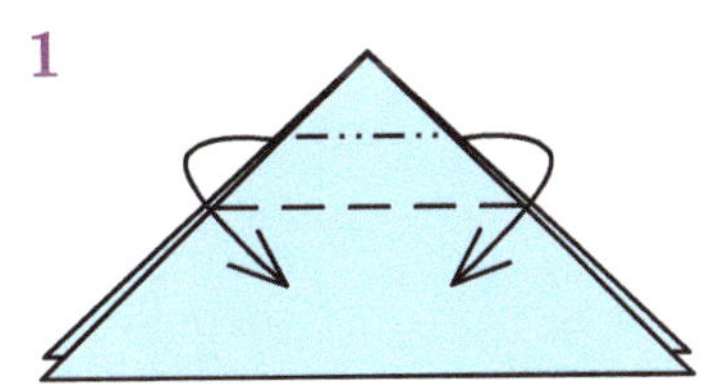

Spread-squash-fold.

2

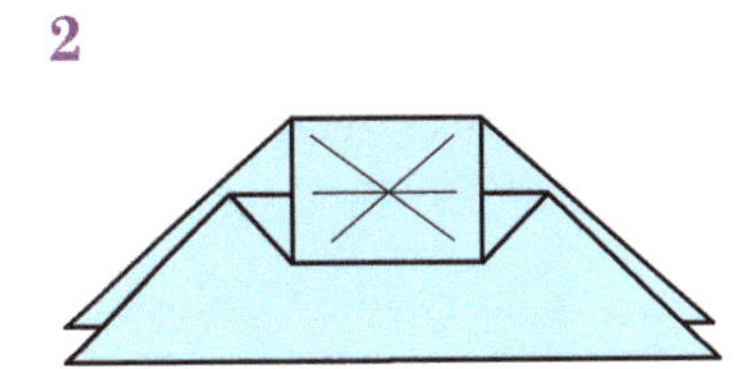

Appreciating Dinosaurs of the Ancient World

The ancient world was filled with creatures that walked, ran, flew, and defended themselves in breathtaking ways. Dinosaurs came in every size and shape, from tiny hatchlings to towering giants, each perfectly suited to its environment.

Even the smallest dinosaurs, like baby hatchlings and early Isanosaurus, remind us that every giant begins with a first step. Their curiosity, hunger, and energy hint at the marvels to come.

The long-necked titans, from Apatosaurus to Brachiosaurus, moved gracefully across plains and forests, grazing treetops and shaping their surroundings. Gentle giants of enormous size, they combined calm strength with timeless presence.

Two-legged walkers, like Coelophysis, Tyrannosaurus, and Parasaurolophus, brought speed, balance, and energy to the land. Some were fierce hunters, others alert herbivores, all showing how upright movement transformed life in the ancient world.

Above, pterosaurs such as Pteranodon and Quetzalcoatlus mastered the skies, some soaring on vast wings, others darting nimbly over water and land. Their flight reminds us that dinosaurs explored every realm of Earth.

Finally, horned and plated dinosaurs like Triceratops, Stegosaurus, and Styracosaurus carried defenses and displays that made them unforgettable. Armor, spikes, and frills added presence, protection, and personality to the ancient world.

Taken together, these chapters show a world of incredible variety and imagination. Dinosaurs were thriving, adaptive creatures, each with its own story. By folding and studying them, we glimpse a past that was enormous, elegant, and endlessly fascinating—a world that continues to inspire curiosity, creativity, and wonder.

Welcome to the Ancient World

First Folds from the Age of Dinosaurs

Every great journey into deep time begins with a first step—and the first fold. In this chapter, you'll meet five dinosaurs that welcome you into the ancient world, from a newly hatched baby dinosaur to some of the most famous giants of prehistory. These models are designed to be friendly, approachable, and rewarding, making them the perfect place to begin your adventure. As you fold, you'll discover how simple structures can grow into powerful forms.

Baby Dinosaur

The baby dinosaur cracks out of its shell and blinks at the ancient world around it. It has no idea how large it will grow, or whether it will one day wear horns, plates, or spikes. For now, it knows only one thing: it is hungry—and whoever feeds it first will be its mother for life.

Origami is especially delightful when a few folds accomplish many things. This model is based on a simple blintz fish base, yet with just a handful of thoughtful folds it achieves several important features at once:
1. A clear dinosaur form, with the body tallest at the center and tapering naturally toward the head and tail.
2. Hind legs positioned near the center for balance and strength.
3. Shorter front legs that suggest early movement.
4. A long, expressive tail that gives the model life and motion.

The structural ideas used in this baby dinosaur appear again and again throughout this collection, forming the foundation for many of the larger and more complex dinosaurs that follow.

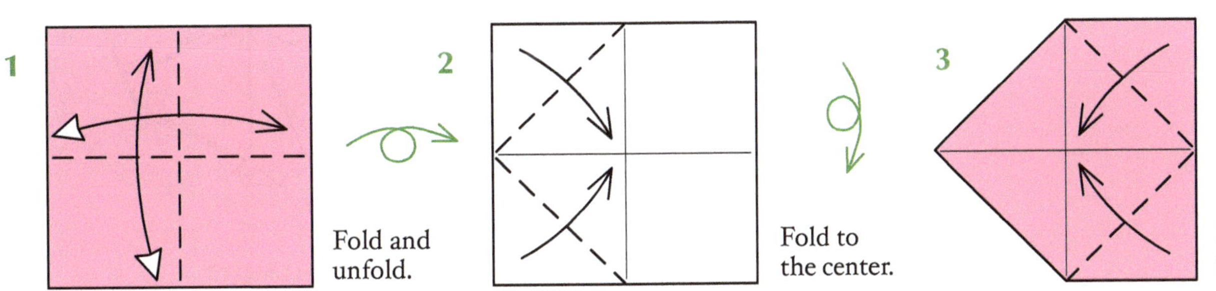

4

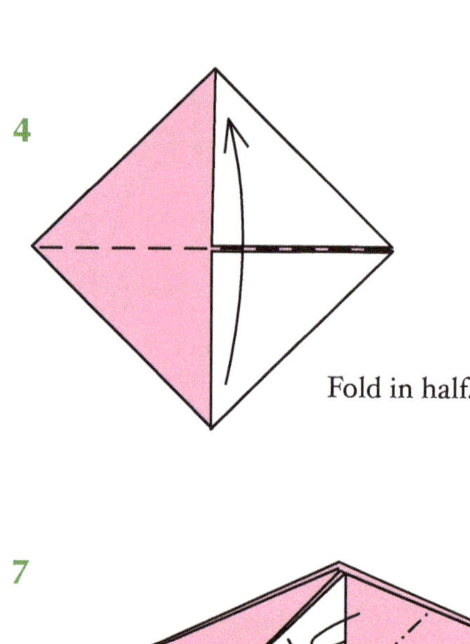

Fold in half.

5

Fold down and swing out from inside.

6

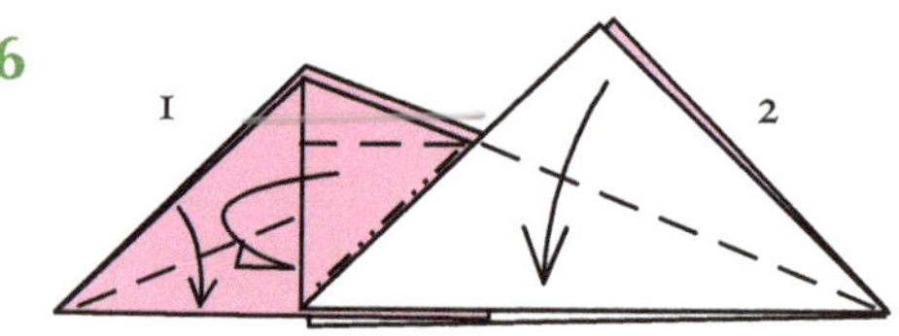

1. Reverse-fold.
2. Fold down.
Repeat behind.

7

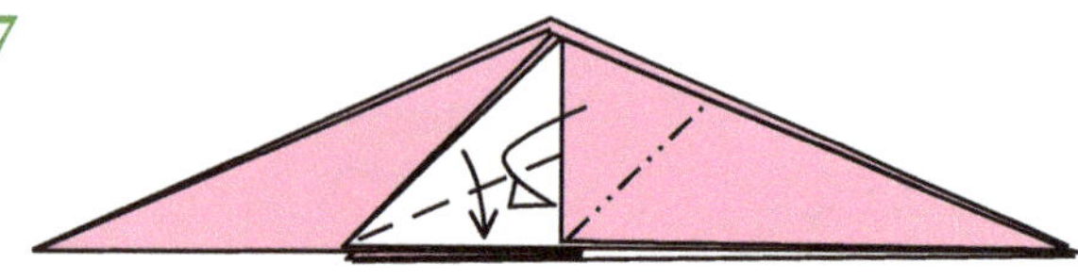

Reverse-fold and repeat behind.

8

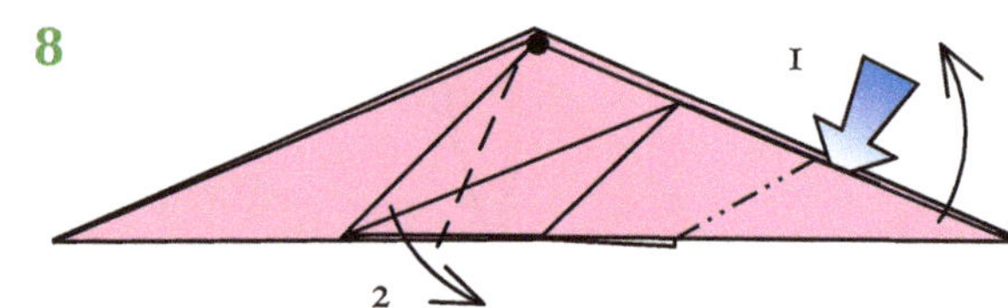

1. Reverse-fold.
2. Fold down close to the dot, repeat behind.

9

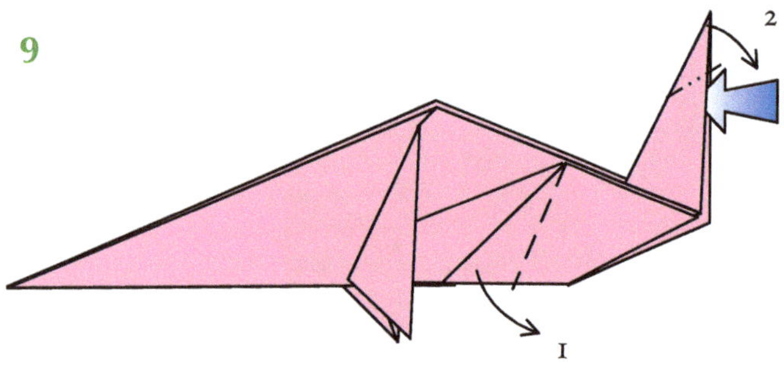

1. Fold the leg, repeat behind.
2. Reverse-fold.

10

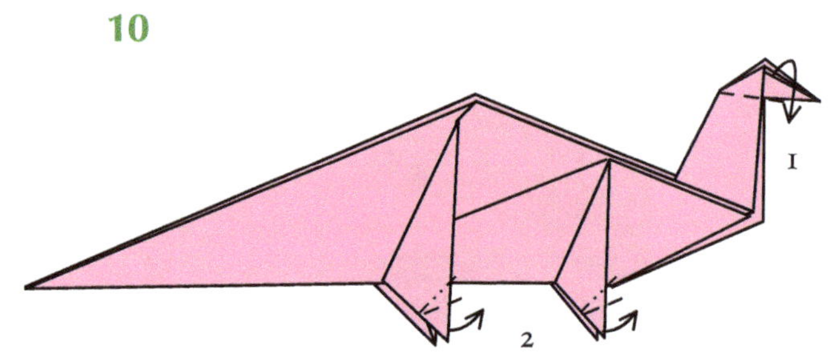

1. Fold a layer down.
2. Make crimp folds.
Repeat behind.

11

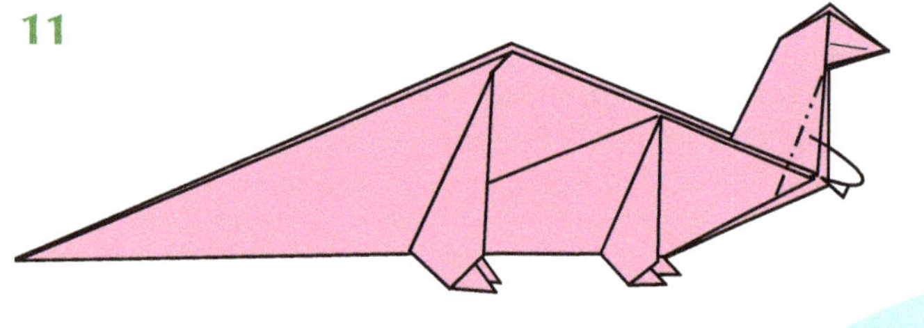

Fold inside and repeat behind.

12

Baby Dinosaur

Isanosaurus

Hop onto Isanosaurus's broad back and enjoy a slow, swaying ride through the ancient forest. One of the earliest known long-necked dinosaurs, Isanosaurus lived during a time when giants were just beginning to appear. It moved steadily and calmly, using its long neck to browse high branches while keeping its massive body safely grounded below.

This model builds directly from the structure used in the baby dinosaur, showing how simple ideas can grow into grand forms. These folds allow for a longer, more graceful neck and a seamless closed back—unlike the open-backed design of the baby dinosaur. In origami animals, closed backs create a more natural appearance.

1

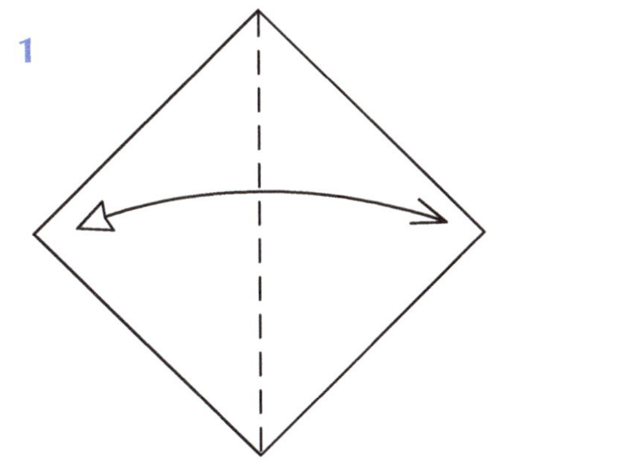

Fold and unfold.

2

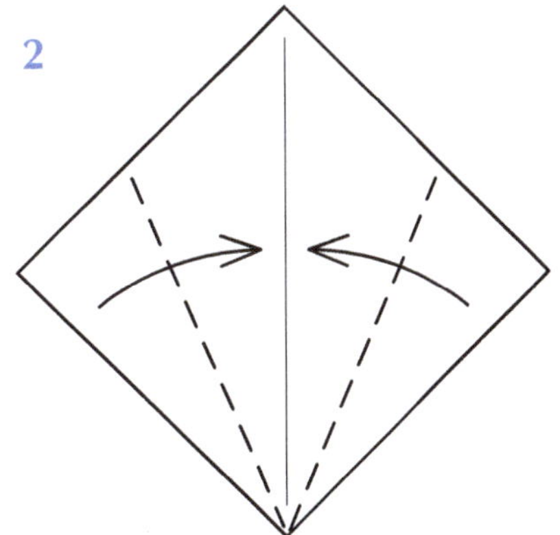

Fold to the center.

3

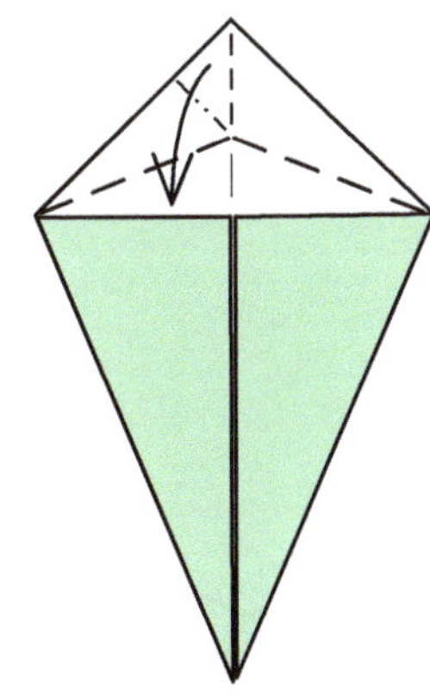

Rabbit-ear.

4 5

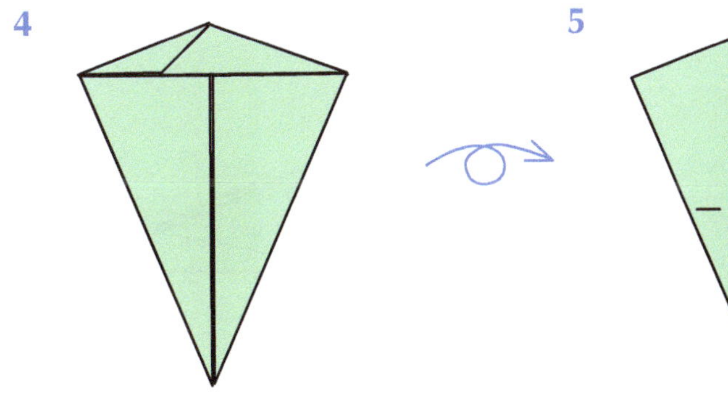

6

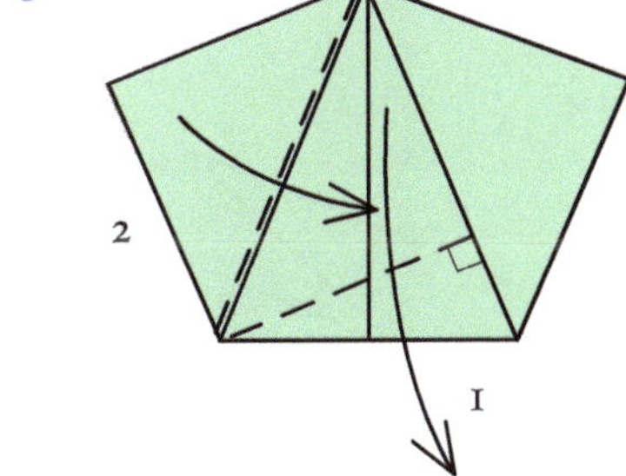

1. Fold down at a right angle.
2. Fold toward the center.

7

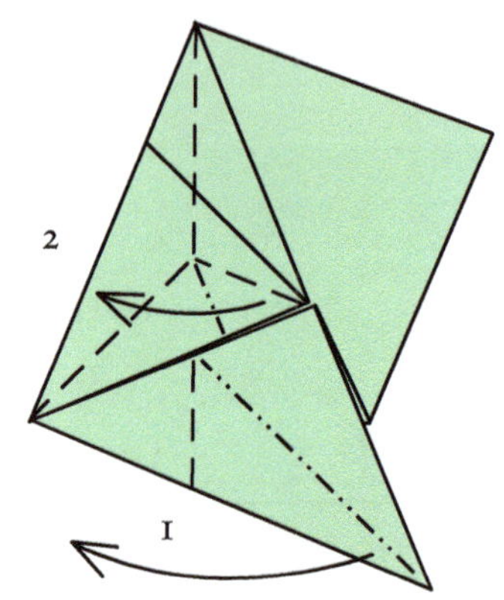

1. Squash-fold.
2. Rabbit-ear.

8

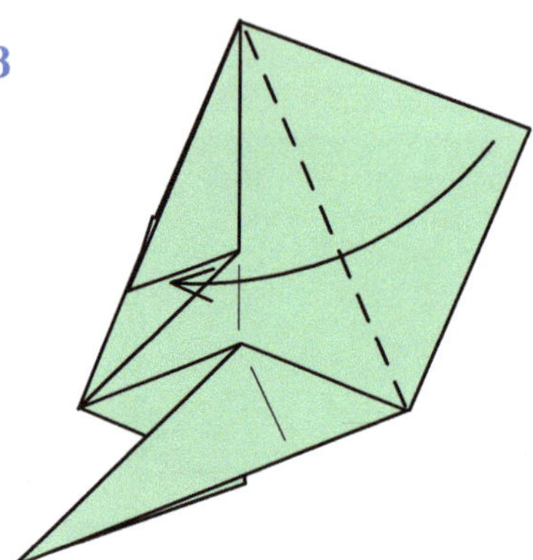

Repeat steps 6–7 on the upper part, on the right.

9

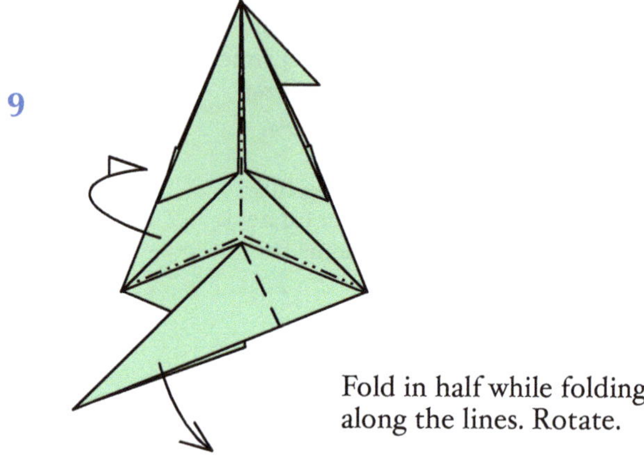

Fold in half while folding along the lines. Rotate.

10

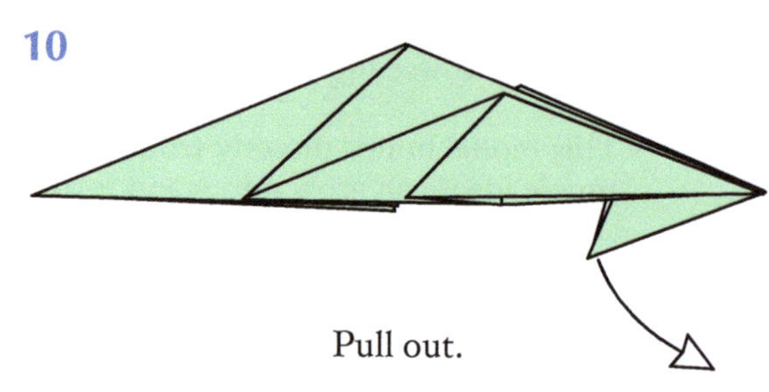

Pull out.

11

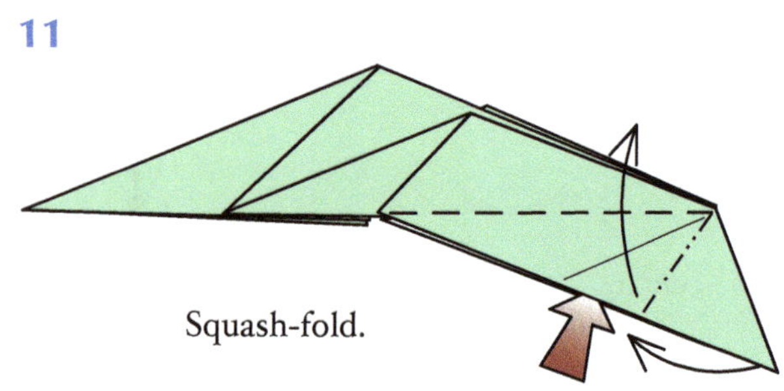

Squash-fold.

12

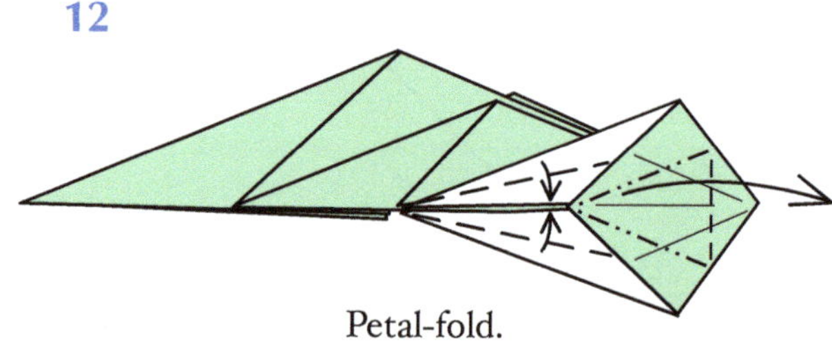

Petal-fold.

13

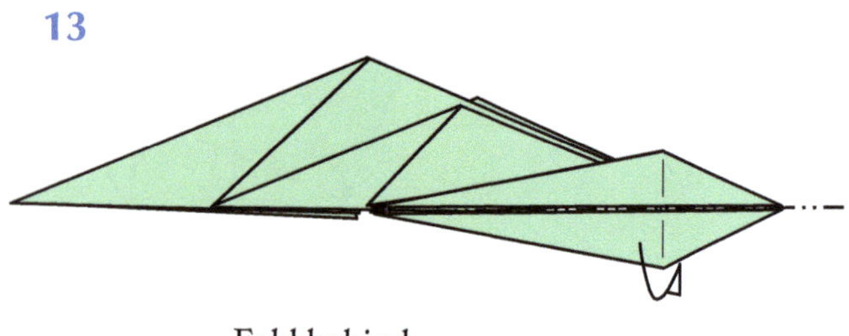

Fold behind.

14

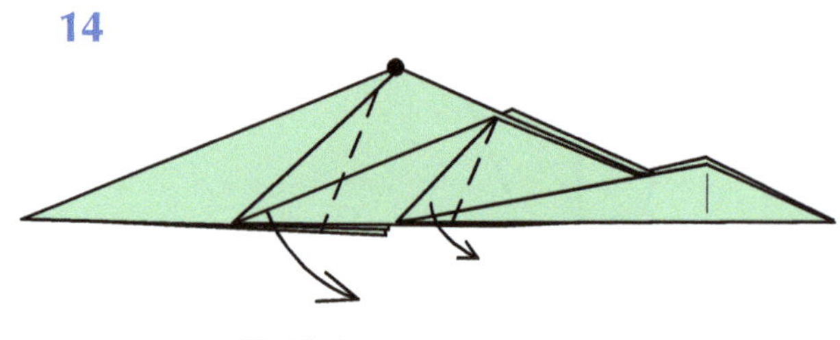

Fold down to the left of the dot. Repeat behind.

15

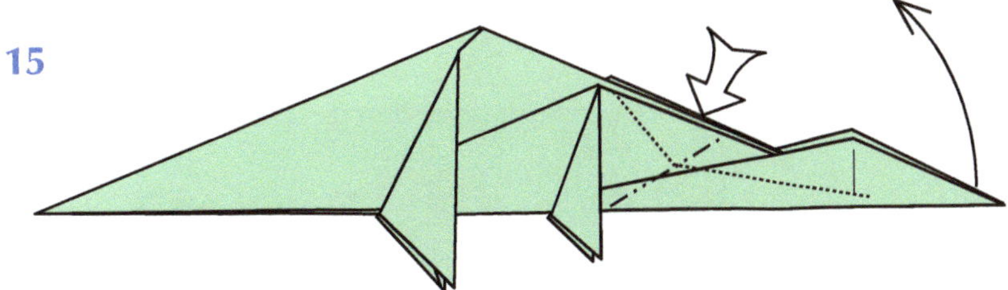

Push in and fold along the dotted lines on the inner layers, for this reverse fold.

16

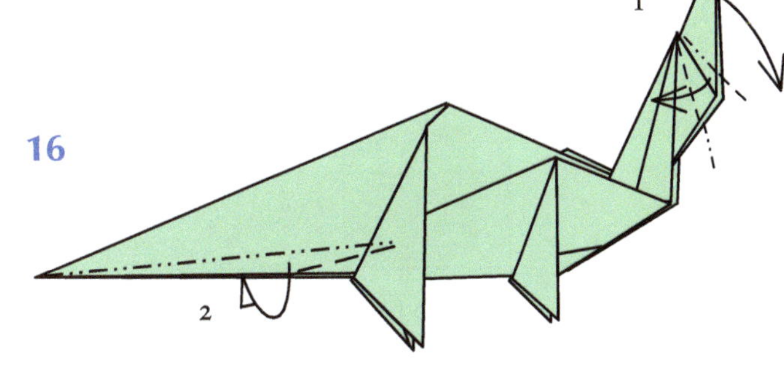

1. Crimp-fold.
2. Fold inside, repeat behind.

17

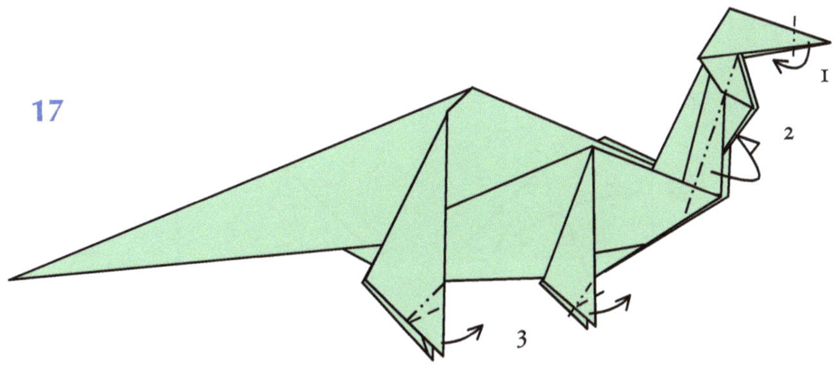

1. Reverse-fold.
2. Fold inside, repeat behind.
3. Make crimp folds, repeat behind.

18

Isanosaurus

Tyrannosaurus

Climb onto the back of the Tyrannosaurus and hold tight—this powerful giant will carry you across vast prehistoric plains and through dense forests. As it roams, its keen senses are always on the lookout for tasty treats, reminding us why Tyrannosaurus was one of the most formidable hunters of the ancient world. With strong legs, a massive head, and a commanding presence, it ruled its landscape with confidence.

Careful design allows this model to capture the Tyrannosaurus in only 16 steps, showing that a few well-chosen folds can create a recognizable dinosaur.

1

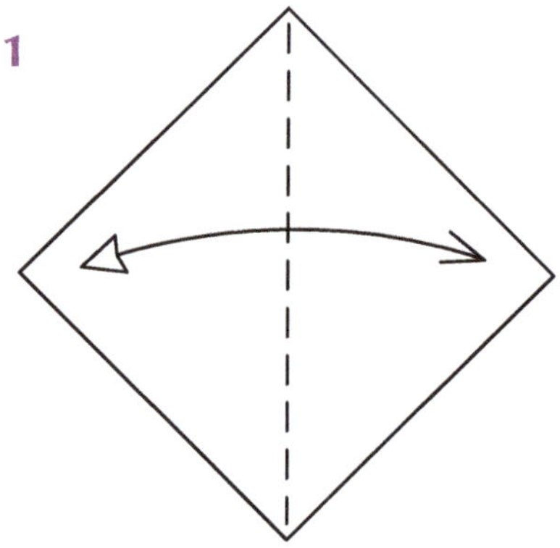

Fold and unfold.

2

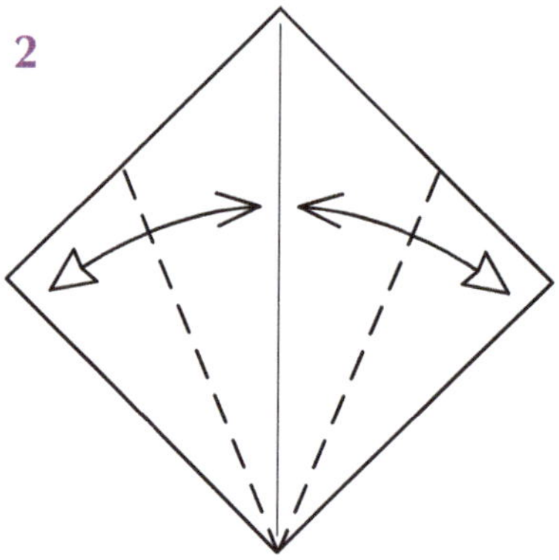

Fold to the center and unfold.

3

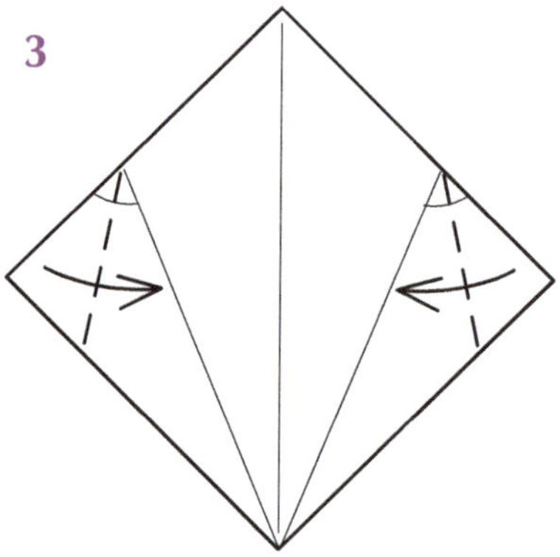

Fold on the left and right.

4

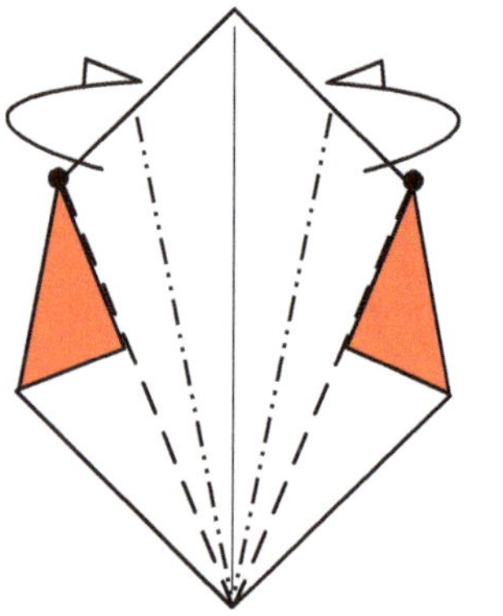

Pleat-fold so the dots meet in the center.

5

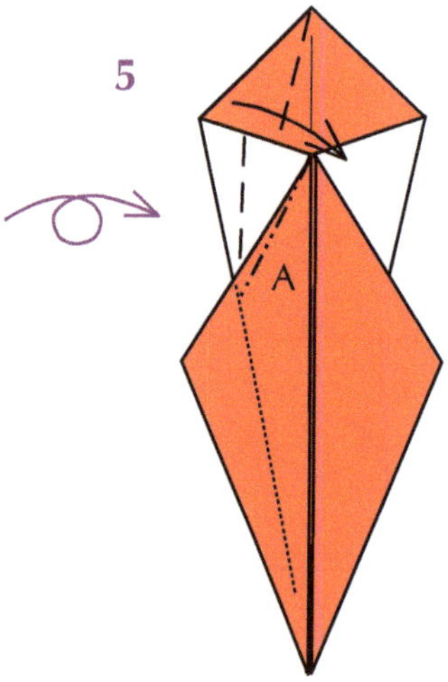

A

Fold under region A for this reverse fold.

6

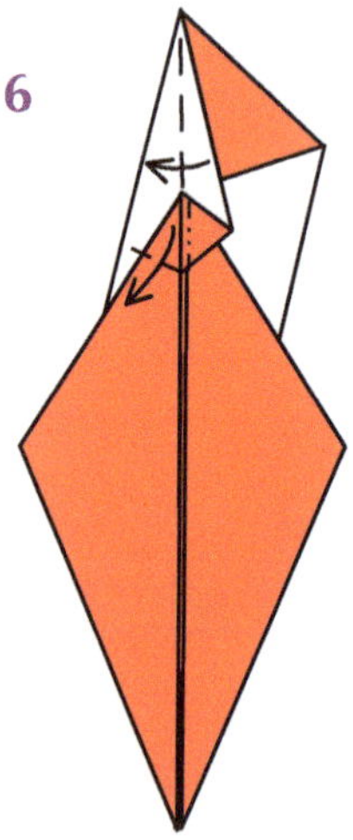

Squash-fold.

7

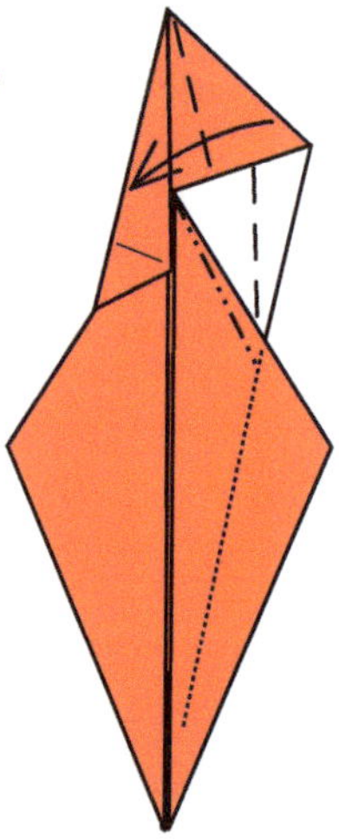

Repeat steps 5–6 on the right.

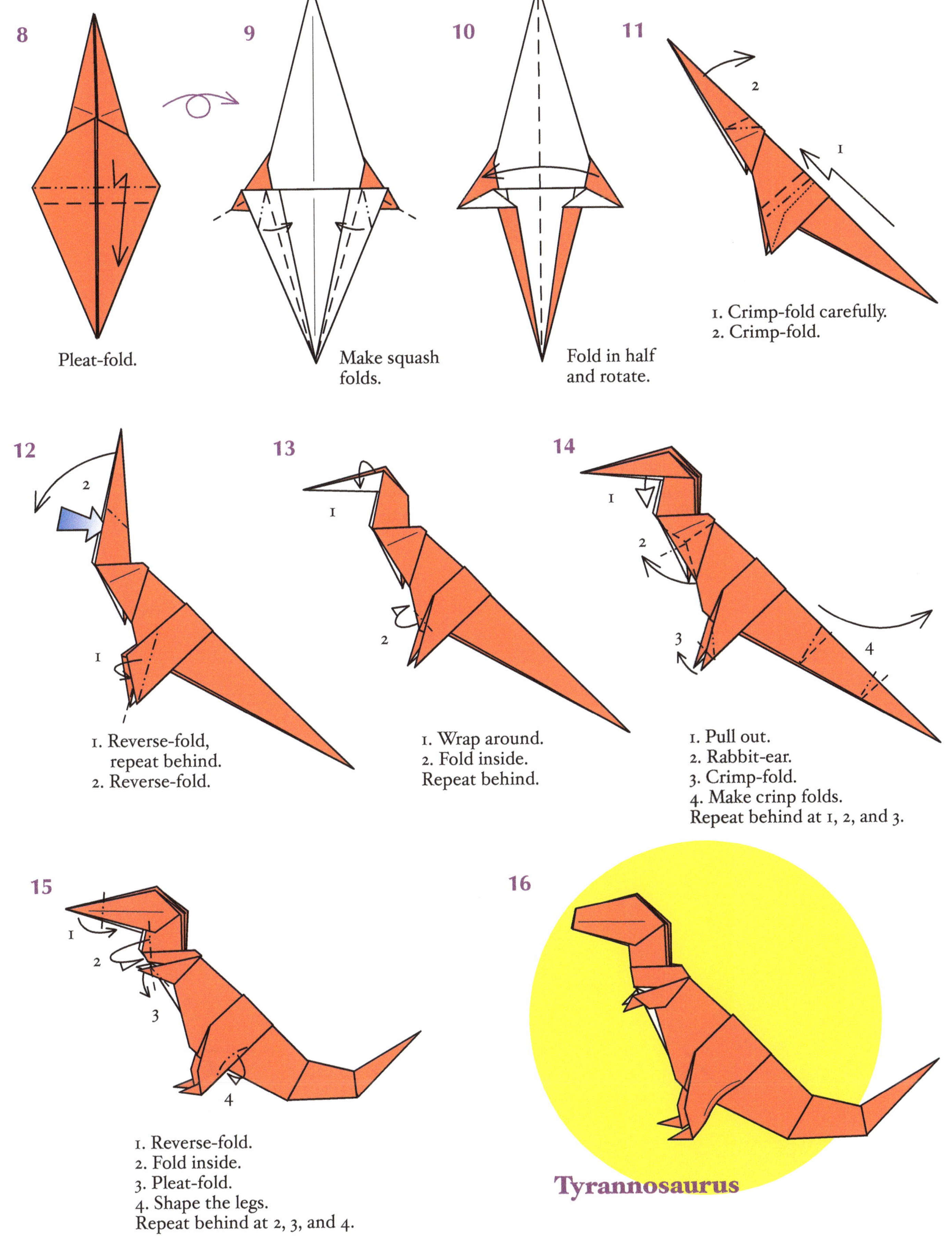
8
9
10
11
2
1
Pleat-fold.
Make squash folds.
Fold in half and rotate.
1. Crimp-fold carefully.
2. Crimp-fold.
12
13
14
2
1
1
2
1
2
3
4
1. Reverse-fold, repeat behind.
2. Reverse-fold.
1. Wrap around.
2. Fold inside.
Repeat behind.
1. Pull out.
2. Rabbit-ear.
3. Crimp-fold.
4. Make crinp folds.
Repeat behind at 1, 2, and 3.
15
16
1
2
3
4
1. Reverse-fold.
2. Fold inside.
3. Pleat-fold.
4. Shape the legs.
Repeat behind at 2, 3, and 4.
Tyrannosaurus

Pterodactylus

Take to the skies with Pterodactylus and enjoy a true flyer's view of the ancient world. Gliding on broad wings, it soars over forests, rivers, and open plains, revealing the vast landscapes of deep time below. As one of the earliest known flying reptiles, Pterodactylus invites you to see the prehistoric world from a new perspective and encourages you to explore further, meet more dinosaurs, and fold even more models along the way.

1

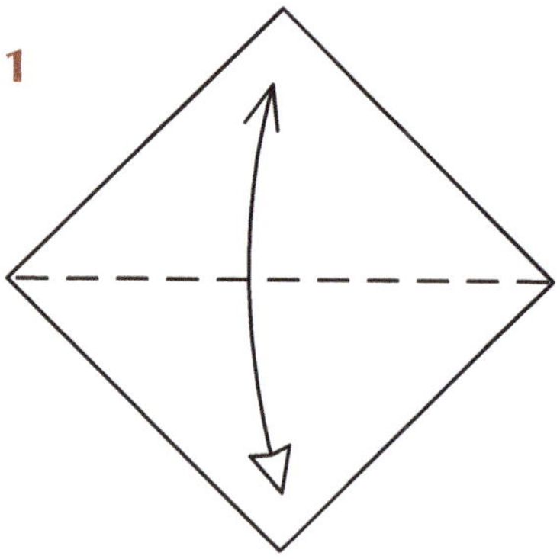

Fold and unfold.

2

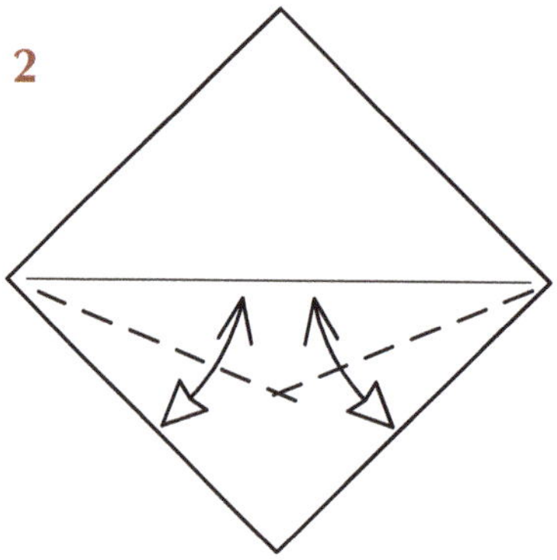

Fold and unfold.
Rotate 180°.

3

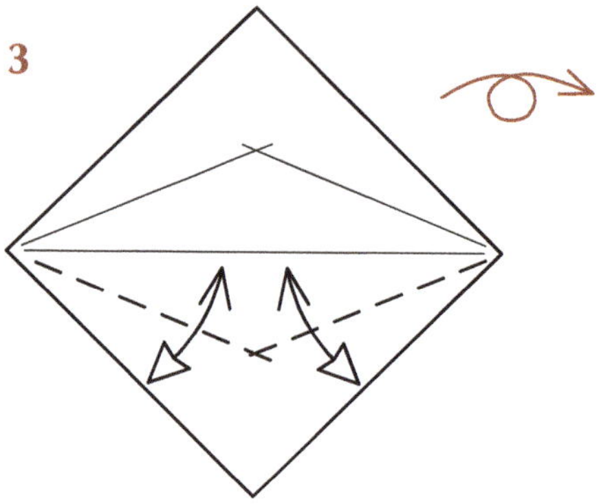

Fold and unfold.
Rotate 90°.

4

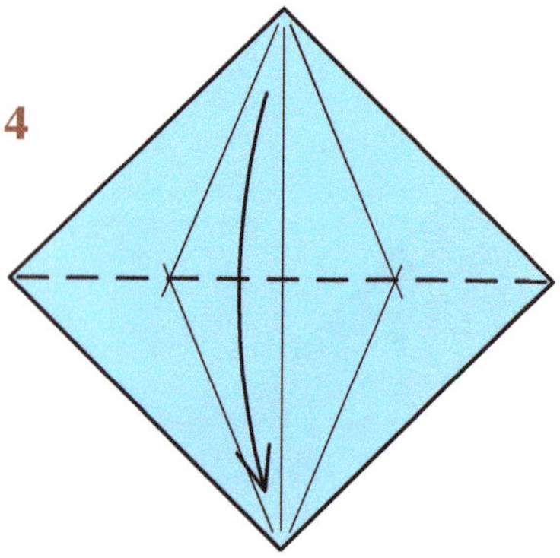

Fold in half.

5

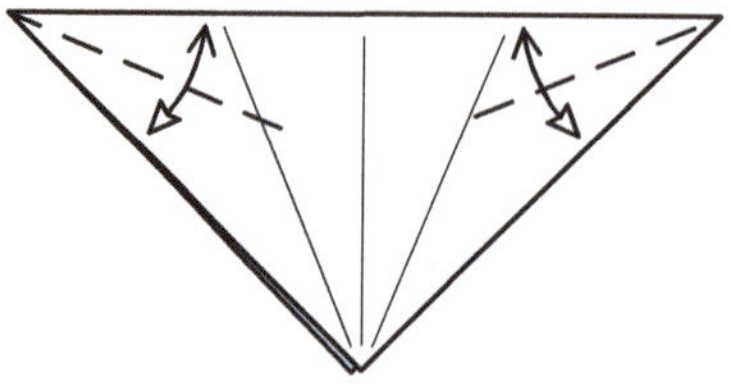

Fold and unfold.
Repeat behind.

6

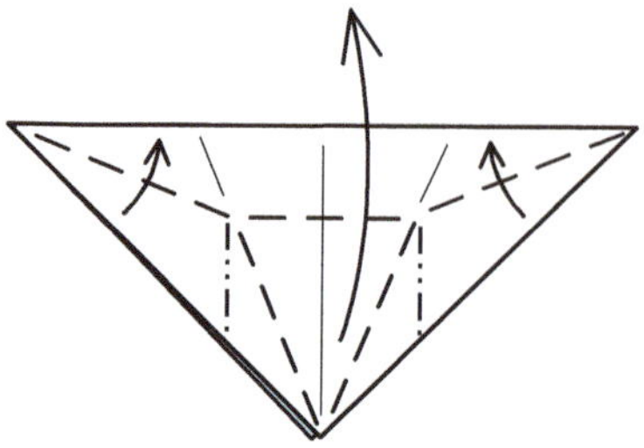

Fold along the creases.
Repeat behind.

7

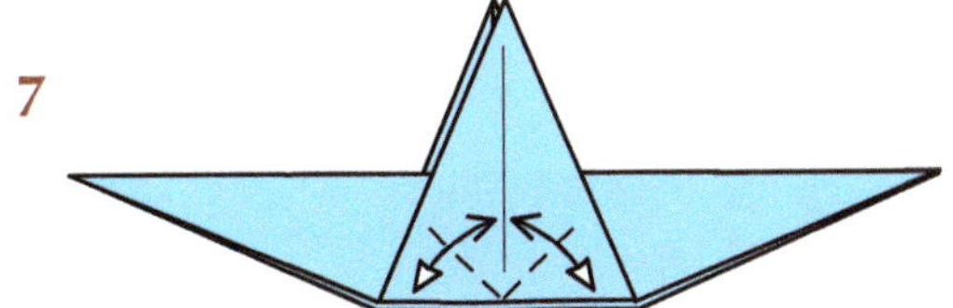

Fold and unfold all the layers.

8

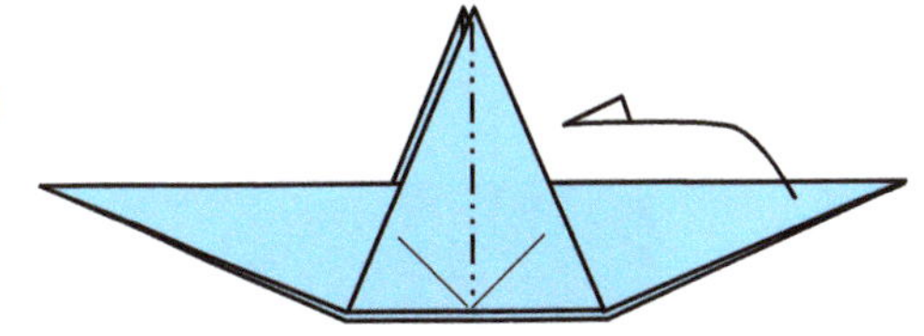

Fold in half and rotate 90°.

9

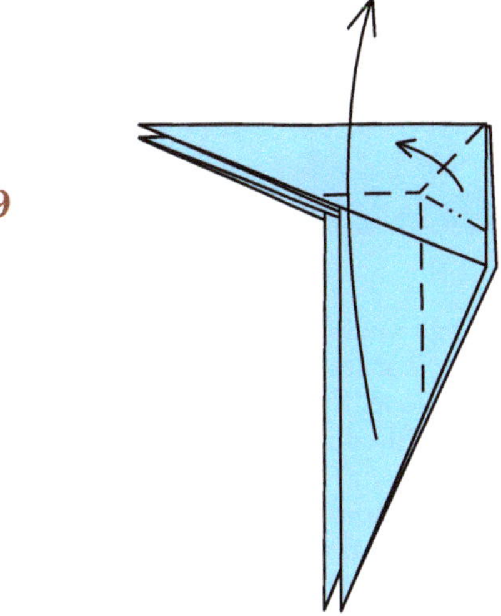

This is similar to a rabbit ear. Repeat behind.

10

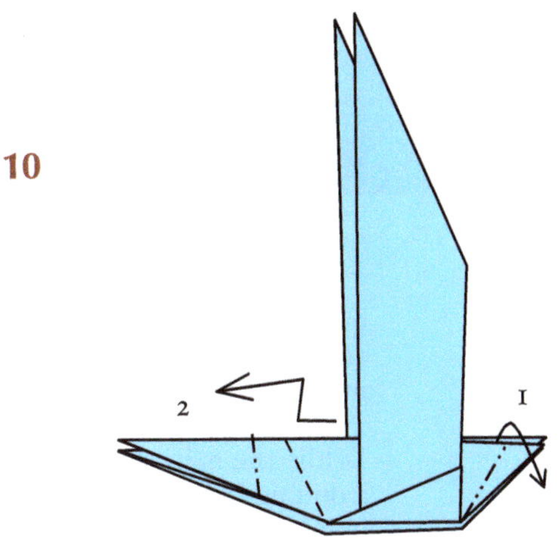

1. Slide out the top flap, repeat behind.
2. Make outside-reverse folds.

11

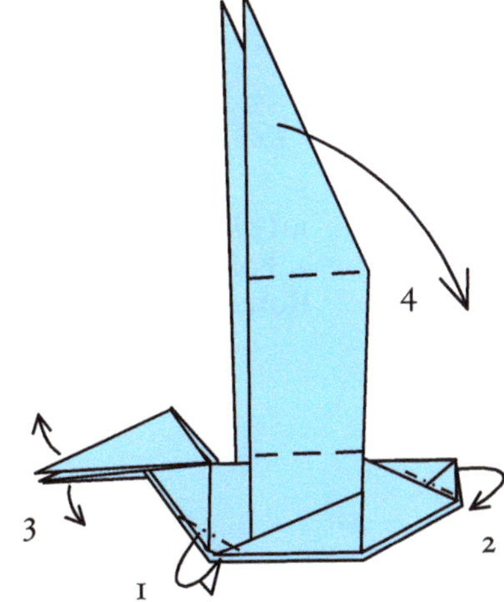

1. Fold inside, repeat behind.
2. Reverse-fold.
3. Spread the head.
4. Fold the wings, repeat behind.

12

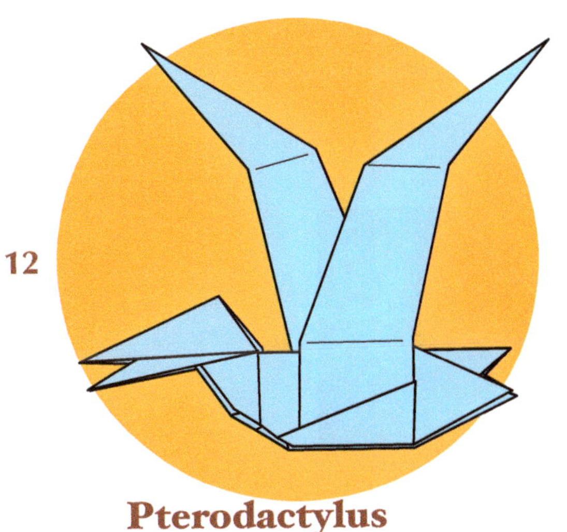

Pterodactylus

Stegosaurus

This young Stegosaurus will walk beside you as you journey through ancient lands, offering quiet protection along the way. The tall plates lining its back make it instantly recognizable and help discourage any curious predators that might wander too close. Though peaceful in nature, Stegosaurus was well prepared to defend itself in a world filled with giants.

While the baby dinosaur model is based on a blintz fish base, this Stegosaurus grows from a double-blintz fish base. Building on the same core structure, additional folds create the iconic plates—all accomplished in under 20 steps. One of the joys of origami is discovering the simplest way to achieve powerful results.

1

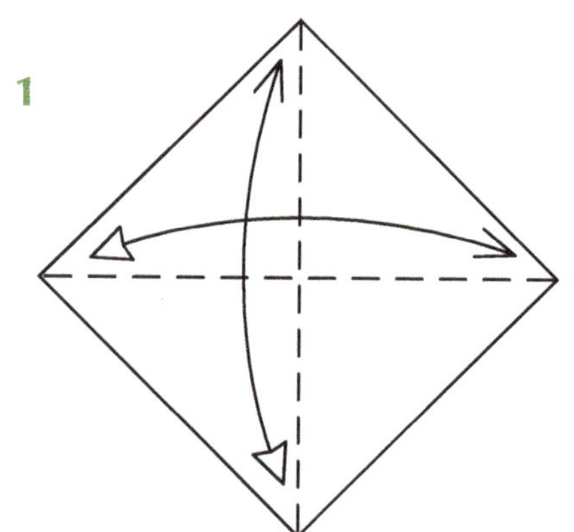

Fold and unfold.

2

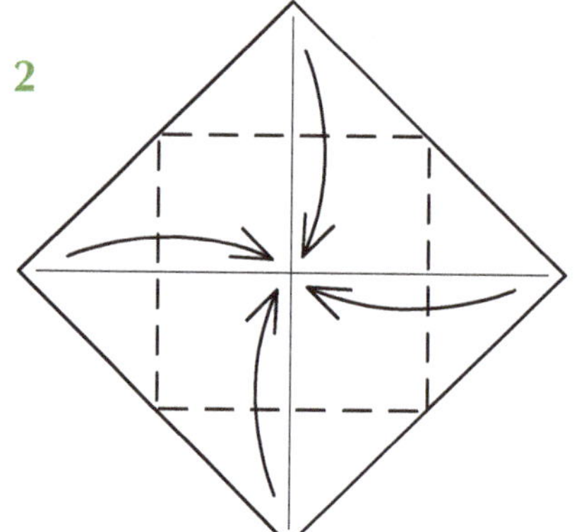

Fold to the center.

3

1. Fold to the center.
2. Fold and unfold.
Rotate 45°.

4

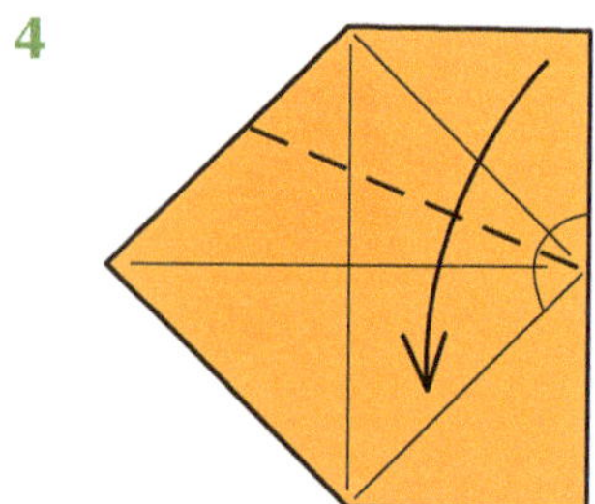

5

Open while folding up.

6

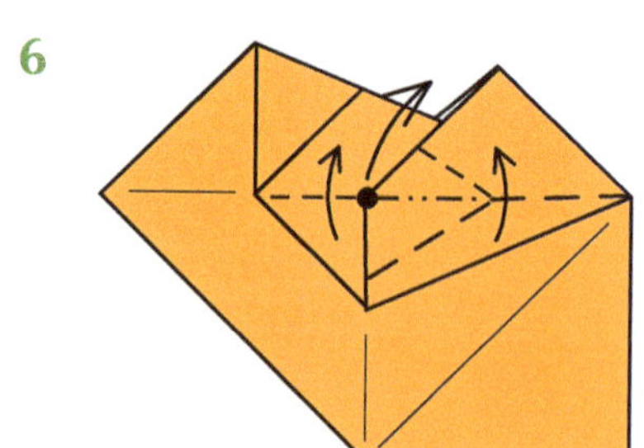

Bring the dot up while folding up.

7

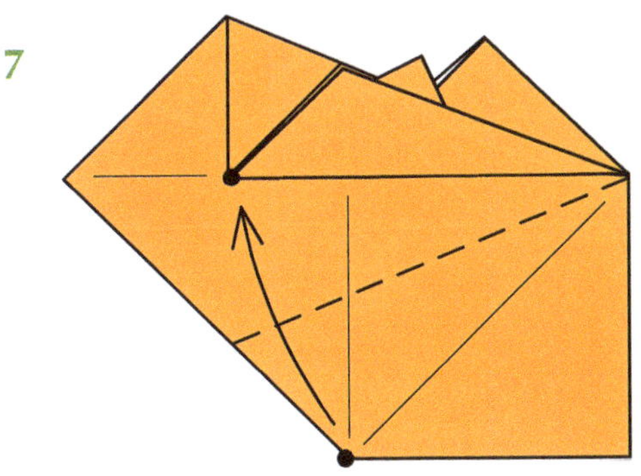

Repeat steps 4–6 on the bottom.

8

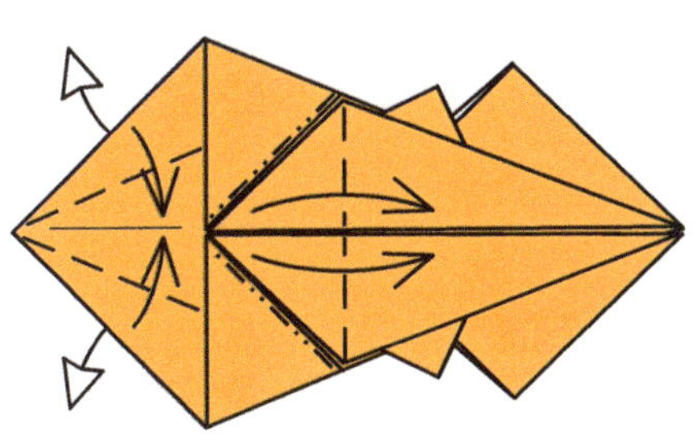

Squash-fold and swing out from behind.

9

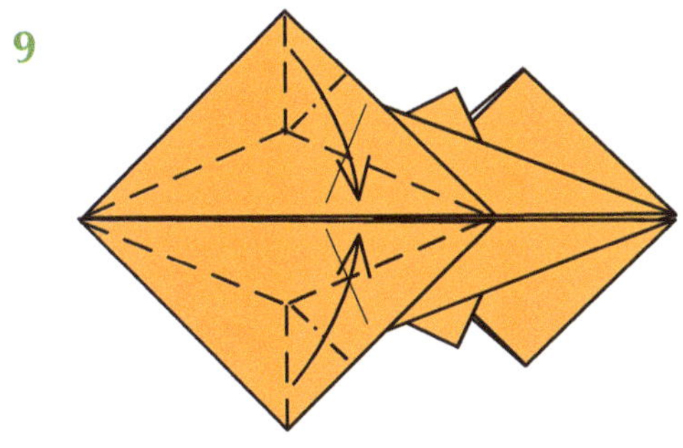

Make rabbit ears.

10

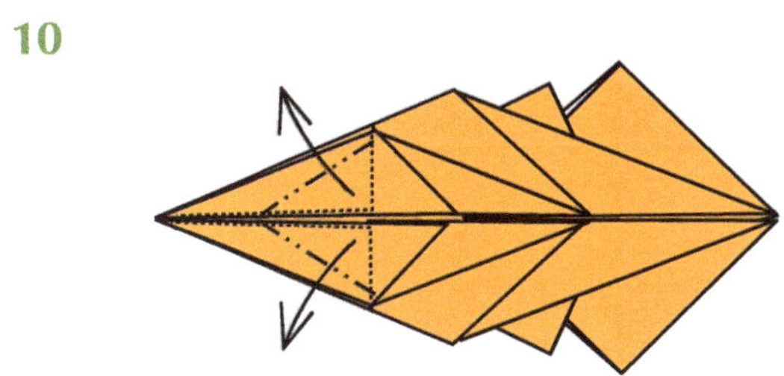

Make reverse folds on the inner layers.

11

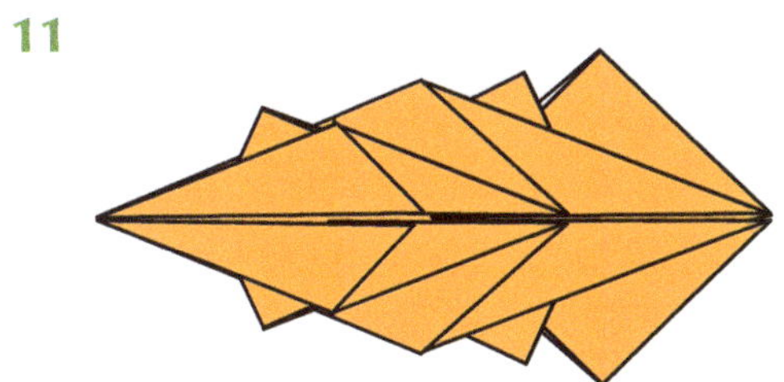

12

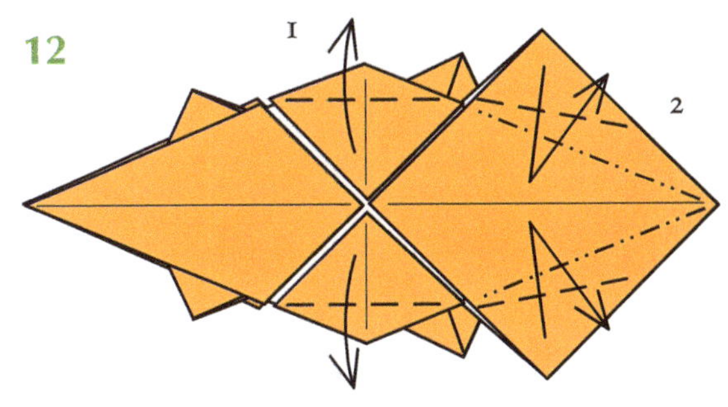

1. Fold the top flaps.
2. Make crimp folds.

13

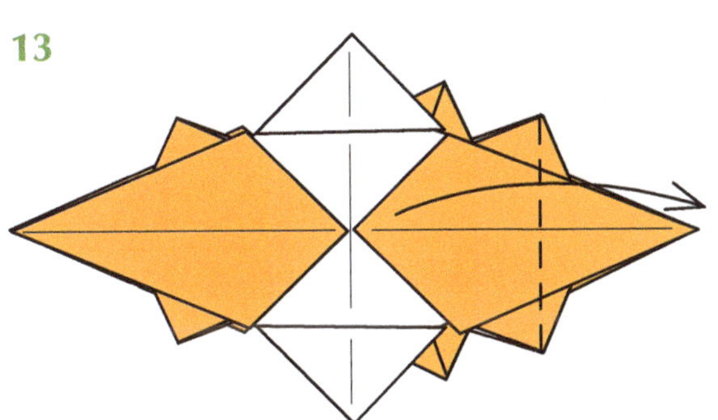

14

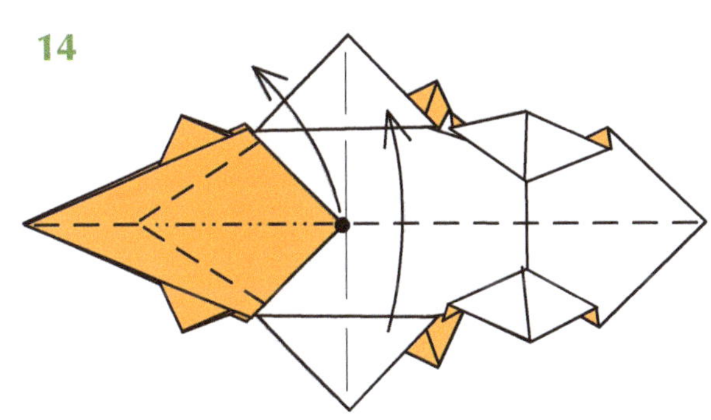

Lift up at the dot while folding in half.

15

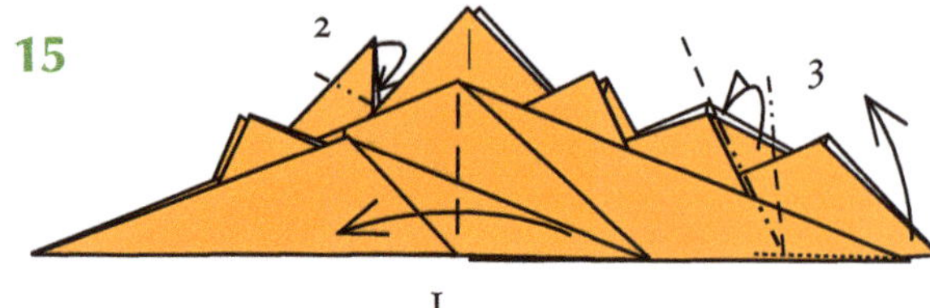

1. Fold the leg, repeat behind.
2. Reverse-fold.
3. Crimp-fold.

16

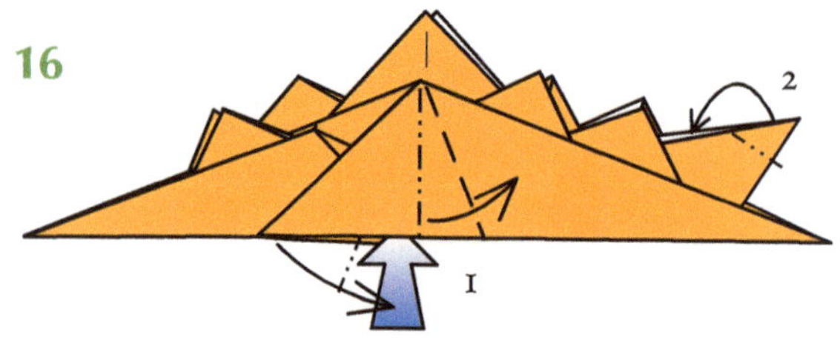

1. Crimp-fold, repeat behind.
2. Reverse-fold.

17

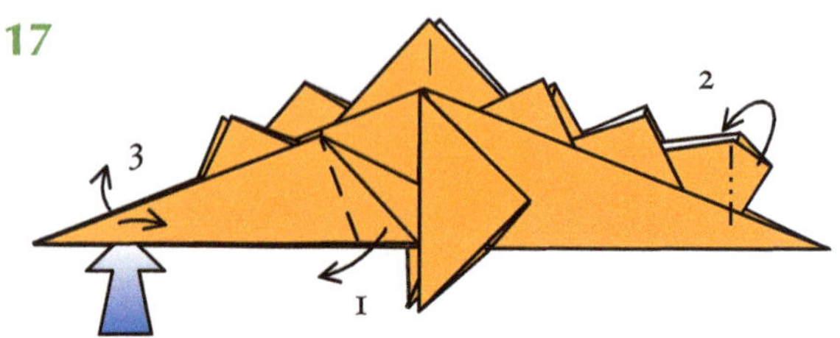

1. Fold the leg, repeat behind.
2. Reverse-fold.
3. Push up and spread the head.

18

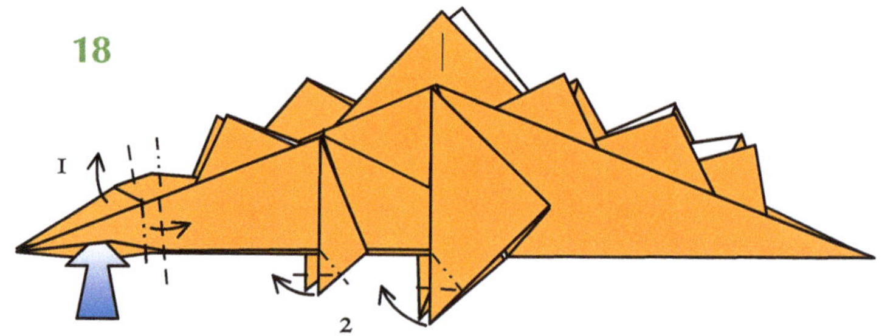

1. The head is 3D. Push in, pull out at the top and flatten with a crimp fold.
2. Make crimp folds, repeat behind.

19

Stegosaurus

The Long-Necked Titans

Sauropods of the Ancient Earth

In this chapter, the Earth grows quiet beneath enormous footsteps. The long-necked titans arrive—giant sauropods whose bodies stretched across the land like living hills and whose necks reached into the treetops of ancient forests. These were some of the largest animals to ever walk on land, and yet many were gentle, plant-eaters. From the early giants to the most massive dinosaurs ever known, these long-necked titans invite you to experience the wonder of deep time.

Apatosaurus

Apatosaurus was one of the true giants of the ancient world—a long-necked titan that moved through prehistoric forests. Stretching up to 75 feet long and weighing as much as several elephants combined, this enormous sauropod lived during the Late Jurassic Period, when giant dinosaurs dominated the land. Despite its massive size, Apatosaurus was a gentle plant-eater, spending much of its day browsing leaves from trees and shrubs. Its long, whip-like tail may have helped with balance—or cracked loudly through the air to warn predators that this giant was not to be disturbed.

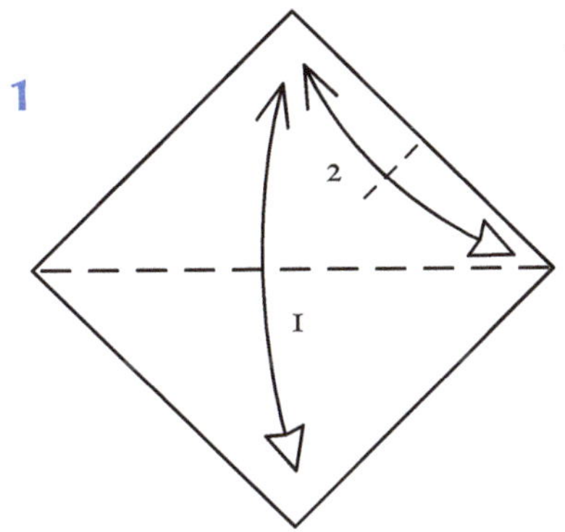

1. Fold and unfold.
2. Fold and unfold on the edge.

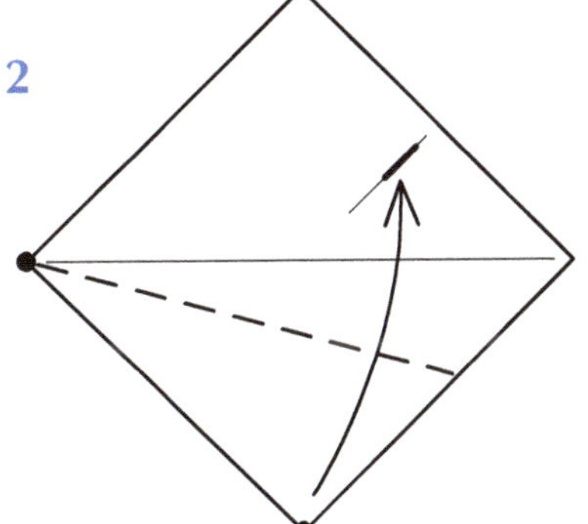

Bring the corner to the line.

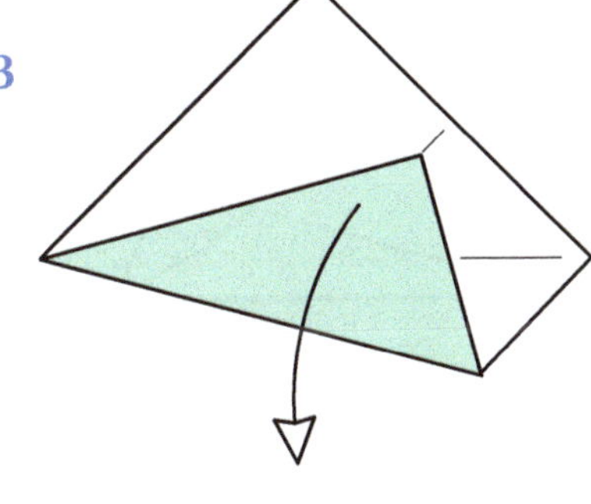

Unfold.

4

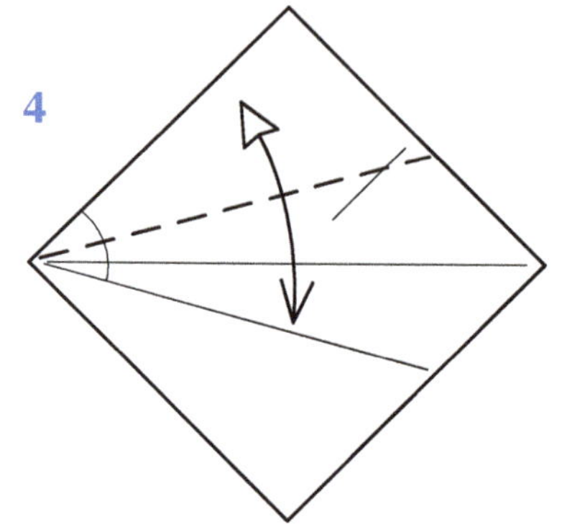

Fold and unfold.

5

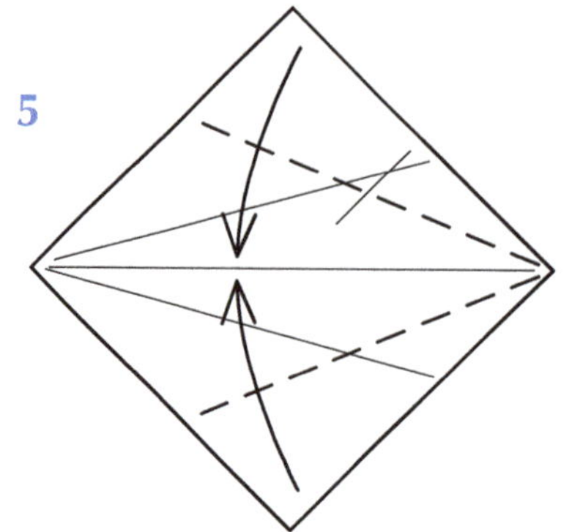

Fold to the center.

6

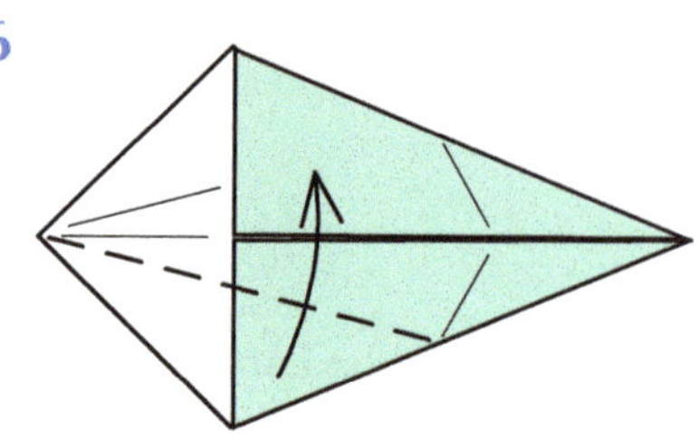

Fold along the crease.

7

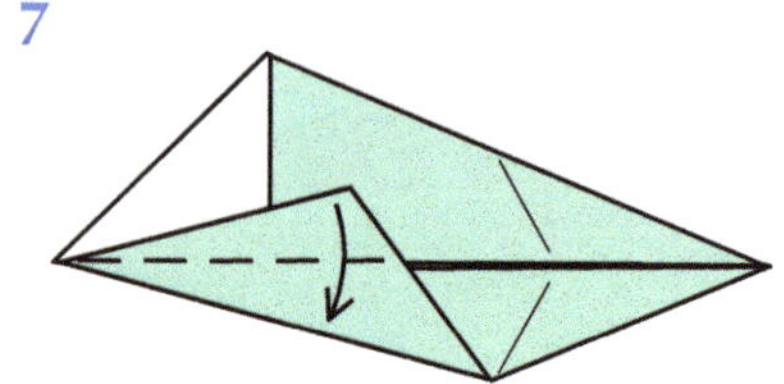

8

Unfold.

9

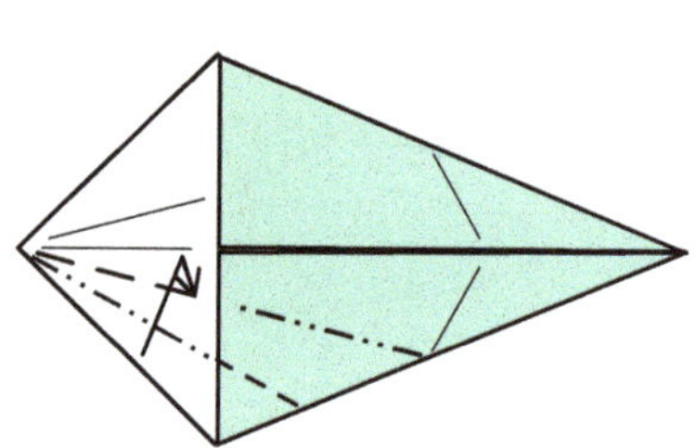

Crimp-fold along the creases.

10

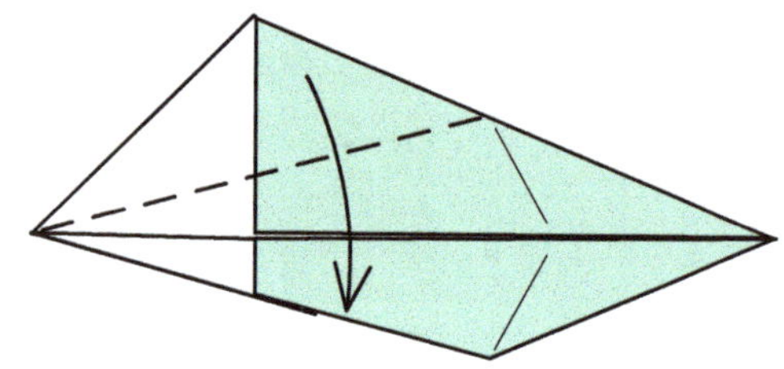

Repeat steps 6–9 on the top.

11

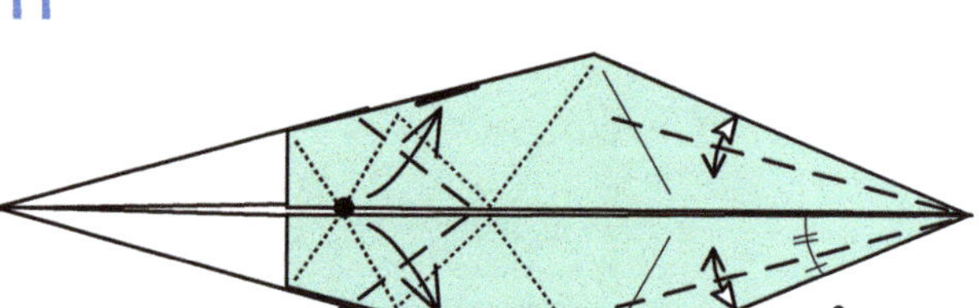

1. The dot will meet the bold lines.
2. Fold and unfold at an angle of 1/3.

12

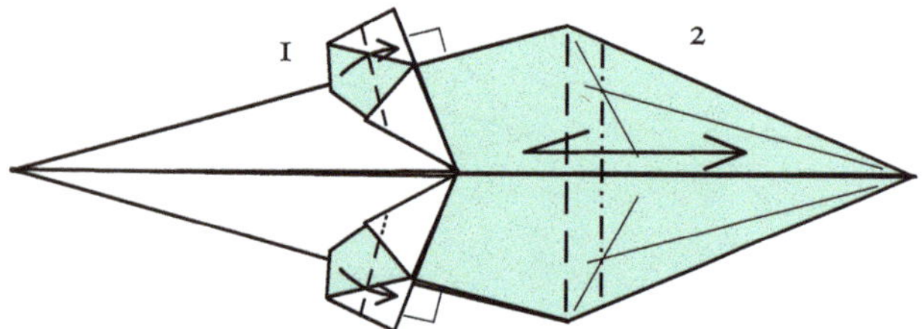

1. Note the right angles.
   Fold under the white triangles.
2. Pleat-fold.

13

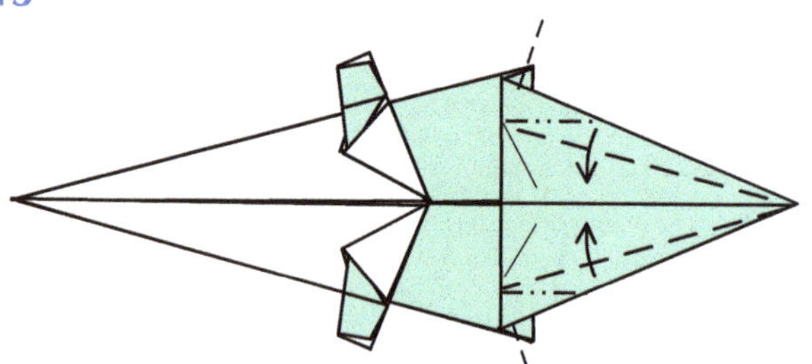

Mak squash folds.

14

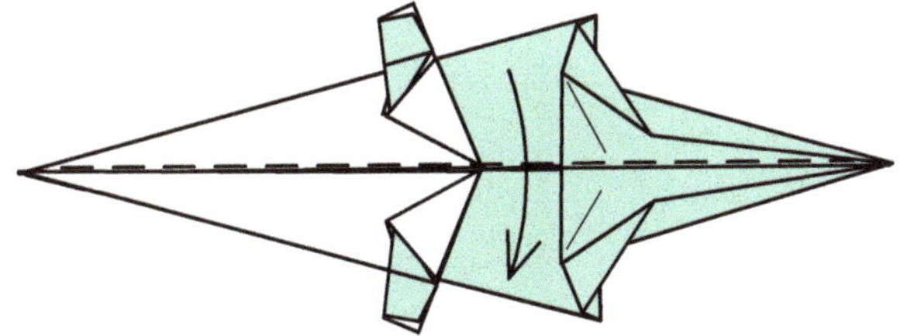

Fold in half.

15

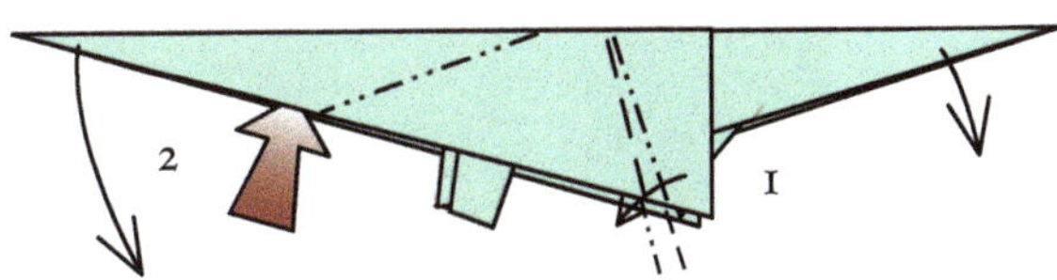

1. Crimp-fold.
2. Reverse-fold.

16

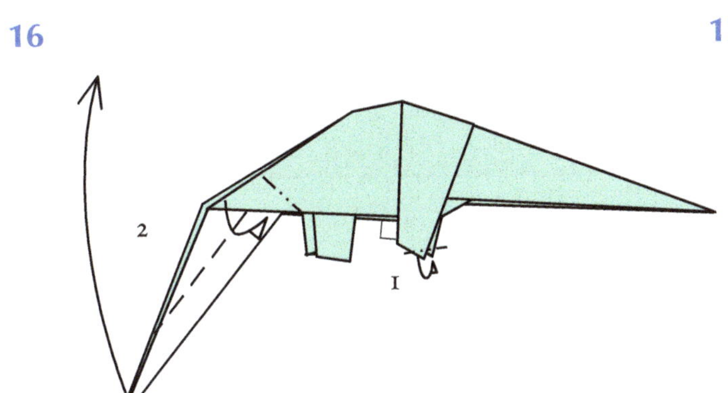

1. Note the right angle. Fold inside, repeat behind.
2. This is similar to a reverse fold.

17

1. Reverse-fold.
2. Shape the legs, repeat behind.
3. Shape the tail.

18

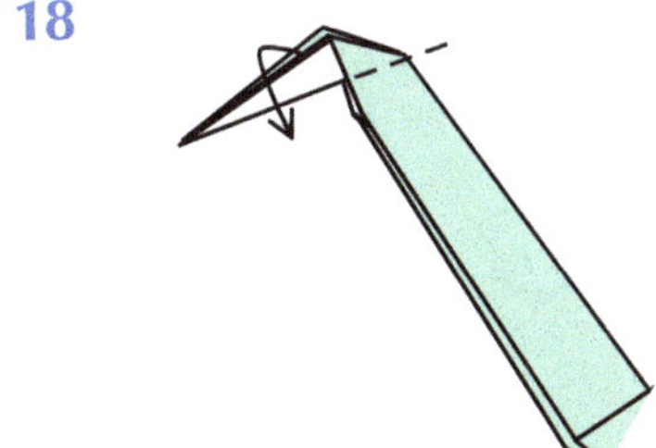

Fold the top layer down.

19

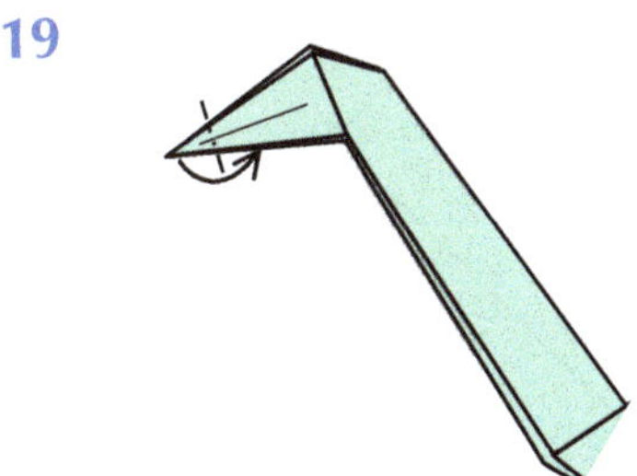

Reverse-fold.

20

Apatosaurus

Diplodocus

Diplodocus was one of the longest dinosaurs to ever walk the Earth, reaching lengths of up to 90 feet. Living during the Late Jurassic Period, it shared its world with many other enormous sauropods, yet stood out for its slender build and incredible length. This peaceful herbivore fed on low-growing plants, using its peg-like teeth to strip leaves rather than chew them. Its extremely long tail may have acted like a whip, possibly creating loud cracking sounds to startle predators from a distance.

1

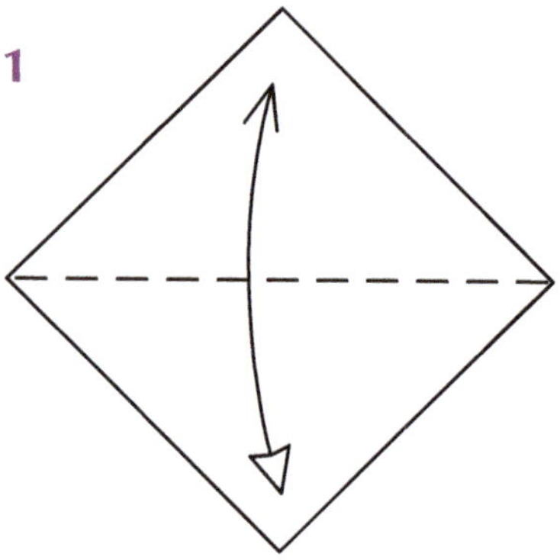

Fold and unfold.

2

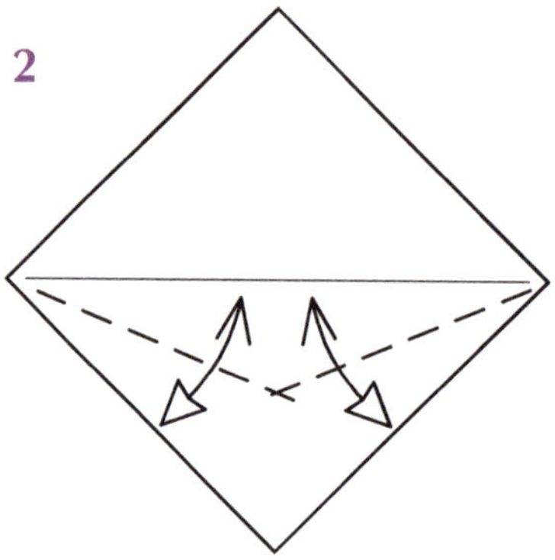

Fold and unfold.
Rotate 180°.

3

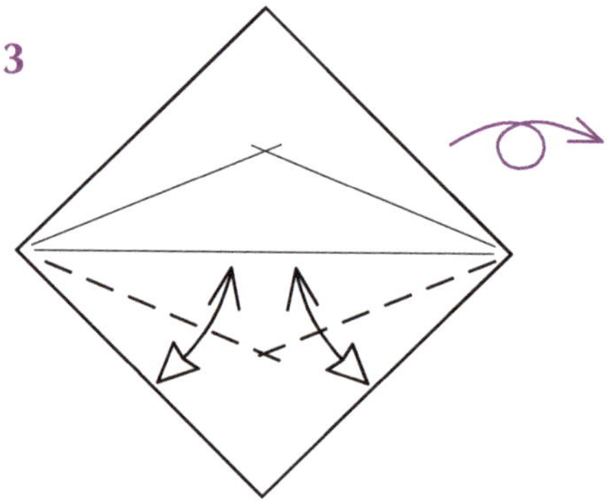

Fold and unfold.

4

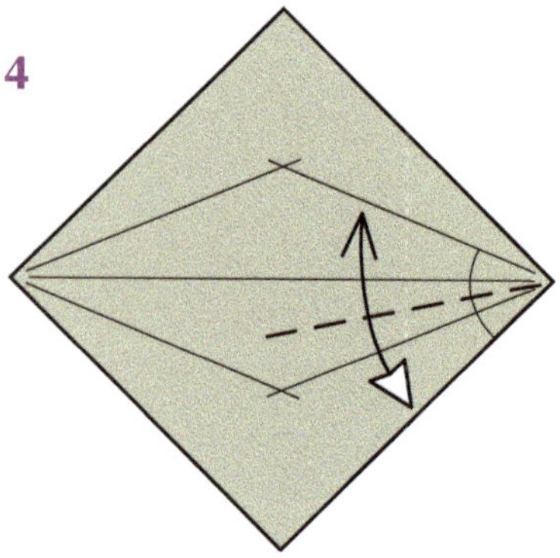

Fold and unfold.

5

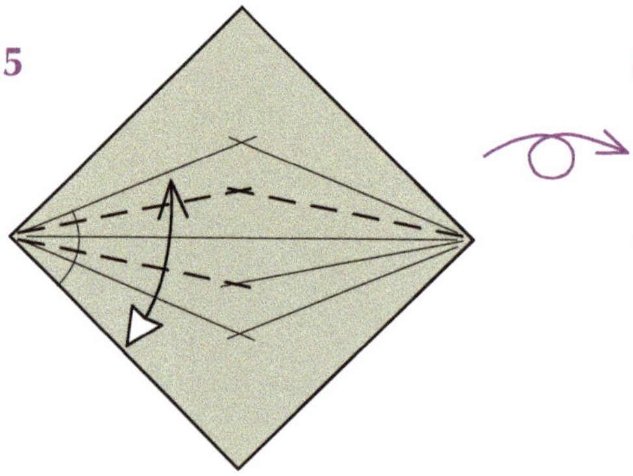

Repeat step 4 three times.

6

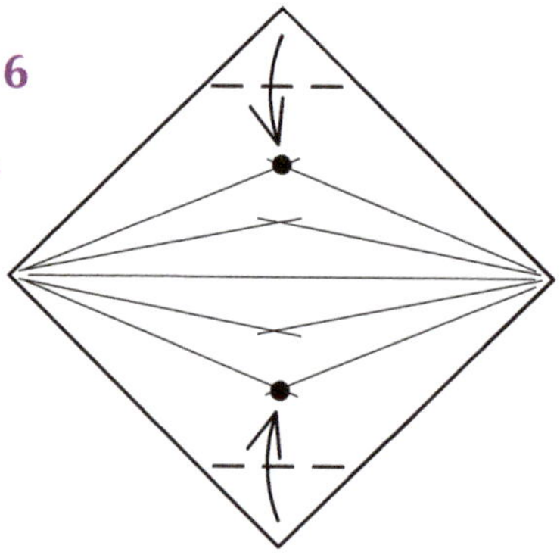

7

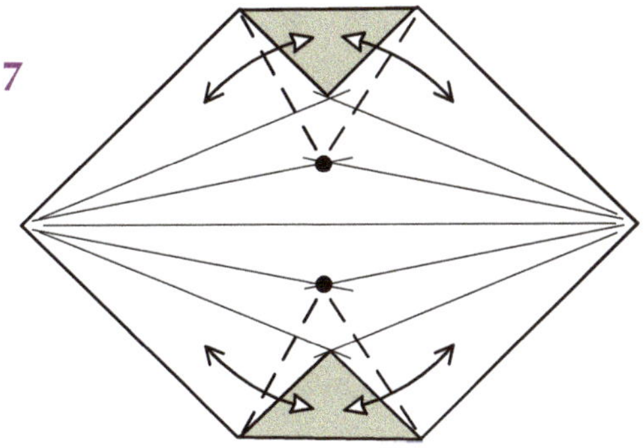

Fold and unfold.

8

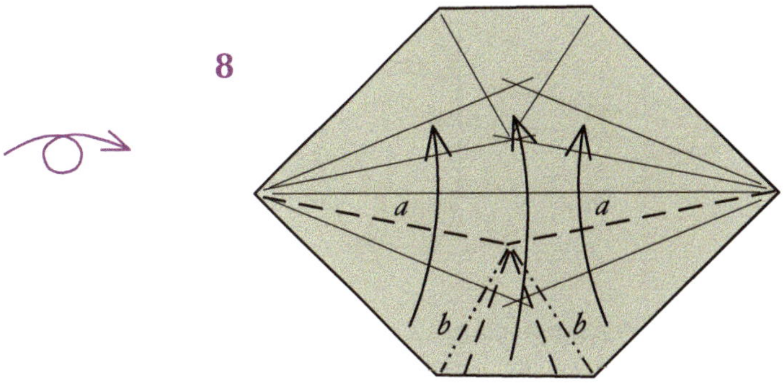

Fold along creases *a* and *b*. Begin by folding up on the left and right, then flatten in the center.

9

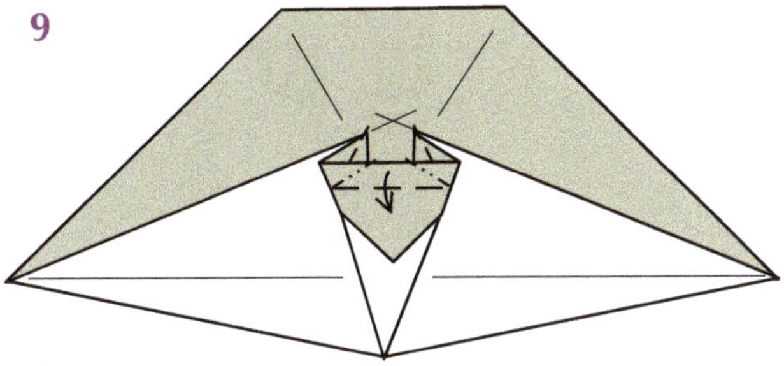

Petal-fold.

10

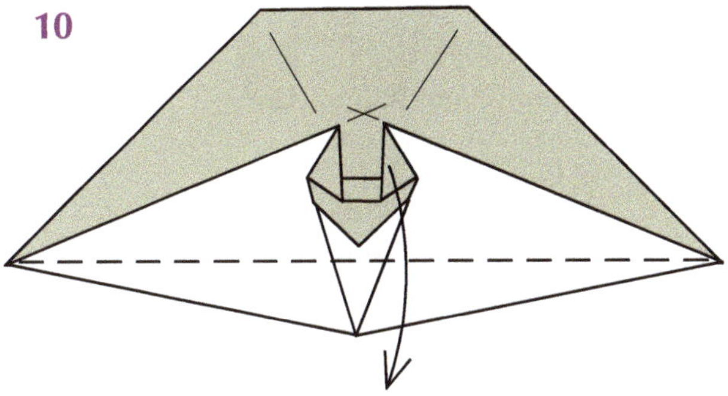

Rotate 180°.

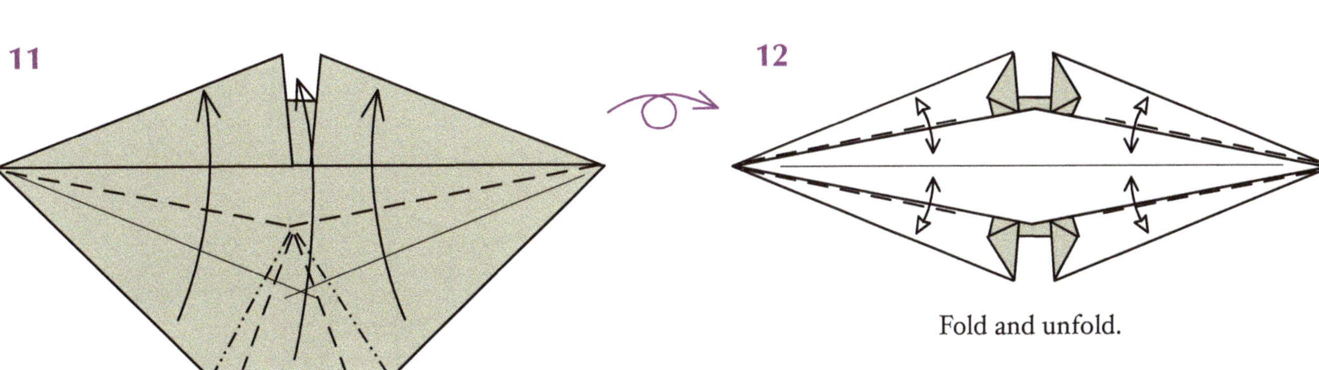

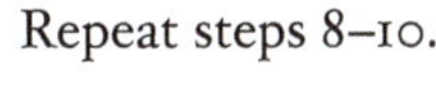

11

Repeat steps 8–10.

12

Fold and unfold.

13

Pleat-fold.

14

Note the bold line is slightly to the left of the legs. Make squash folds.

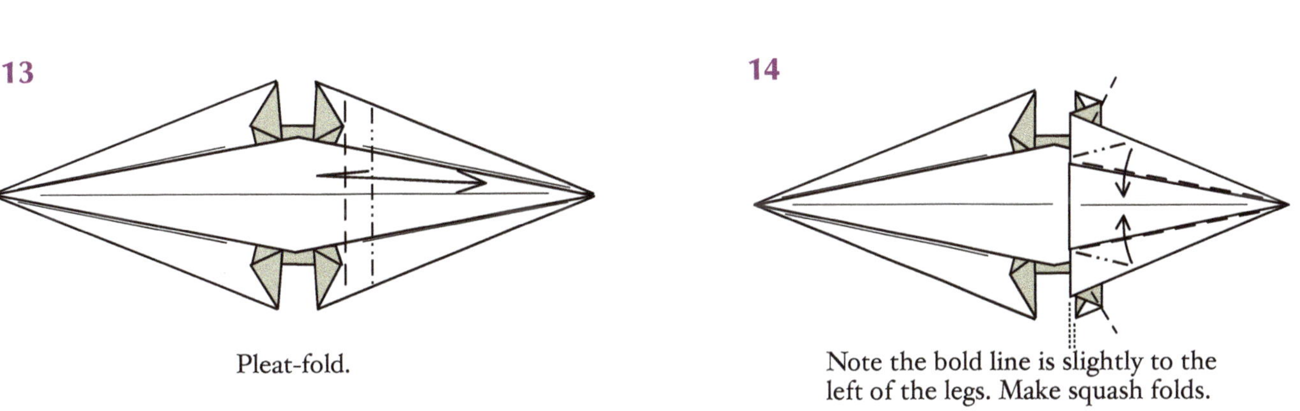

15

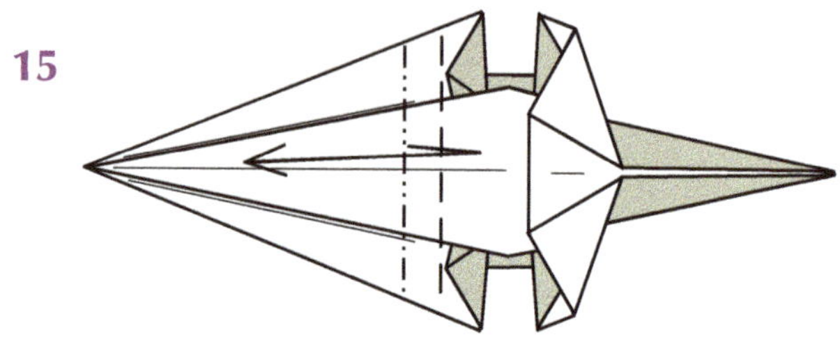

Repeat steps 13–14 on the left.

16

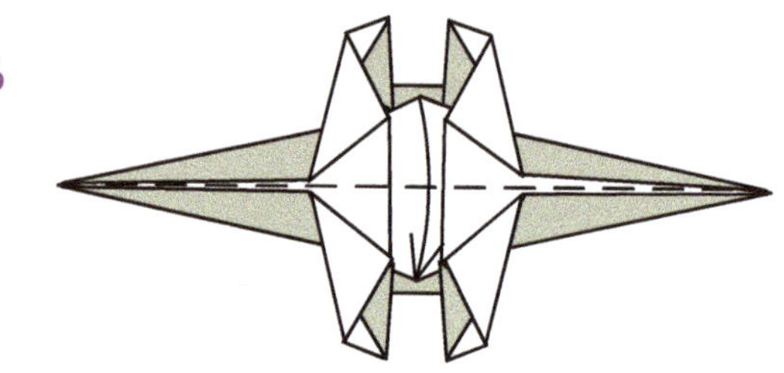

Fold in half.

17

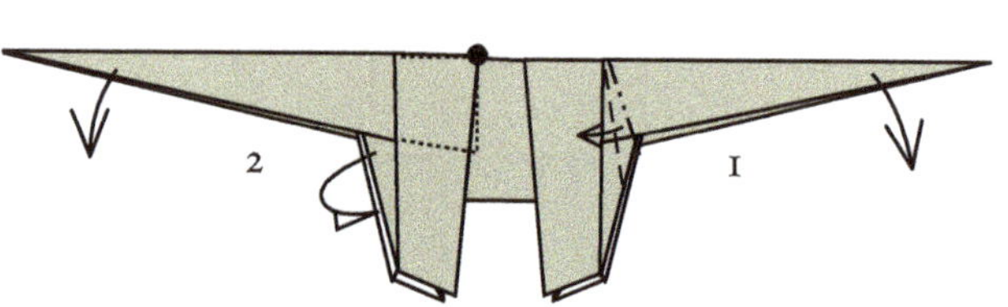

1. Crimp-fold.
2. Slide the neck down from the dot, while sliding the paper into the legs.

18

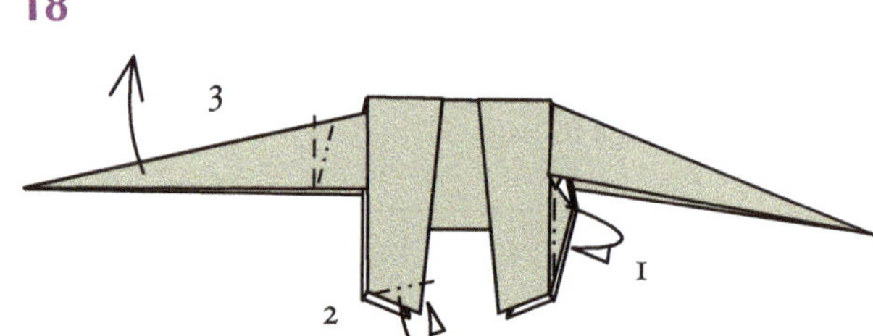

1. Fold inside, repeat behind.
2. Fold inside, repeat behind.
3. Crimp-fold.

19

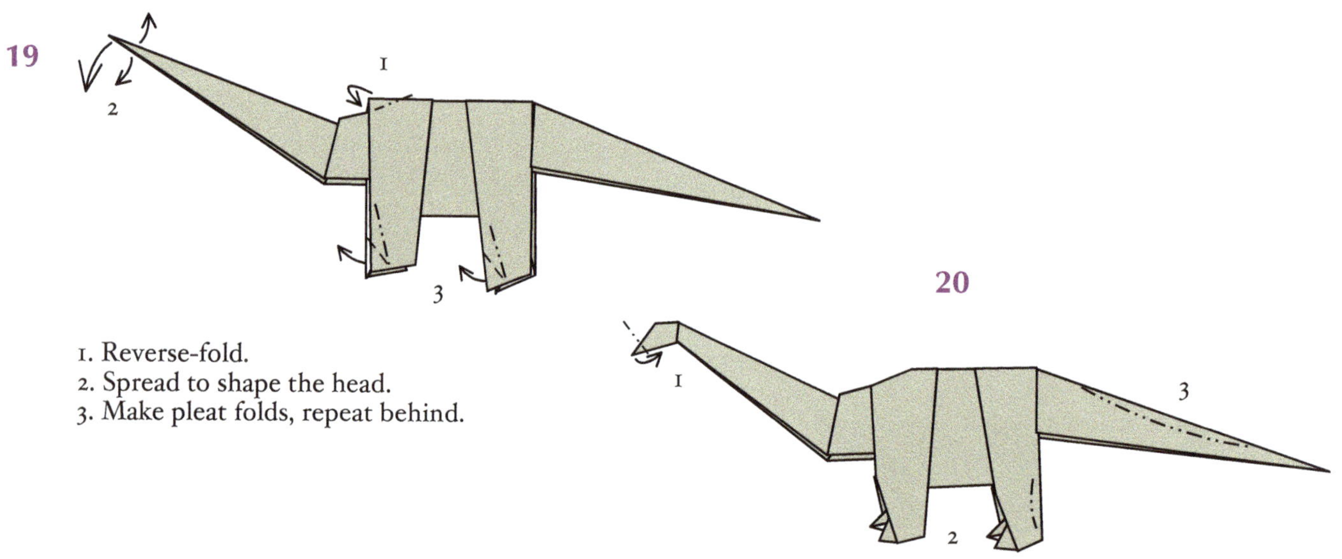

1. Reverse-fold.
2. Spread to shape the head.
3. Make pleat folds, repeat behind.

20

1. Reverse-fold.
2. Shape the legs, repeat behind.
3. Shape the tail.

21

Plateosaurus

Plateosaurus lived much earlier than most giant sauropods, during the Late Triassic Period, when dinosaurs were just beginning to grow large. At up to 35 feet long, it was impressive for its time, even though it was smaller than later giants. A primarily plant-eater, Plateosaurus likely fed on leaves and soft vegetation. It may have been able to stand on its hind legs to reach higher plants, showing an early experiment in size and feeding that would later lead to the enormous sauropods.

1

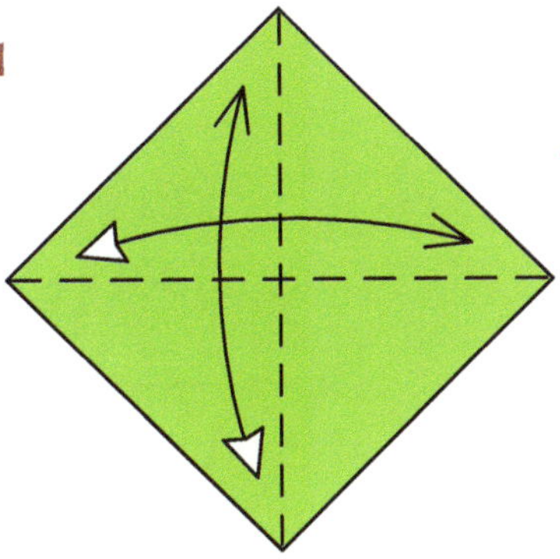

Fold and unfold.

2

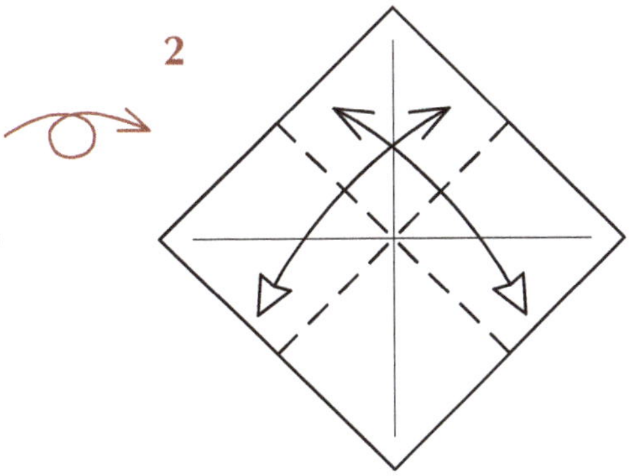

Fold and unfold.

3

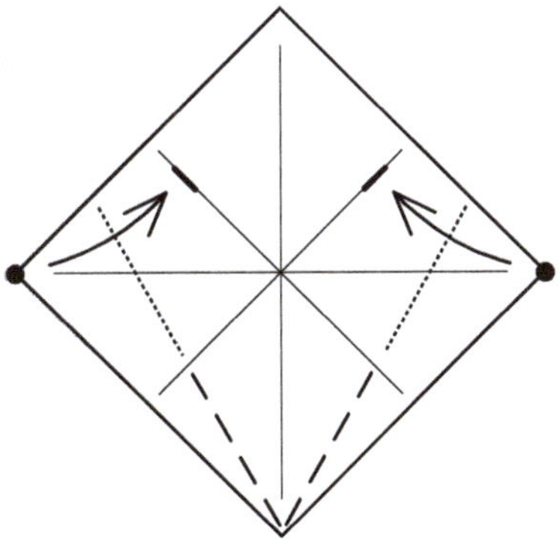

Bring the corners to the creases.

4

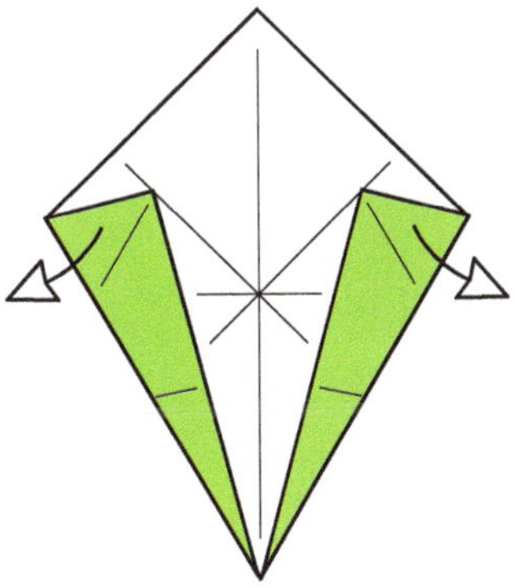

Unfold and rotate 90°.

5

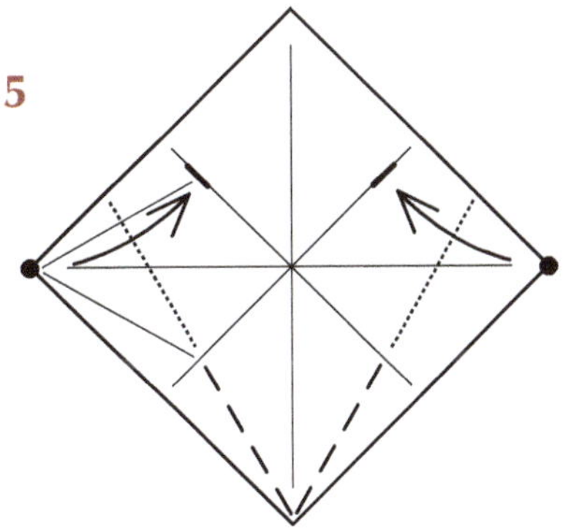

Repeat steps 3–4 three times.

6

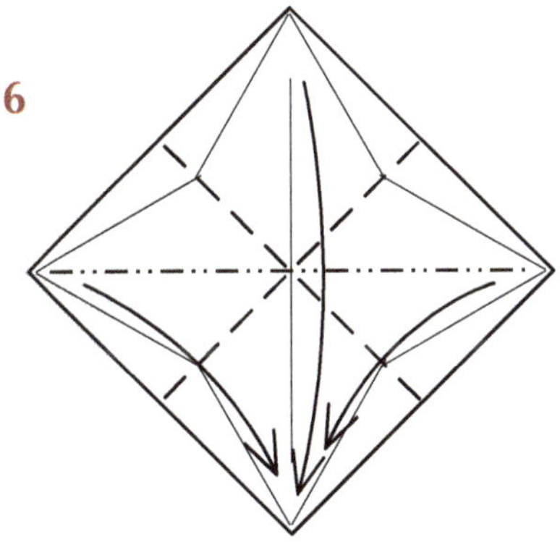

Fold along the creases.

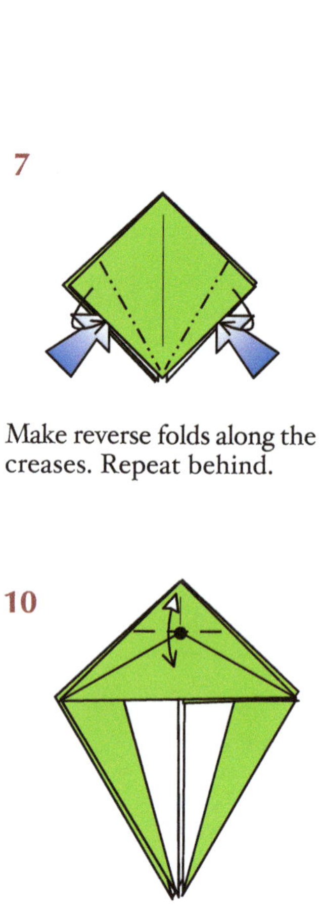

7

Make reverse folds along the creases. Repeat behind.

8

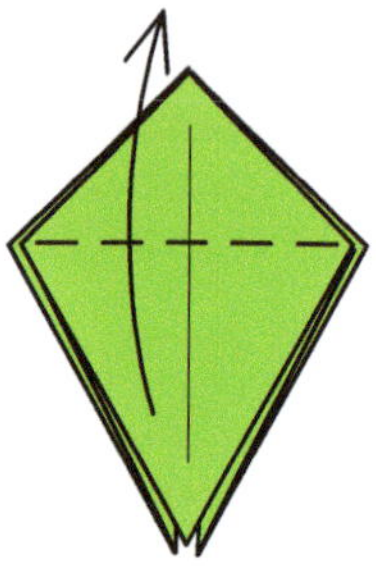

Fold the top flap up.

9

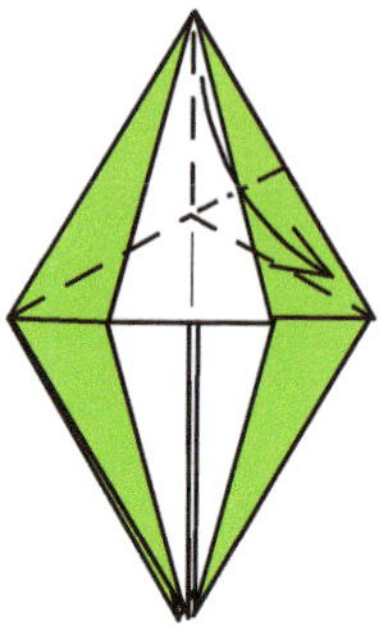

Rabbit-ear.

10

Fold and unfold.

11

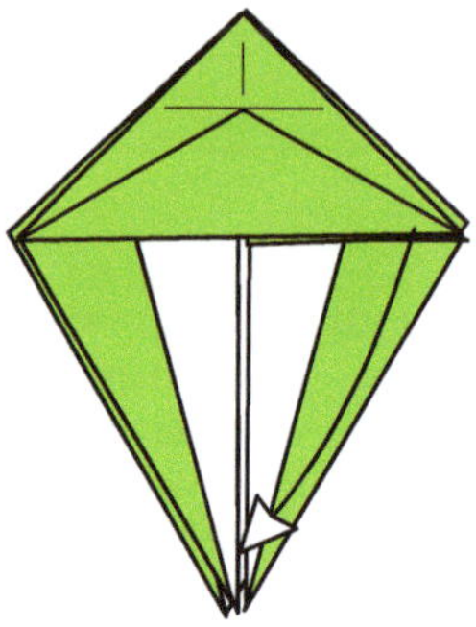

Unfold.

12

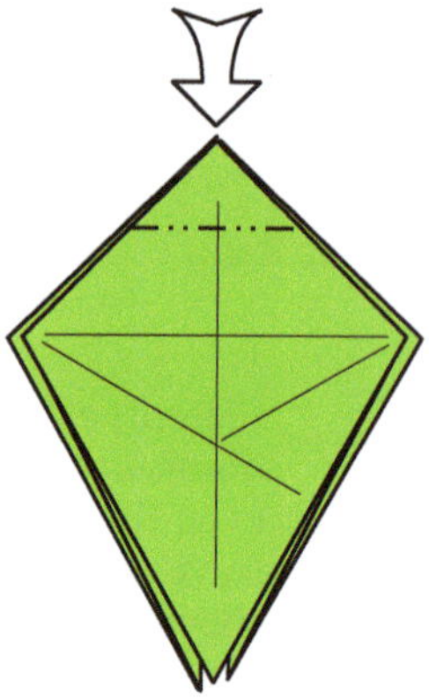

Spread to sink.

13

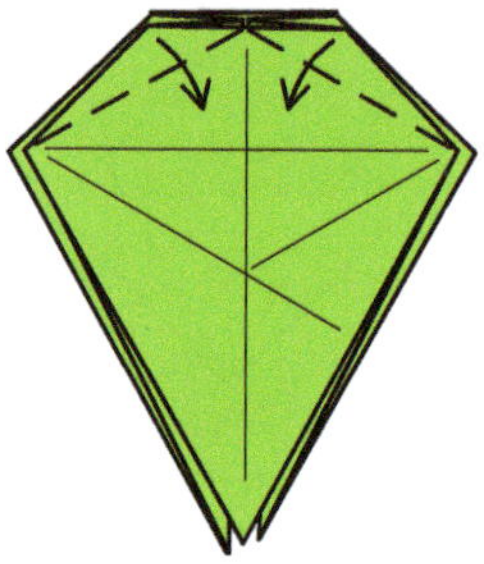

Repeat behind.

14

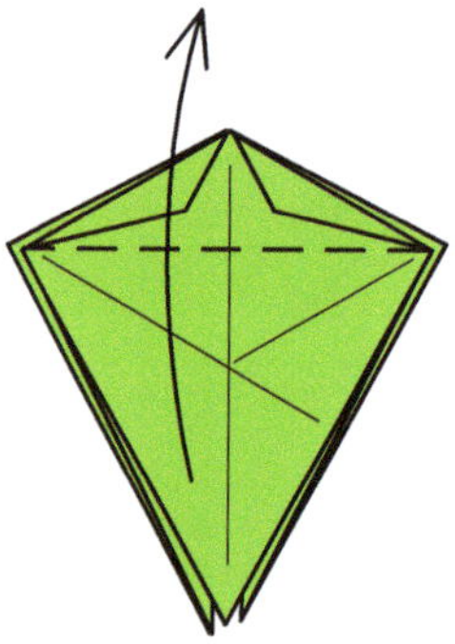

Repeat behind.

15

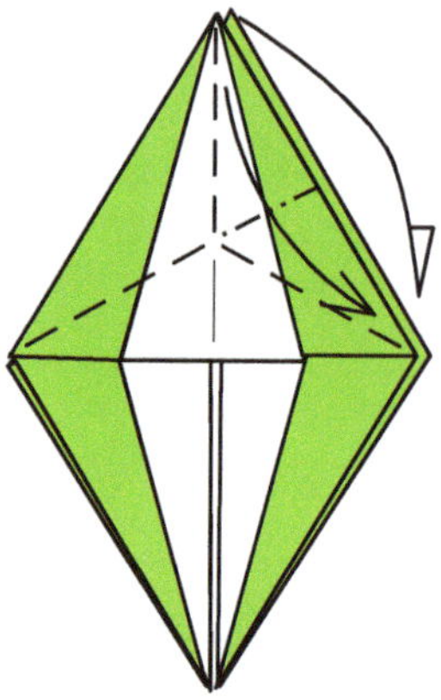

Rabbit-ear and repeat behind.

16

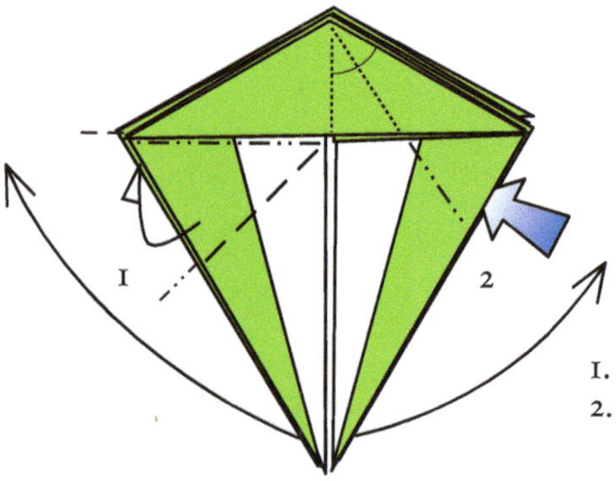

1. Crimp-fold.
2. Reverse-fold.

17

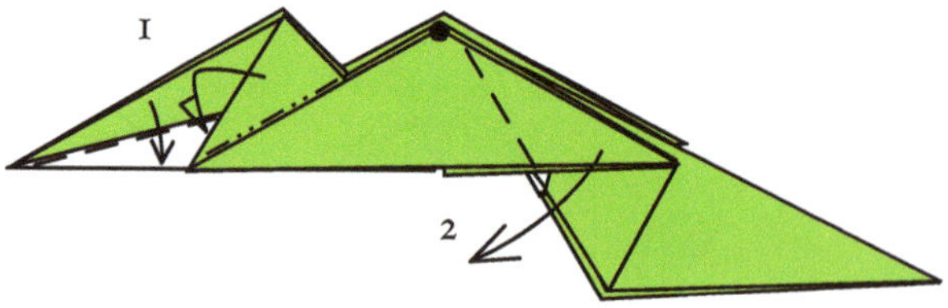

1. Reverse-fold.
2. Valley-fold to the right of the dot.

Repeat behind.

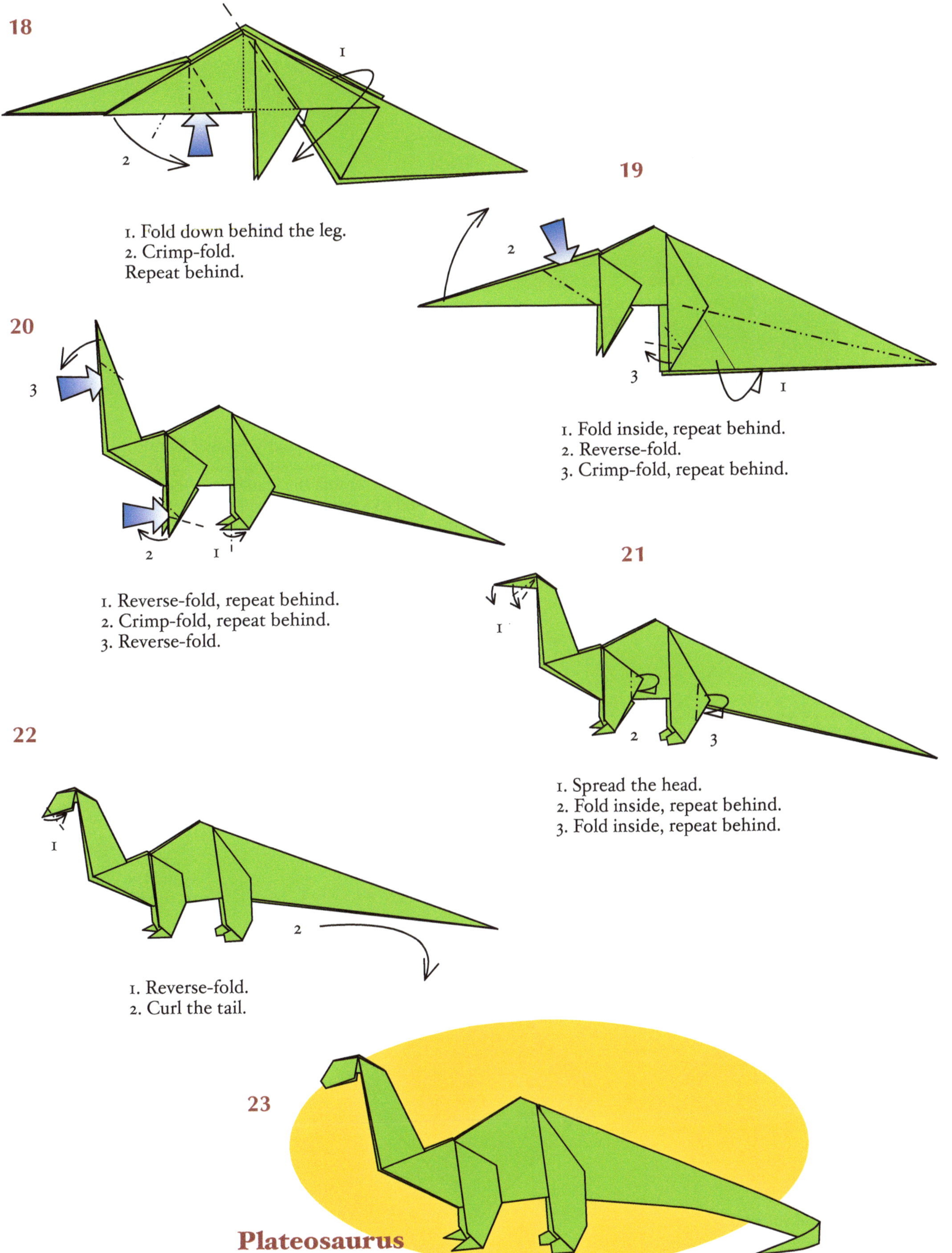
18
1. Fold down behind the leg.
2. Crimp-fold.
Repeat behind.
19
1. Fold inside, repeat behind.
2. Reverse-fold.
3. Crimp-fold, repeat behind.
20
1. Reverse-fold, repeat behind.
2. Crimp-fold, repeat behind.
3. Reverse-fold.
21
1. Spread the head.
2. Fold inside, repeat behind.
3. Fold inside, repeat behind.
22
1. Reverse-fold.
2. Curl the tail.
23
Plateosaurus

Barapasaurus

Barapasaurus was an early sauropod that lived during the Early Jurassic Period, a time when dinosaurs were rapidly increasing in size. Measuring around 45 feet long, it was one of the first dinosaurs to truly resemble the classic long-necked giants. A steady herbivore, Barapasaurus used its strong legs to support its heavy body as it slowly moved across the landscape. Its name means "big-legged lizard," a fitting description for a dinosaur built to carry great weight.

1

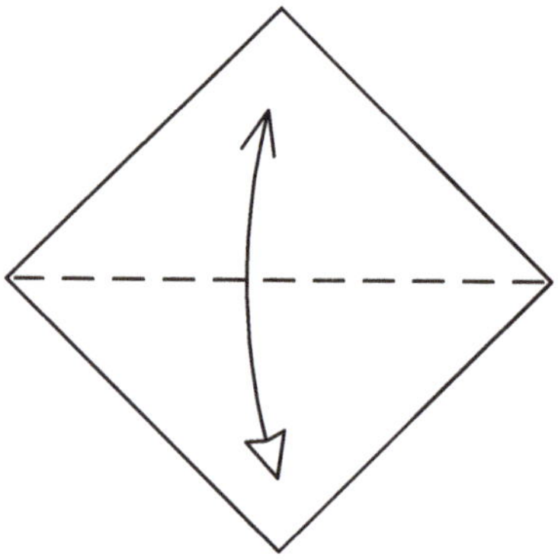

Fold and unfold.

2

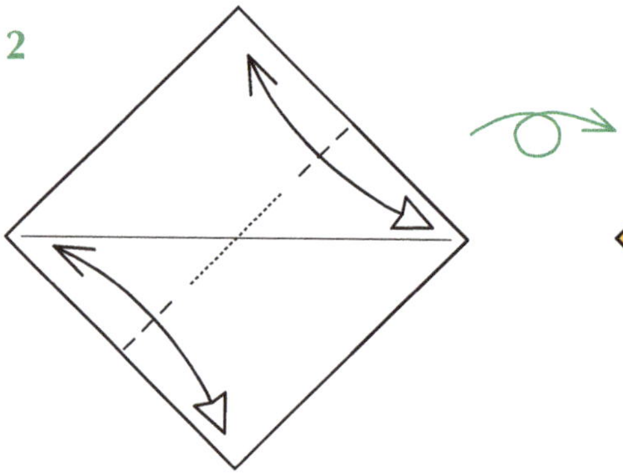

Fold and unfold.

3

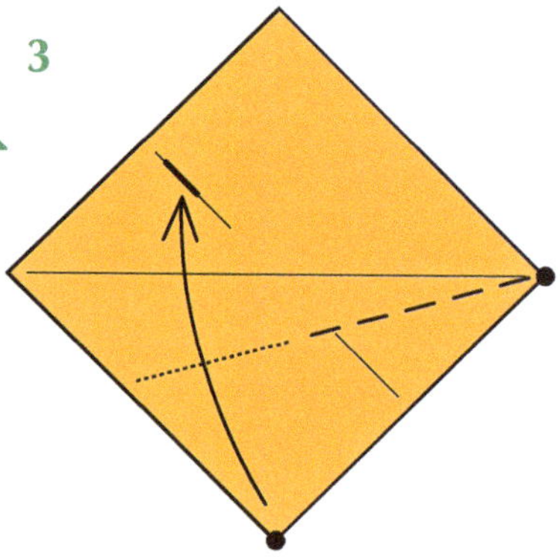

Bring the corner to the line.

4

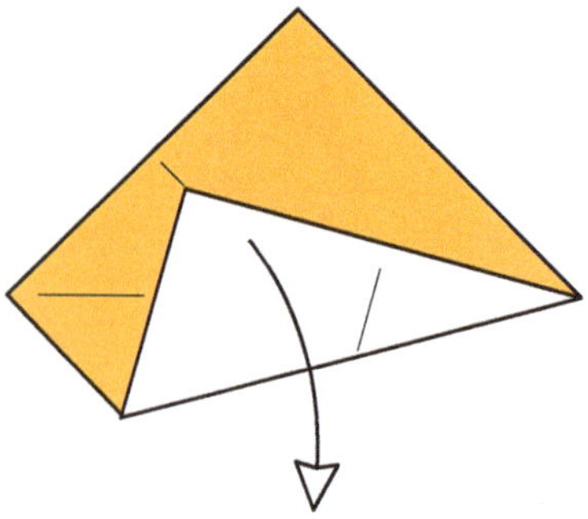

Unfold and rotate 180°.

5

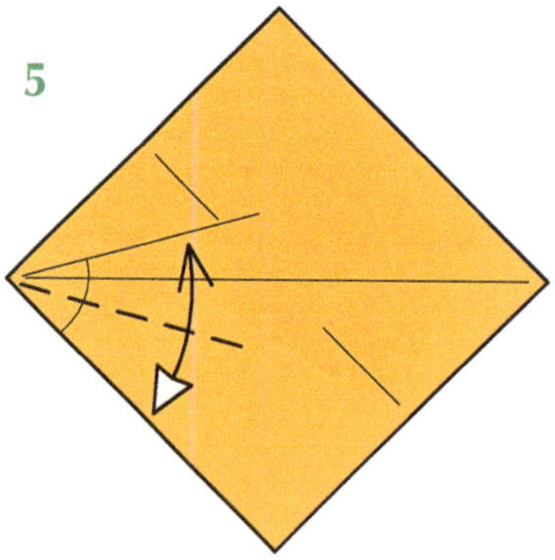

Fold and unfold.

6

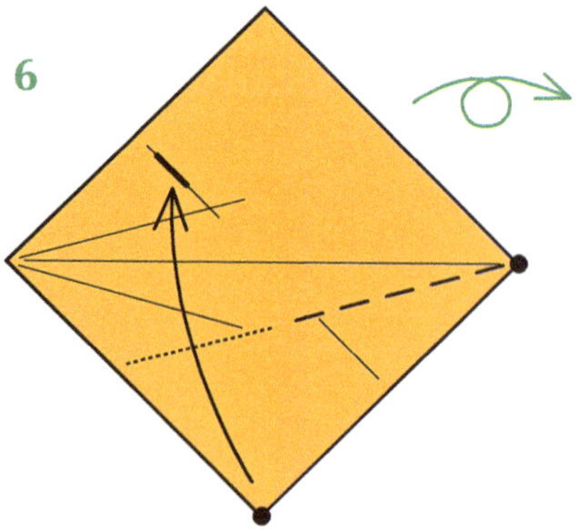

Repeat steps 3–5.

7

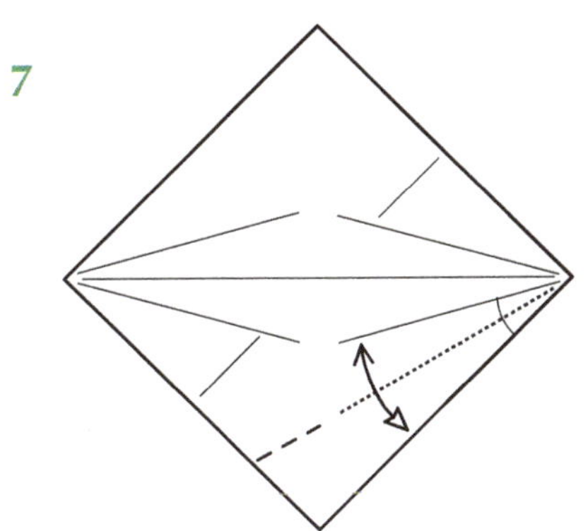

Fold and unfold on the edge.

8

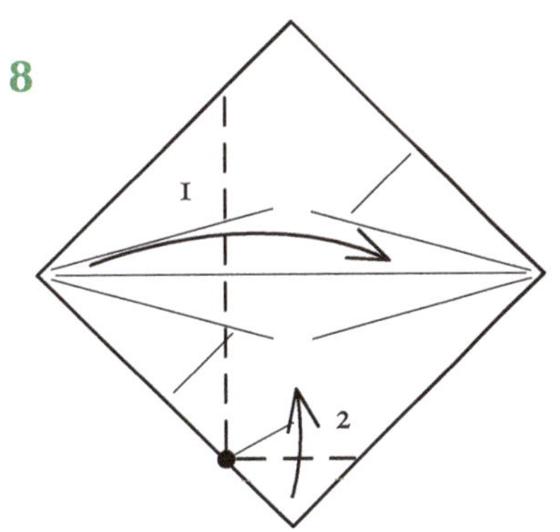

Fold in order.

9

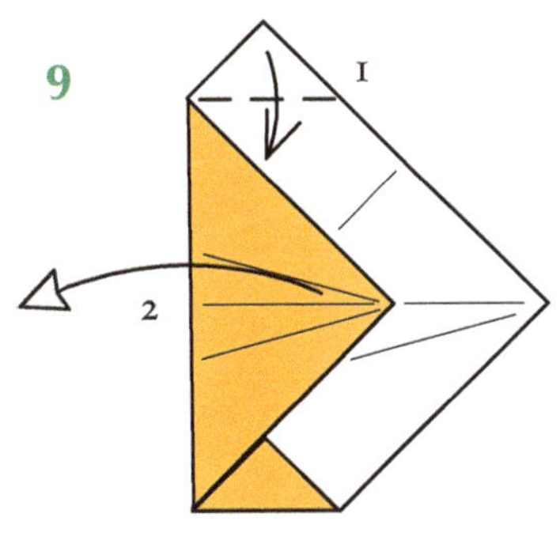

1. Fold down.
2. Unfold.

10

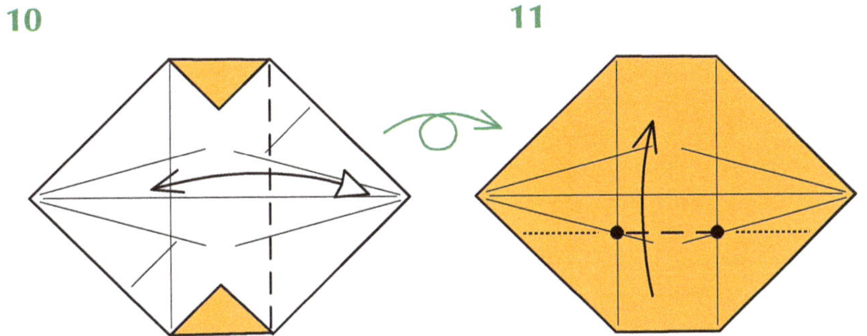

Fold and unfold.

11

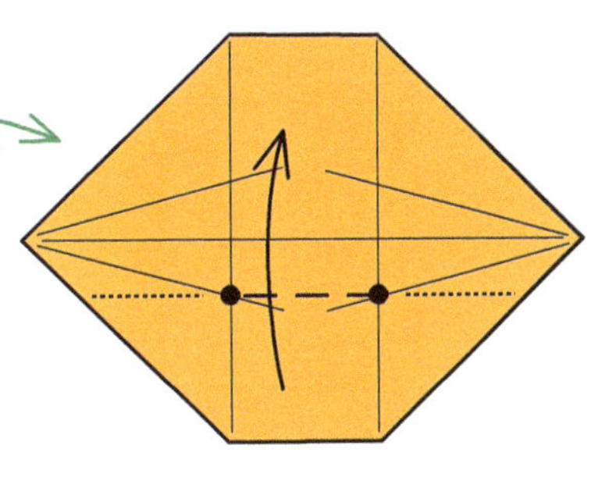

Crease between the dots.

12

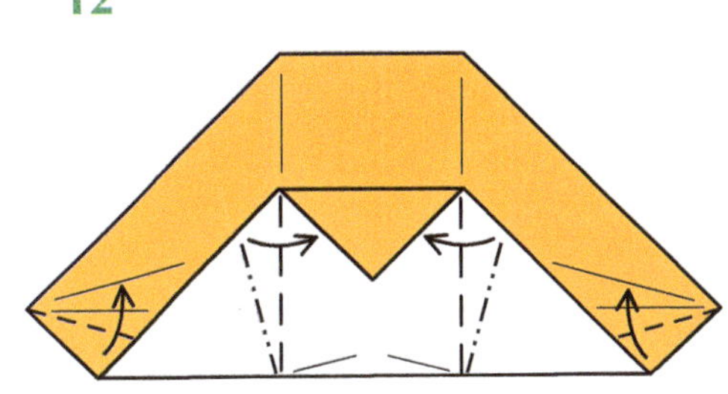

Valley-fold along the creases for these squash folds.

13

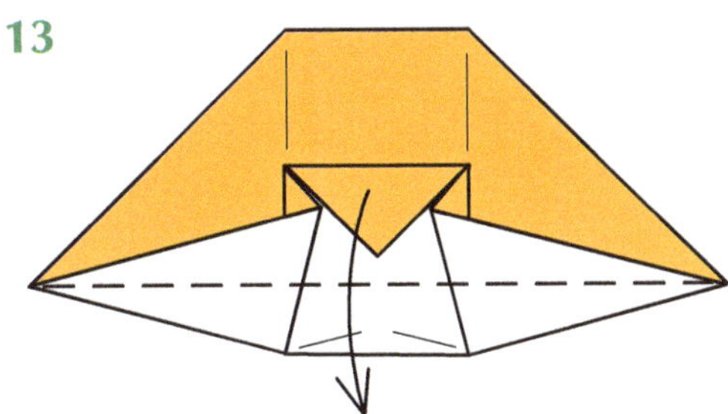

Fold down and rotate 180°.

14

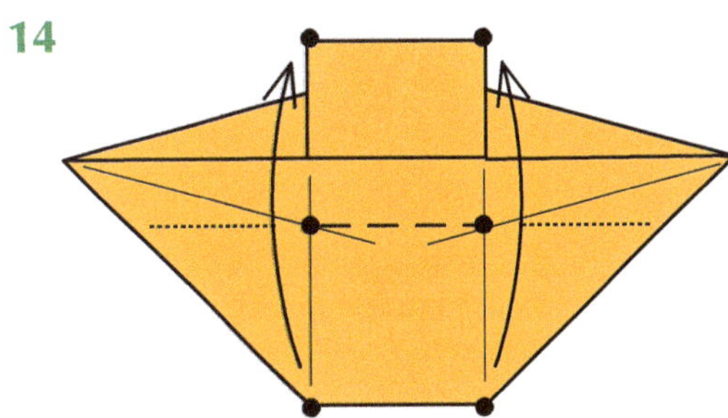

Repeat steps 11–13.

15

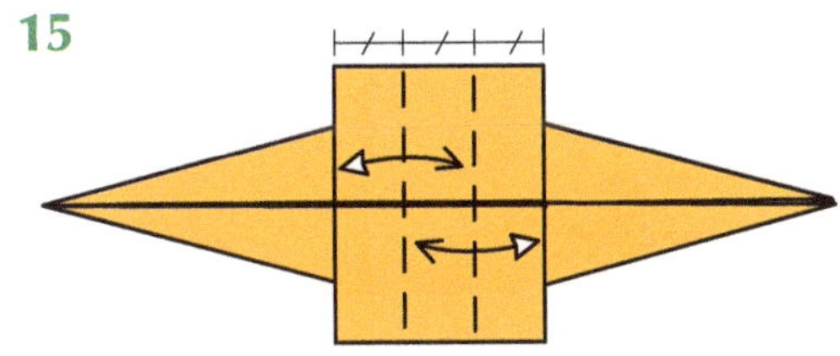

Divide in thirds. Fold and unfold.

16

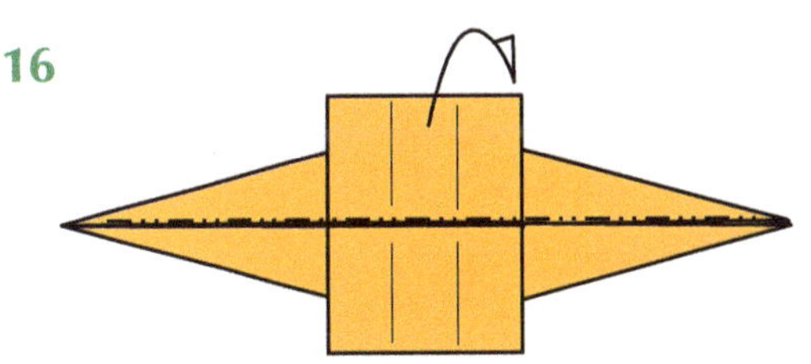

Fold in half.

17

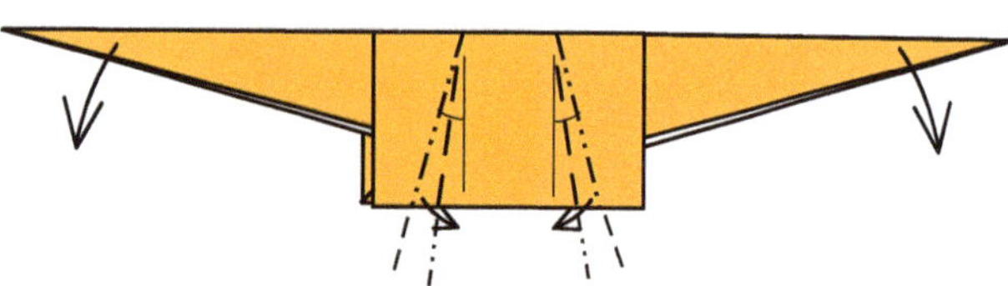

Make crimp folds.

18

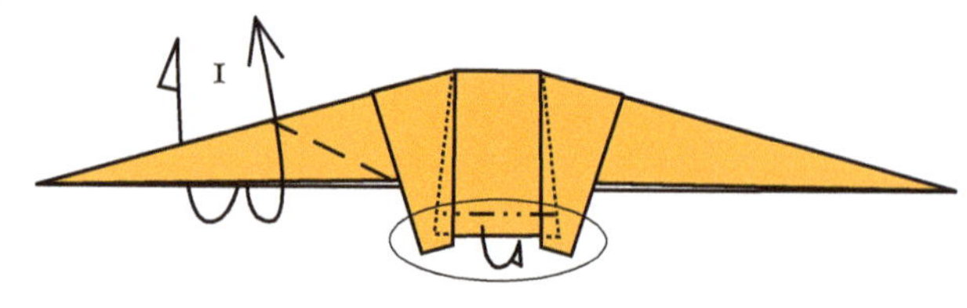

1. Outside-reverse-fold.
2. Petal-fold, repeat behind.

View of inside.

19

1. Wrap around from inside.
2. Fold behind.
Repeat behind.

20

1. Ouside-reverse-fold and spread the head.
2. Shape the legs, repeat behind.
3. Shape the tail.

21

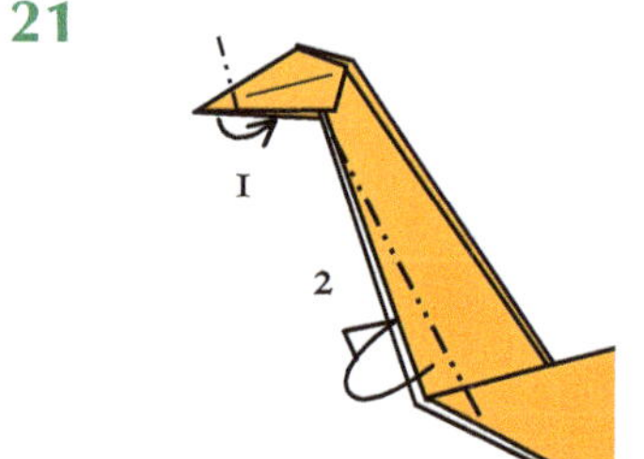

1. Reverse-fold.
2. Fold inside, repeat behind.

22

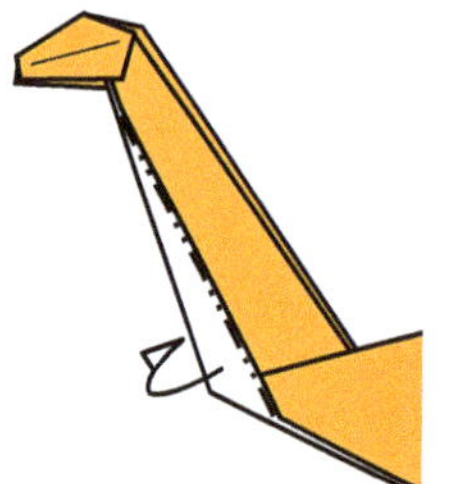

Fold inside.

23

Barapasaurus

Camarasaurus

Camarasaurus was a powerfully built sauropod from the Late Jurassic Period, reaching lengths of about 60 feet. Unlike many of its relatives, it had a shorter neck and tail, giving it a stockier, more muscular appearance. This plant-eater had strong, spoon-shaped teeth that allowed it to chew tougher vegetation. Its sturdy skull and jaw made Camarasaurus one of the best-equipped sauropods for handling coarse plant material.

1

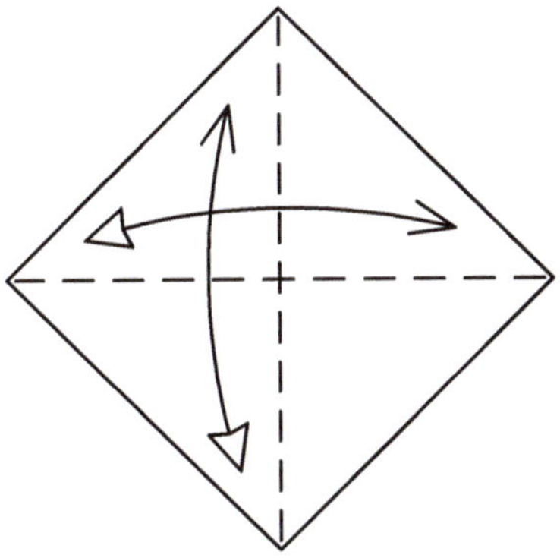

Fold and unfold.

2

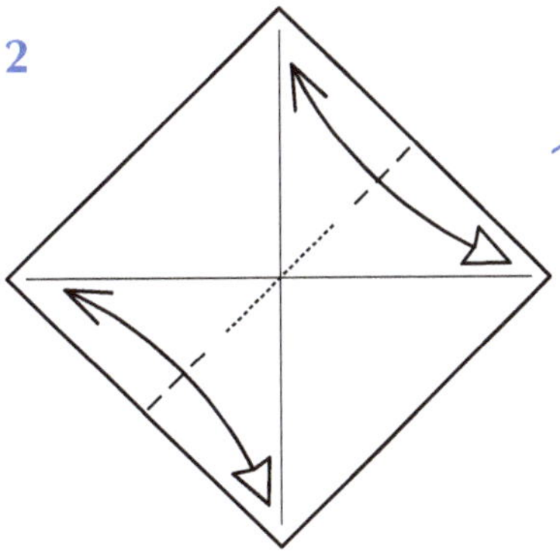

Fold and unfold.

3

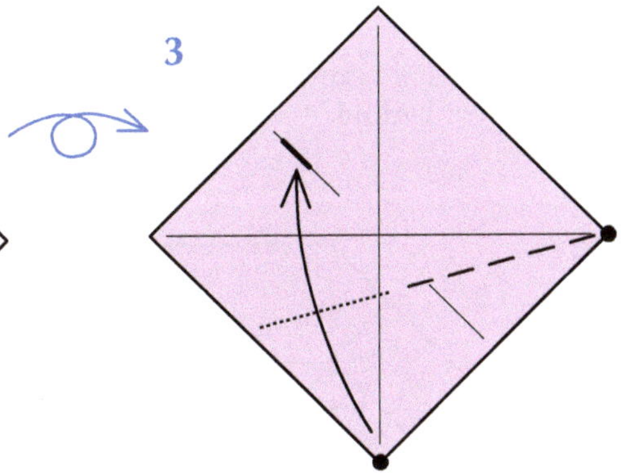

Bring the corner to the line.

4

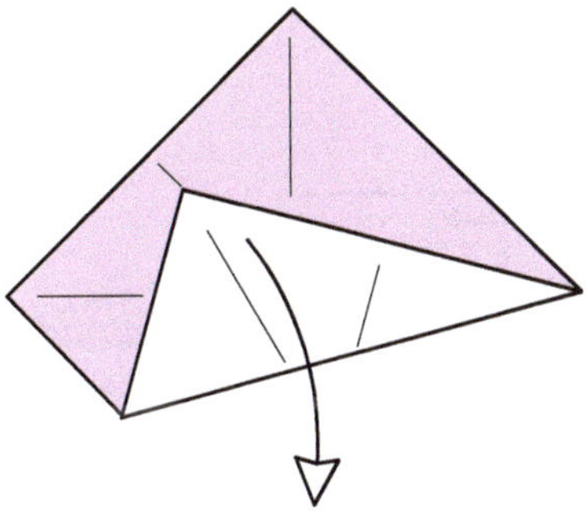

Unfold and rotate 180°.

5

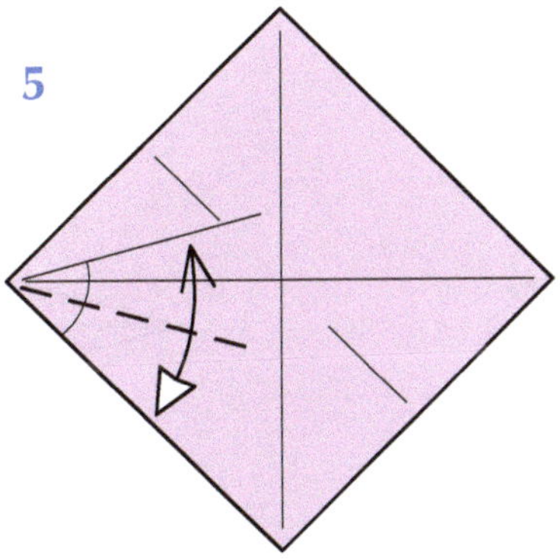

Fold and unfold.

6

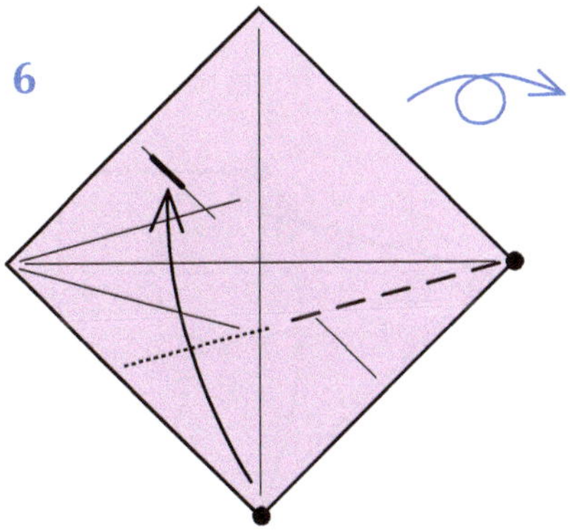

Repeat steps 3–5.

7

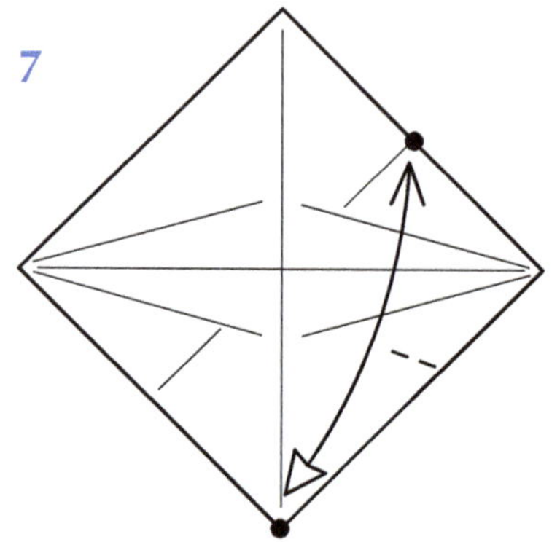

Fold and unfold on the edge.

8

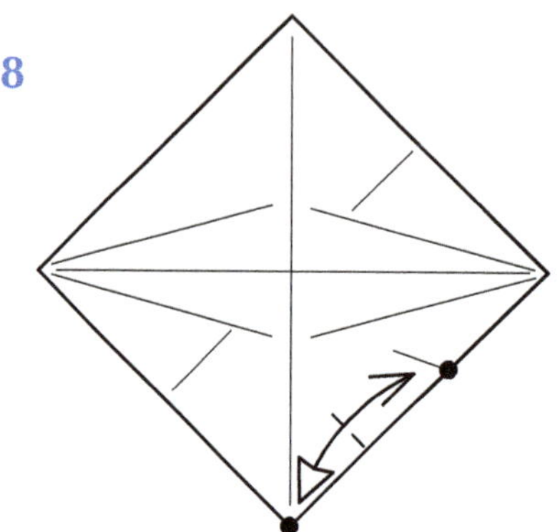

Fold and unfold on the edge.

9

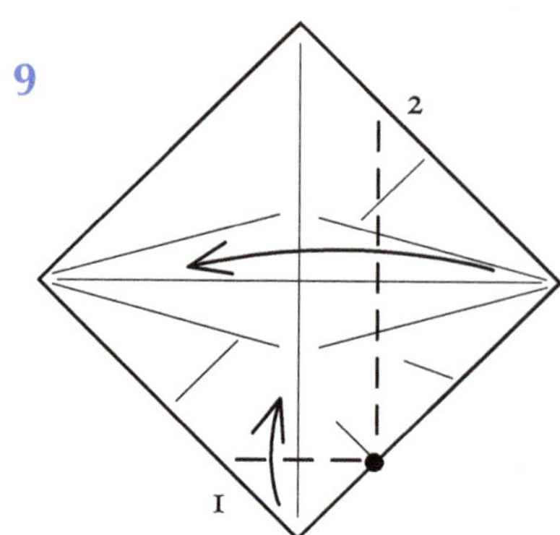

10

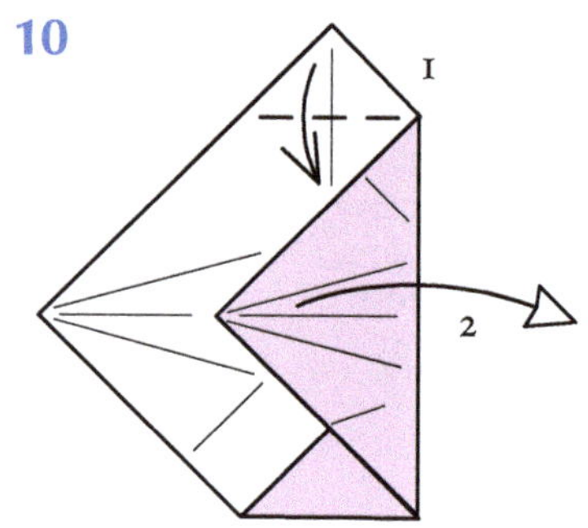

1. Fold down.
2. Unfold.

11

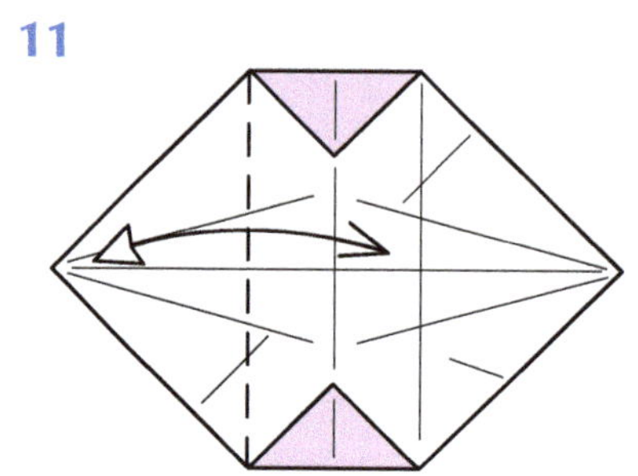

Fold and unfold.

12

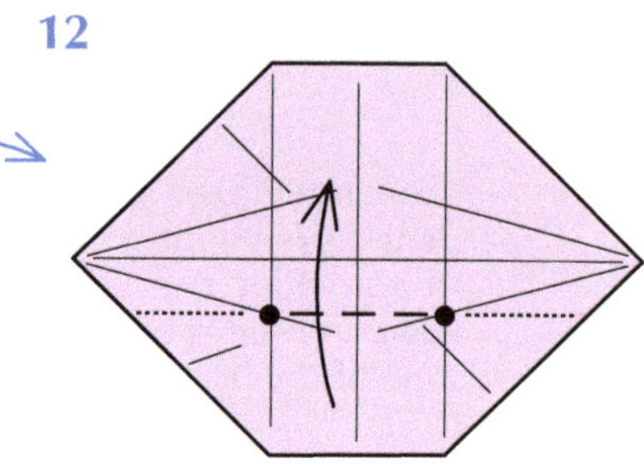

Crease between the dots.

13

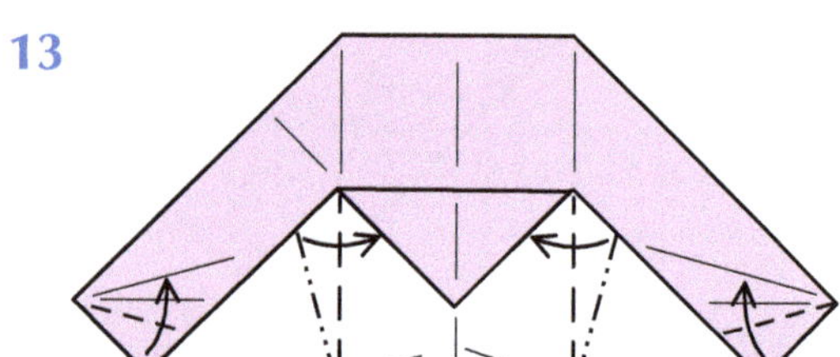

Valley-fold along the creases for these squash folds.

14

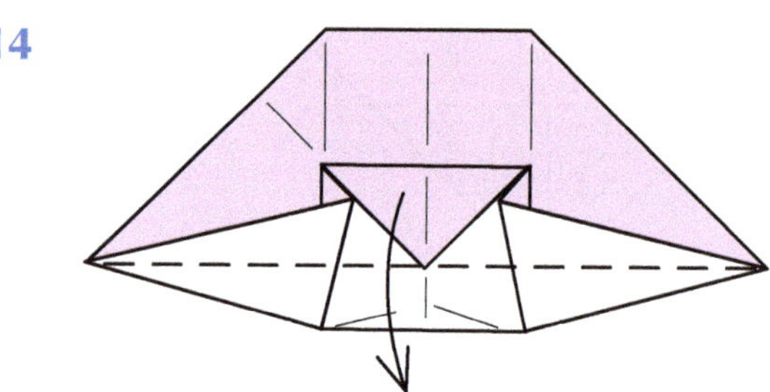

Fold down and rotate 180°.

15

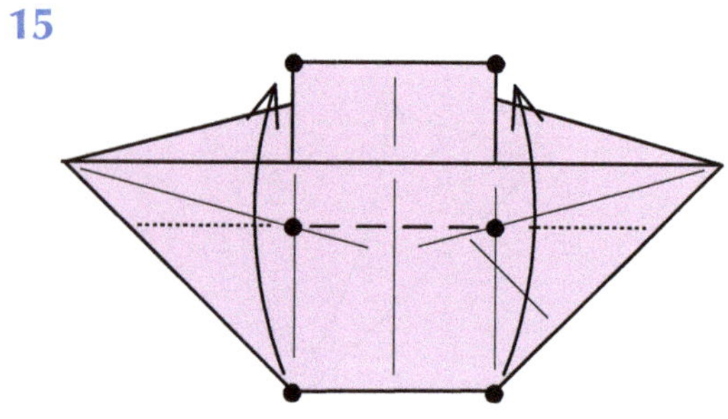

Repeat steps 12–14.

16

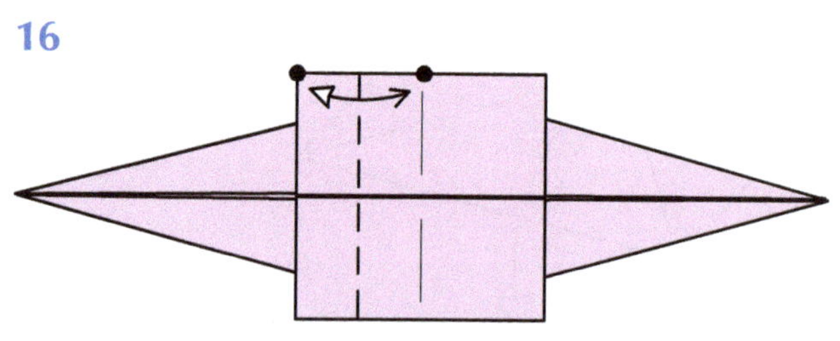

Fold and unfold.

17

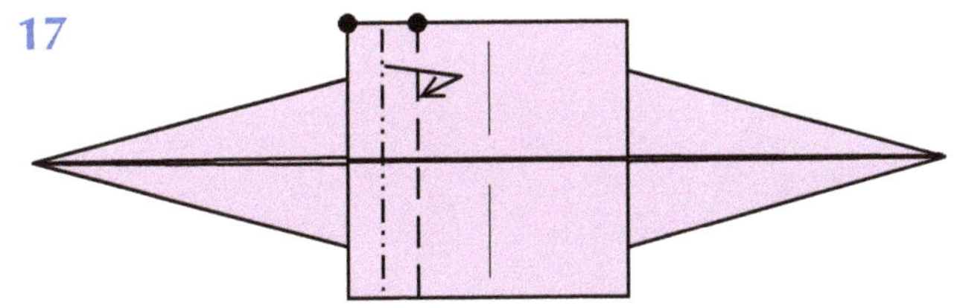

Pleat-fold so the dots meet.

18

Repeat steps 16–17 on the right.

19

20

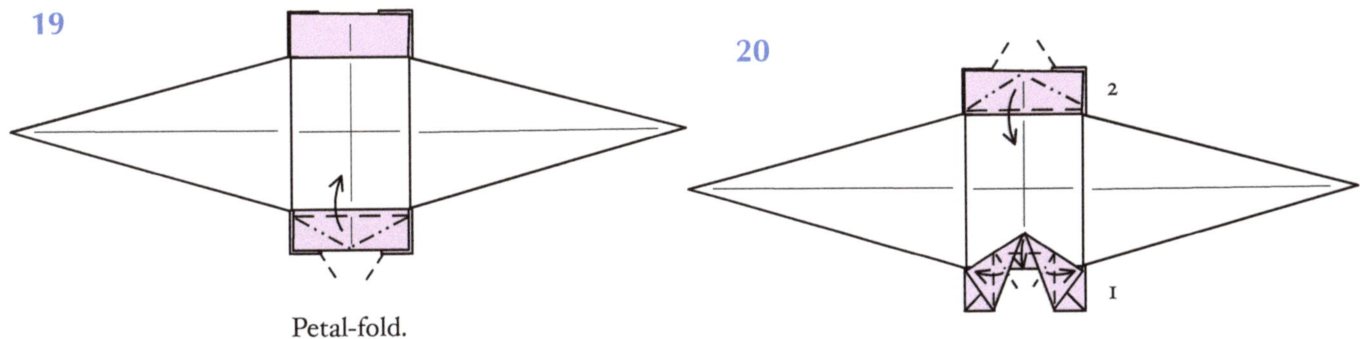

Petal-fold.

1. Petal-fold.
2. Repeat steps 19–20 on the top.

21

22

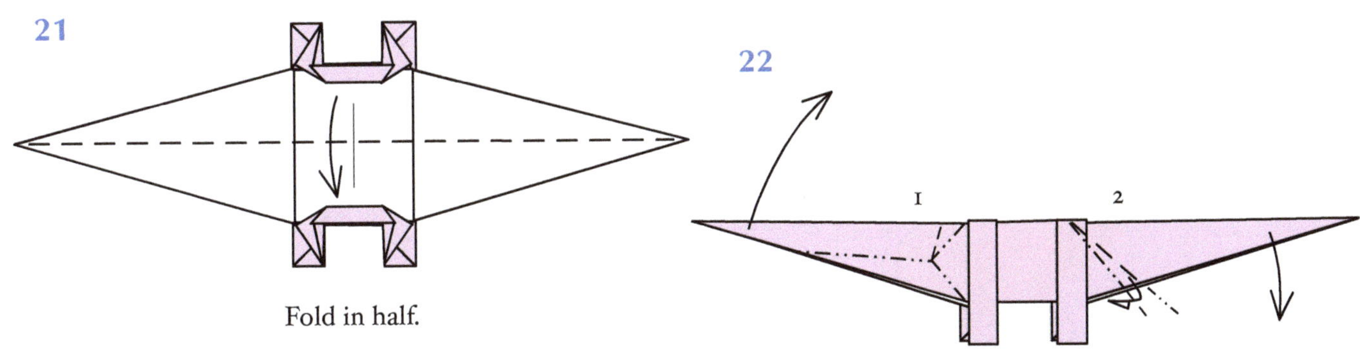

Fold in half.

1. Double-rabbit-ear.
2. Crimp-fold.

23

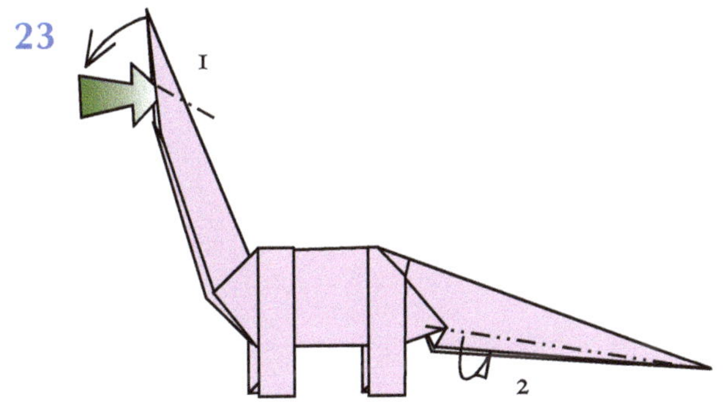

1. Reverse-fold.
2. Fold inside, repeat behind.

24

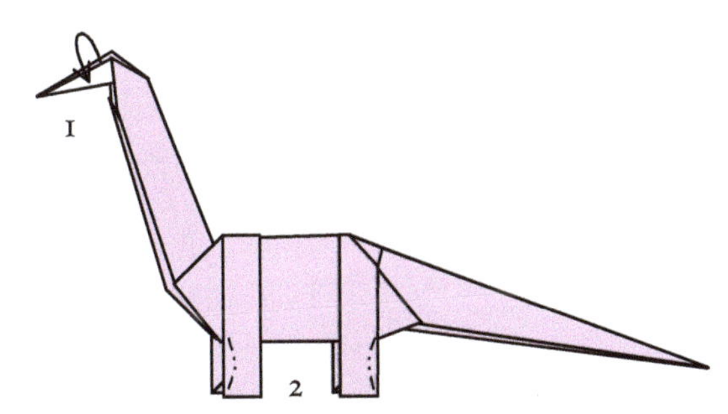

1. Wrap around.
2. Shape the legs.
Repeat behind.

25

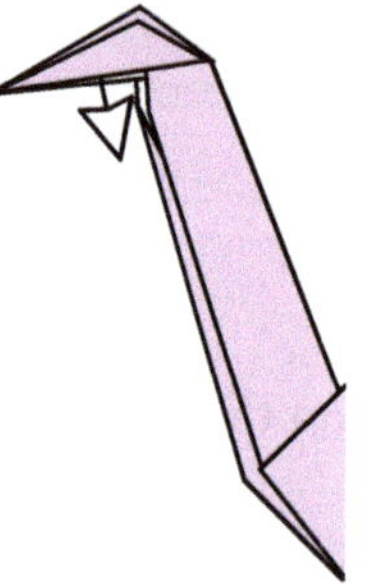

Pull out from inside.
Repeat behind.

26

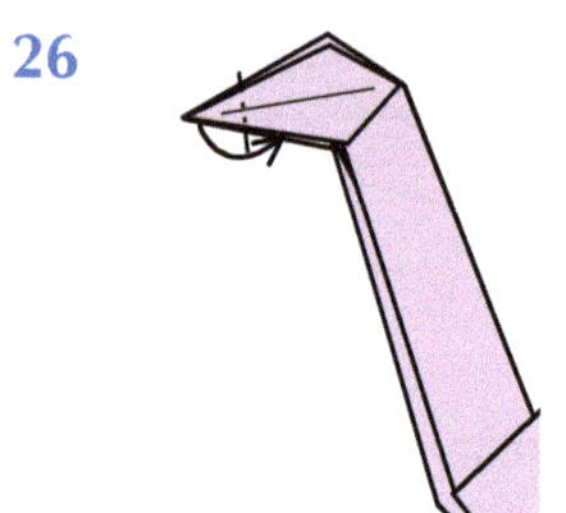

Fold inside.

27

Camarasaurus

Brachiosaurus

Brachiosaurus lived during the Late Jurassic Period and stood out thanks to its unusually long front legs, which lifted its shoulders higher than its hips. This gave it a towering posture, allowing it to reach leaves high in the treetops. It could grow up to 85 feet long and stand over 40 feet tall when stretching upward. A devoted plant-eater, Brachiosaurus fed at heights few other dinosaurs could reach, making it one of the tallest and most inspiring animals of the ancient world.

1

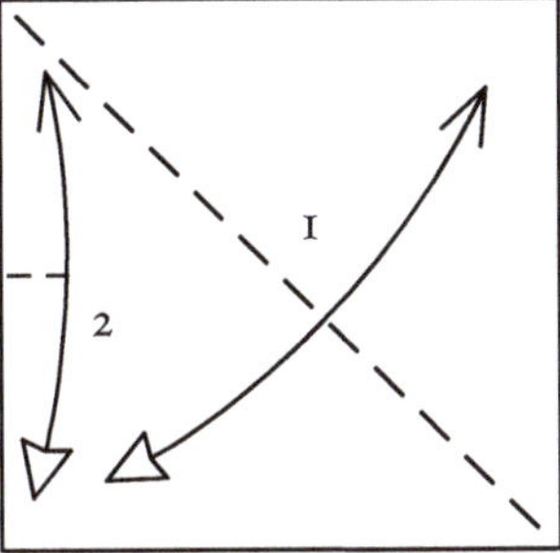

1. Fold and unfold.
2. Fold and unfold on the left.

2

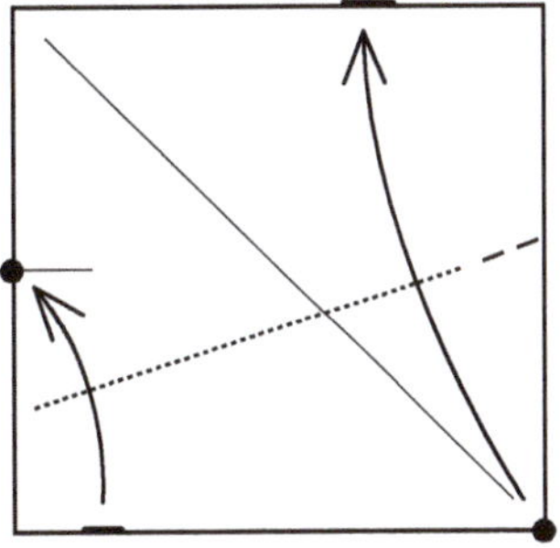

Bring the bottom edge to the left dot and the bottom right corner to the top. Crease on the right.

3

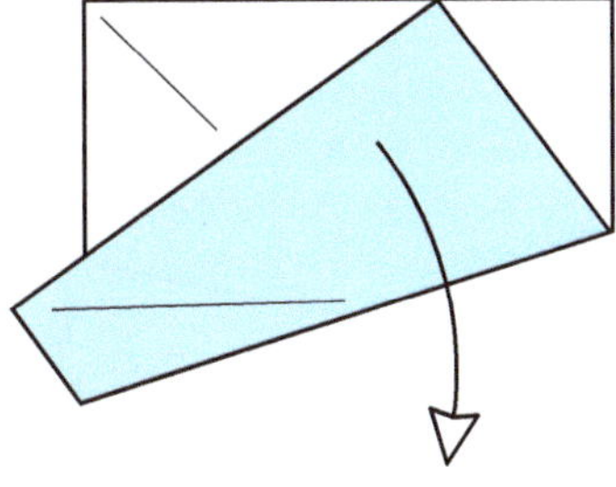

Unfold.

4

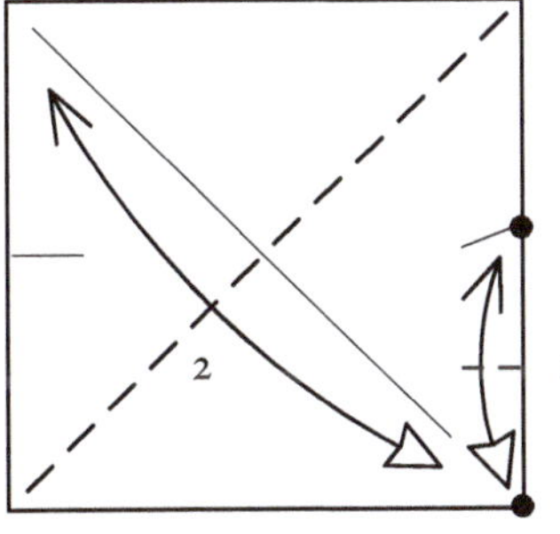

1. Fold and unfold on the right.
2. Fold and unfold.

5

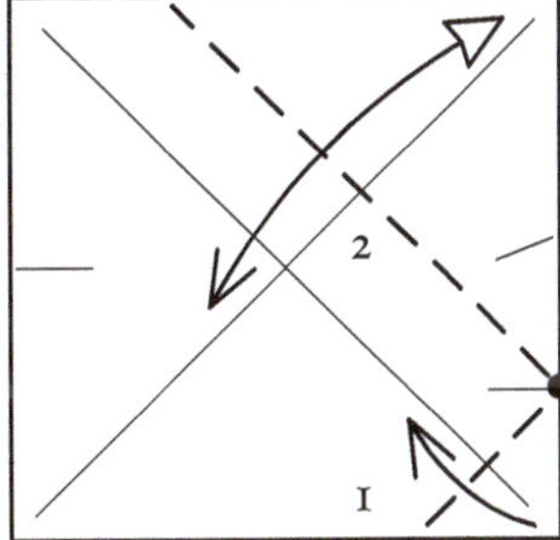

1. Fold up.
2. Fold and unfold.
Rotate.

6

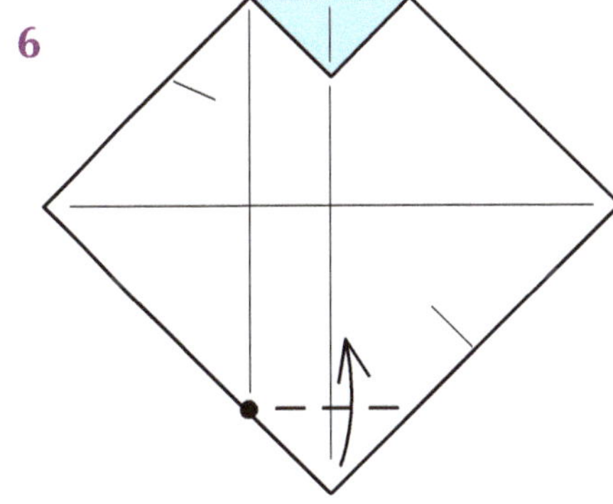

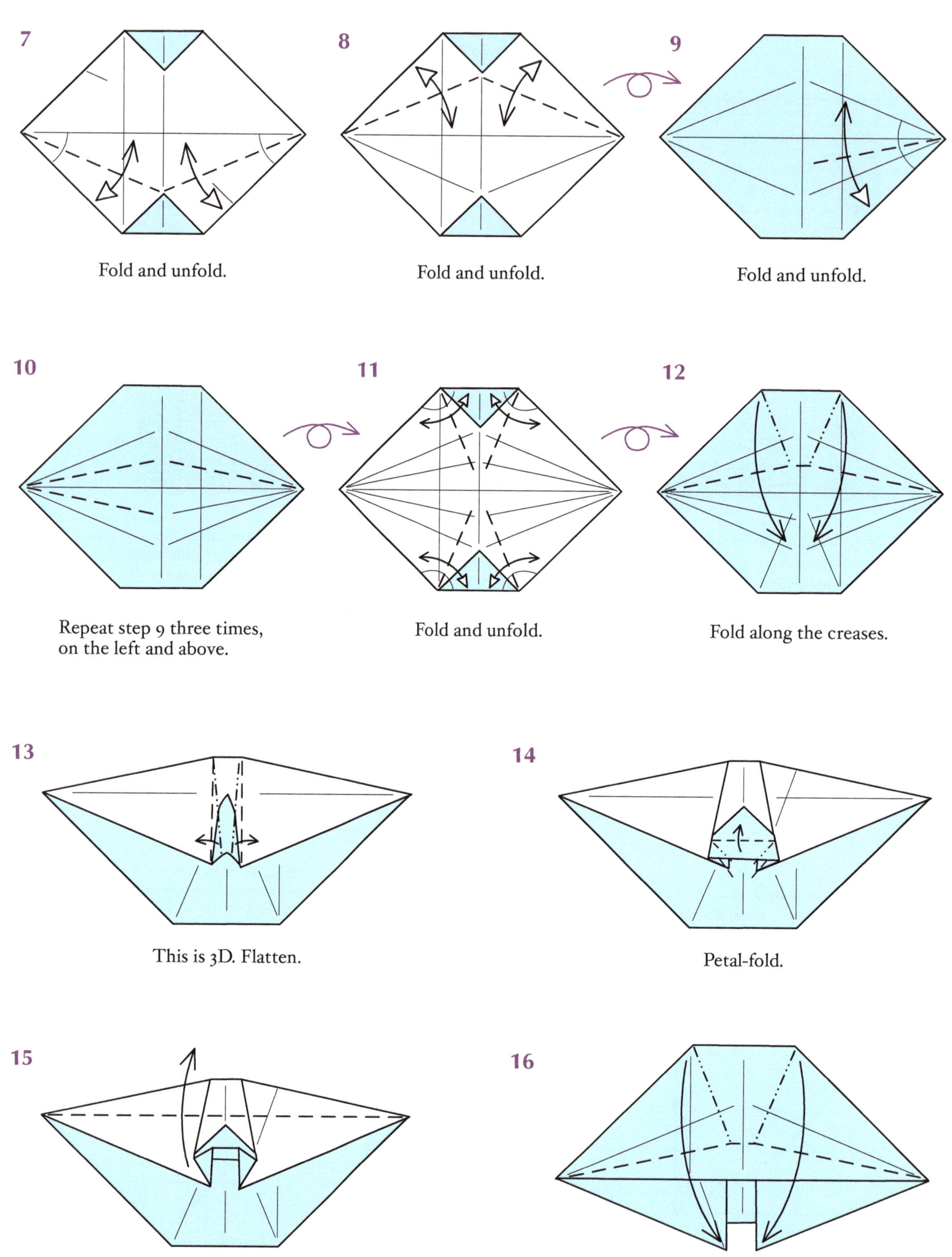
7
Fold and unfold.
8
Fold and unfold.
9
Fold and unfold.
10
Repeat step 9 three times,
on the left and above.
11
Fold and unfold.
12
Fold along the creases.
13
This is 3D. Flatten.
14
Petal-fold.
15
Rotate 180°.
16
Repeat steps 12–15.

17

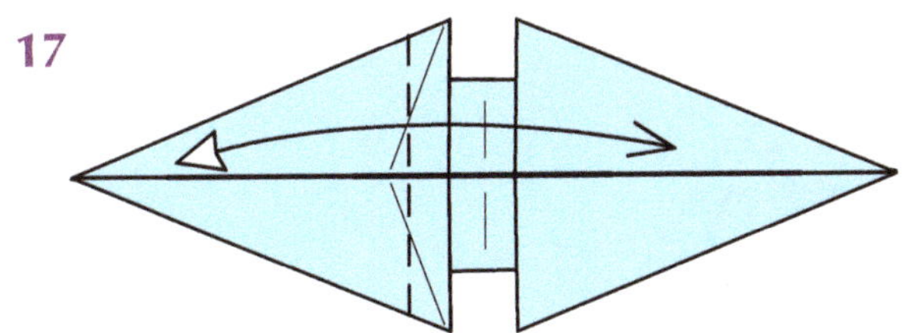

Fold and unfold.

18

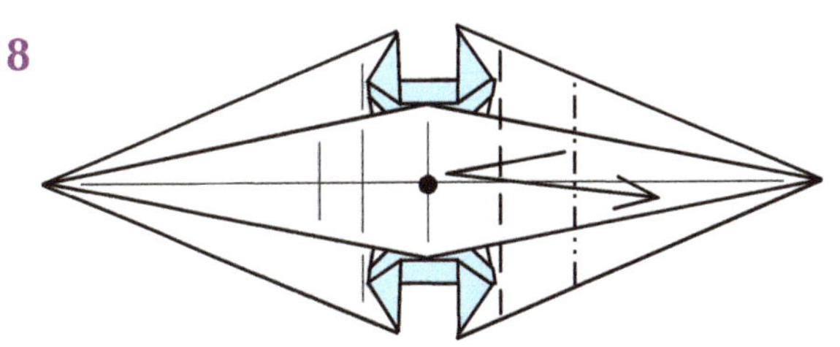

Pleat-fold to the dot.

19

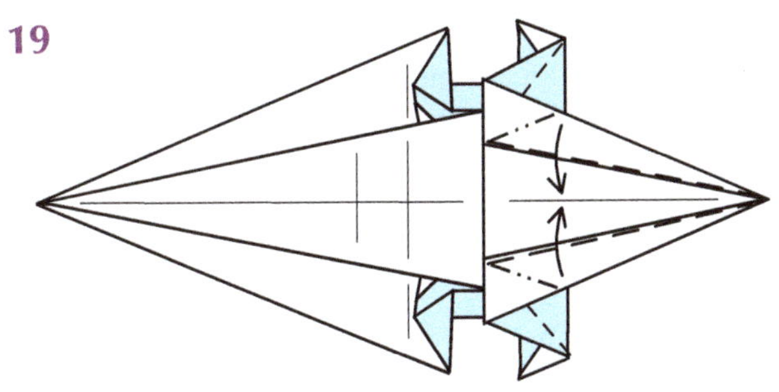

Make squash folds.

20

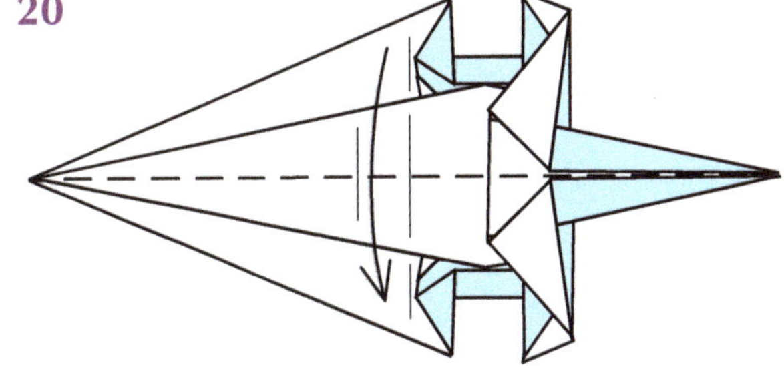

Fold in half.

21

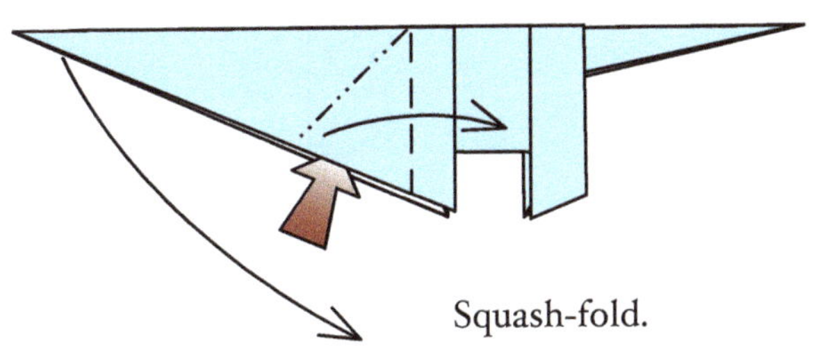

Squash-fold.

22

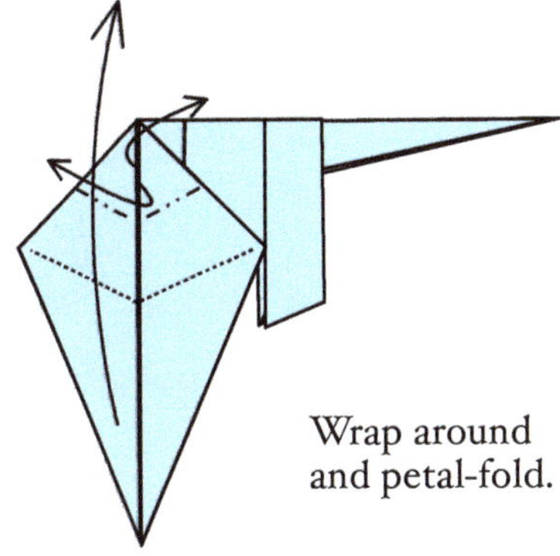

Wrap around and petal-fold.

23

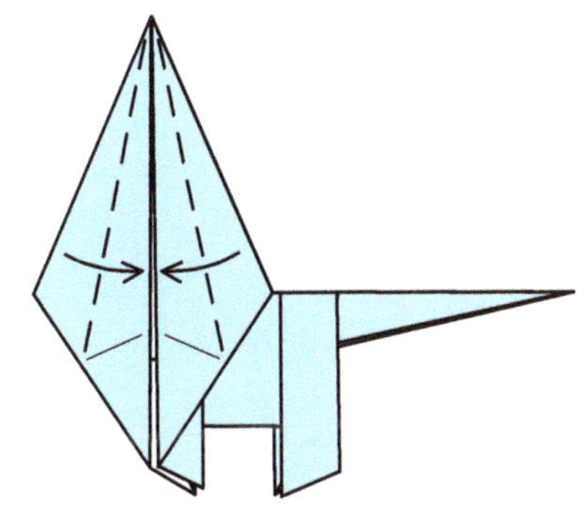

Fold to the center.

24

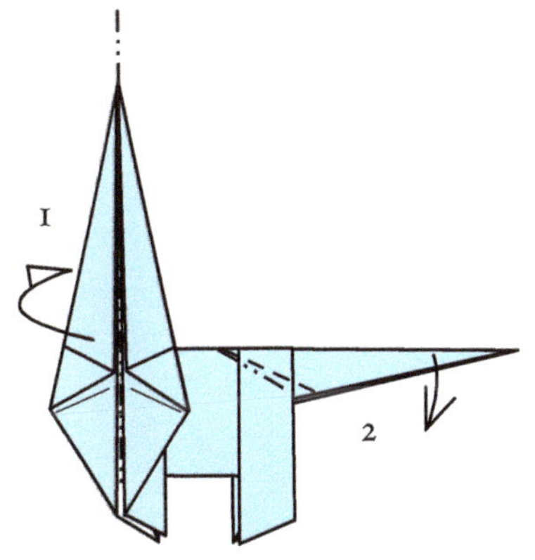

1. Fold behind.
2. Crimp-fold.

25

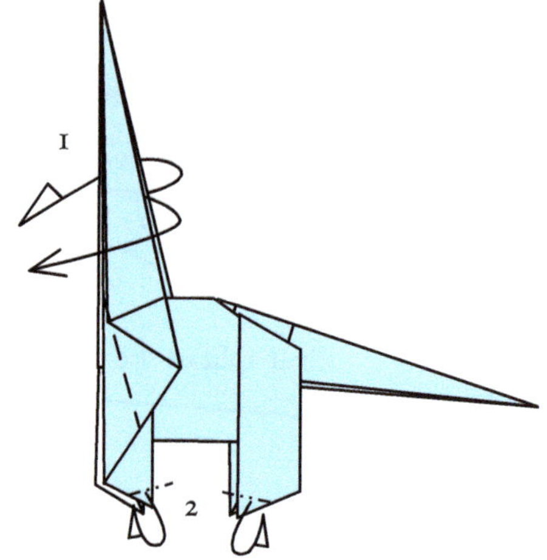

1. Outside-reverse-fold.
2. Fold inside, repeat behind.

26

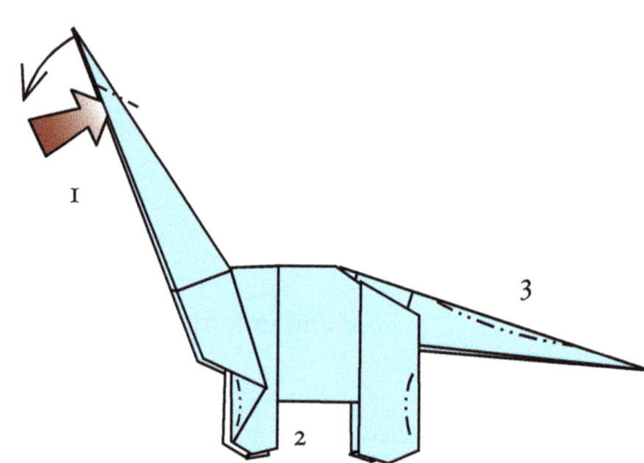

1. Reverse-fold.
2. Shape the legs, repeat behind.
3. Shape the tail.

27

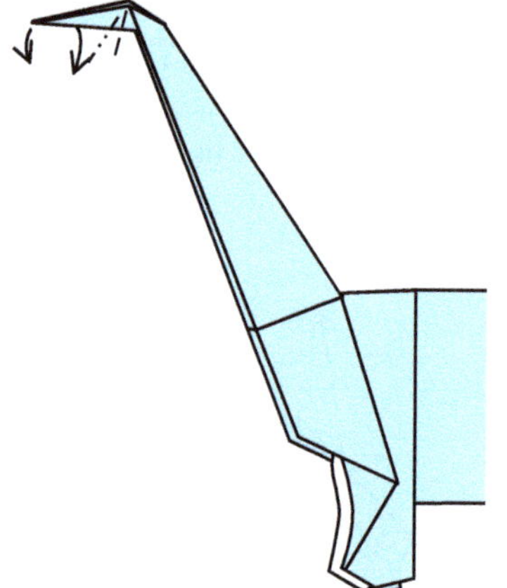

Open and spread the head.

28

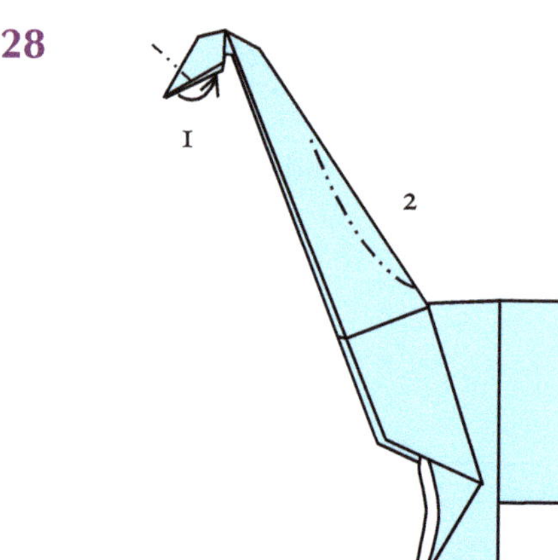

1. Reverse-fold.
2. Shape the neck.

29

Brachiosaurus

Seismosaurus

Seismosaurus, whose name means "earth-shaking lizard," lived during the Late Jurassic Period and was built on an astonishing scale. Some estimates suggest it may have stretched over 100 feet long, making it one of the longest dinosaurs ever discovered. This massive herbivore likely moved slowly and deliberately, its footsteps sending vibrations through the ground. With its long neck and sweeping tail, Seismosaurus represents the peak of sauropod size and the incredible extremes reached by dinosaurs in deep time.

1

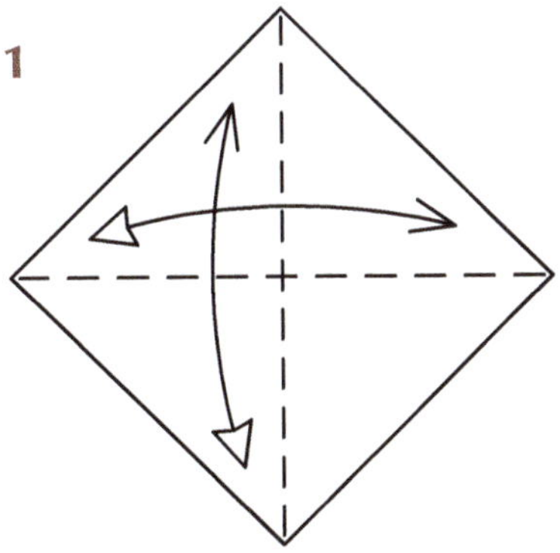

Fold and unfold.

2

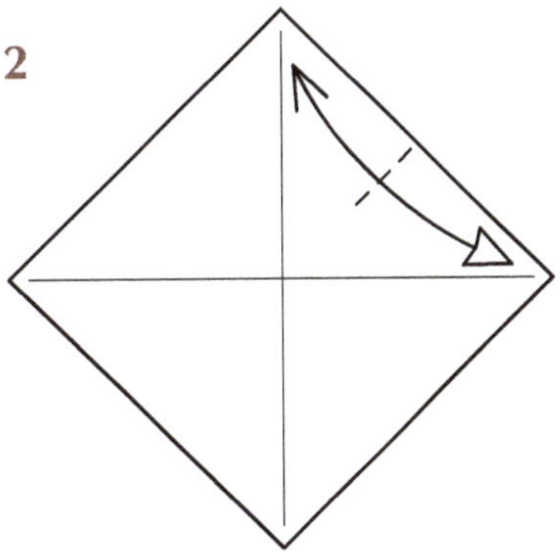

Fold and unfold on the edge.

3

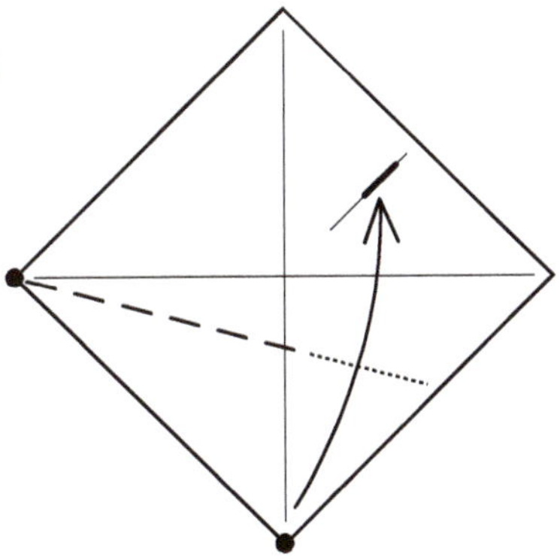

Bring the corner to the line.

4

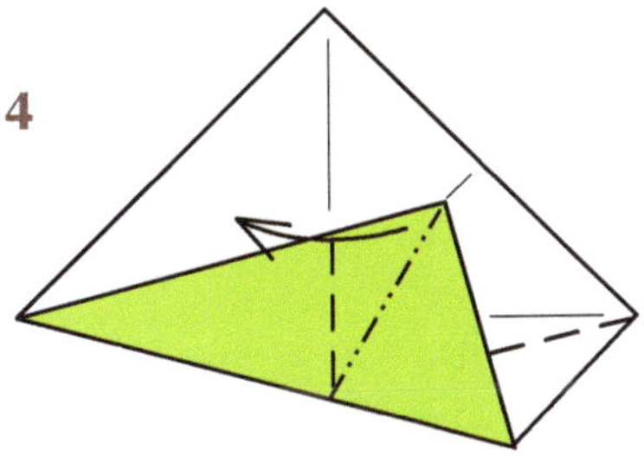

Squash-fold.

5

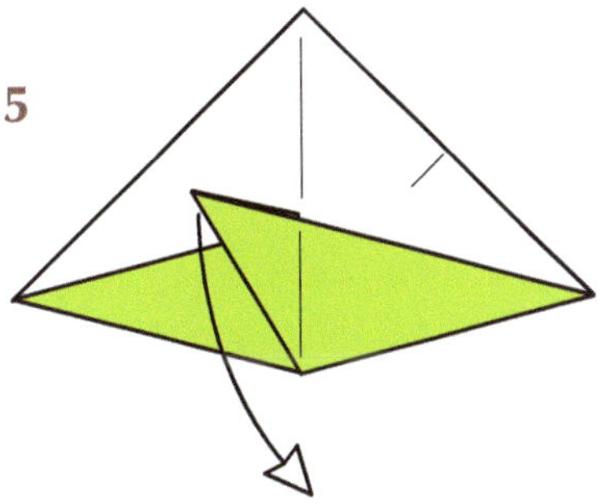

Unfold.

6

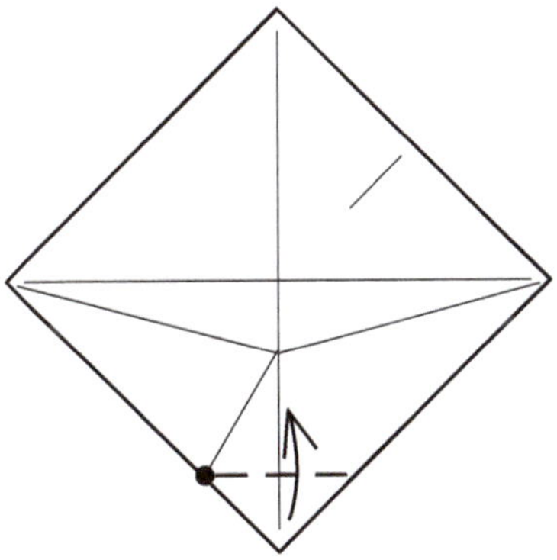

Rotate 180°.

7

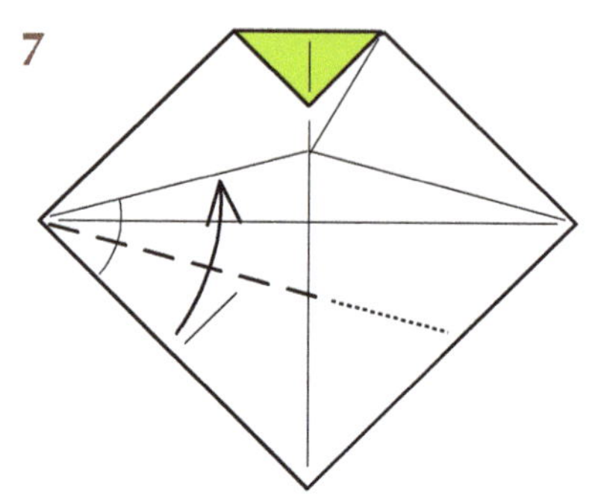

Repeat steps 3–6.

8

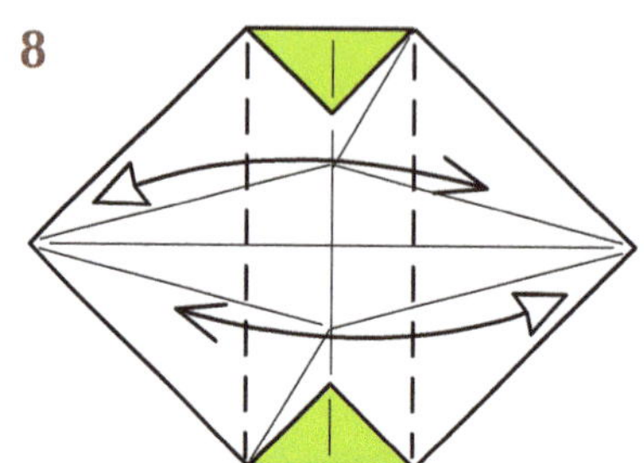

Fold and unfold.

9

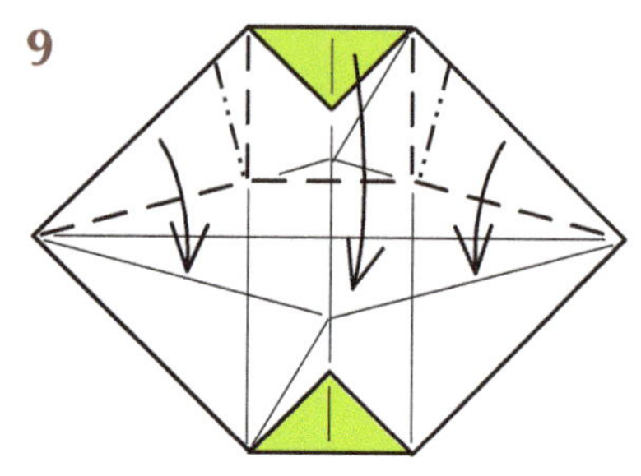

Fold along several of the creases.

10

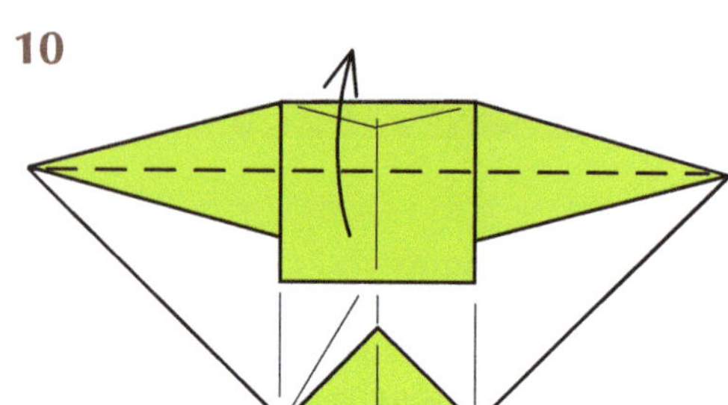

11

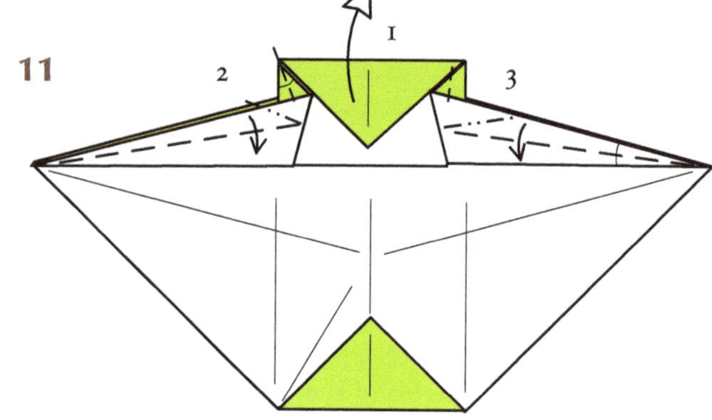

1. Unfold.
2. Bisect the angle at the top for this squash fold.
3. Bisect the angle on the white layer for this squash fold.

12

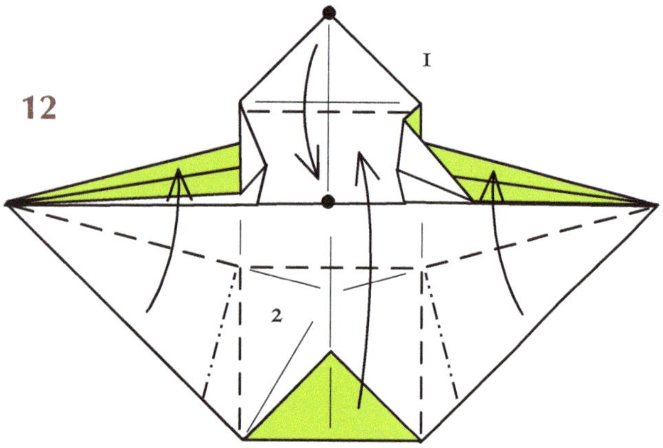

1. Fold down.
2. Repeat steps 9–12 on the bottom.

13

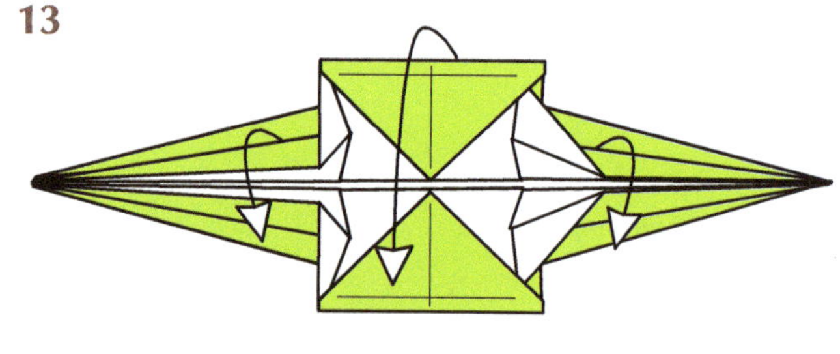

Unfold.

14

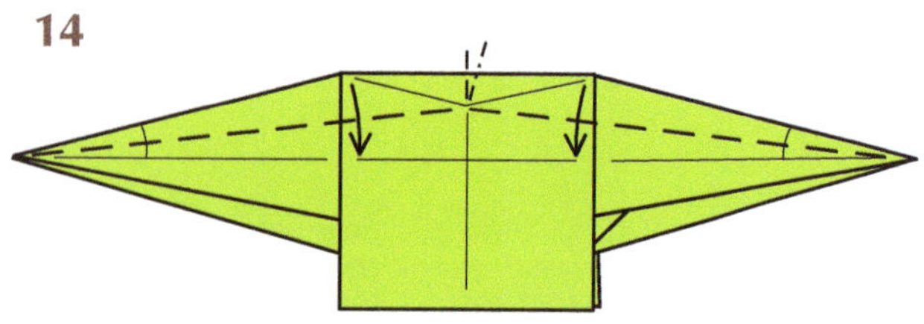

Bisect the angles.

15

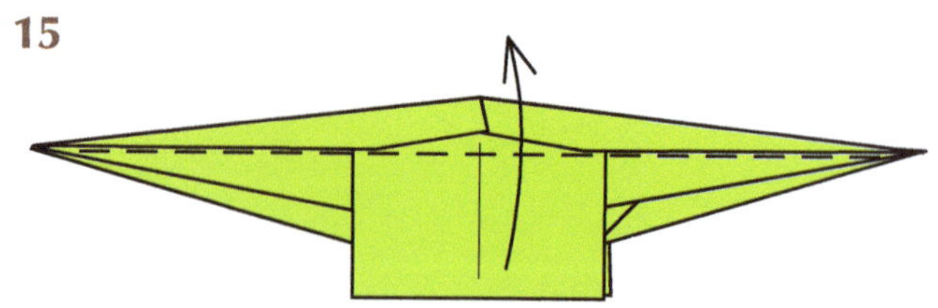

16

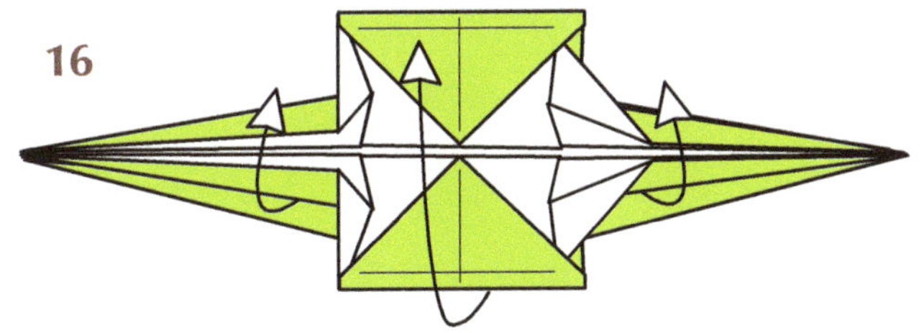

Repeat steps 13–15 on the bottom.

17

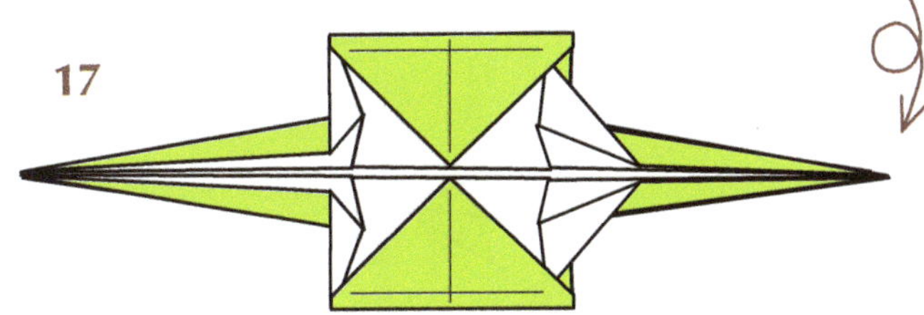

18

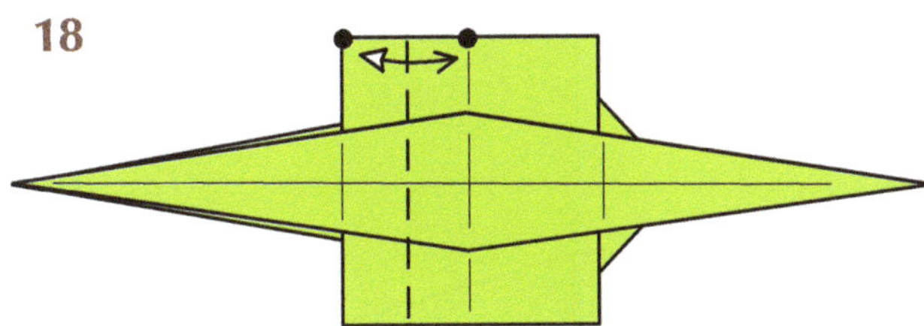

Fold and unfold.

19

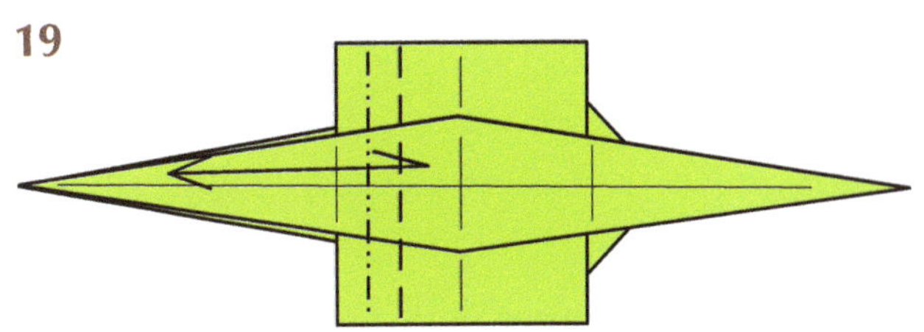

Valley-fold along the crease for this pleat fold.

20

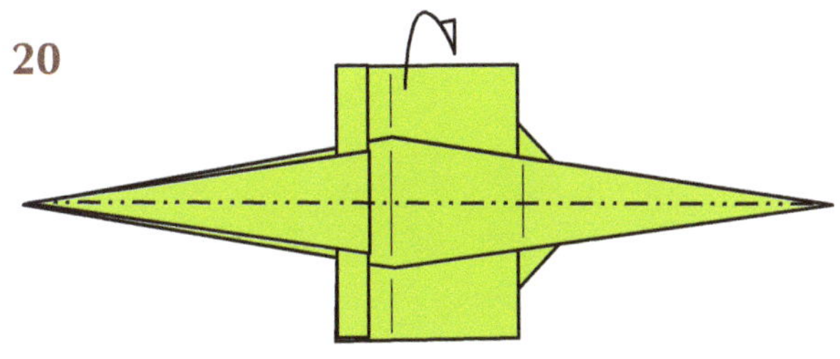

Fold in half.

21

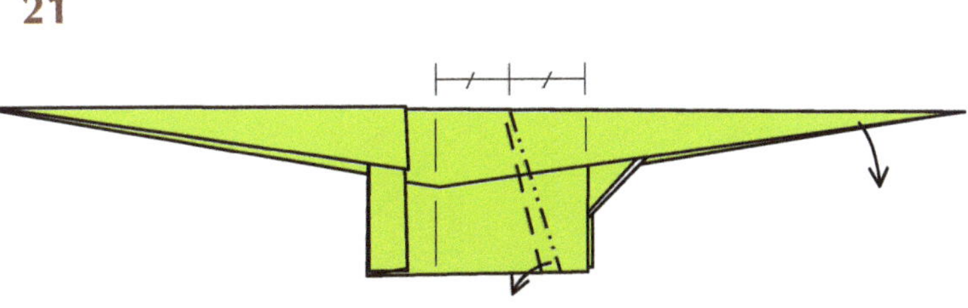

Crimp-fold.

22

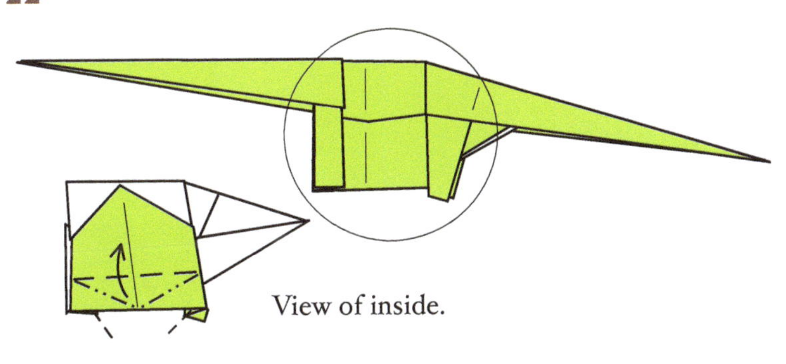

View of inside.

Petal-fold

23

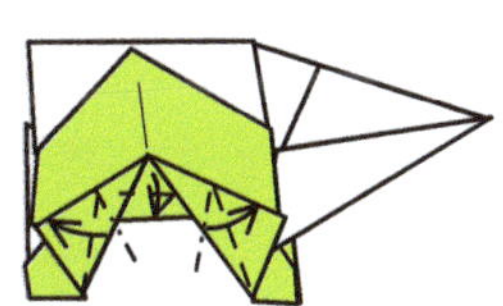

Petal-fold. Repeat steps 22–23 on the other side.

24

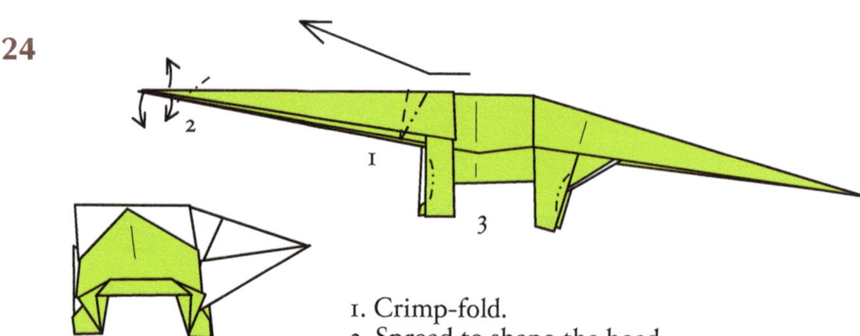

1. Crimp-fold.
2. Spread to shape the head.
3. Shape the legs, repeat behind.

25

1. Reverse-fold.
2. Shape the neck.
3. Curl and shape the tail.

26

Seismosaurus

The Great Two-Legged Walkers

Striding Giants of the Ancient Earth

In this chapter, the pace quickens and the landscape comes alive with motion. The great two-legged walkers stride across plains, forests, and riverbanks, leaving narrow tracks that speak of speed, balance, and power. Walking upright on strong hind legs, these dinosaurs were among the most agile and adaptable creatures of the ancient world. Whether hunting, grazing, or traveling in groups, the great two-legged walkers represent energy and innovation in deep time.

Magnosaurus

Magnosaurus was an early large meat-eating dinosaur that walked confidently on two powerful legs during the Middle Jurassic Period. Measuring about 20 feet long, it was built for speed and strength during a time when large predators were just beginning to appear. As a carnivore, Magnosaurus hunted other dinosaurs, using sharp teeth and strong legs to chase prey across open land. Though not as famous as later predators, it represents an important step in the rise of large two-legged hunters.

1

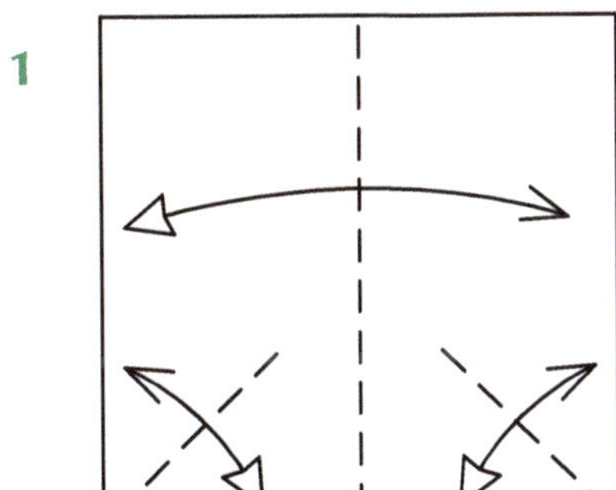

Fold and unfold.

2

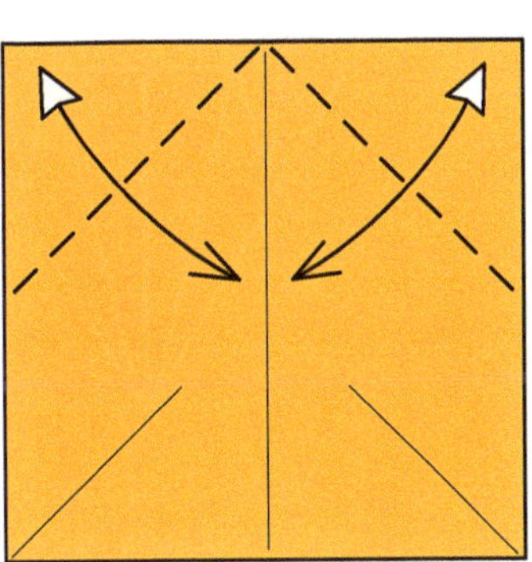

Fold to the center and unfold.

3

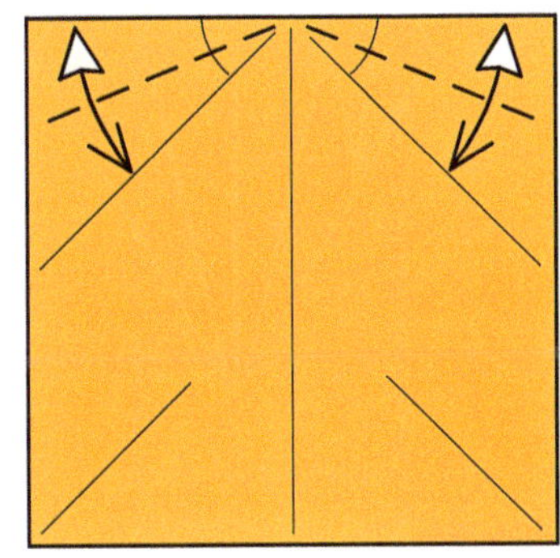

Fold and unfold.

4

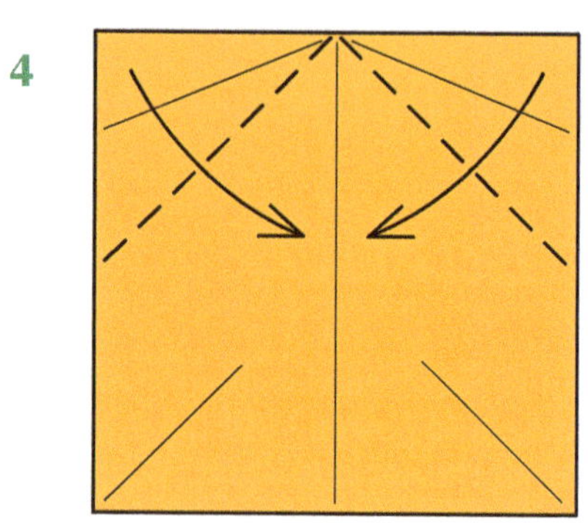

Fold along the creases.

5

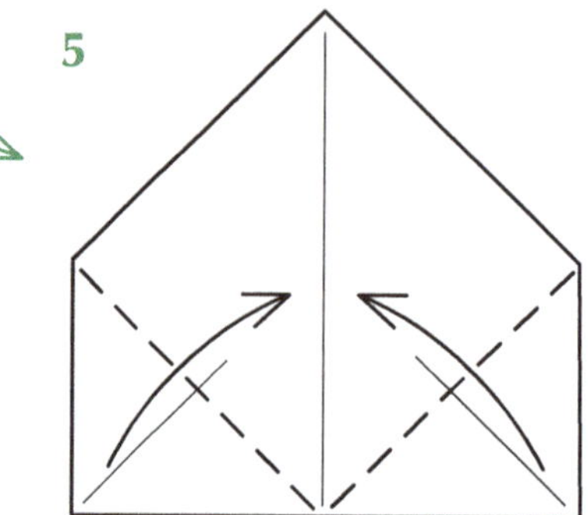

Fold to the center.

6

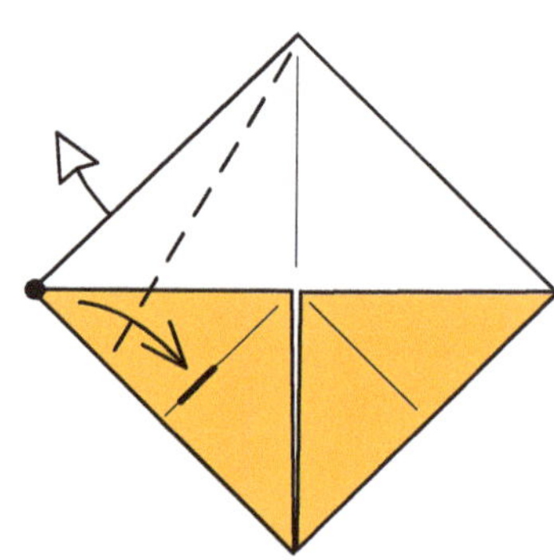

Bring the dot to the line and swing out from behind.

7

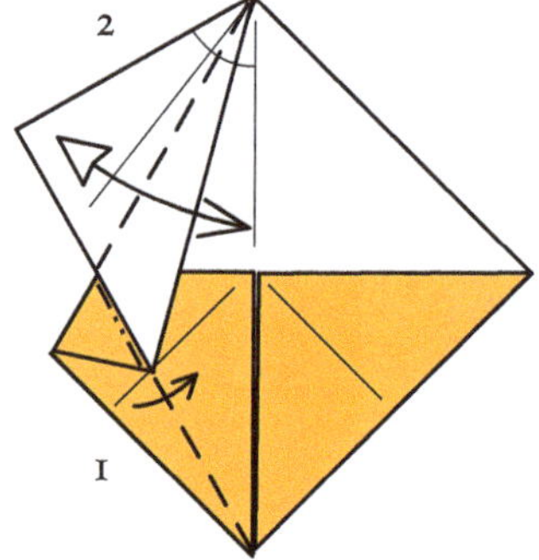

1. Reverse-fold.
2. Fold and unfold.

8

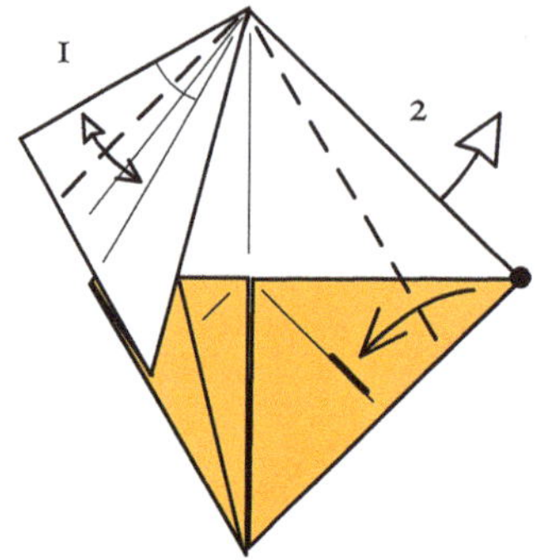

1. Fold and unfold.
2. Repeat steps 6–8 on the right.

9

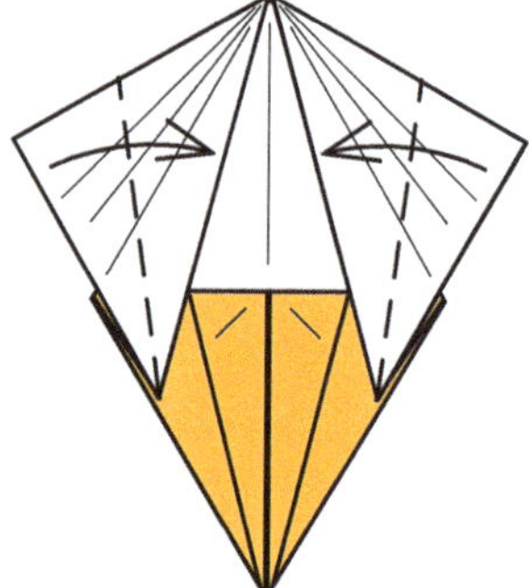

10

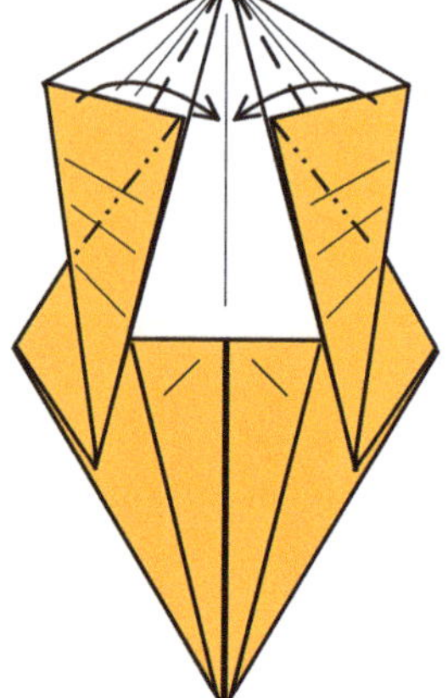

Valley-fold along the creases for these reverse folds.

11

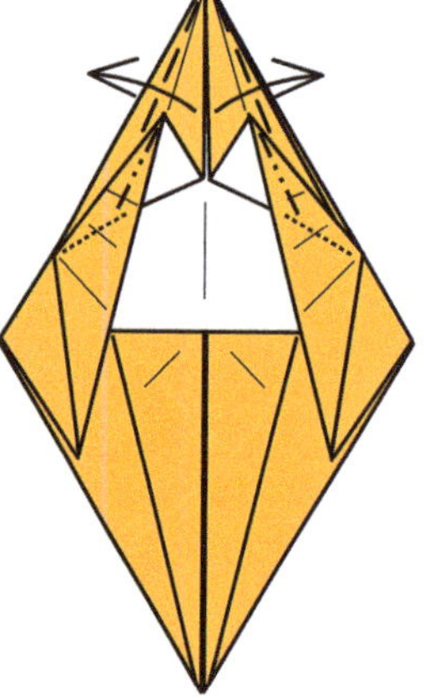

Valley-fold along the creases for these reverse folds.

12

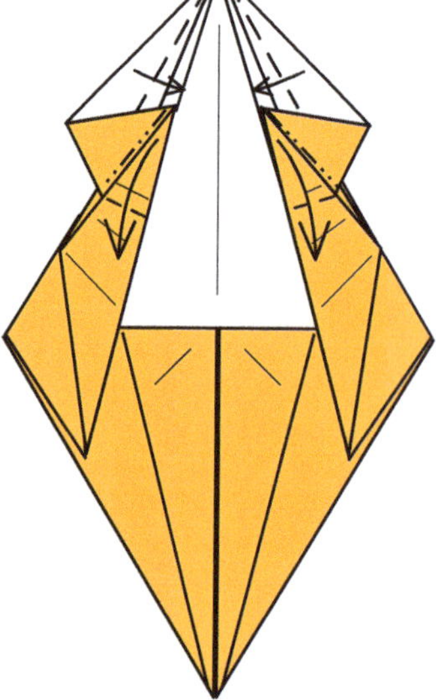

Valley-fold along the creases at the top for these squash folds.

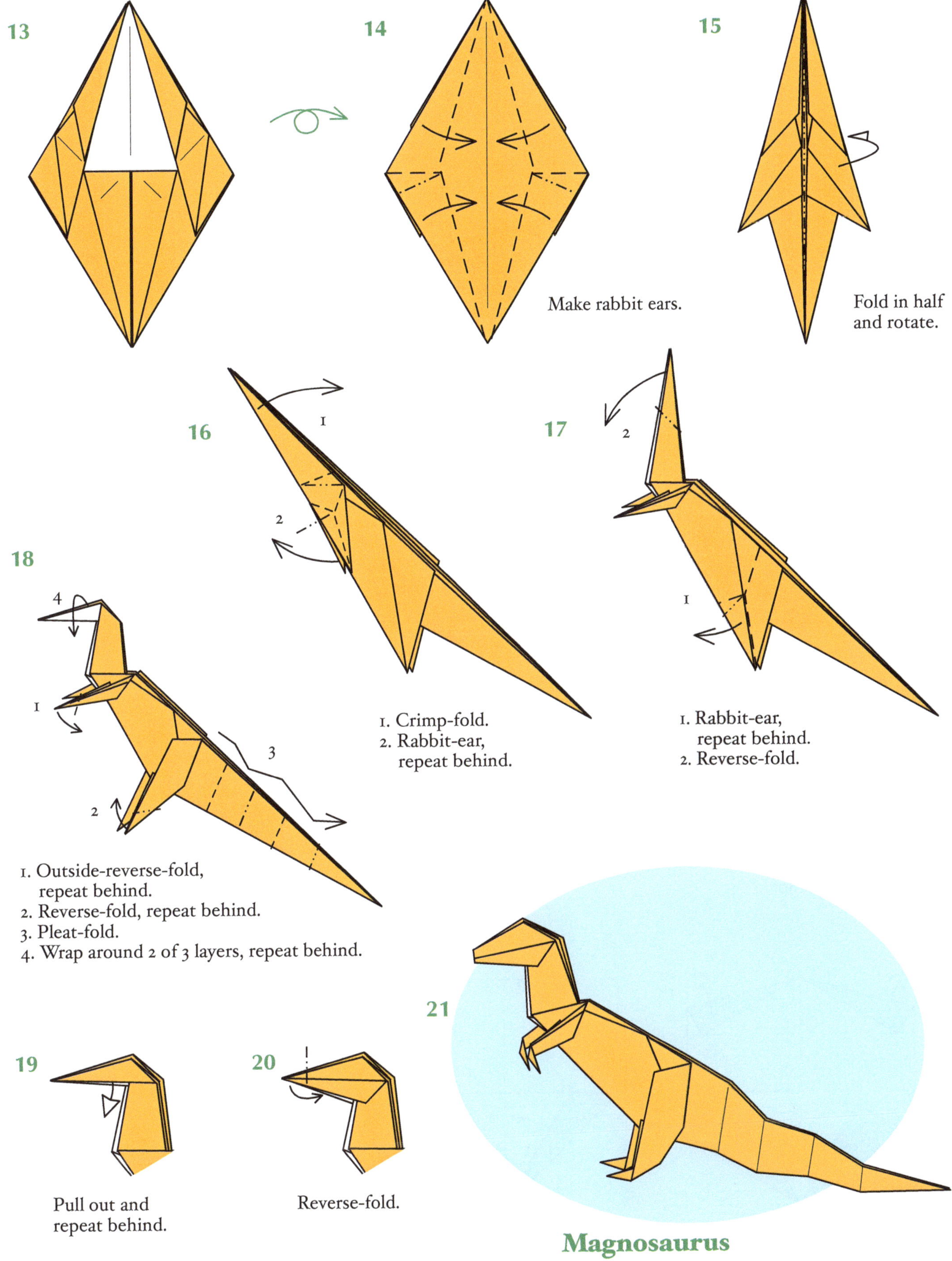
13
14
15
Make rabbit ears.
Fold in half
and rotate.
16
17
1. Crimp-fold.
2. Rabbit-ear,
repeat behind.
1. Rabbit-ear,
repeat behind.
2. Reverse-fold.
18
1. Outside-reverse-fold,
repeat behind.
2. Reverse-fold, repeat behind.
3. Pleat-fold.
4. Wrap around 2 of 3 layers, repeat behind.
19
Pull out and
repeat behind.
20
Reverse-fold.
21
Magnosaurus

Syntarsus

Syntarsus was a small, lightweight dinosaur built for speed. At only about 6 feet long, it darted across the landscape on long legs, making it one of the quickest dinosaurs during the Late Triassic to Early Jurassic Period. A meat-eater, Syntarsus likely fed on insects, small animals, and anything it could catch. Its agility and alert nature helped it survive in a rapidly changing prehistoric world.

1

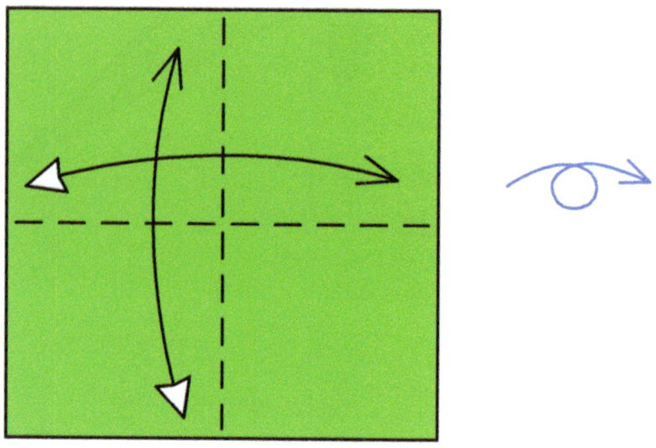

Fold and unfold.

2

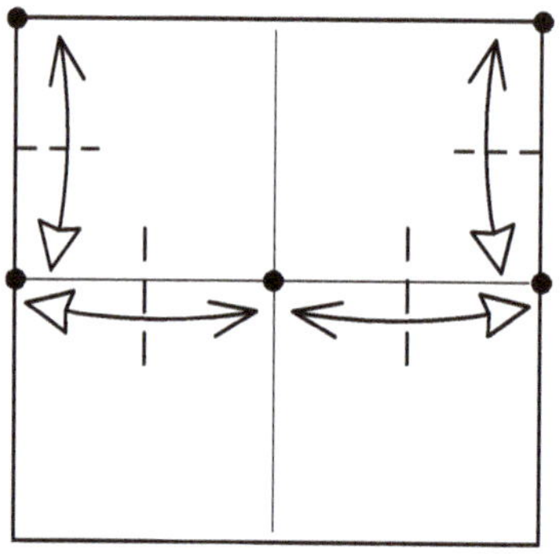

Fold and unfold.

3

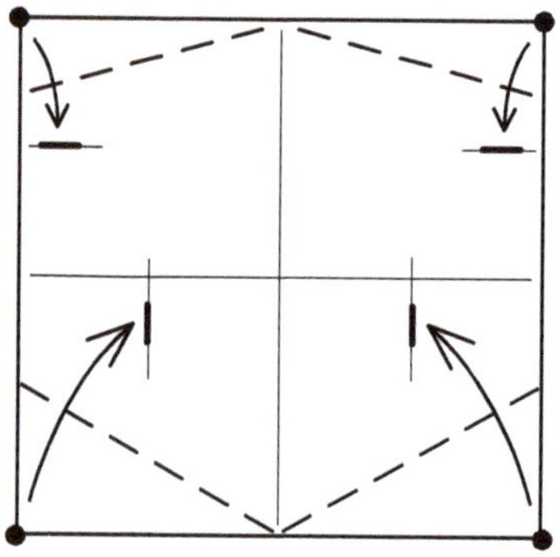

Bring the corners to the lines.

4

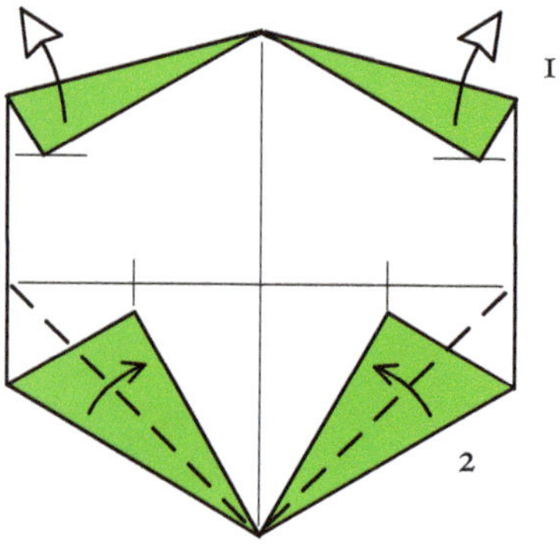

1. Unfold.
2. Make valley folds.

5

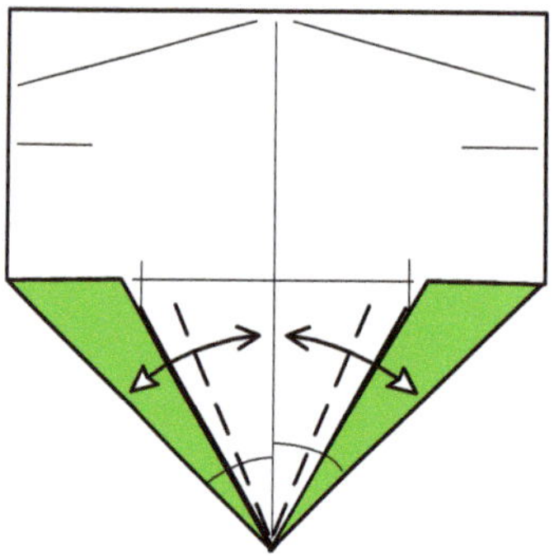

Fold and unfold.

6

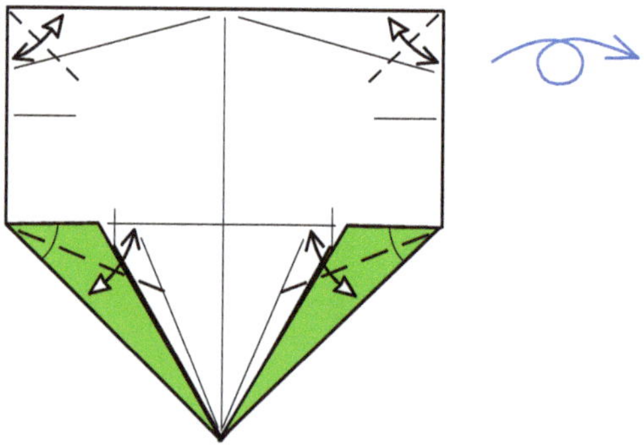

Fold and unfold.

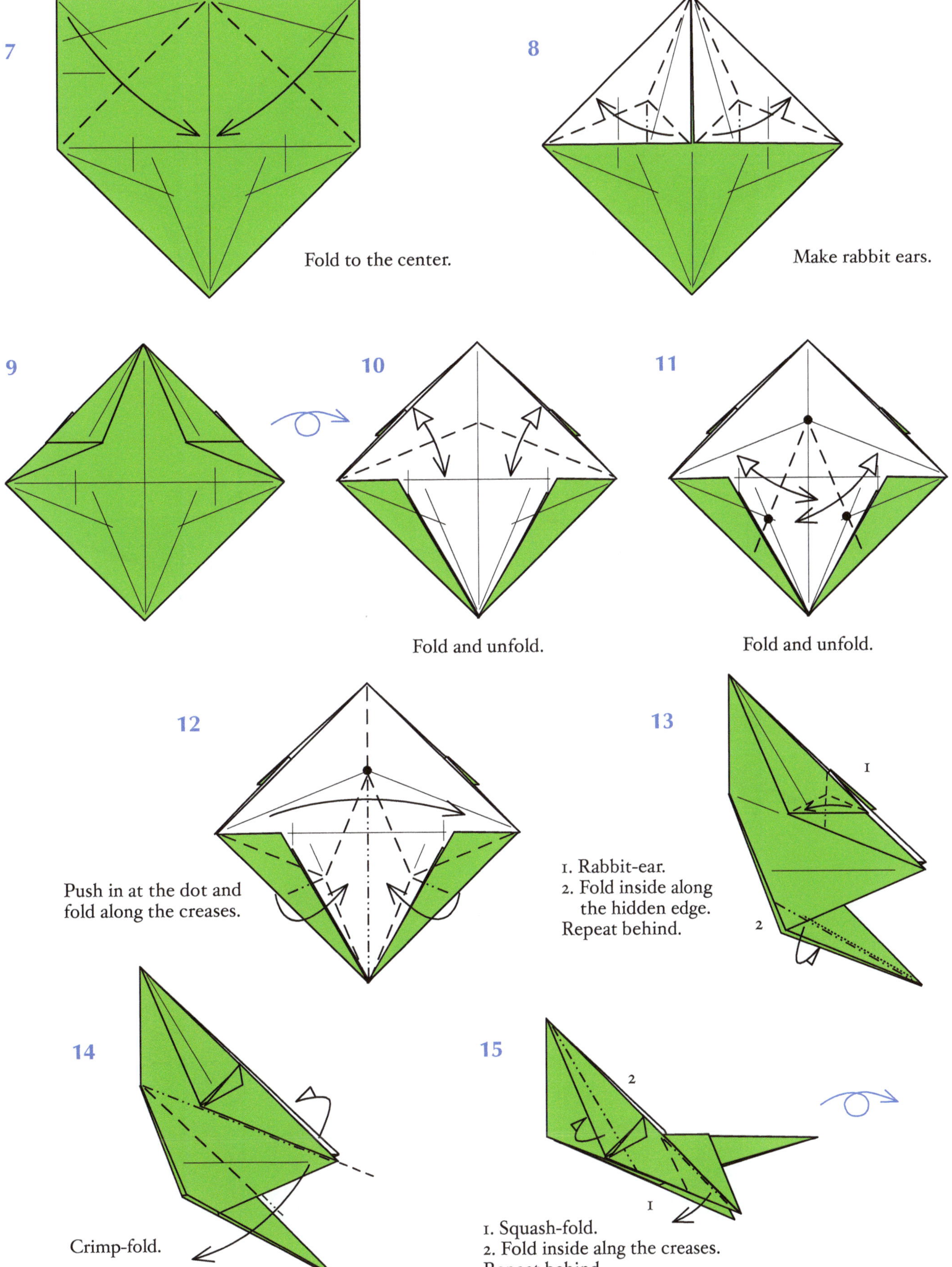
7
Fold to the center.
8
Make rabbit ears.
9
10
Fold and unfold.
11
Fold and unfold.
12
Push in at the dot and
fold along the creases.
13
1
2
1. Rabbit-ear.
2. Fold inside along
the hidden edge.
Repeat behind.
14
Crimp-fold.
15
2
1
1. Squash-fold.
2. Fold inside alng the creases.
Repeat behind.

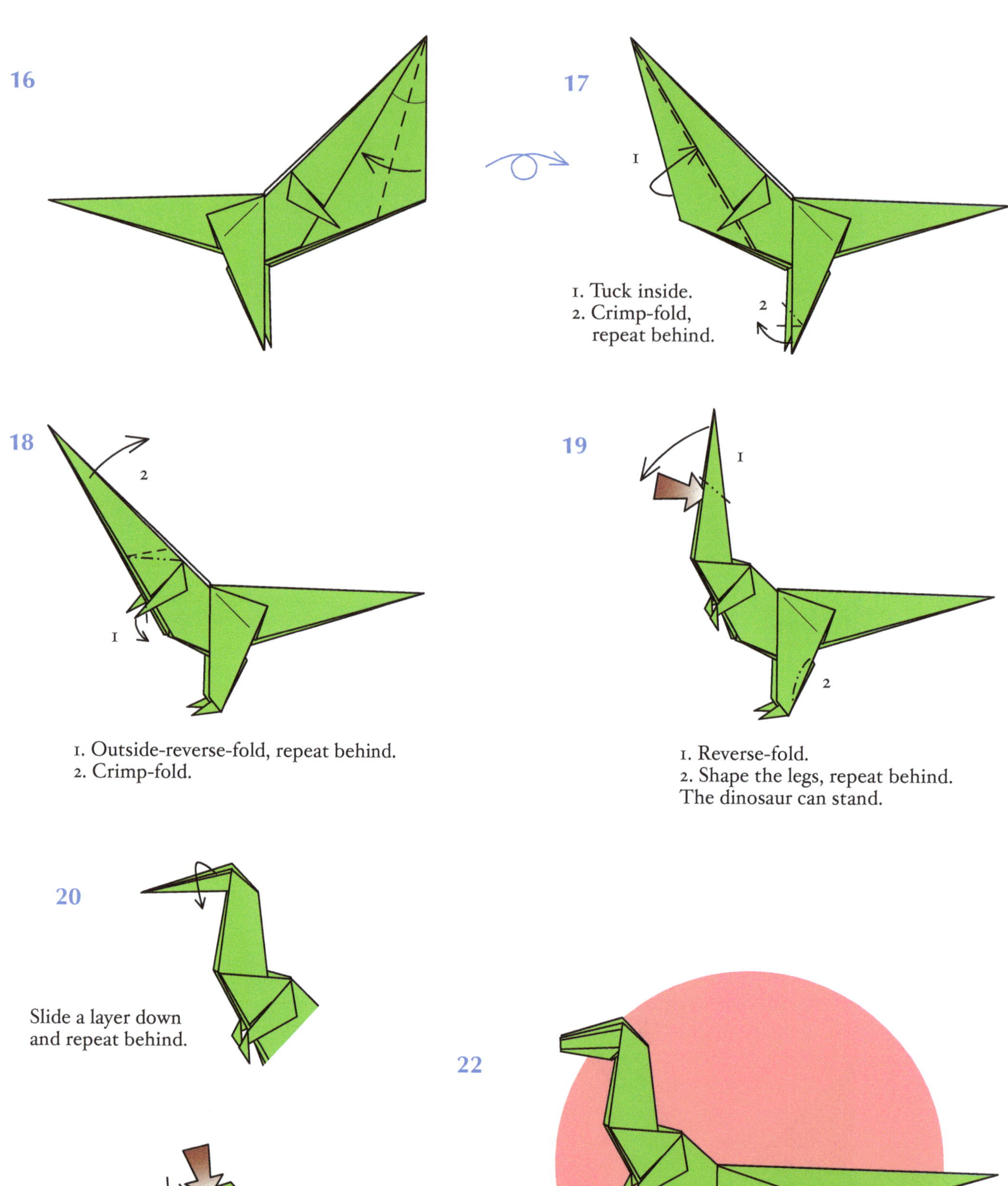

21

Reverse-fold.

22

Syntarsus

Neovenator

Neovenator was a fast and intelligent predator that lived during the Early Cretaceous Period. Growing up to 25 feet long, it combined speed with sharp senses, making it a dangerous hunter. This carnivore likely relied on agility rather than brute force, using quick movements to surprise prey. Neovenator shows how predators continued to evolve even after the age of the Jurassic giants.

1

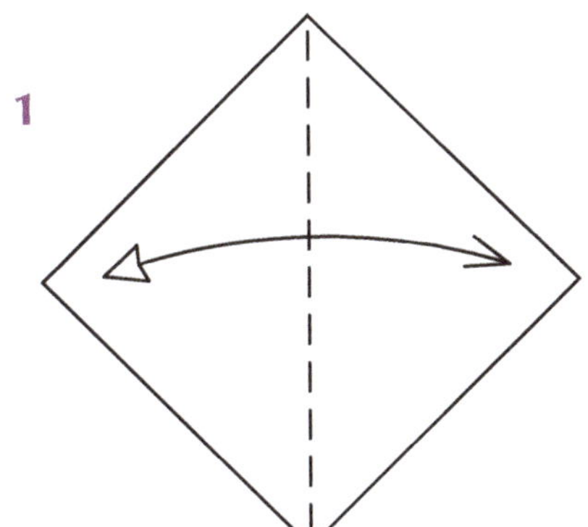

Fold and unfold.

2

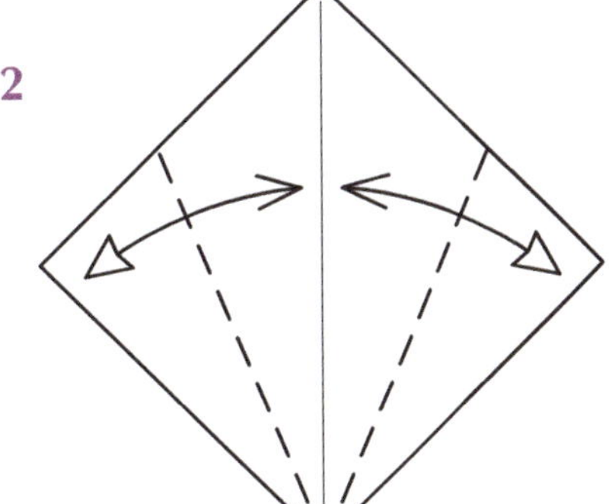

Fold to the center and unfold.

3

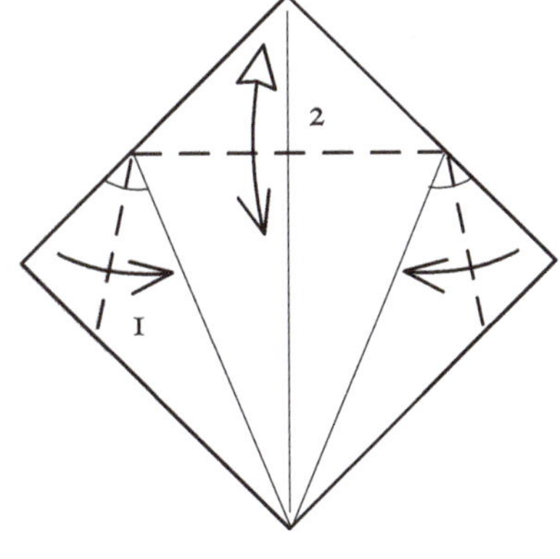

1. Fold on the left and right.
2. Fold and unfold.

4

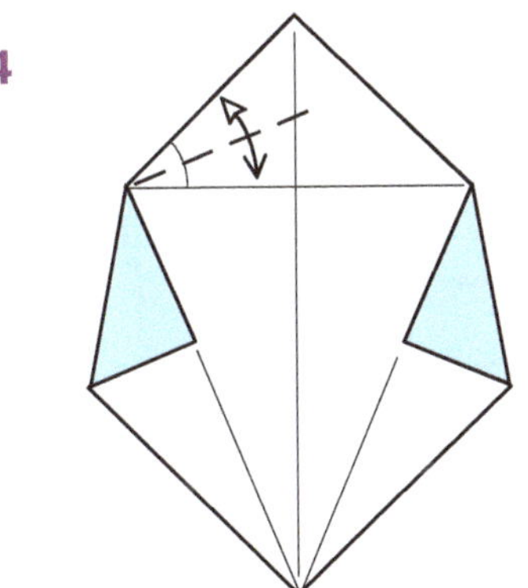

Fold and unfold.

5

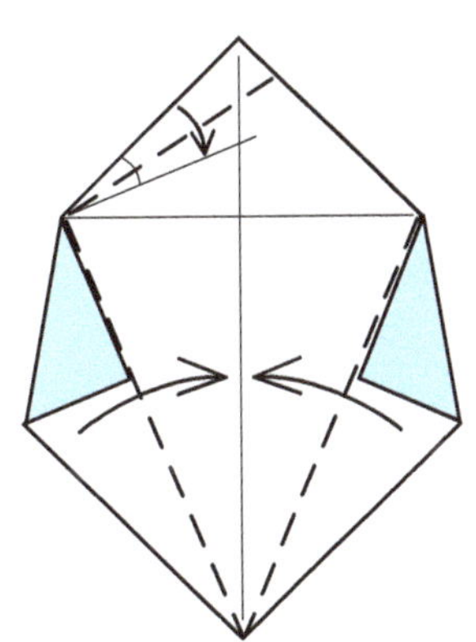

6

Squash-fold.

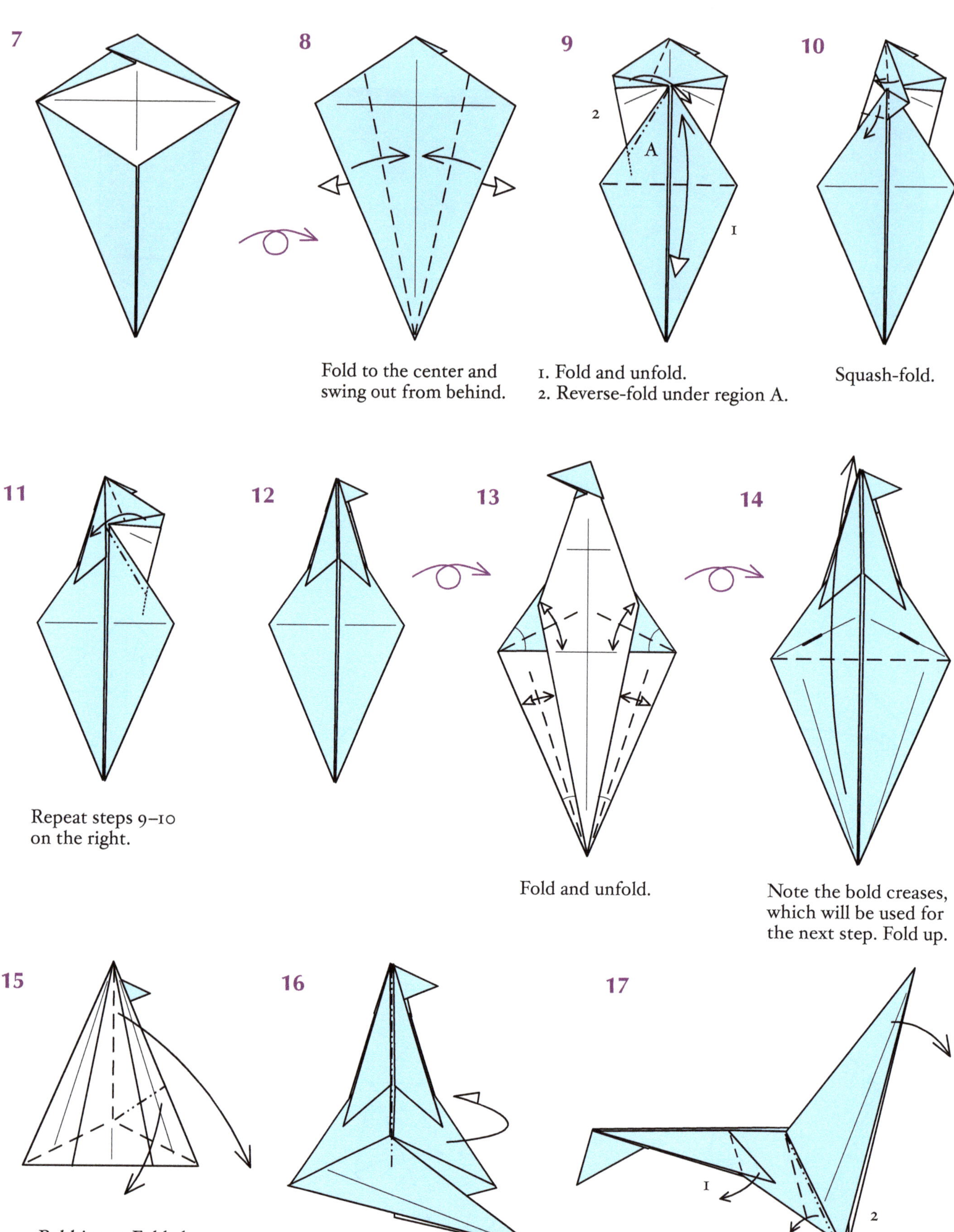

Fold to the center and swing out from behind.

1. Fold and unfold.
2. Reverse-fold under region A.

Squash-fold.

Repeat steps 9–10 on the right.

Fold and unfold.

Note the bold creases, which will be used for the next step. Fold up.

Rabbit-ear. Fold along the bold creases shown in step 14.

Fold in half and rotate 90°.

1. Fold the arm down, repeat behind.
2. Crimp-fold.

18

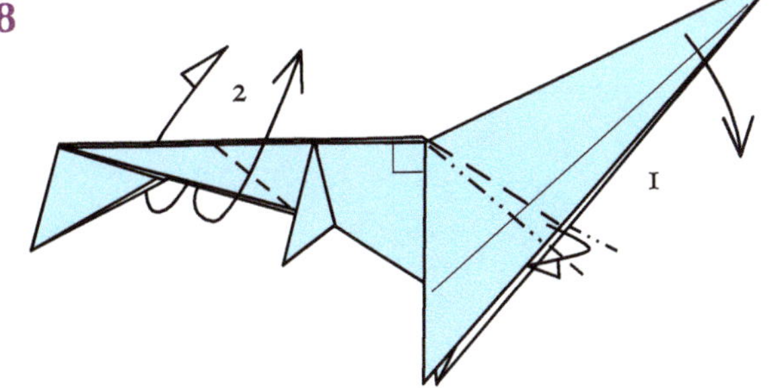

Note the right angle.
1. Crimp-fold.
2. Outside-reverse-fold.

19

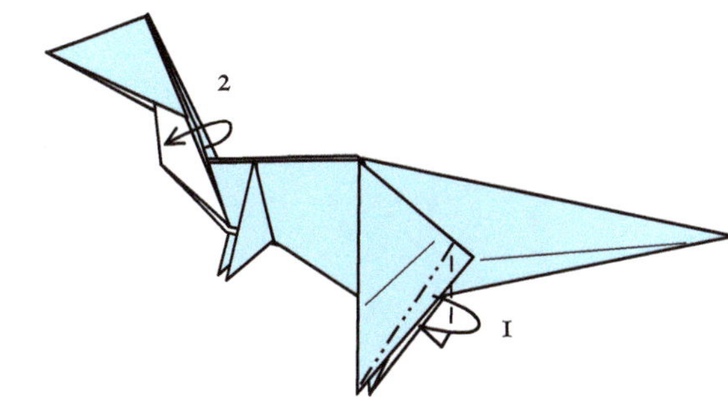

1. Fold inside with a small reverse fold at the top. Fold along the hidden edge.
2. Wrap around.

Repeat behind.

20

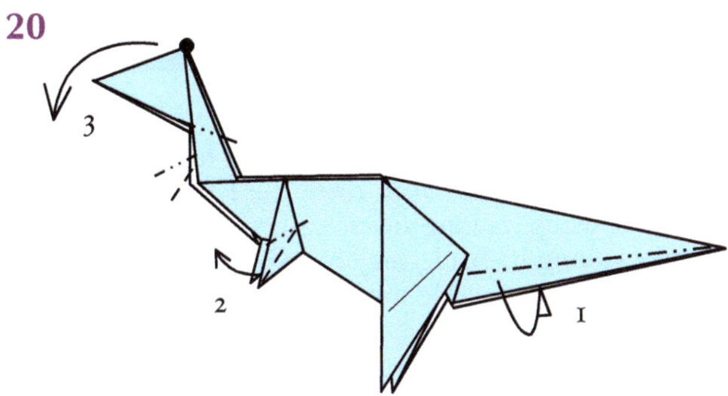

1. Fold inside along the crease, repeat behind.
2. Thin the arm, repeat behind.
3. Pivot the head and move it down at the dot. There will be some folds hidden in the neck.

21

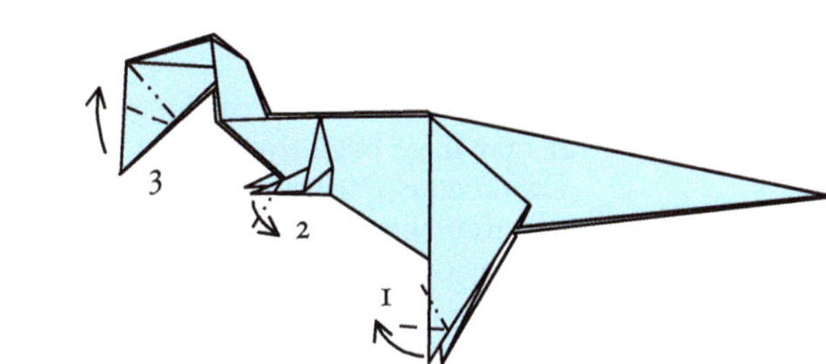

1. Crimp-fold, repeat behind.
2. Reverse-fold, repeat behind.
3. Crimp-fold.

22

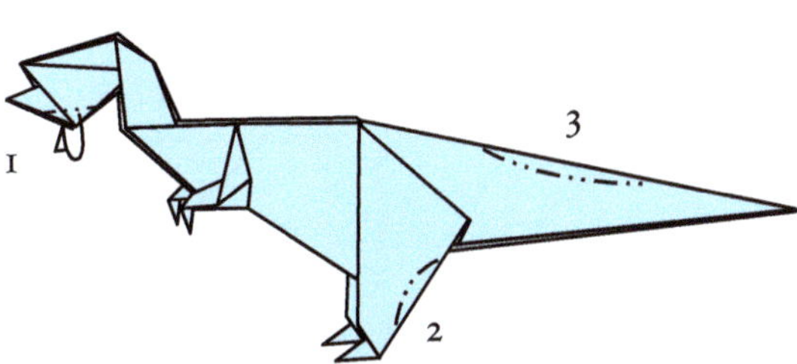
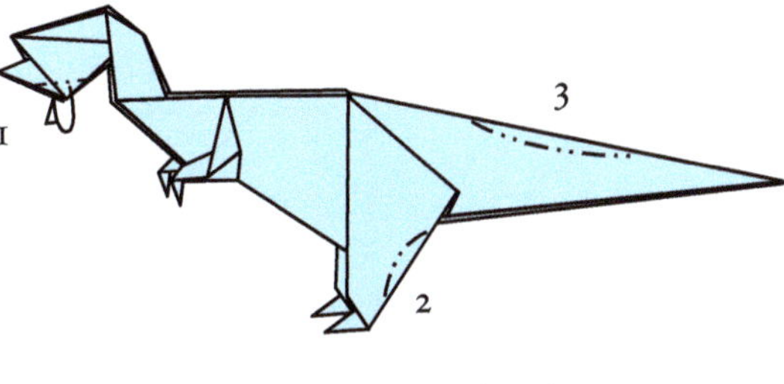

1. Fold inside, repeat behind.
2. Shape the legs, repeat behind.
3. Shape the tail.

This dinosaur can balance on its legs.

23

Neovenator

Spinosaurus

Spinosaurus was one of the most unusual dinosaurs ever discovered. Stretching over 50 feet long, it may have been the longest meat-eating dinosaur of all time. A carnivore from the Late Cretaceous Period, Spinosaurus likely fed mainly on fish, using its long snout and conical teeth to catch slippery prey. Its tall sail, formed by long spines along its back, may have been used for display or temperature control, making it one of the most recognizable dinosaurs in history.

1

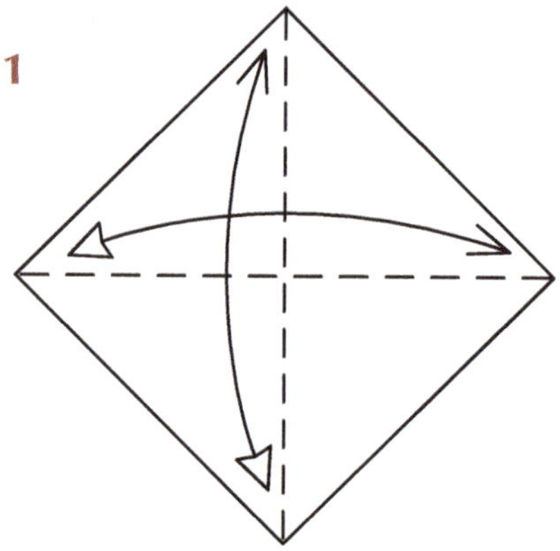

Fold and unfold.

2

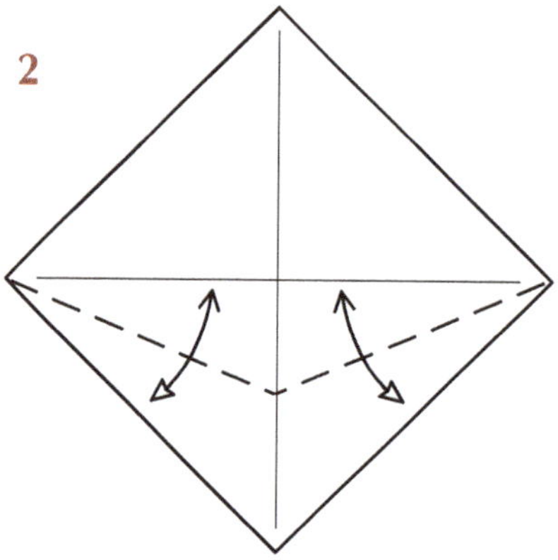

Fold and unfold.

3

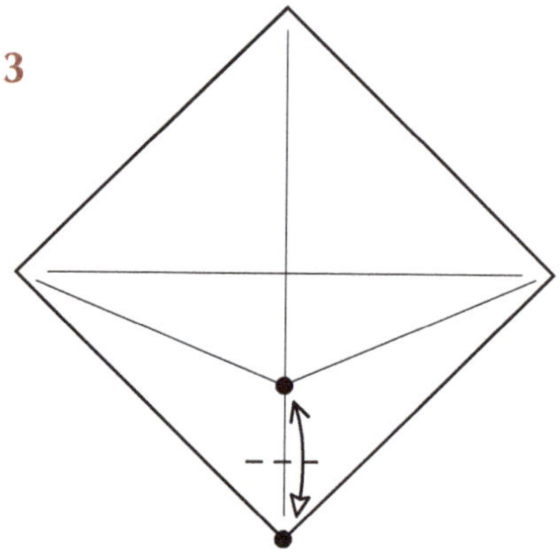

Fold and unfold.

4

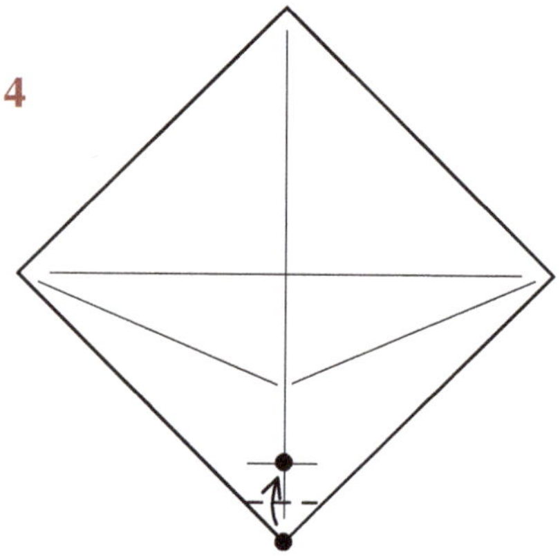

5

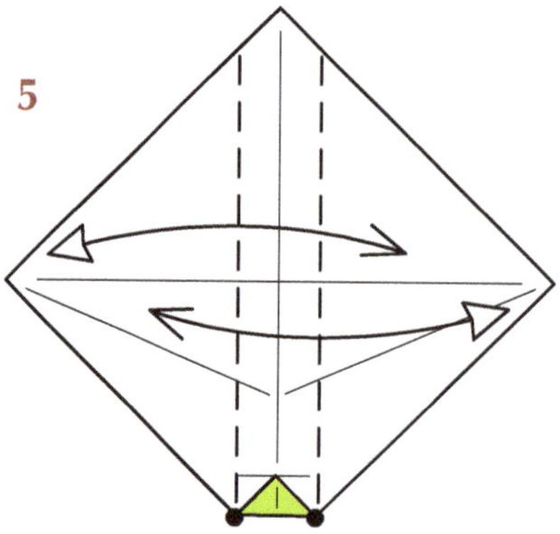

Fold and unfold.
Rotate 180°.

6

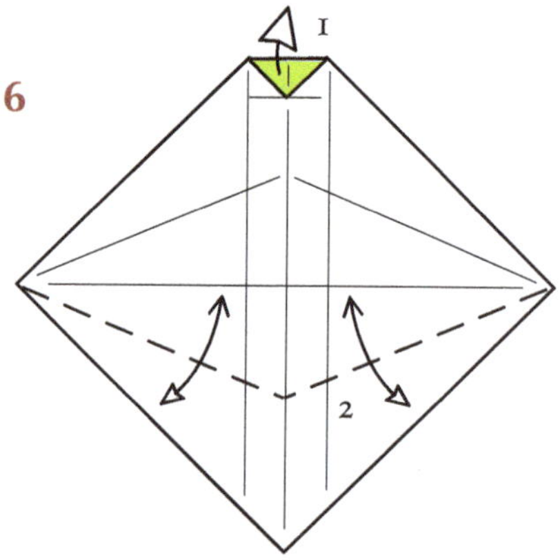

1. Unfold.
2. Fold and unfold.

7

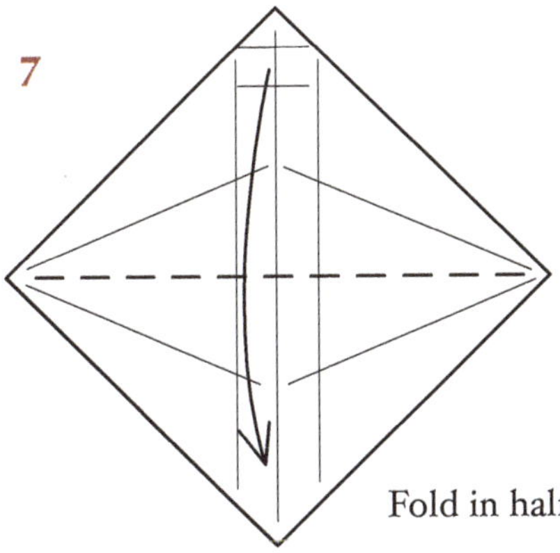

Fold in half.

8

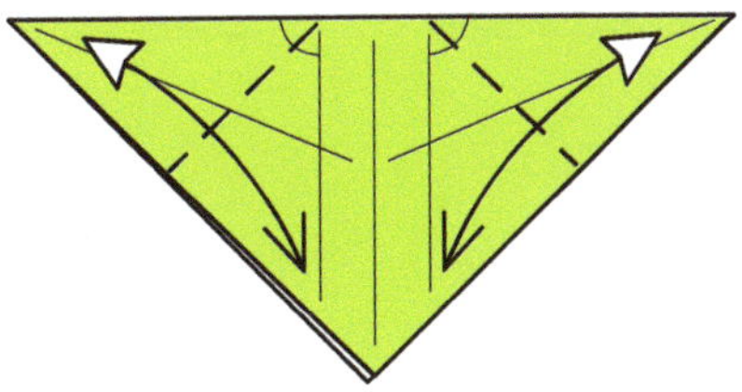

Fold and unfold.

9

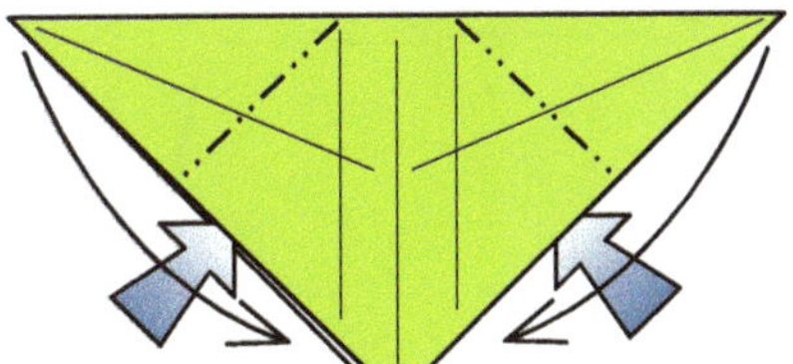

Make reverse folds.

10

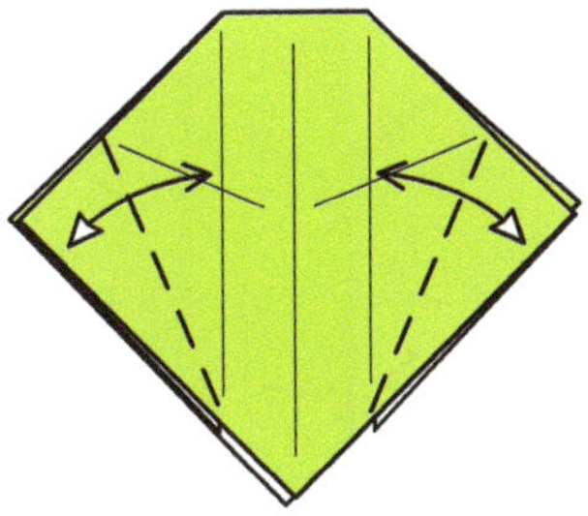

Fold and unfold the top flaps. Repeat behind.

11

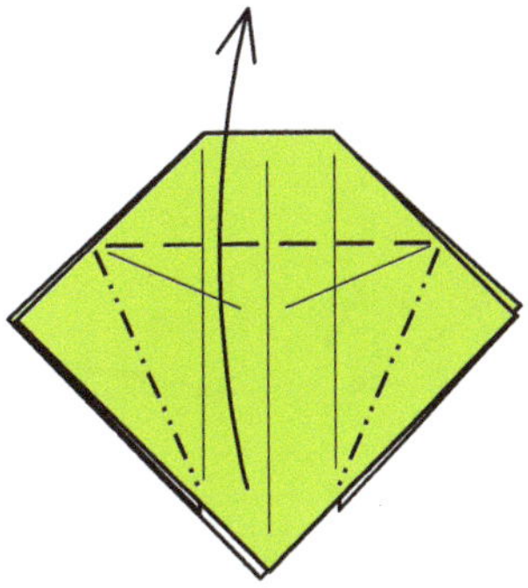

Petal-fold and repeat behind.

12

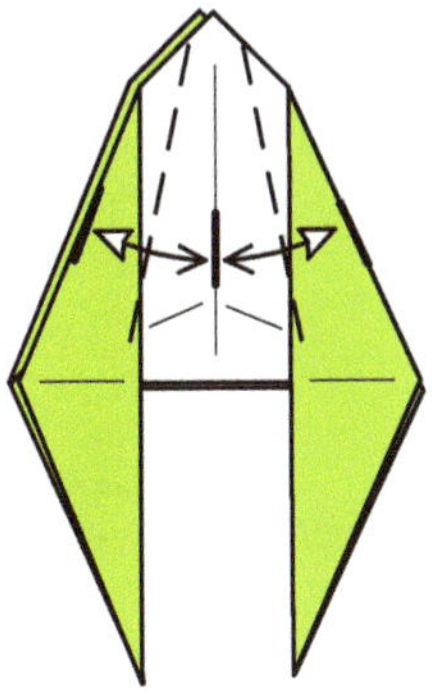

Fold and unfold the edges to the center. Repeat behind.

13

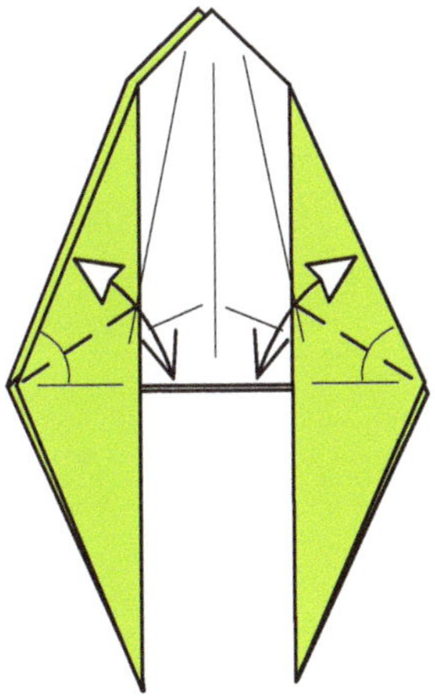

Fold and unfold. Repeat behind.

14

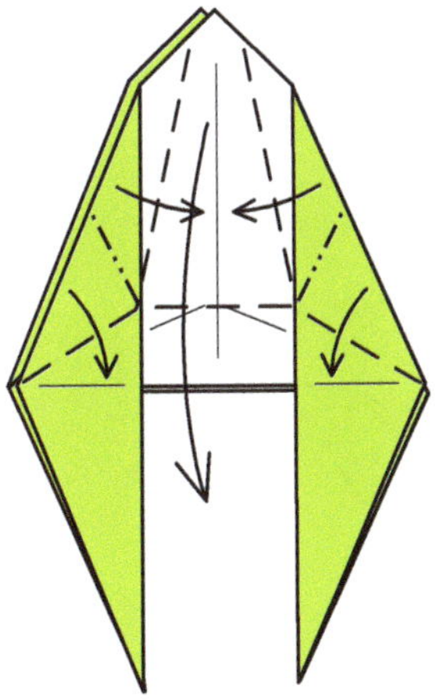

Fold along several of the creases. Repeat behind.

15

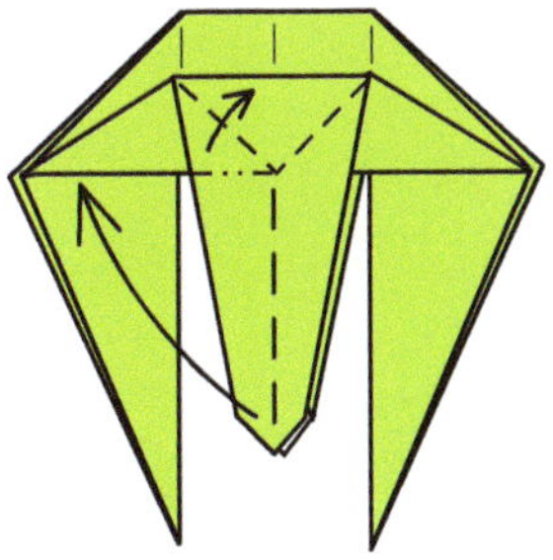

Rabbit-ear and repeat behind.

16

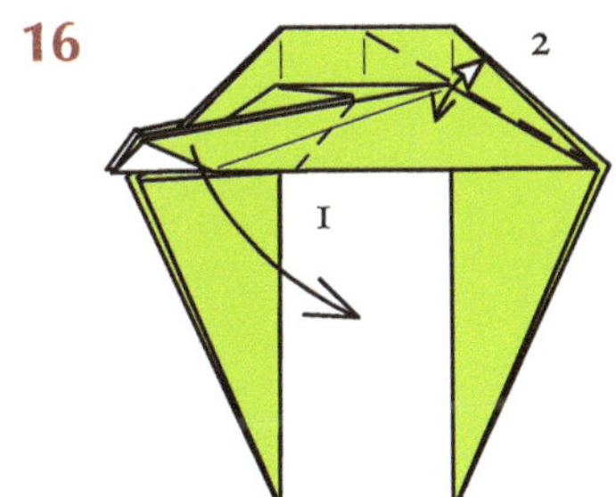

1. Fold down, repeat behind.
2. Fold and unfold.

17

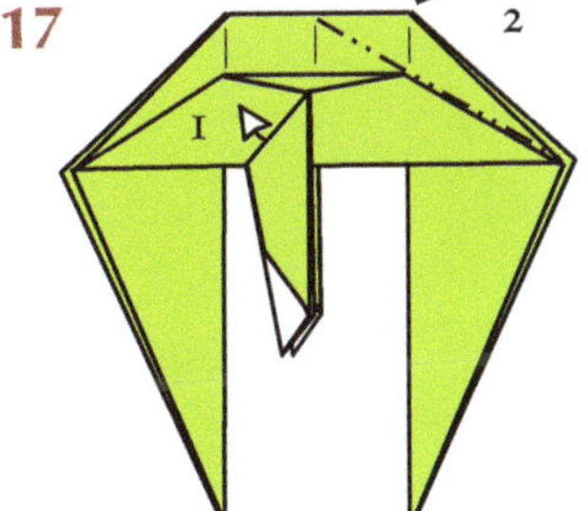

1. Pull out, repeat behind.
2. Spread the paper to sink.

18

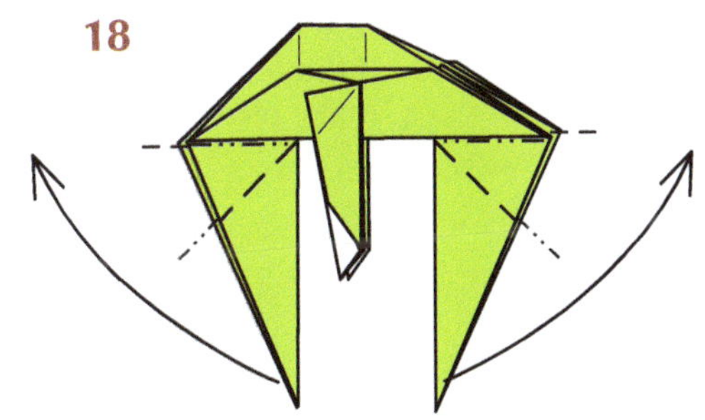

Make crimp folds.

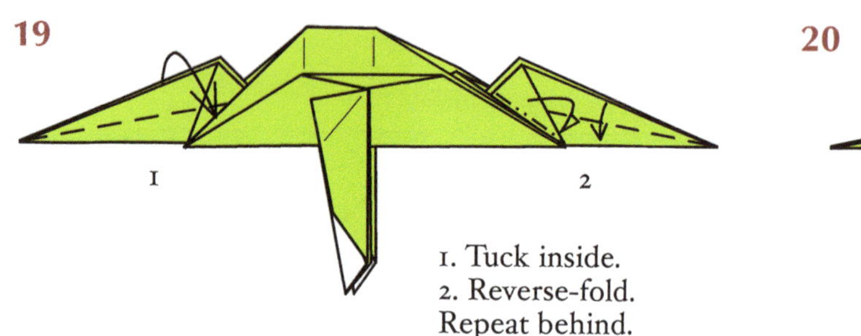

19

1. Tuck inside.
2. Reverse-fold.

Repeat behind.

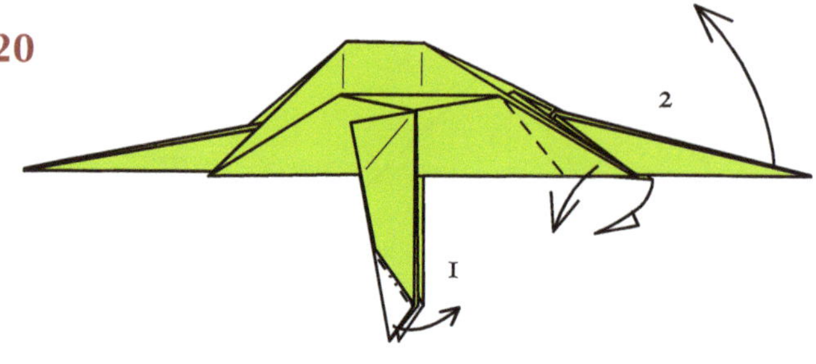

20

1. Reverse-fold, repeat behind.
2. Fold the arms down while sliding the neck up.

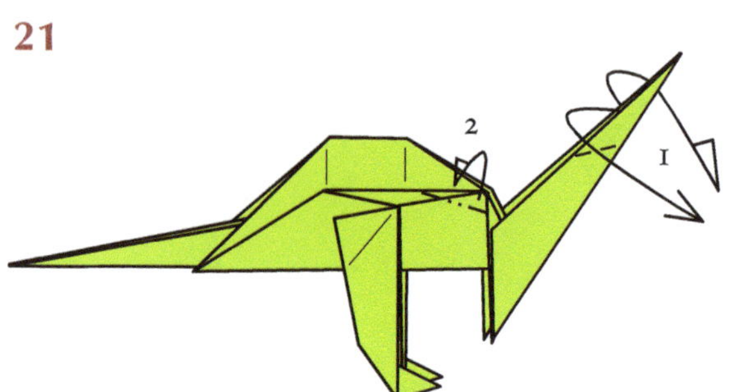

21

1. Outside-reverse-fold.
2. Fold inside, repeat behind.

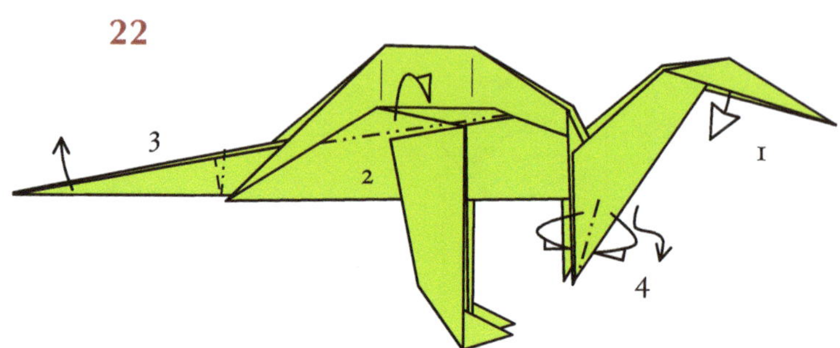

22

1. Pull out, repeat behind.
2. Fold inside, repeat behind.
3. Crimp-fold.
4. Thin and shape the arm, repeat behind.

23

1. Reverse-fold.
2. Crimp-fold, repeat behind.
3. Fold inside on both sides of the feet, repeat behind.
4. Make pleat folds.

24

Spinosaurus

Tyrannosaurus

Tyrannosaurus was the undisputed heavyweight of two-legged predators. At up to 40 feet long, it ruled the land during the Late Cretaceous Period. This powerful carnivore had massive jaws and incredible bite strength, allowing it to crush bone with ease. Despite its small arms, Tyrannosaurus was a balanced, efficient hunter—and one of the most famous dinosaurs ever discovered.

This dinosaur builds off of the structure from the earlier Tyrannosaurus and adds a large, open mouth.

1

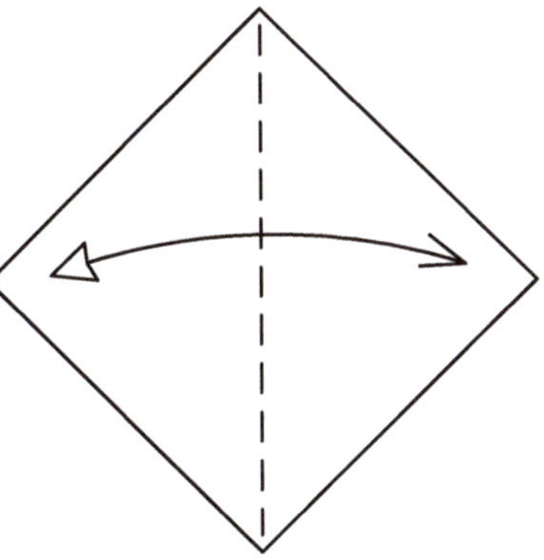

Fold and unfold.

2

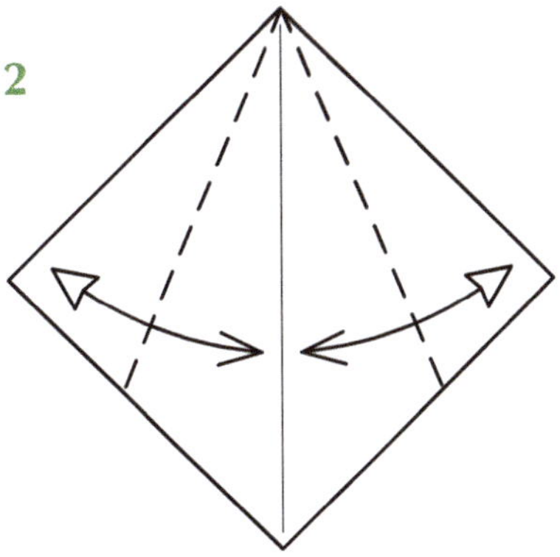

Fold to the center and unfold.

3

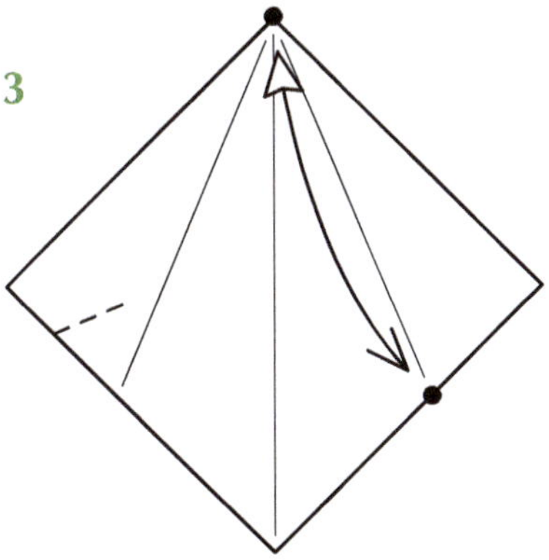

Fold and unfold on the edge.

4

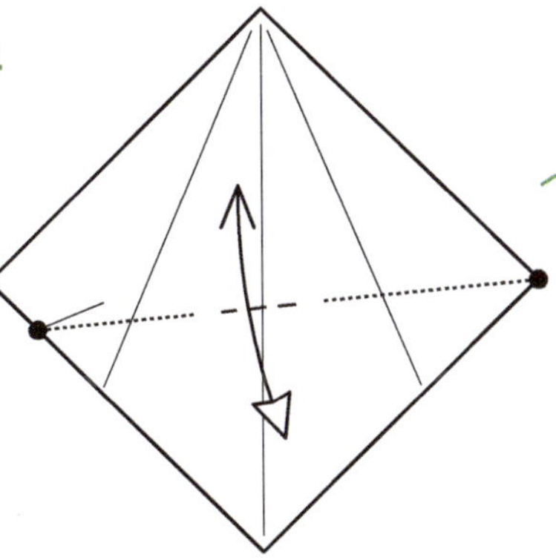

Fold and unfold on the diagonal.

5

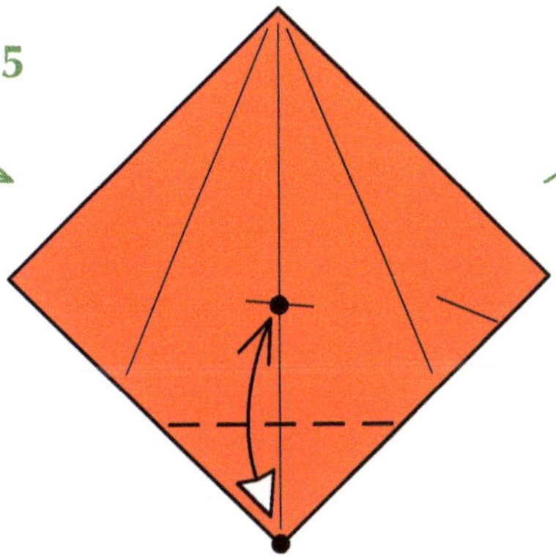

Fold and unfold.

6

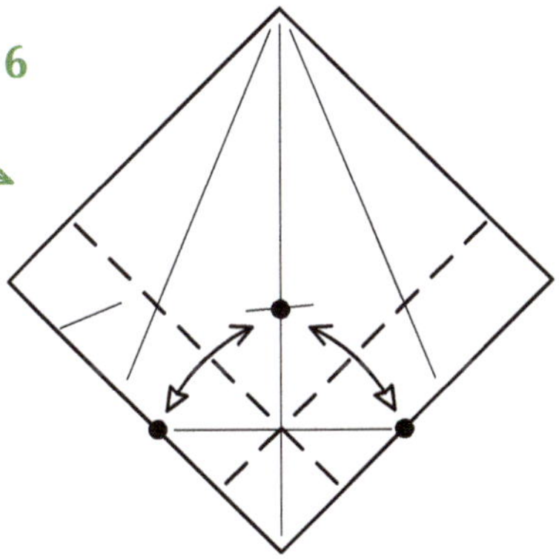

Fold and unfold.

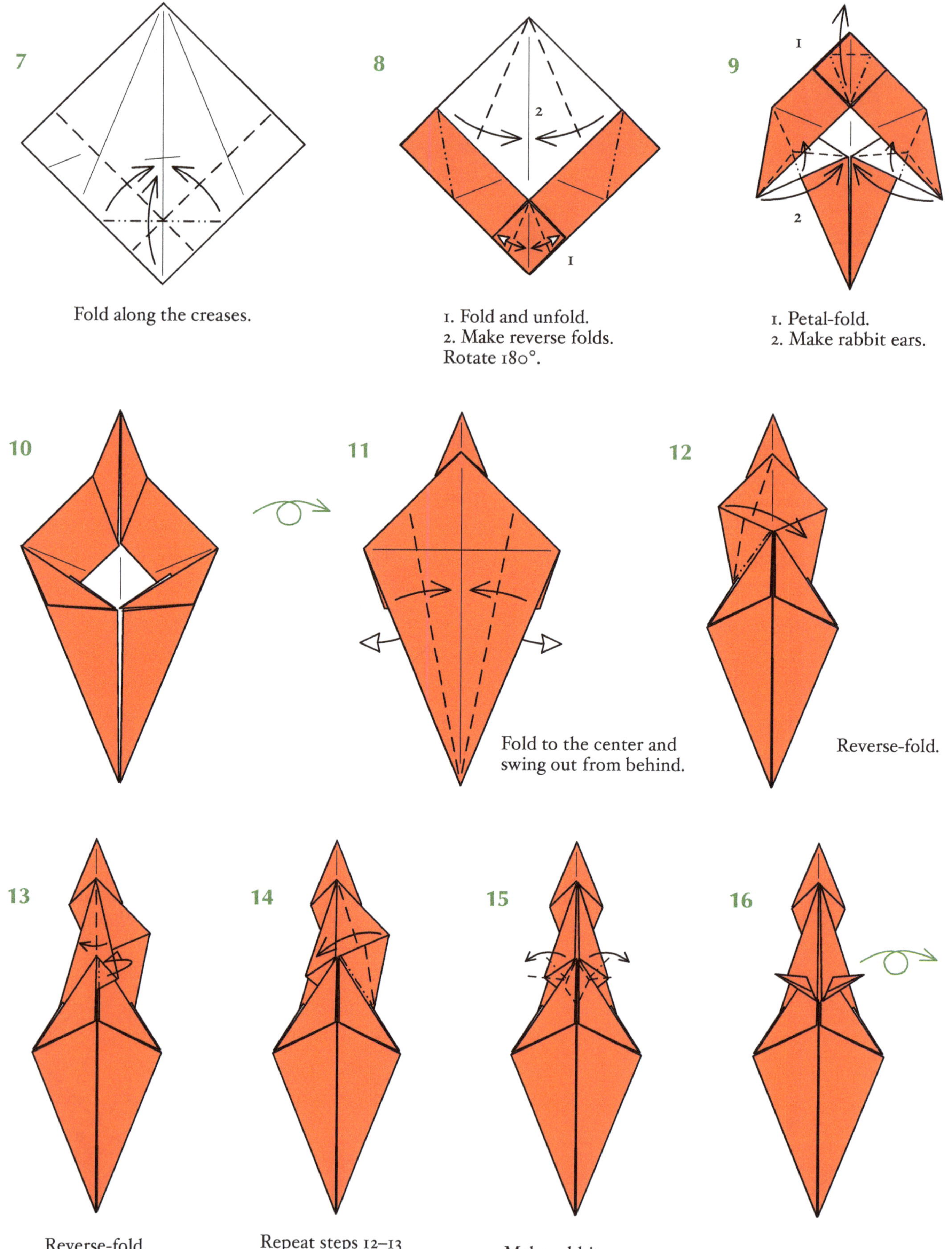
7
Fold along the creases.
8
1. Fold and unfold.
2. Make reverse folds.
Rotate 180°.
9
1. Petal-fold.
2. Make rabbit ears.
10
11
Fold to the center and
swing out from behind.
12
Reverse-fold.
13
Reverse-fold.
14
Repeat steps 12–13
on the right.
15
Make rabbit ears.
16

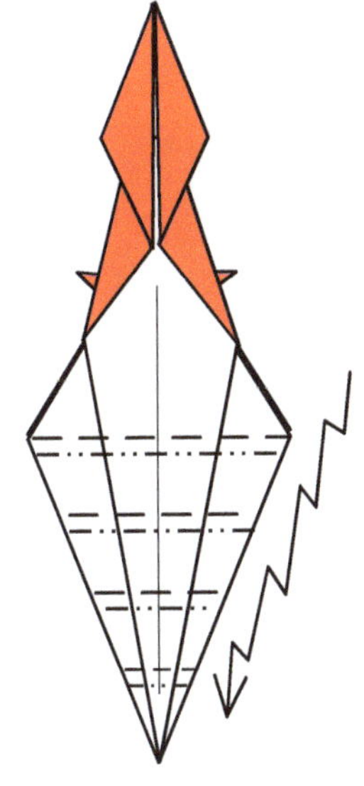

Make four pleat folds.

18

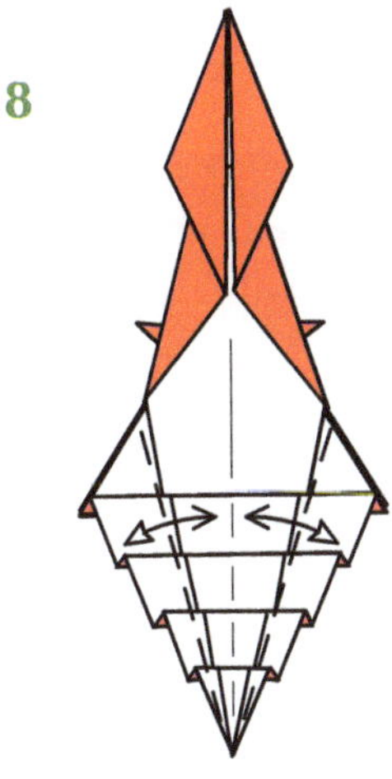

Fold toward the center and unfold.

19

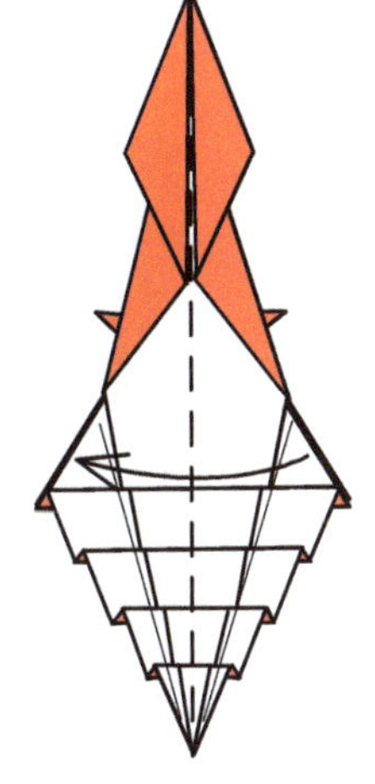

Fold in half and rotate.

20

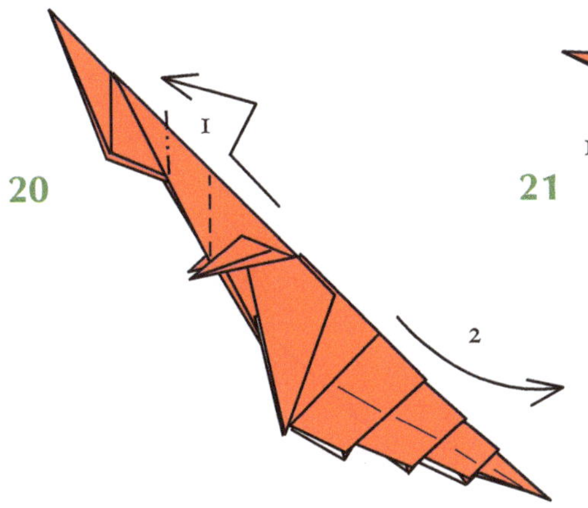

1. Make outside-reverse folds.
2. Slide each segment up.

21

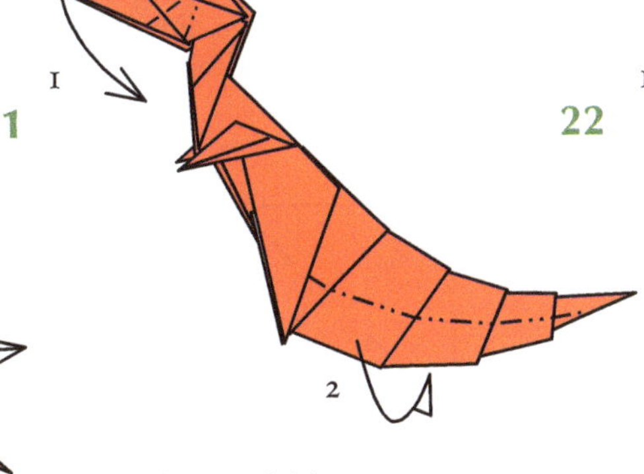

1. Crimp-fold.
2. Fold inside, repeat behind. Note it does not come to a point.

22

1. Fold inside.
2. Pleat-fold.
3. Reverse-fold.

Repeat behind.

23

1. Outside-reverse-fold.
2. Curl the arms, repeat behind.
3. Fold inside, repeat behind.
4. Shape the legs, repeat behind.

24

Tyrannosaurus

Coelophysis

Coelophysis was a slender, lightweight dinosaur that lived very early in dinosaur history, during the Late Triassic Period. Measuring about 10 feet long, it moved quickly and gracefully on long legs. A meat-eater, Coelophysis likely hunted small animals and insects. Fossils suggest it may have lived in groups, making it one of the earliest dinosaurs to show social behavior.

1 Fold and unfold.

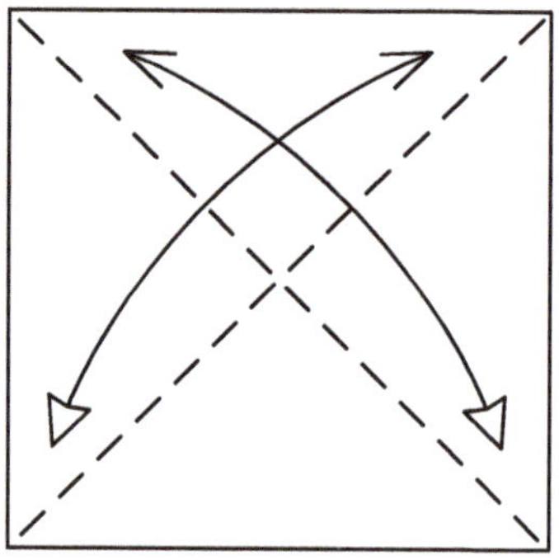

2 Fold to the center.

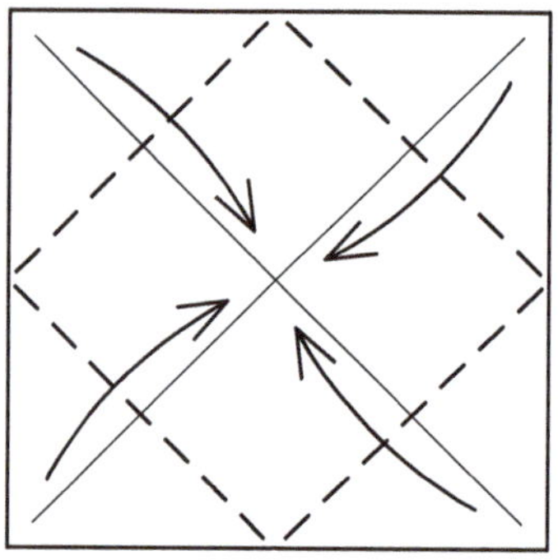

3 Bring the corner to the line.

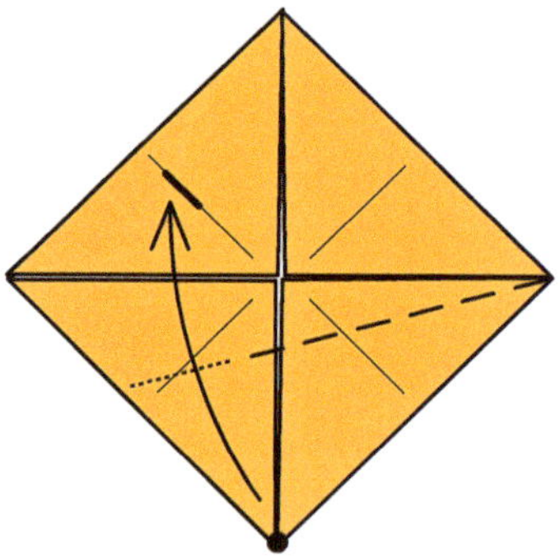

4 Unfold.

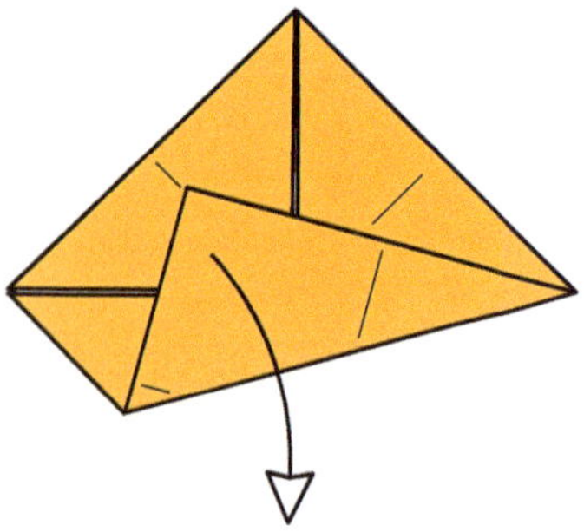

5 Repeat steps 3–4 on the left.

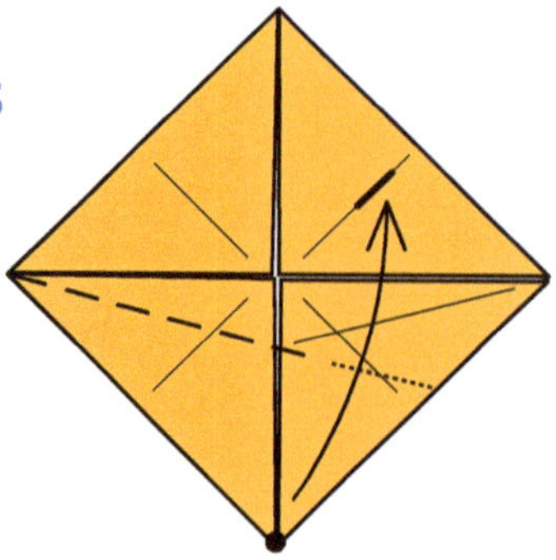

6 Unfold.

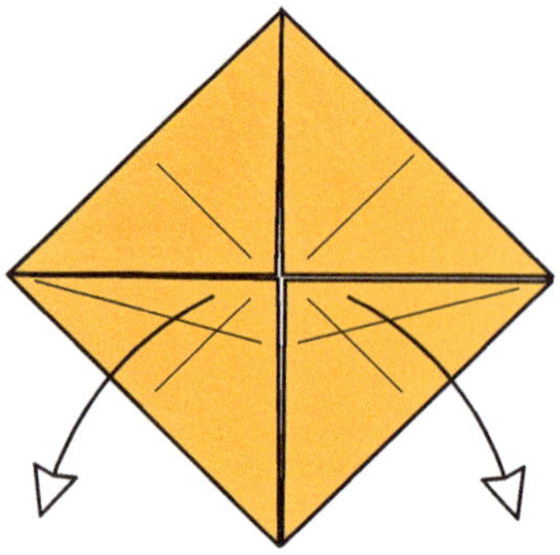

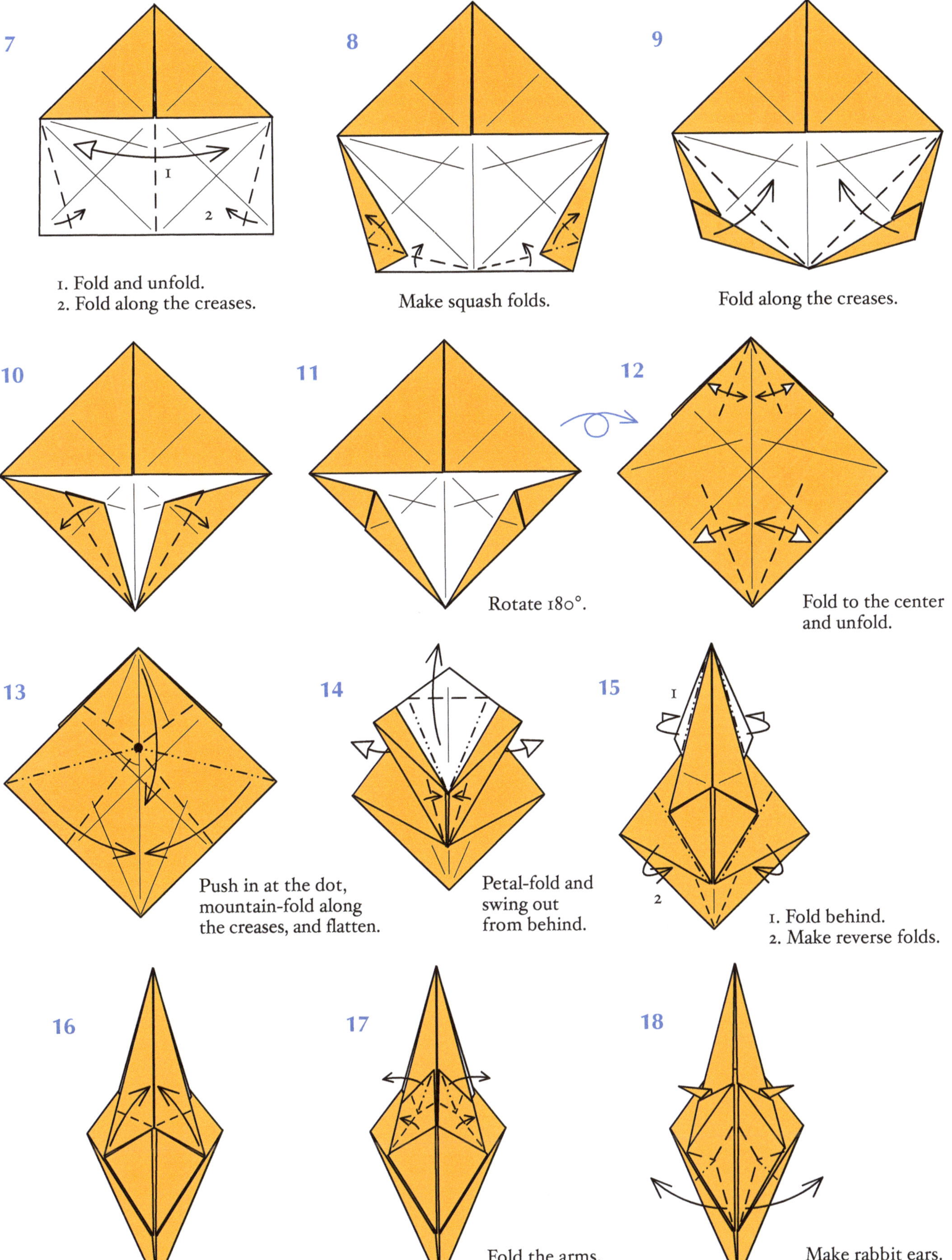
7
1. Fold and unfold.
2. Fold along the creases.
8
Make squash folds.
9
Fold along the creases.
10
11
Rotate 180°.
12
Fold to the center and unfold.
13
Push in at the dot, mountain-fold along the creases, and flatten.
14
Petal-fold and swing out from behind.
15
1. Fold behind.
2. Make reverse folds.
16
17
Fold the arms.
18
Make rabbit ears.

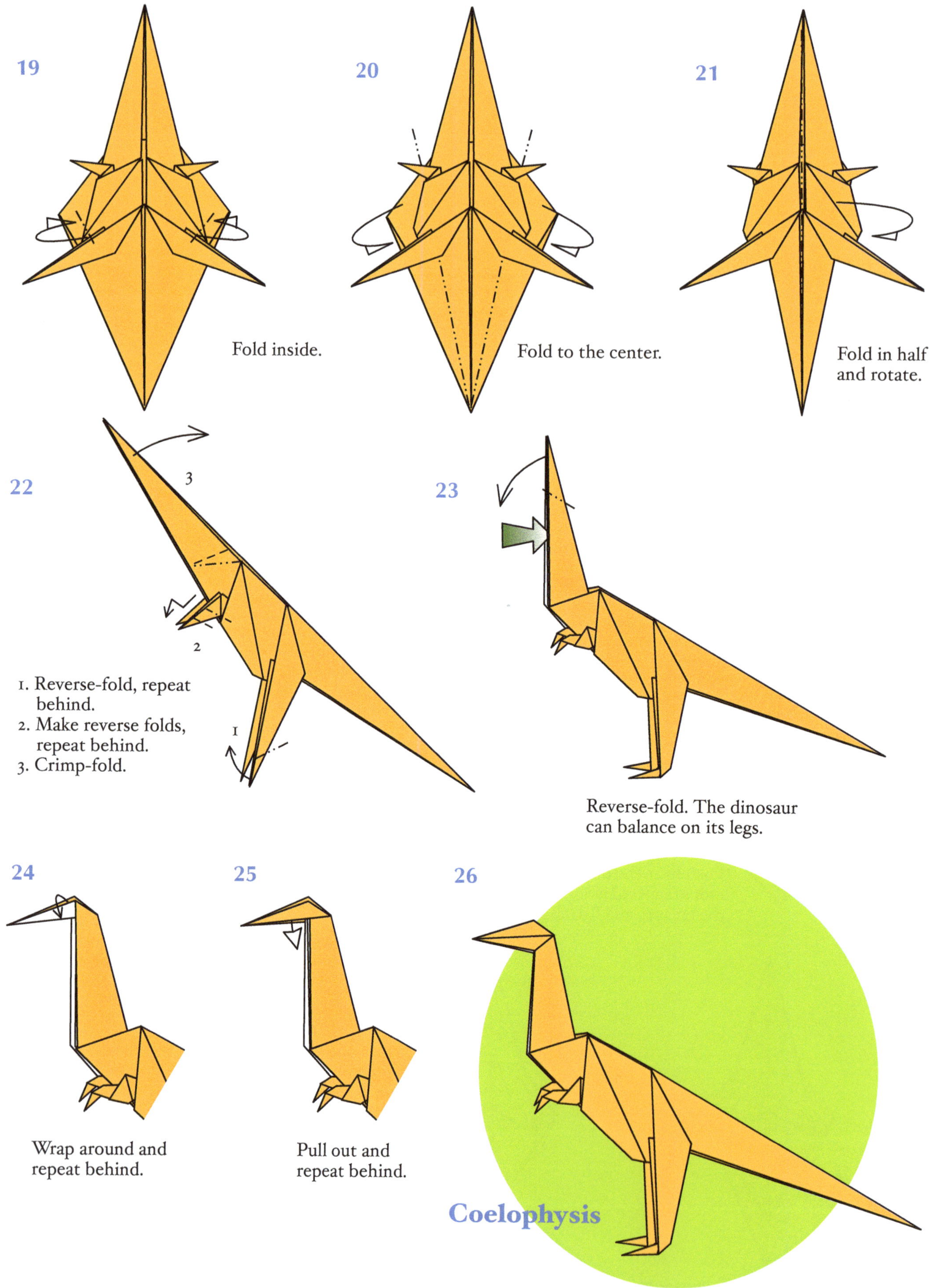
19
Fold inside.
20
Fold to the center.
21
Fold in half
and rotate.
22
3
2
1
1. Reverse-fold, repeat
behind.
2. Make reverse folds,
repeat behind.
3. Crimp-fold.
23
Reverse-fold. The dinosaur
can balance on its legs.
24
Wrap around and
repeat behind.
25
Pull out and
repeat behind.
26
Coelophysis

Aralosaurus

From the Late Cretaceous Period, Aralosaurus was a duck-billed dinosaur that walked on two legs and sometimes on all fours. Growing up to 20 feet long, it roamed wide plains in search of food. A peaceful plant-eater, Aralosaurus used its broad beak to crop vegetation. It may have had a small crest, hinting at early experiments in display among duck-billed dinosaurs.

1

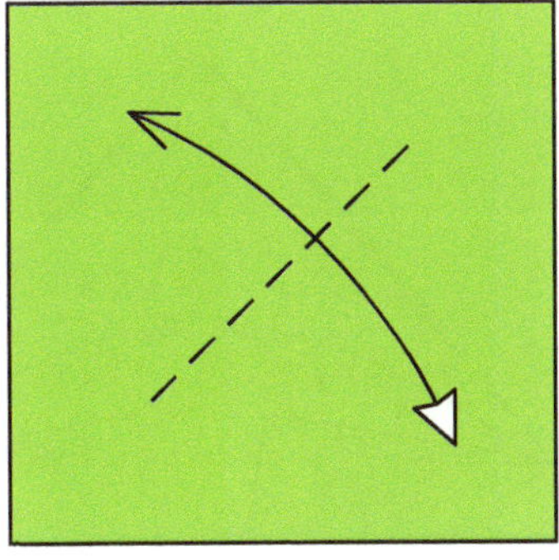

Fold and unfold in the center.

2

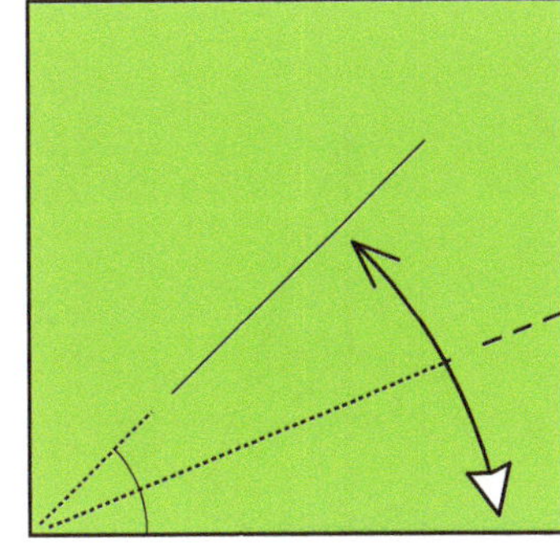

Fold and unfold on the right.

3

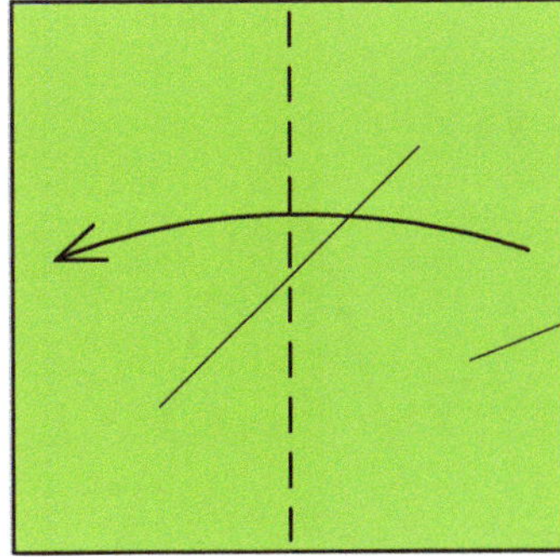

Fold in half.

4

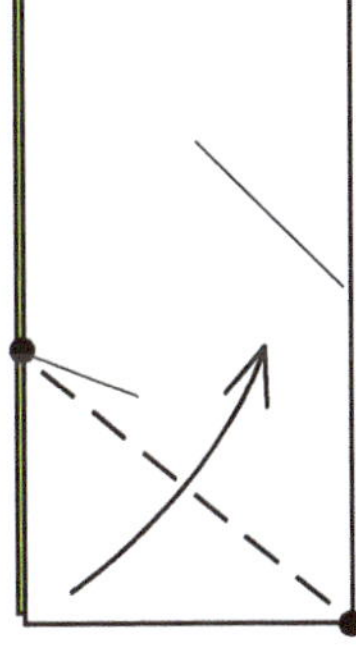

Repeat behind.

5

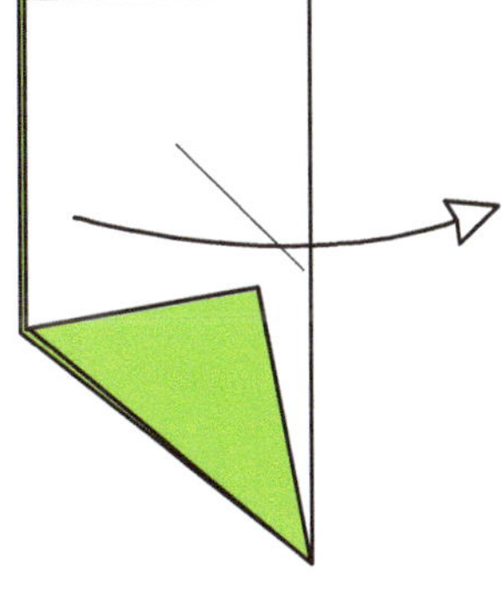

Unfold.

6

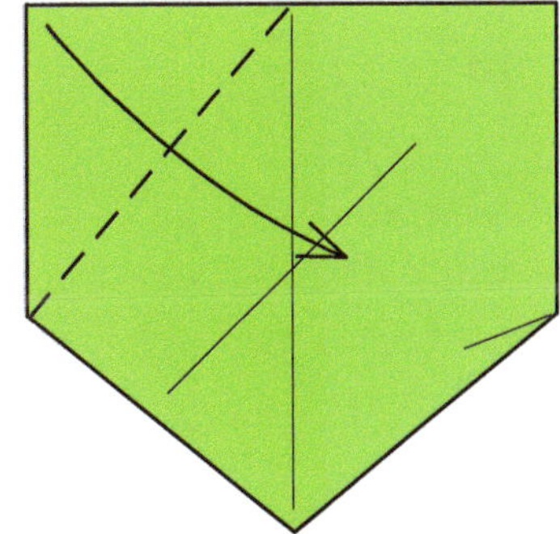

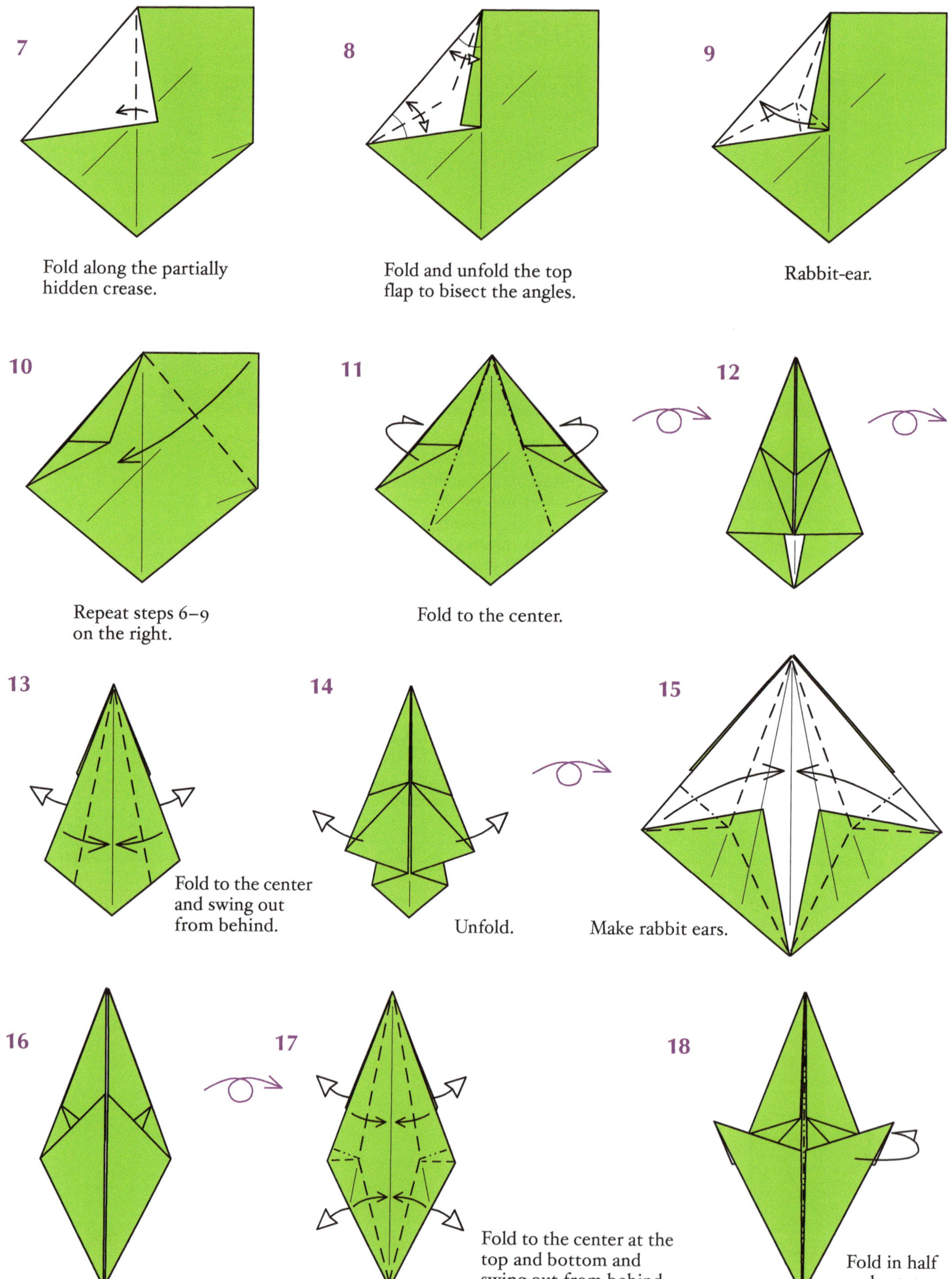
7
Fold along the partially hidden crease.
8
Fold and unfold the top flap to bisect the angles.
9
Rabbit-ear.
10
Repeat steps 6–9 on the right.
11
Fold to the center.
12
13
Fold to the center and swing out from behind.
14
Unfold.
15
Make rabbit ears.
16
17
Fold to the center at the top and bottom and swing out from behind.
18
Fold in half and rotate.

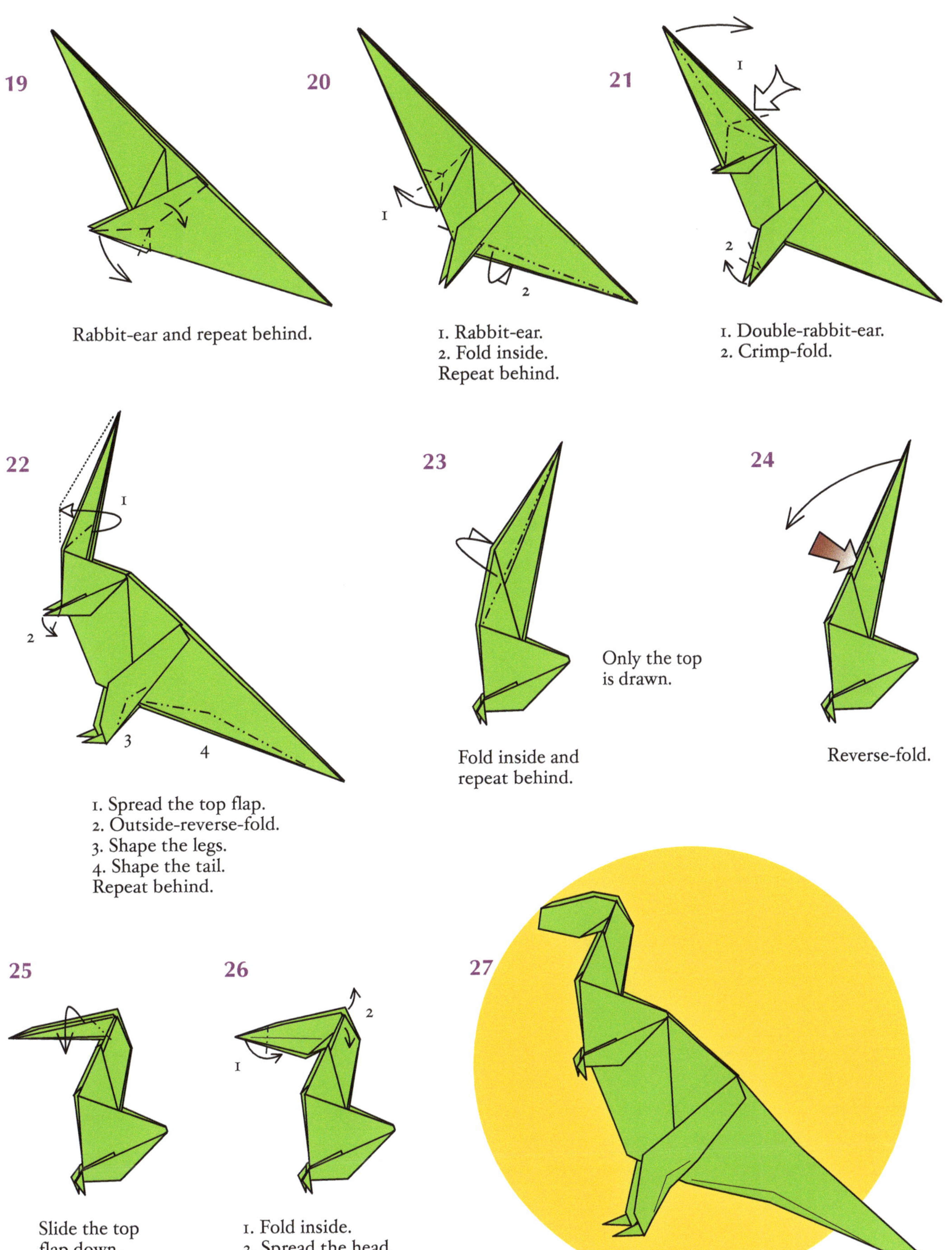

19

Rabbit-ear and repeat behind.

20

1. Rabbit-ear.
2. Fold inside.

Repeat behind.

21

1. Double-rabbit-ear.
2. Crimp-fold.

22

1. Spread the top flap.
2. Outside-reverse-fold.
3. Shape the legs.
4. Shape the tail.

Repeat behind.

23

Fold inside and repeat behind.

24

Reverse-fold.

25

Slide the top flap down.

26

1. Fold inside.
2. Spread the head.

27

Gilmoreosaurus

Gilmoreosaurus was a sturdy, medium-sized dinosaur reaching about 20 feet long. It walked mostly on two legs and was well adapted for long-distance travel. This herbivore fed on low-growing plants and shrubs. Its strong build suggests it could move efficiently across large areas while grazing, avoiding predators through awareness rather than speed. It lived during the Late Cretaceous Period.

1

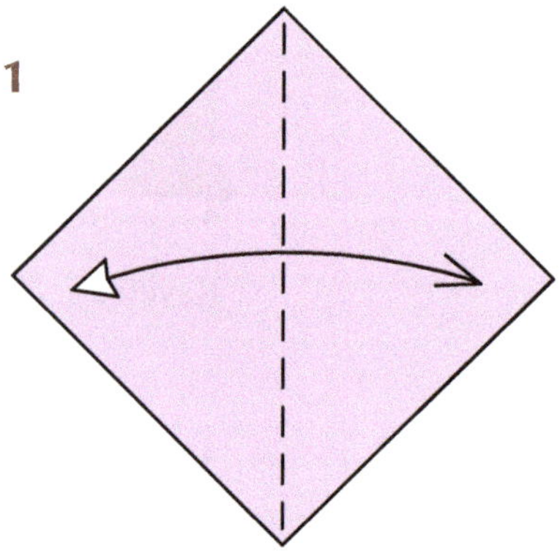

Fold and unfold.

2

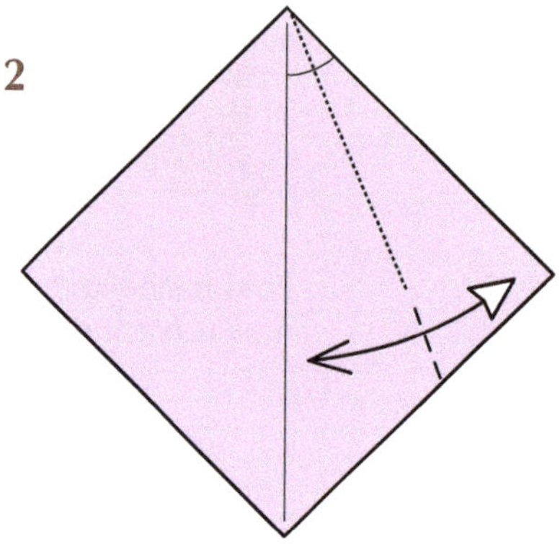

Fold and unfold on the edge.

3

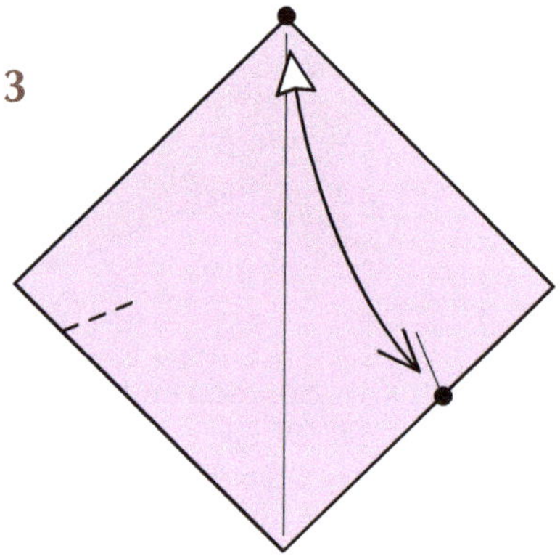

Fold and unfold on the edge.

4

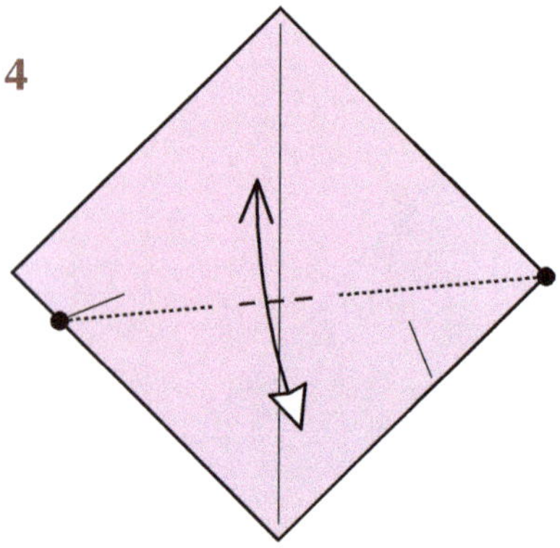

Fold and unfold on the diagonal.

5

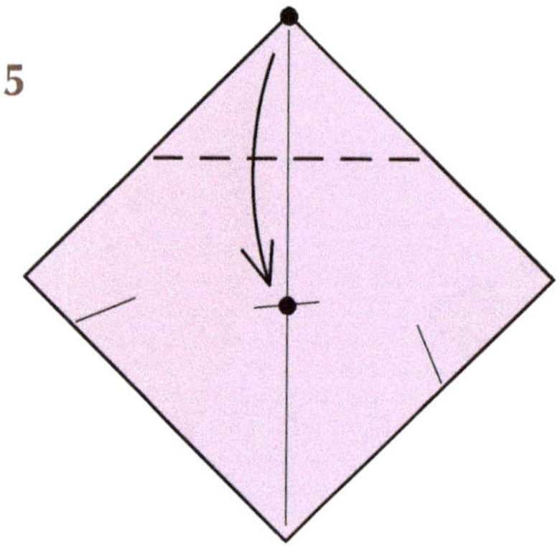

6

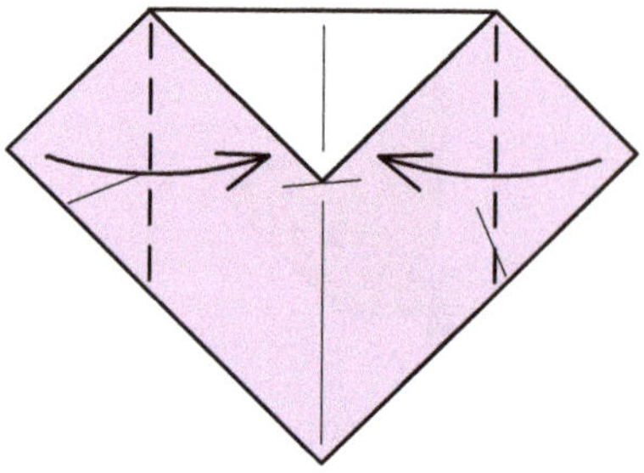

7

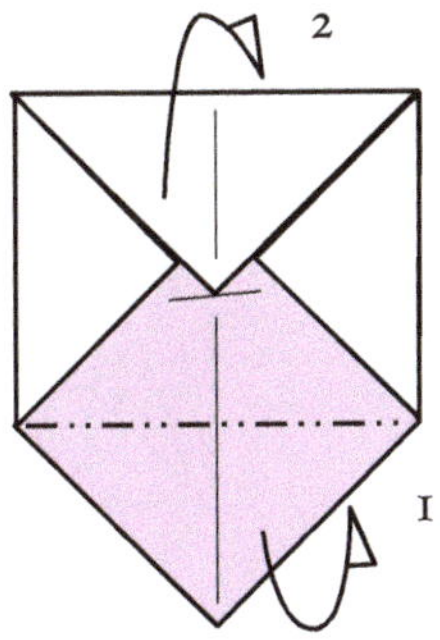

1. Fold behind.
2. Wrap around.

8

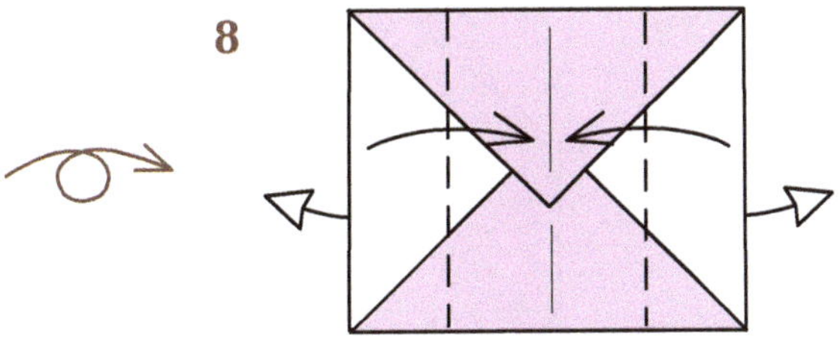

Fold to the center and swing out from behind.

9

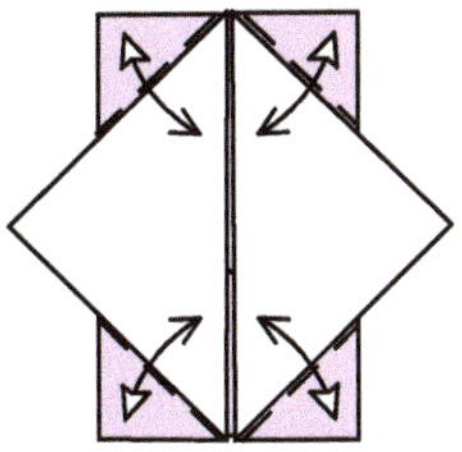

Fold and unfold.

10

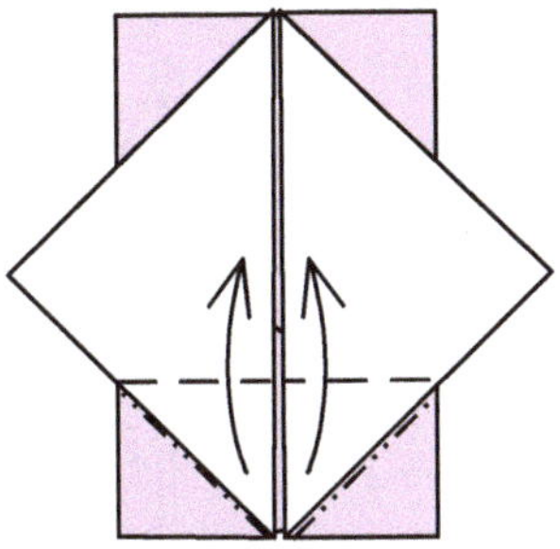

Make squash folds.

11

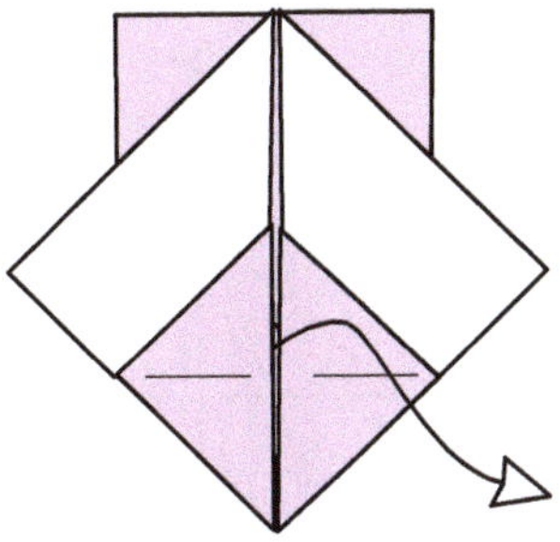

Pull out the hidden corner.

12

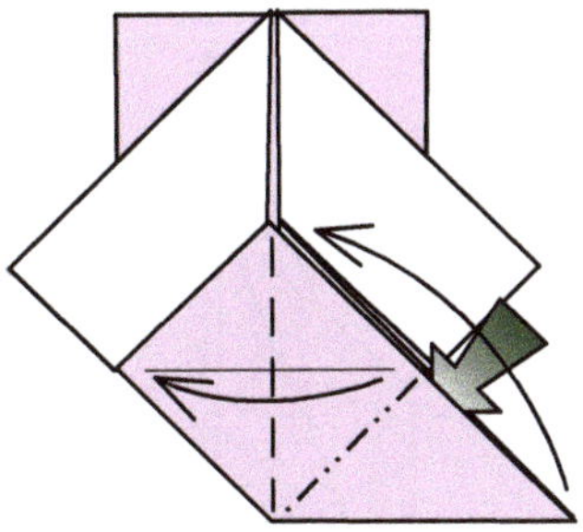

Squash-fold.

13

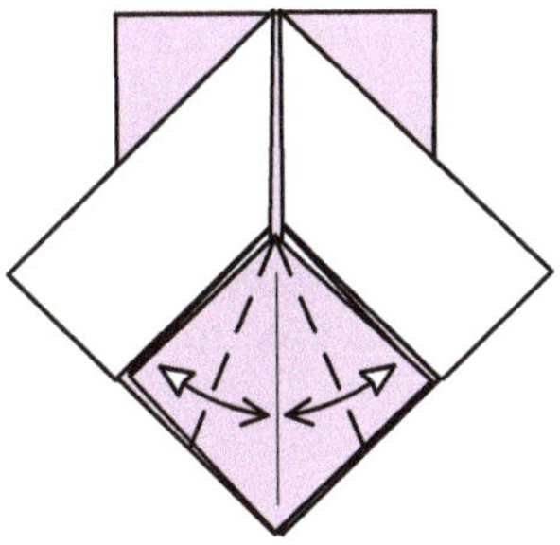

Fold and unfold.

14

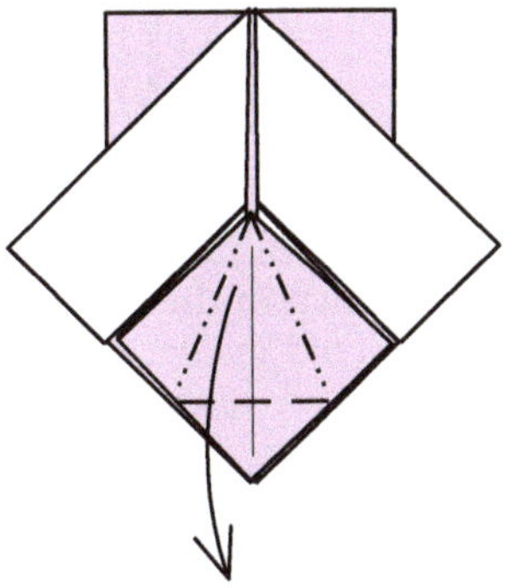

Petal-fold.

15

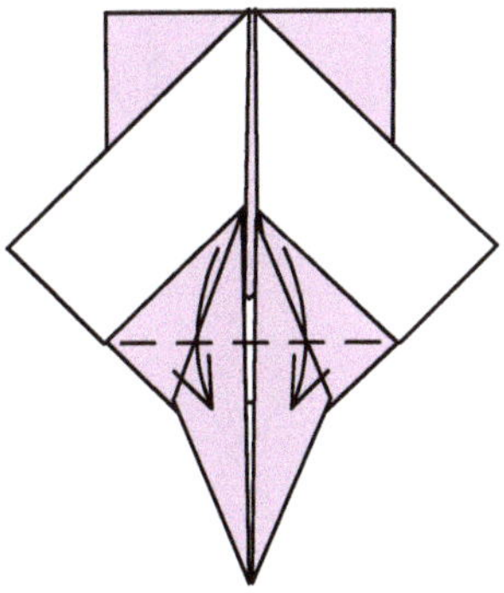

Rotate 180°.

16

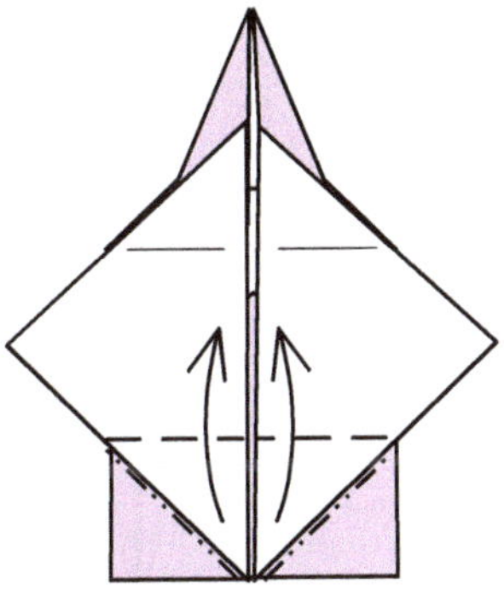

Repeat steps 10–15.

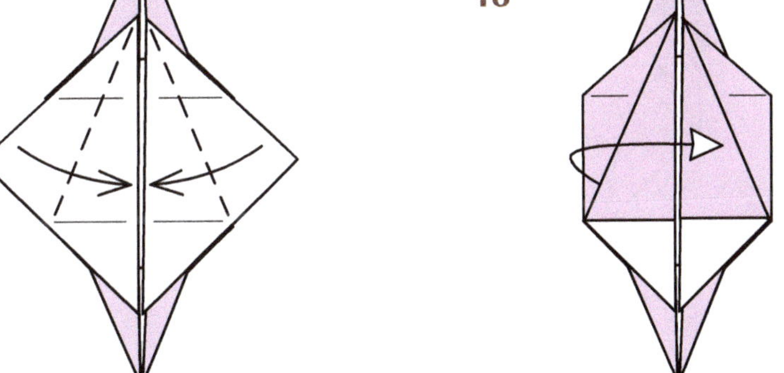

17

Fold to the center.

18

Unfold the top flap.

19

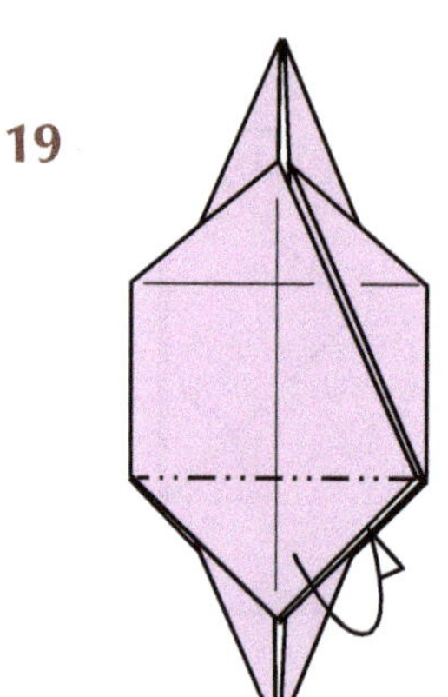

Fold inside.

20

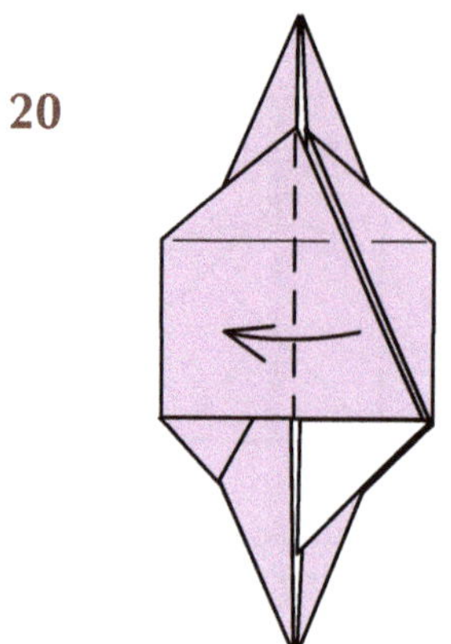

21

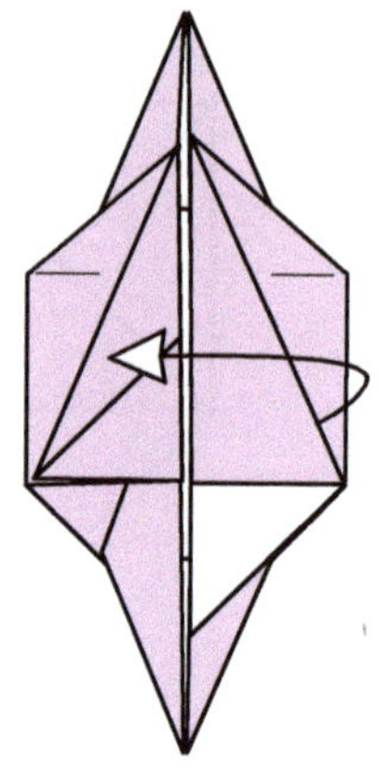

Repeat steps 18–20
on the right.

22

Make squash folds.

23

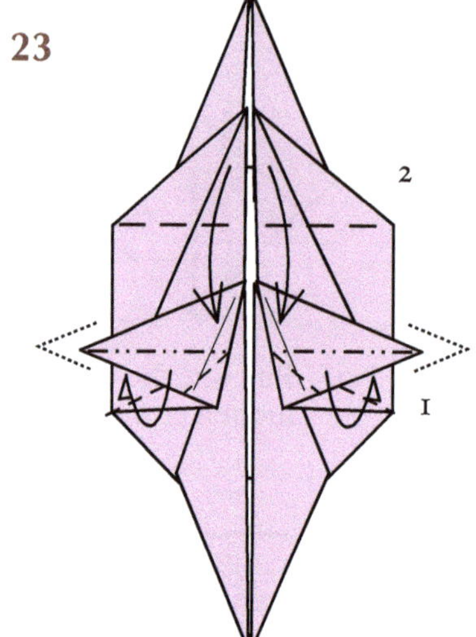

Note the angle of the legs,
shown in the dotted lines.
1. Fold inside.
2. Fold down.

24

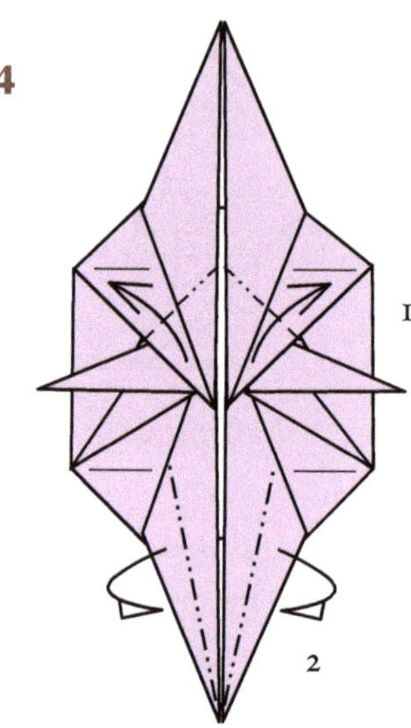

1. Make reverse folds.
2. Fold to the center.

25

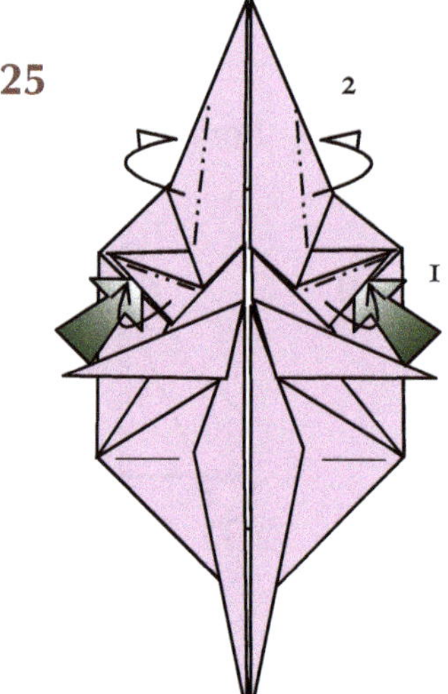

1. Make reverse folds.
2. Fold inside.

26

27

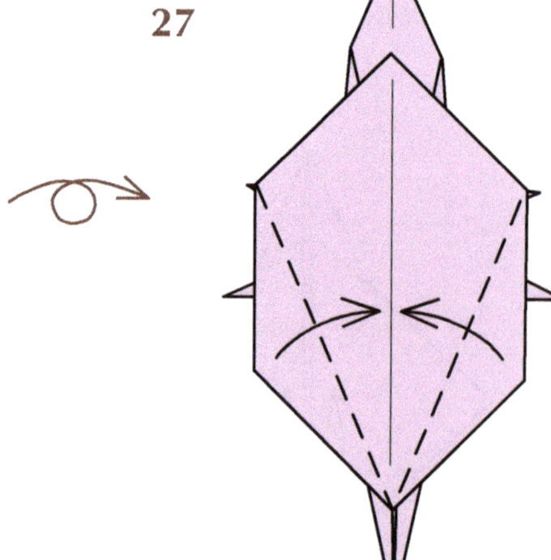

Fold to the center.

28

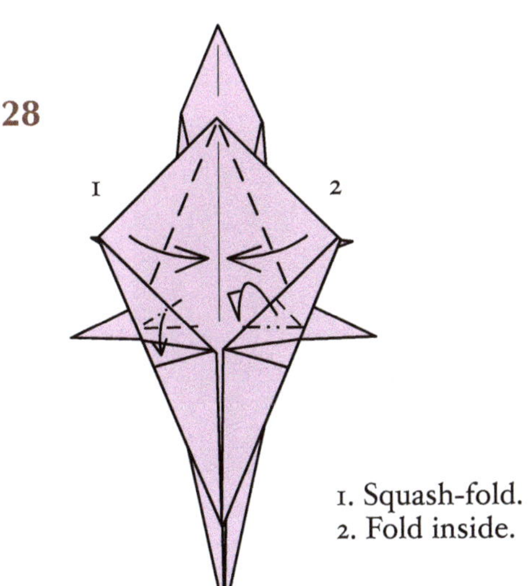

1. Squash-fold.
2. Fold inside.

29

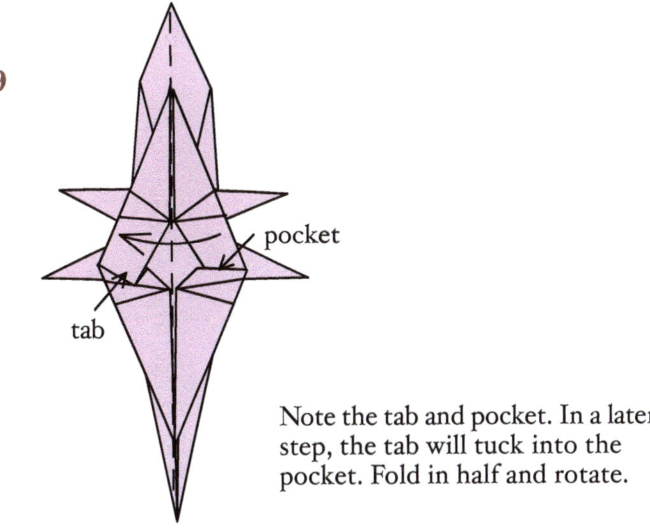

Note the tab and pocket. In a later step, the tab will tuck into the pocket. Fold in half and rotate.

30

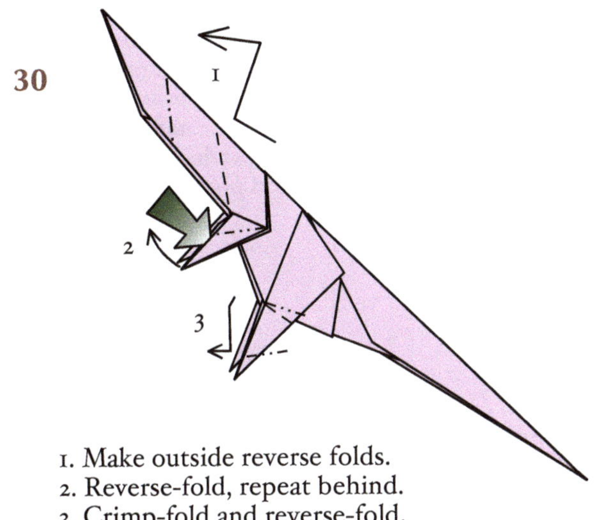

1. Make outside reverse folds.
2. Reverse-fold, repeat behind.
3. Crimp-fold and reverse-fold, repeat behind.

31

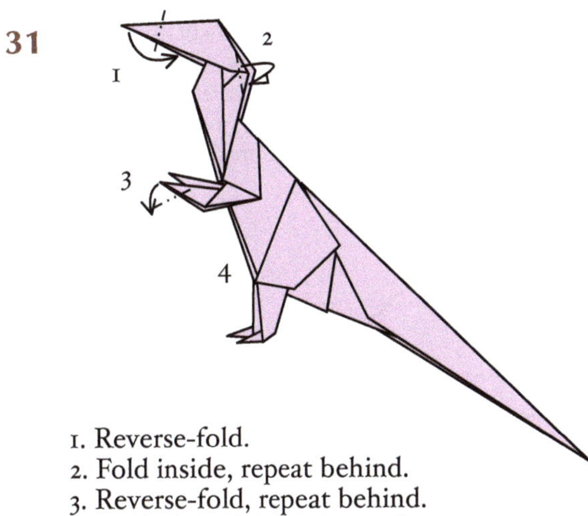

1. Reverse-fold.
2. Fold inside, repeat behind.
3. Reverse-fold, repeat behind.
4. Tuck the tab into the pocket to lock the model.

32

Gilmoreosaurus

Carcharodontosaurus

Carcharodontosaurus was one of the largest meat-eating dinosaurs to ever walk the Earth. Measuring up to 45 feet long, this powerful predator lived during the Late Cretaceous Period in what is now North Africa. A fierce carnivore, Carcharodontosaurus had long, sharp teeth shaped like the blades of a shark—its name means "shark-toothed lizard." These slicing teeth were perfect for cutting through flesh, allowing it to hunt large prey with efficiency. With its massive skull and strong legs, Carcharodontosaurus stood among the top predators of its time, rivaling even Tyrannosaurus in size and power.

1

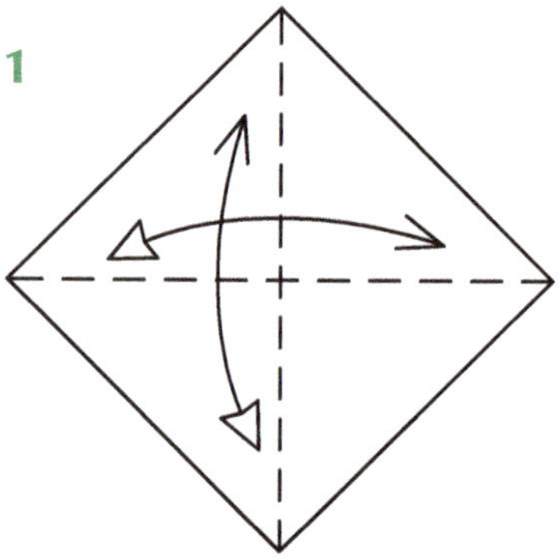

Fold and unfold.

2

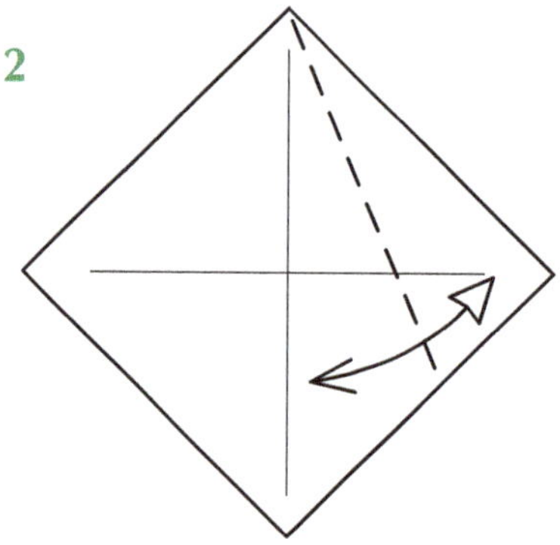

Fold and unfold.

3

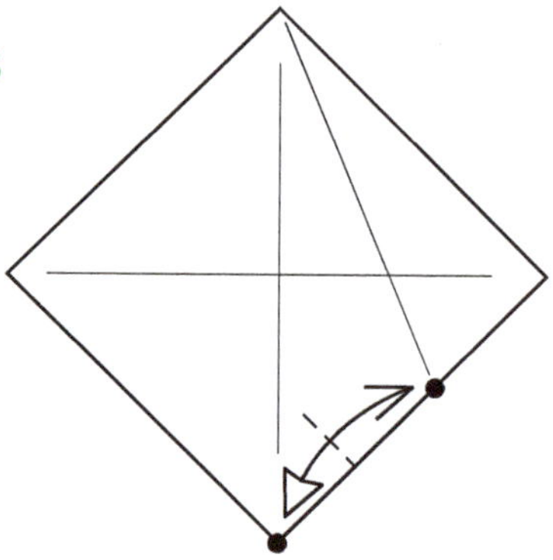

Fold and unfold on the edge.

4

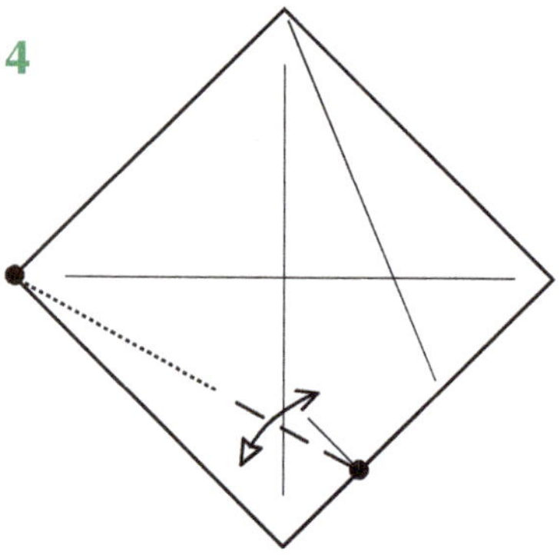

Fold and unfold on the diagonal.

5

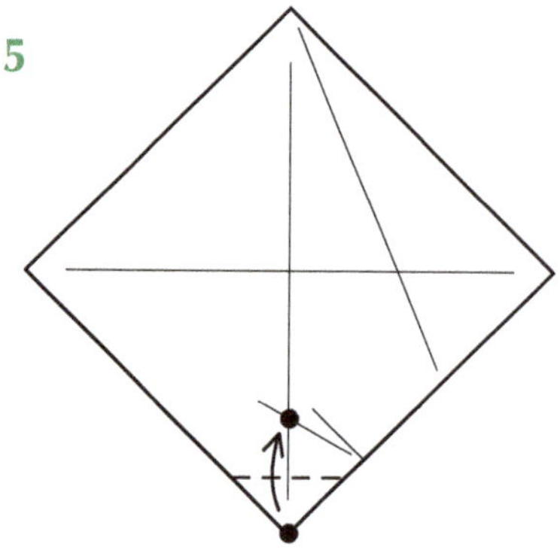

6

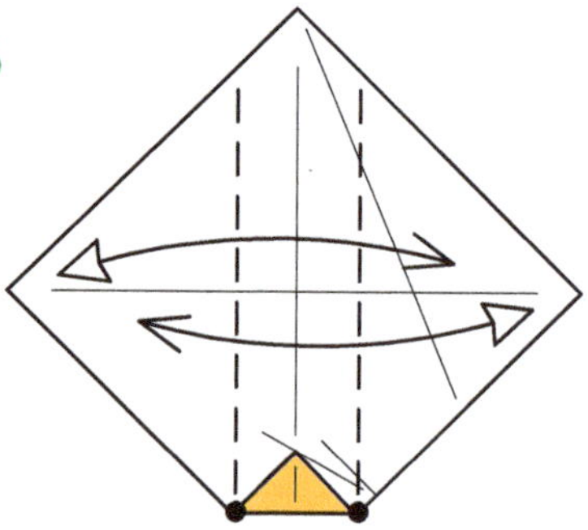

Fold and unfold.

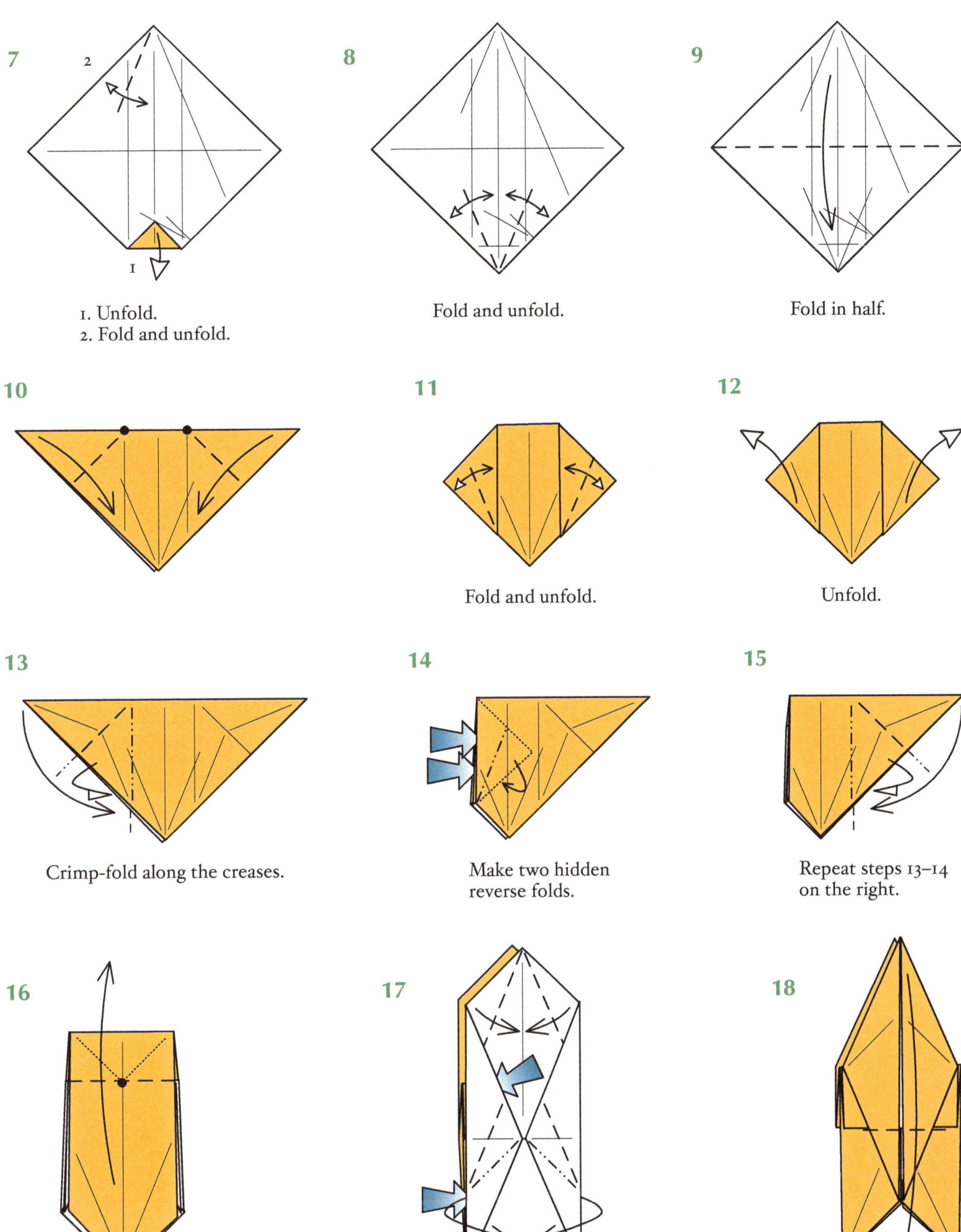
7
2
1
1. Unfold.
2. Fold and unfold.
8
Fold and unfold.
9
Fold in half.
10
11
Fold and unfold.
12
Unfold.
13
Crimp-fold along the creases.
14
Make two hidden
reverse folds.
15
Repeat steps 13–14
on the right.
16
Fold up and
repeat behind.
17
Begin by pushing in a the upper
large arrow. Repeat behind.
18

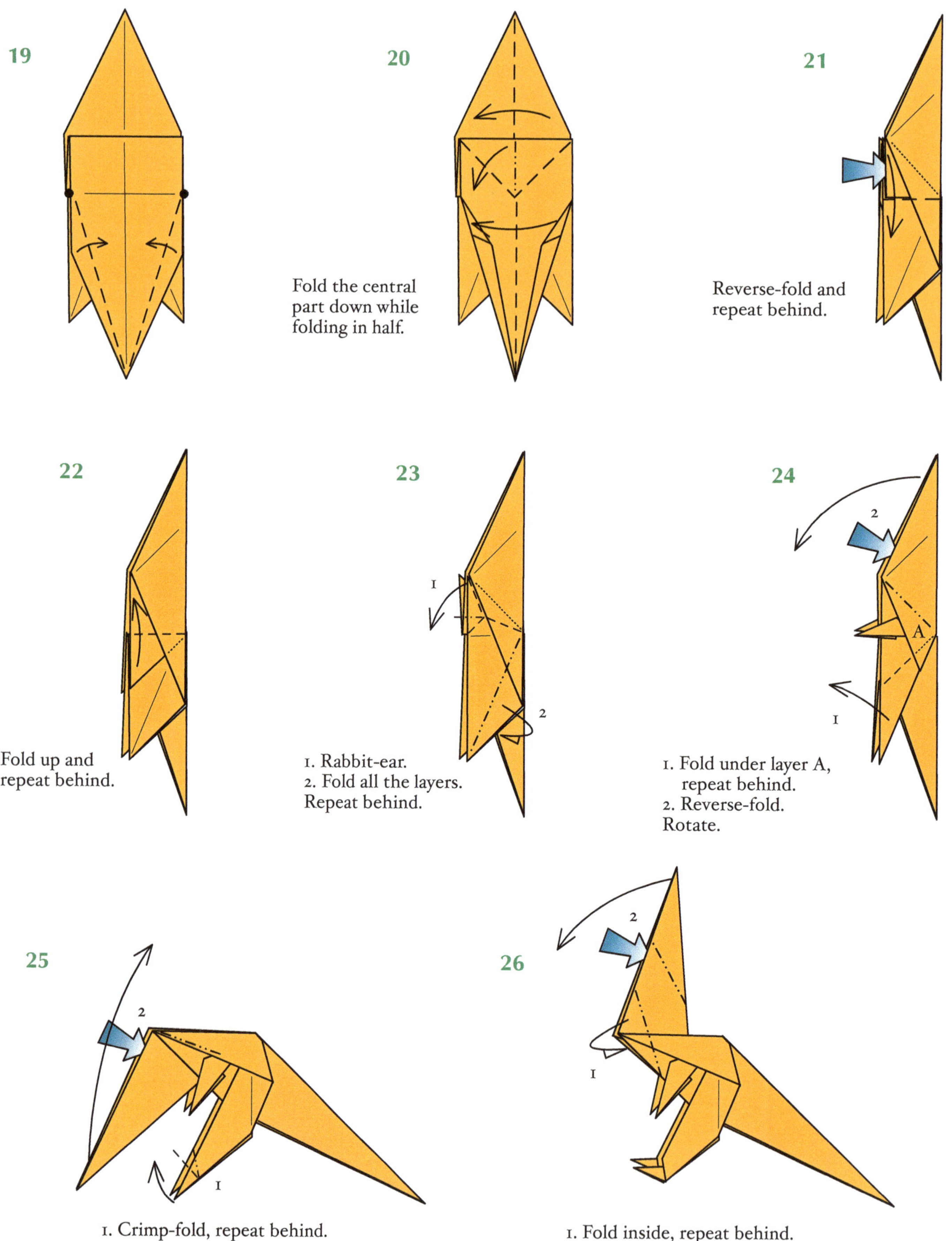
19
20
Fold the central part down while folding in half.
21
Reverse-fold and repeat behind.
22
Fold up and repeat behind.
23
1
2
1. Rabbit-ear.
2. Fold all the layers.
Repeat behind.
24
2
A
1
1. Fold under layer A, repeat behind.
2. Reverse-fold.
Rotate.
25
2
1
1. Crimp-fold, repeat behind.
2. Reverse-fold.
26
2
1
1. Fold inside, repeat behind.
2. Reverse-fold.

27

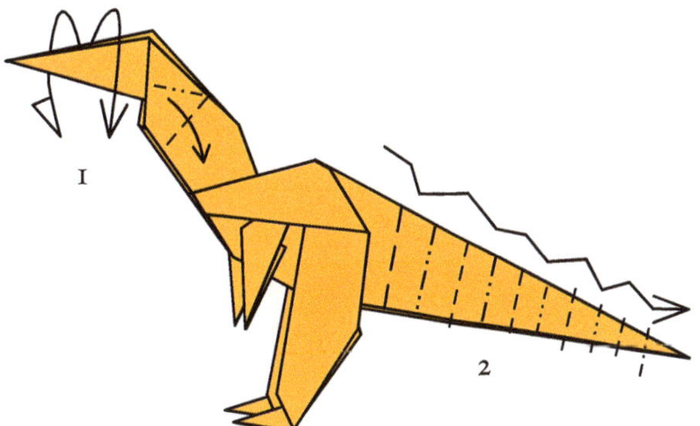

1. Outside-reverse-fold and spread the paper.
2. Pleat-fold.

28

1. Crimp-fold.
2. Shape the arms, repeat behind.

29

1. Fold inside.
2. Shape the legs.
Repeat behind. The model can balance on its legs.

30

Carcharodontosaurus

Parasaurolophus

Parasaurolophus is famous for the long, curved crest extending from the back of its head. Measuring up to 30 feet long, it walked on two legs and sometimes four. A gentle plant-eater from the Late Cretaceous Period, Parasaurolophus likely used its crest to produce sounds, possibly to communicate with others of its kind. Its musical appearance makes it one of the most beloved dinosaurs of all.

1

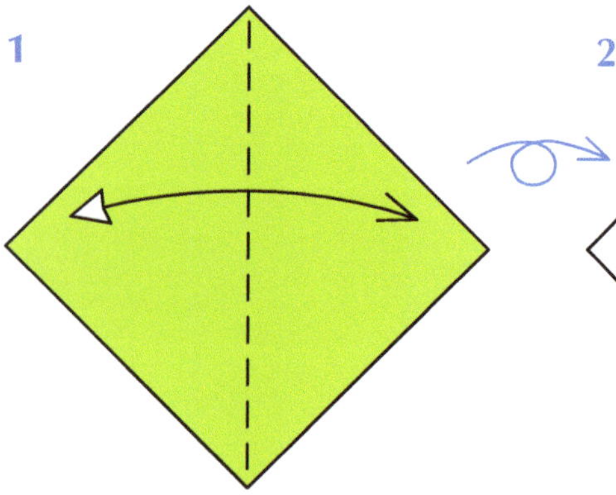

Fold and unfold.

2

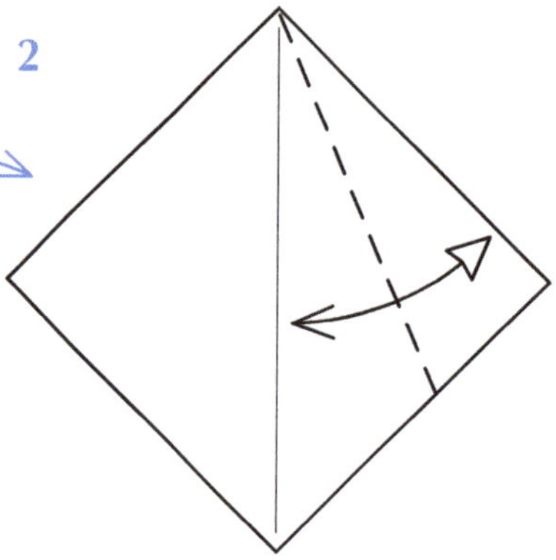

Fold and unfold.

3

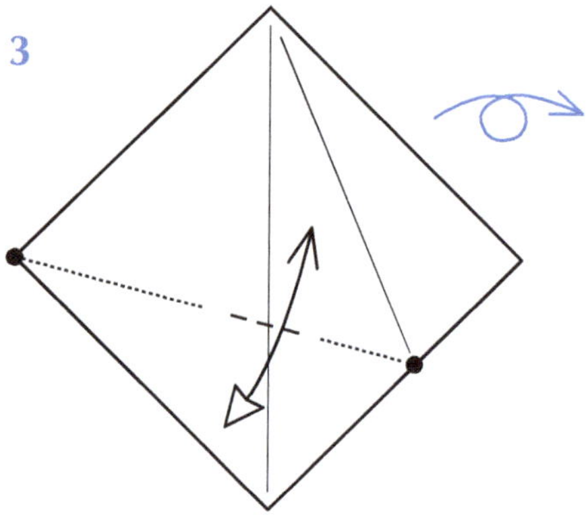

Fold and unfold on the diagonal.

4

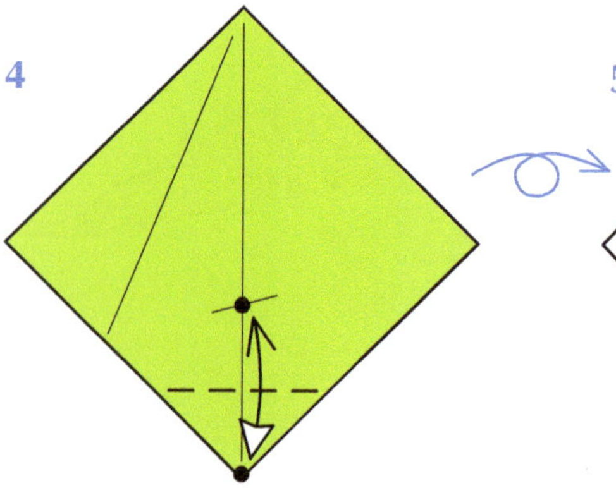

Fold and unfold.

5

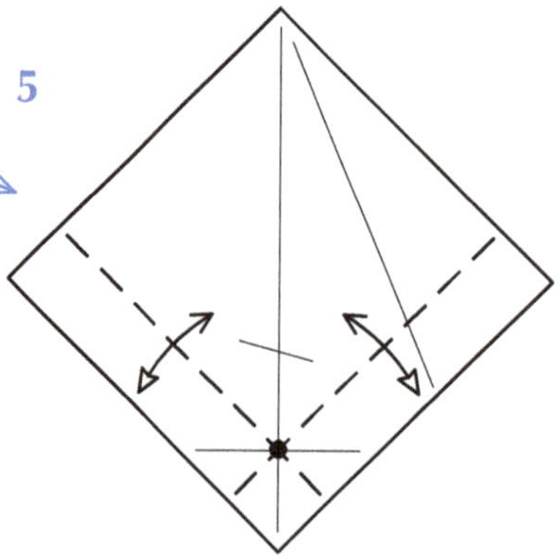

Fold and unfold.

6

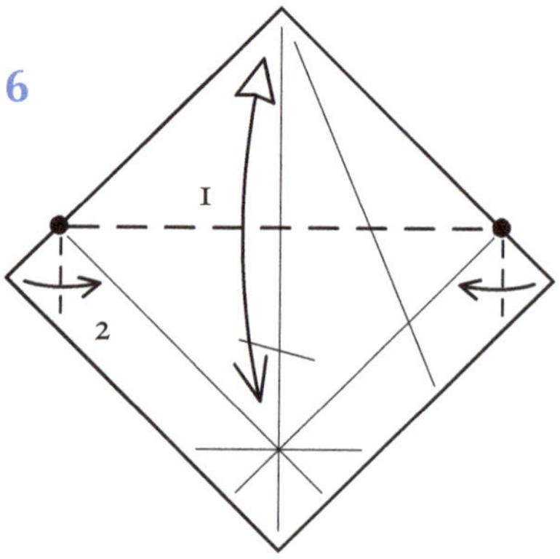

1. Fold and unfold.
2. Fold on the left and right.

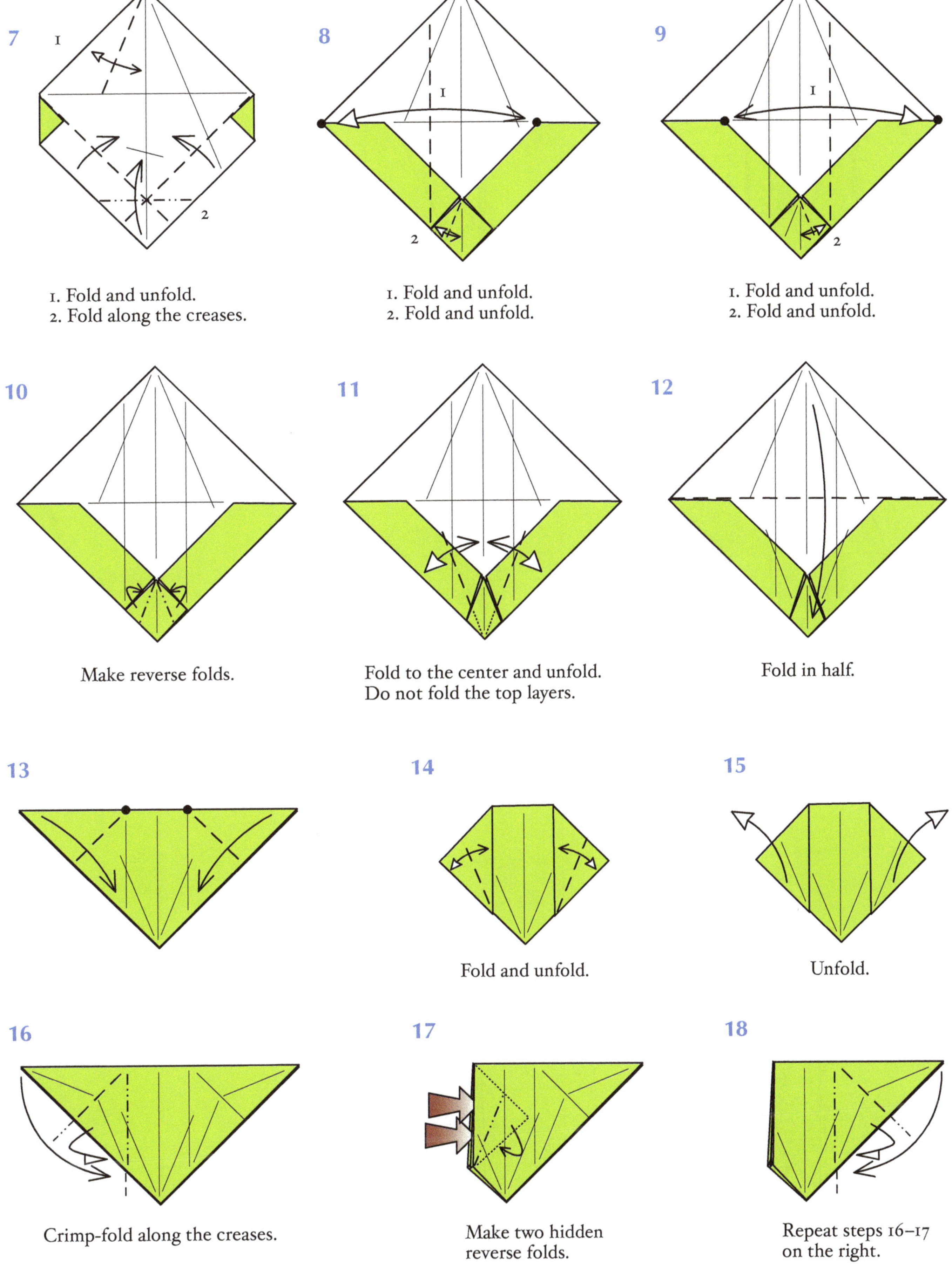
7
1
2
1. Fold and unfold.
2. Fold along the creases.
8
1
2
1. Fold and unfold.
2. Fold and unfold.
9
1
2
1. Fold and unfold.
2. Fold and unfold.
10
Make reverse folds.
11
Fold to the center and unfold.
Do not fold the top layers.
12
Fold in half.
13
14
Fold and unfold.
15
Unfold.
16
Crimp-fold along the creases.
17
Make two hidden
reverse folds.
18
Repeat steps 16–17
on the right.

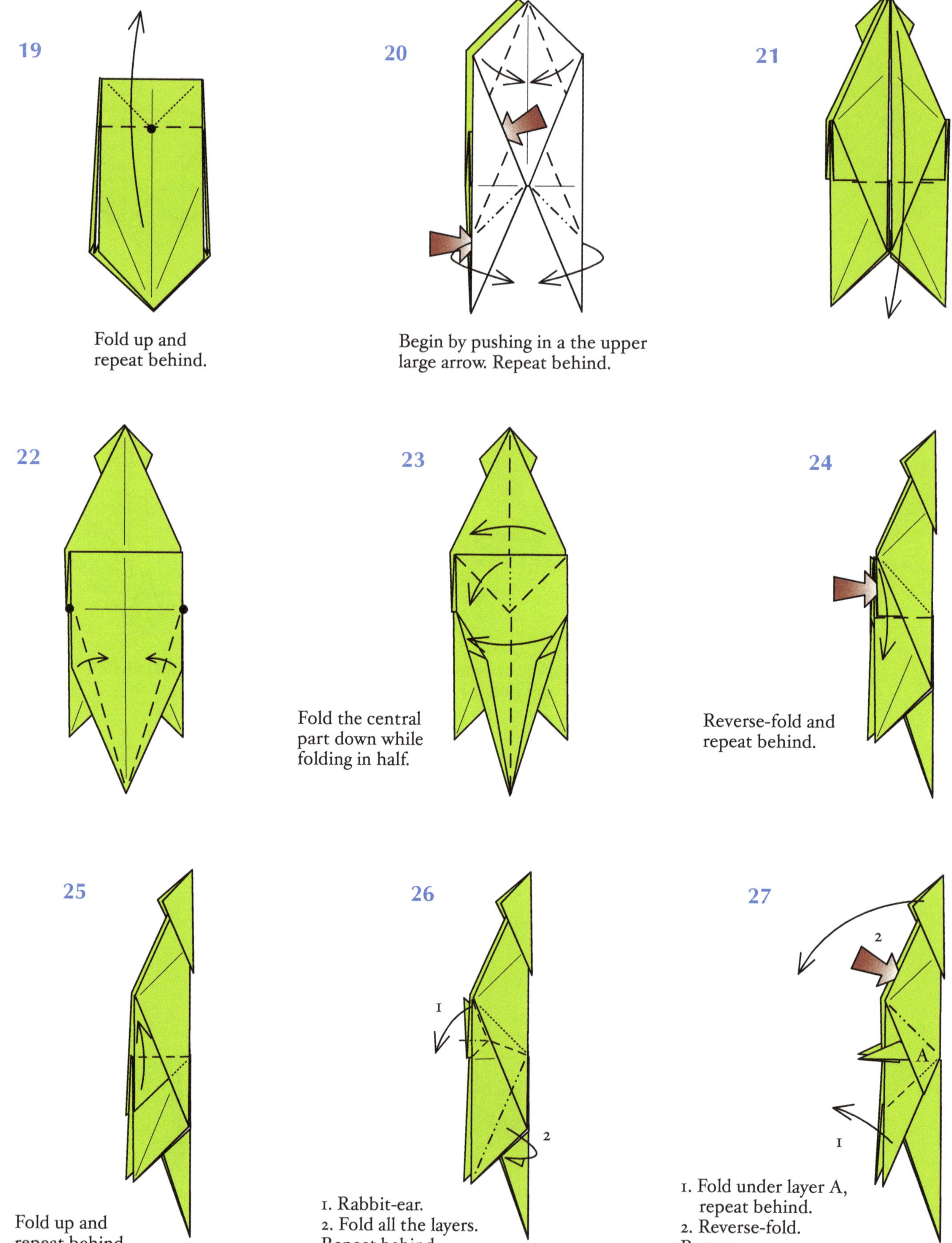
19
Fold up and
repeat behind.
20
Begin by pushing in a the upper
large arrow. Repeat behind.
21
22
23
Fold the central
part down while
folding in half.
24
Reverse-fold and
repeat behind.
25
Fold up and
repeat behind.
26
1
2
1. Rabbit-ear.
2. Fold all the layers.
Repeat behind.
27
2
A
1
1. Fold under layer A,
repeat behind.
2. Reverse-fold.
Rotate.

28

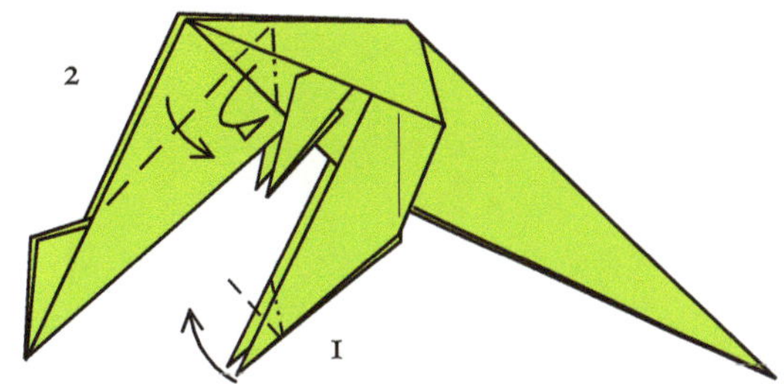

1. Crimp-fold.
2. Reverse-fold.
Repeat behind.

29

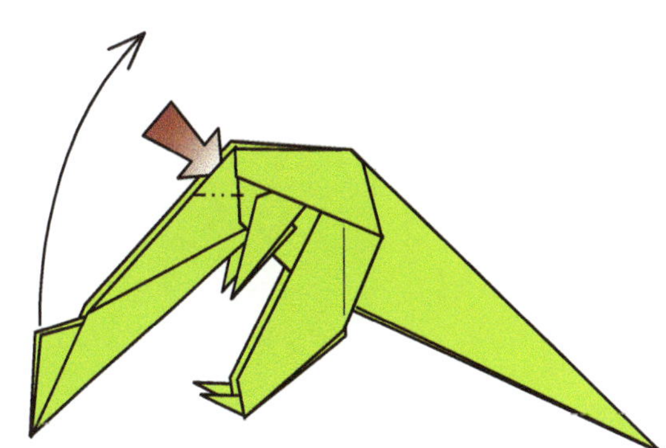

Reverse-fold.

30

1. Crimp-fold.
2. Shape the arms, repeat behind.

31

1. Crimp-fold.
2. Shape the legs, repeat behind.
The model can balance on its legs.

32

Parasaurolophus

Tarascosaurus

Tarascosaurus was a large meat-eating dinosaur from the Late Cretaceous Period, reaching lengths of about 30 feet. Though known from only limited fossil remains, it was clearly built as a powerful predator, with strong legs and sharp teeth suited for hunting large prey.

Much about Tarascosaurus remains a mystery, reminding us that many impressive dinosaurs are still known only in fragments. This leaves room for curiosity, discovery, and imagination. For this model, artistic license was used to add ornamental details, celebrating the unknown and honoring the idea that science and creativity often meet where the fossil record is incomplete.

1

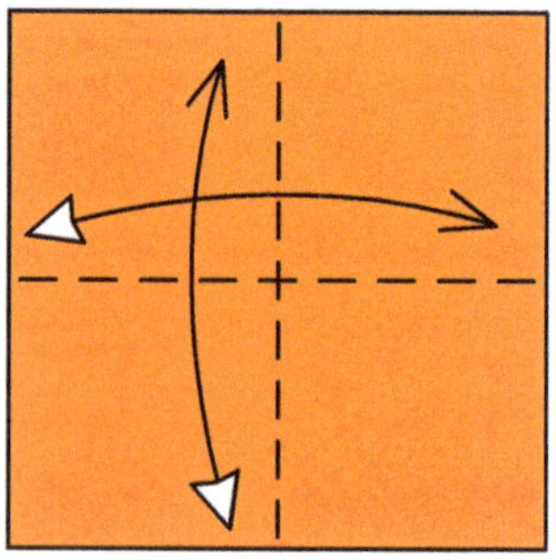

Fold and unfold.

2

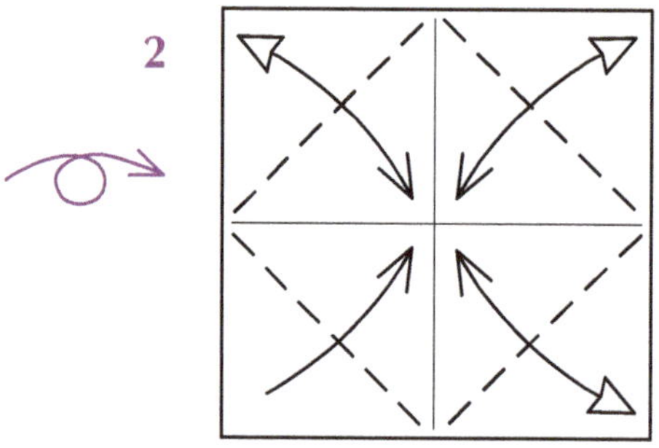

Fold the four corners to the center and unfold on three sides.

3

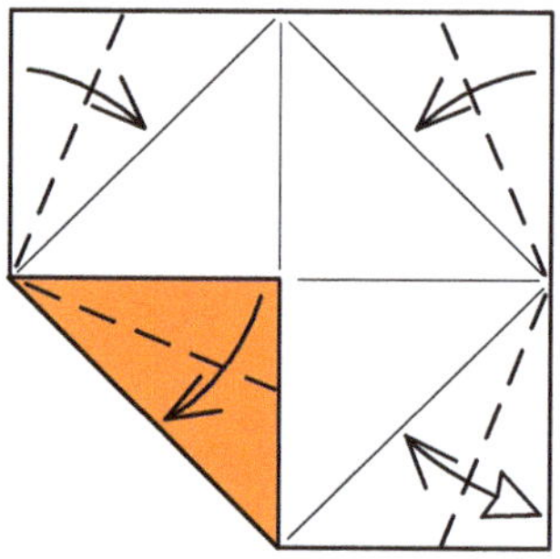

Fold and unfold on one side.

4

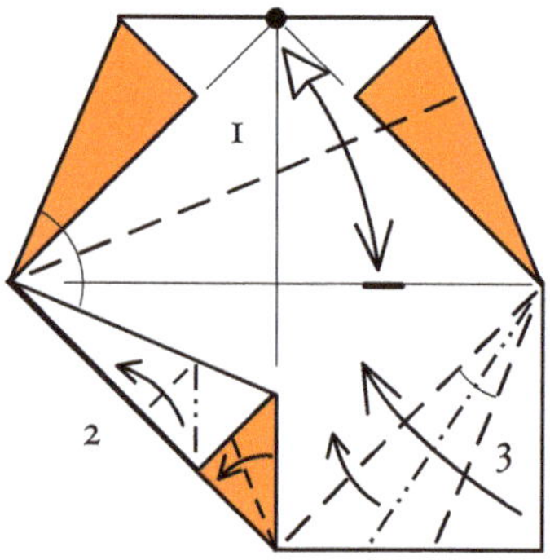

1. Fold and unfold.
2. Squash-fold.
3. Pleat-fold.

5

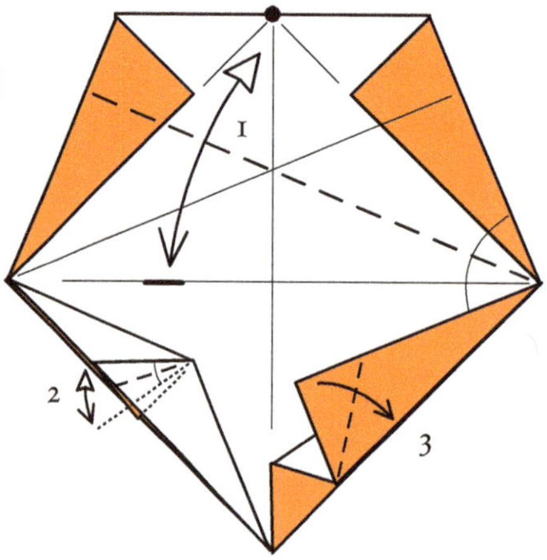

1. Fold and unfold.
2. Fold and unfold, close to the center.
3. Fold the top layer.

6

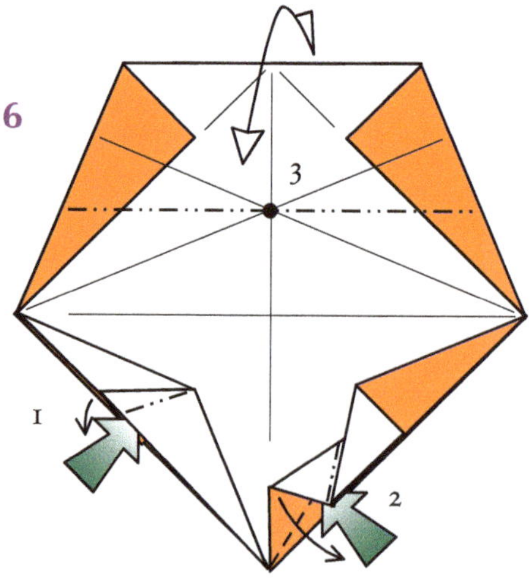

1. Reverse-fold.
2. Reverse-fold.
3. Fold and unfold.

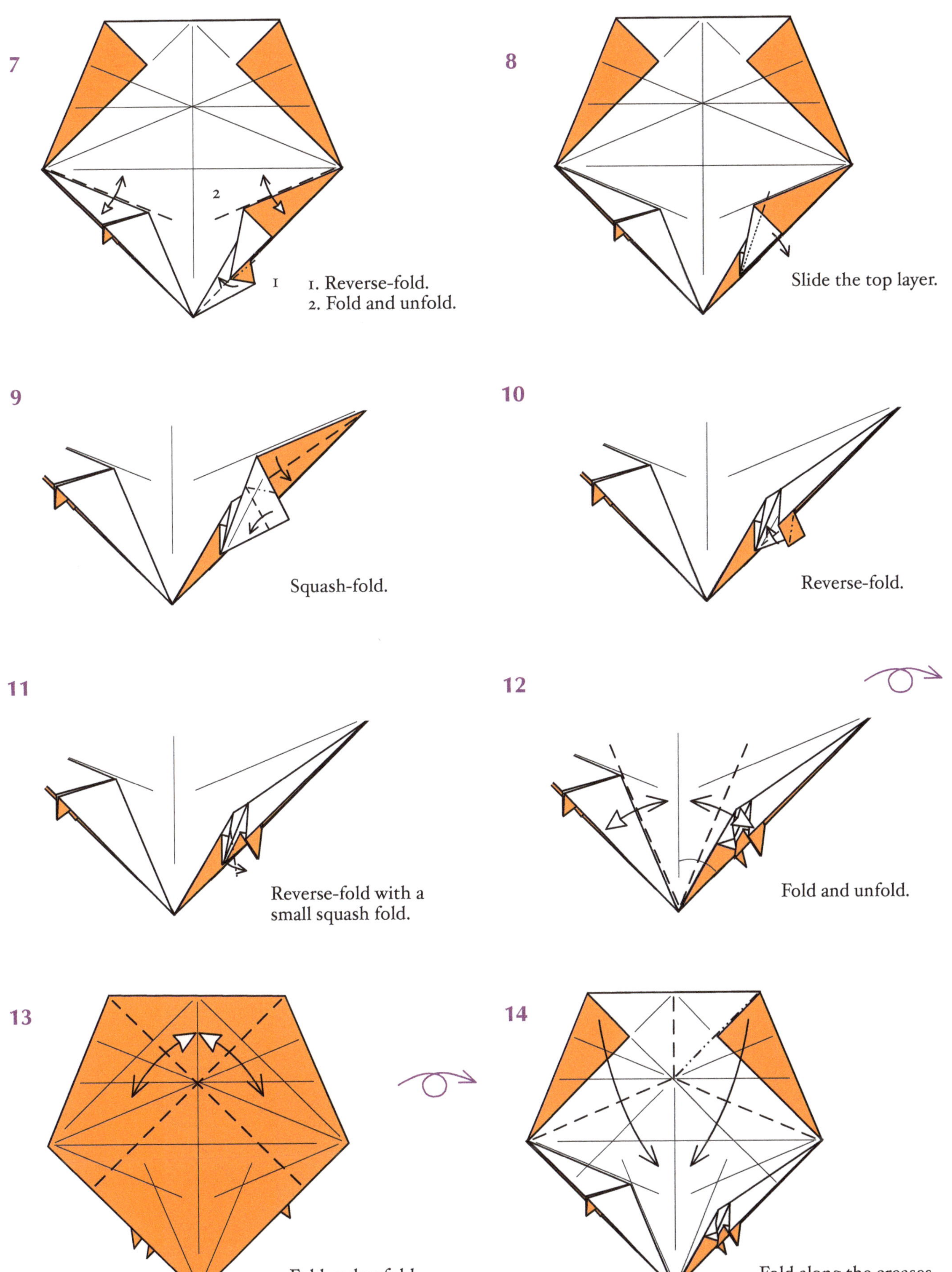
7
1
2
1. Reverse-fold.
2. Fold and unfold.
8
Slide the top layer.
9
Squash-fold.
10
Reverse-fold.
11
Reverse-fold with a small squash fold.
12
Fold and unfold.
13
Fold and unfold.
14
Fold along the creases.

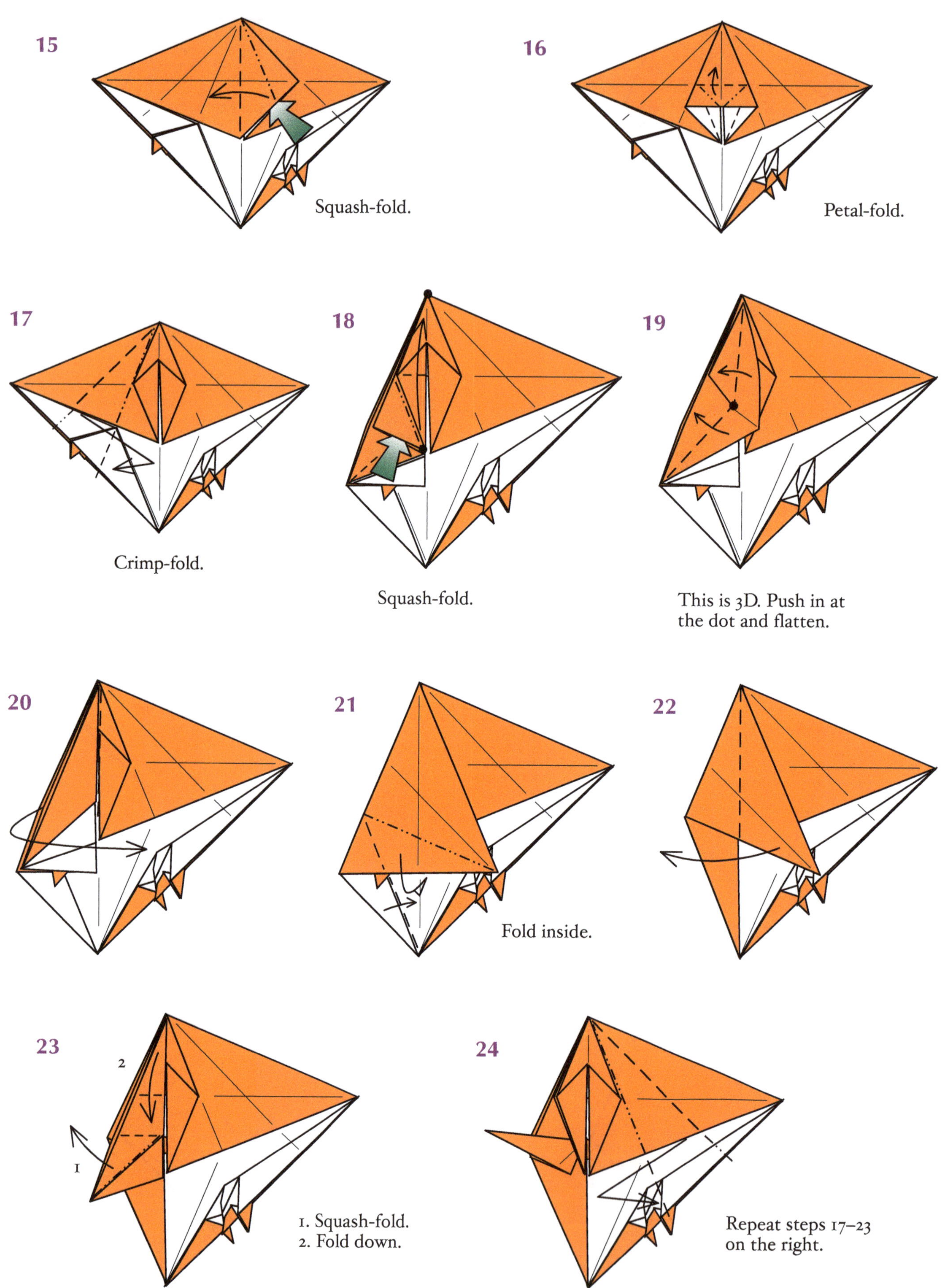
15
Squash-fold.
16
Petal-fold.
17
Crimp-fold.
18
Squash-fold.
19
This is 3D. Push in at the dot and flatten.
20
21
Fold inside.
22
23
2
1
1. Squash-fold.
2. Fold down.
24
Repeat steps 17–23 on the right.

25

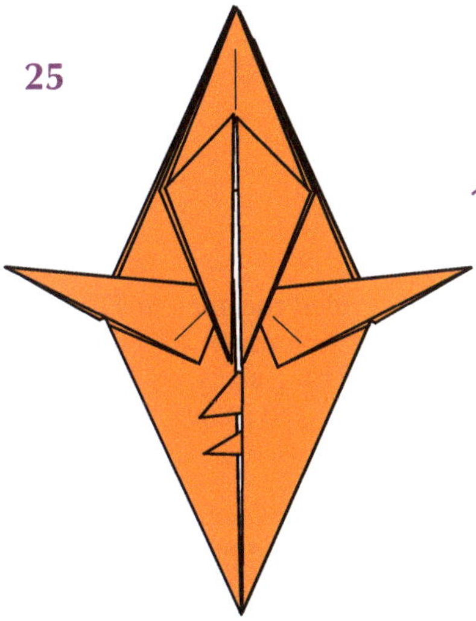

26

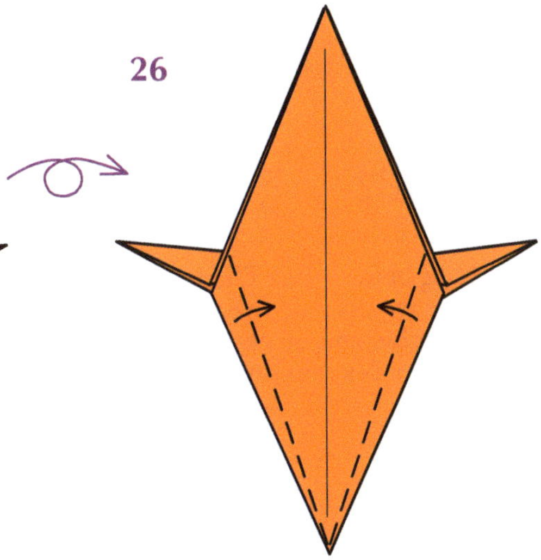

Fold toward the center.

27

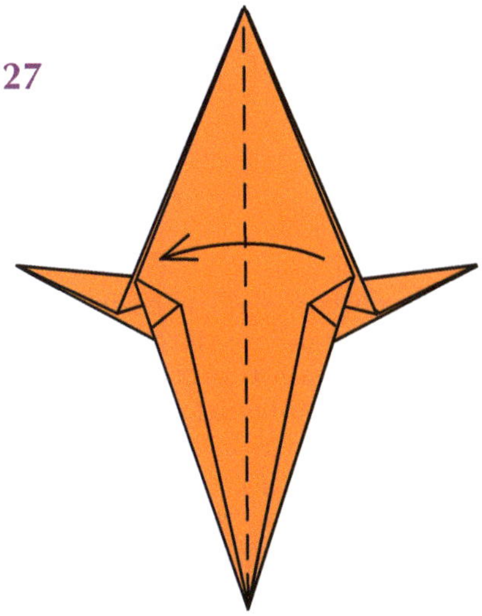

Fold in half and rotate.

28

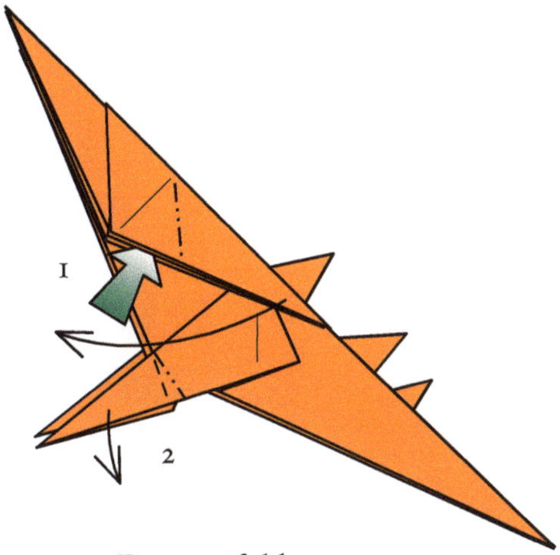

1. Reverse-fold.
2. Crimp-fold.

Repeat behind.

29

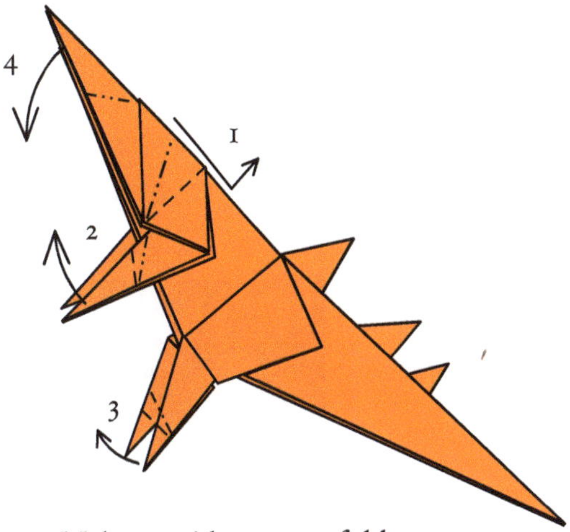

1. Make outside-reverse folds.
2. Crimp-fold, repeat behind.
3. Crimp-fold, repeat behind.
4. Reverse-fold.

30

1. Reverse-fold, repeat behind.
2. Fold two of four layers down, repeat behind.
3. Crimp-fold.

31

Tarascosaurus

Wings Over the Ancient World

The Flyers of Deep Time

In this chapter, the Earth lifts its gaze to the sky. Long before birds filled the air, winged reptiles ruled the ancient heavens, gliding over oceans, forests, and rocky shores. These remarkable flyers stretched vast wings, turning warm air and ocean winds into pathways across the world. Some were nimble and quick, while others grew to astonishing sizes, standing as tall as giants even before taking flight. These flying reptiles remind us that dinosaurs were not limited to land alone.

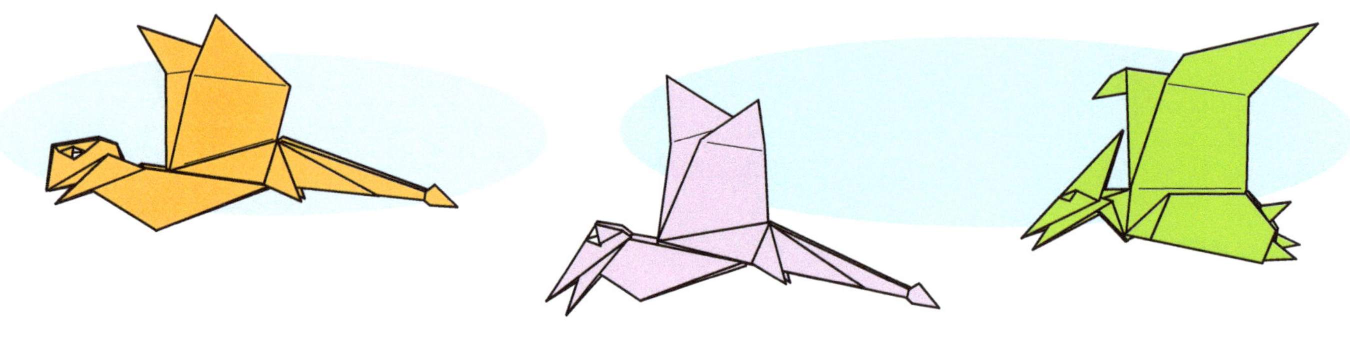

Quetzalcoatlus

Quetzalcoatlus was one of the largest flying animals to ever exist. With a wingspan that may have reached 35-40 feet, it stood as tall as a giraffe when on the ground and dominated the skies of the Late Cretaceous. Though capable of flight, Quetzalcoatlus likely spent much of its time walking on land, using its long beak to snatch small animals. Its immense size and powerful wings made it a true ruler of the ancient air, blurring the line between sky and ground.

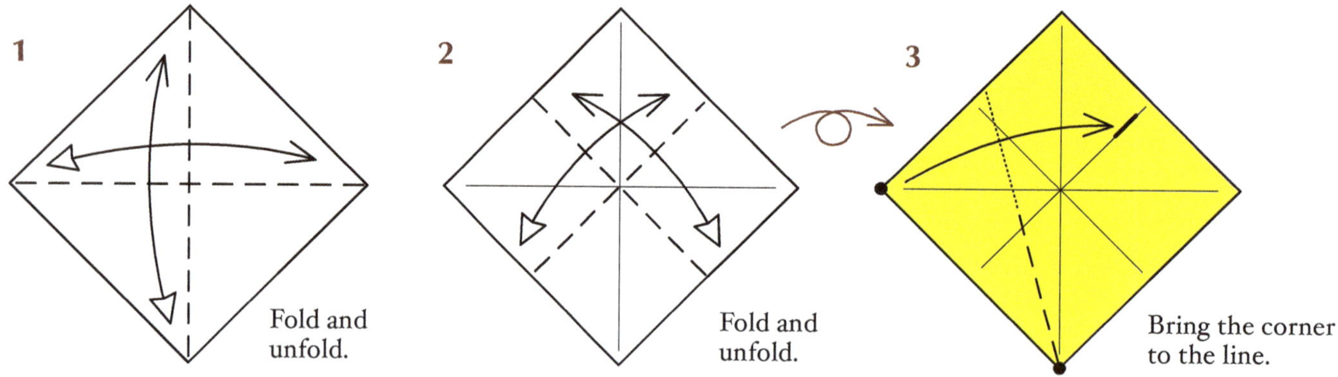

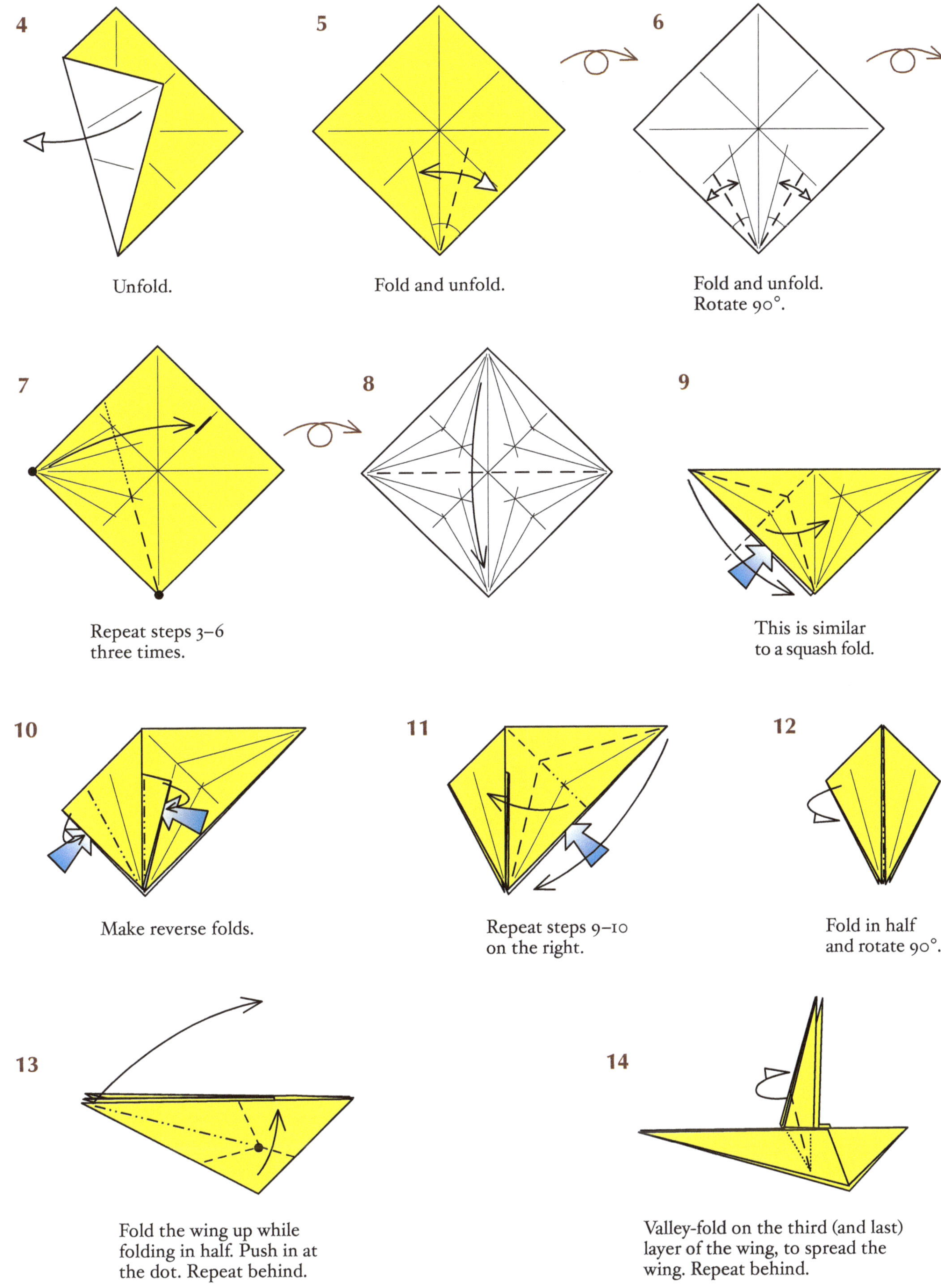
4
Unfold.
5
Fold and unfold.
6
Fold and unfold.
Rotate 90°.
7
Repeat steps 3–6
three times.
8
9
This is similar
to a squash fold.
10
Make reverse folds.
11
Repeat steps 9–10
on the right.
12
Fold in half
and rotate 90°.
13
Fold the wing up while
folding in half. Push in at
the dot. Repeat behind.
14
Valley-fold on the third (and last)
layer of the wing, to spread the
wing. Repeat behind.

15

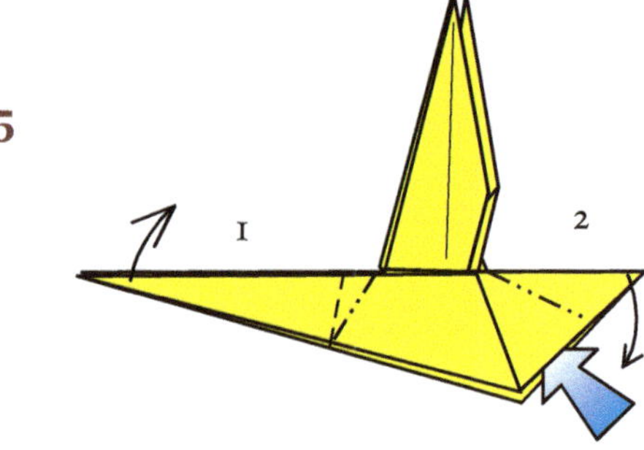

1. Crimp-fold.
2. Reverse-fold.

16

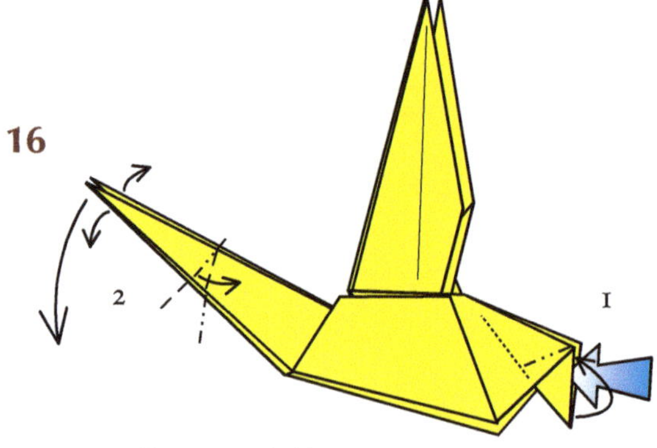

1. Reverse-fold.
2. Crimp-fold and open the mouth.

17

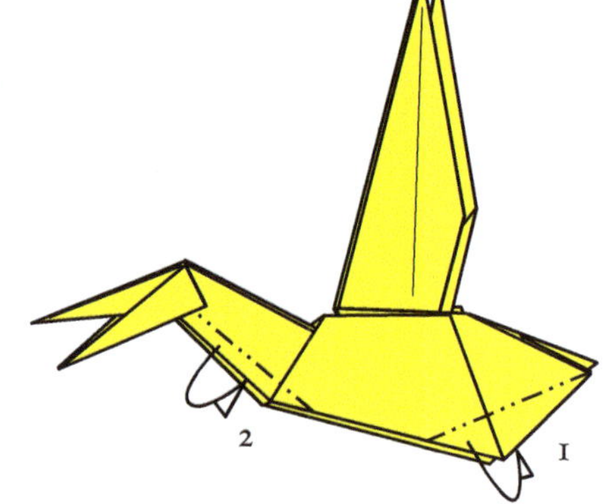

1. Fold inside.
2. Fold inside.
Repeat behind.

18

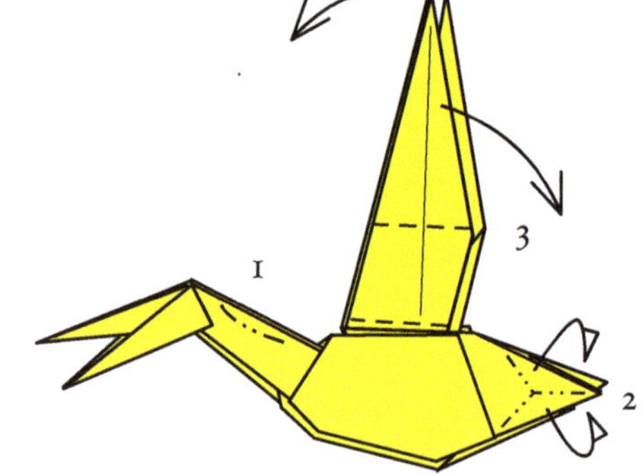

1. Shape the neck.
2. Thin the legs, repeat behind.
3. Spread the wings, repeat behind.

19

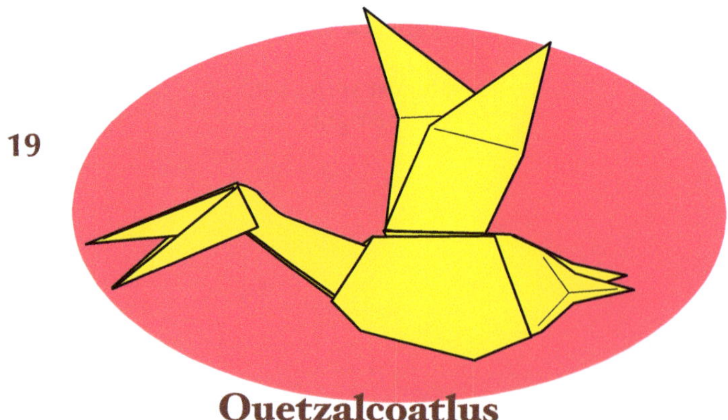

Quetzalcoatlus

Rhamphorynchus

Rhamphorhynchus was a small, agile flier with a long tail ending in a diamond-shaped vane. With a wingspan of about 3 feet, it darted over water and land with quick, fluttering movements. A fish-eater of the Late Jurassic Period, Rhamphorhynchus used its sharp teeth to catch slippery prey near the surface of lakes and seas. Its long tail helped stabilize its flight, making it one of the most graceful and balanced pterosaurs of its time.

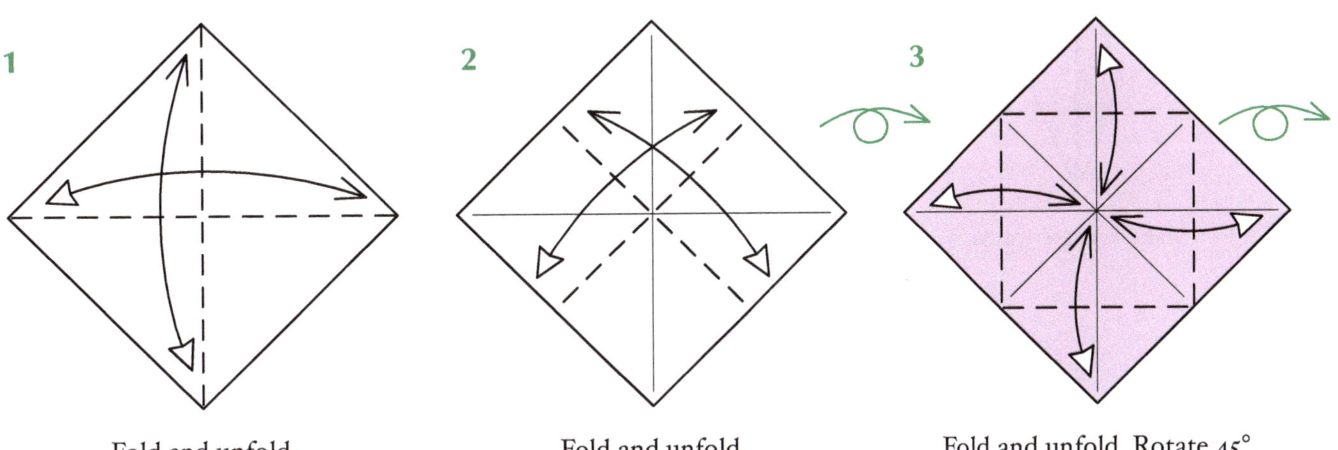

1 Fold and unfold.

2 Fold and unfold.

3 Fold and unfold. Rotate 45°.

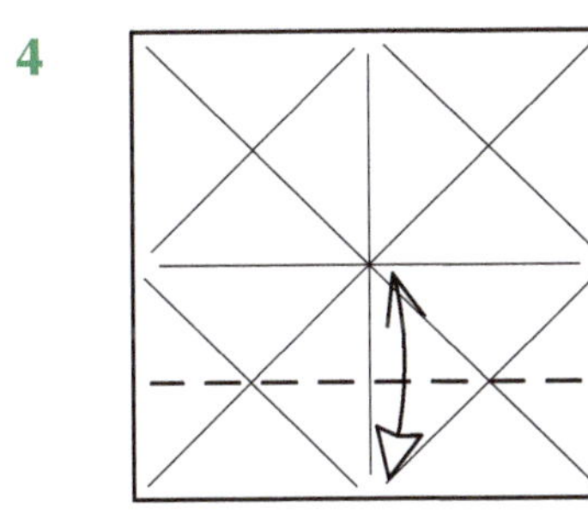

4 Fold and unfold. Rotate 90°.

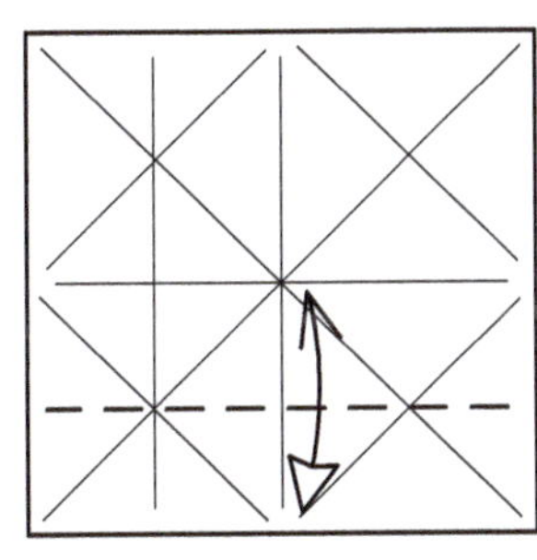

5 Repeat steps 4 three times. Rotate 45°.

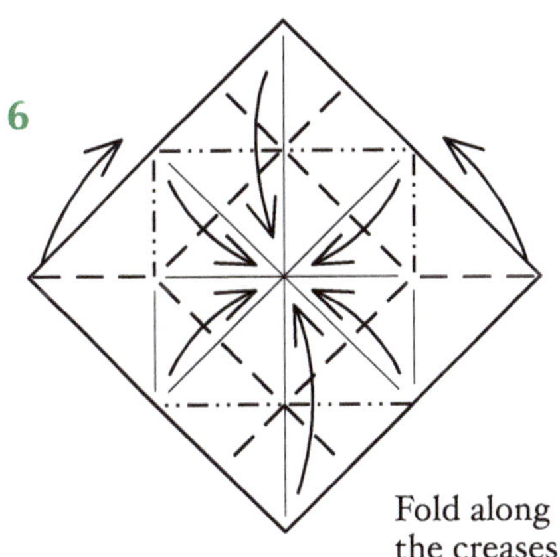

6 Fold along the creases.

7

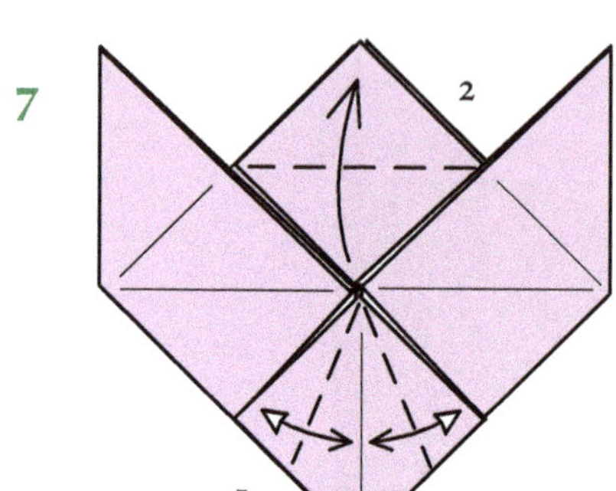

1. Fold and unfold.
2. Fold up.

8

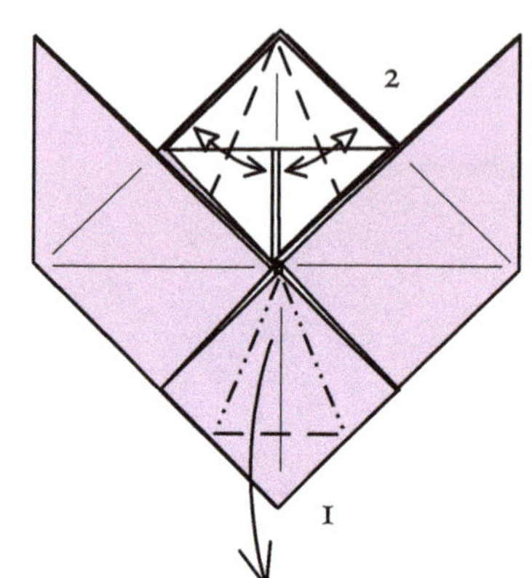

1. Petal-fold.
2. Fold and unfold.

9

Unfold.

10

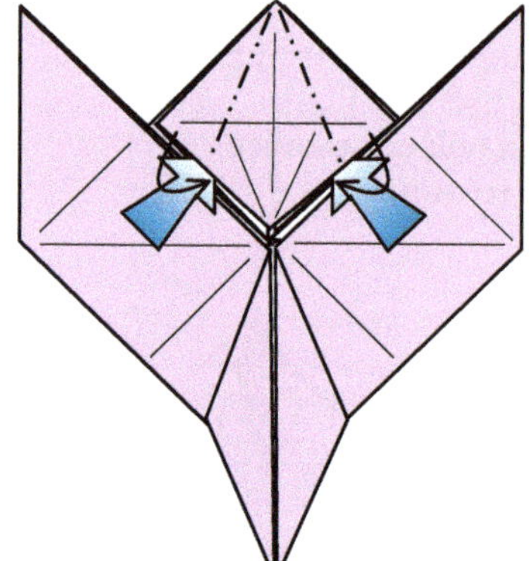

Make reverse folds.

11

Petal-fold.

12

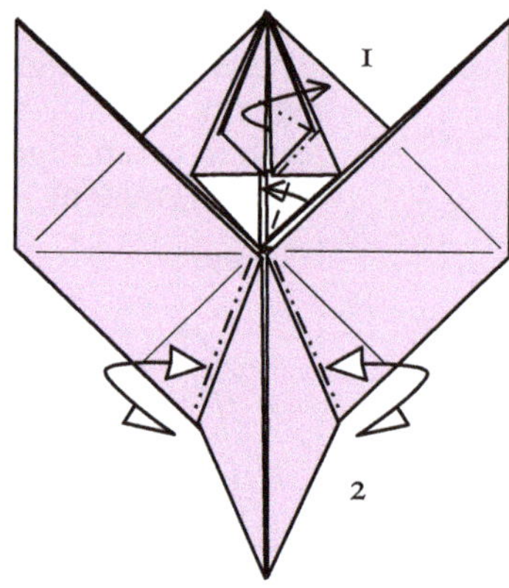

1. Open at the top for this squash fold.
2. Fold and unfold.

13

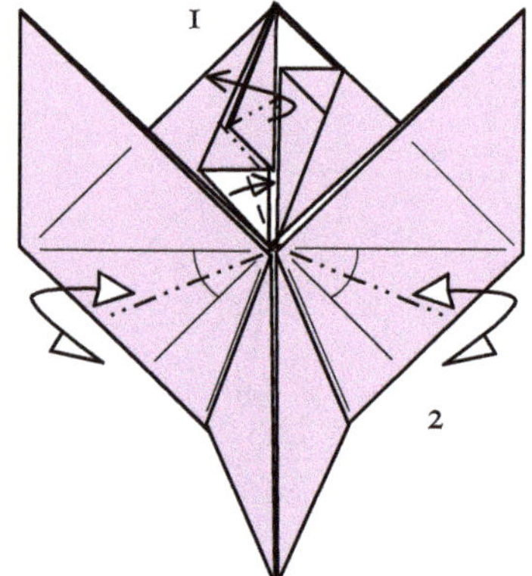

1. Repeat on the left.
2. Fold and unfold.

14

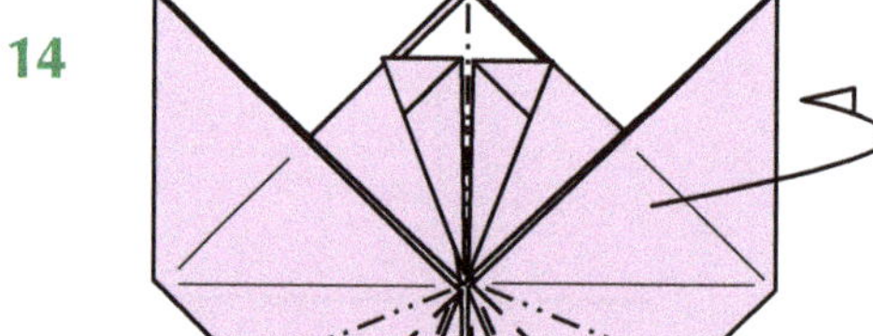

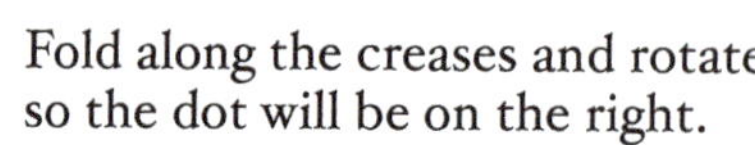

Fold along the creases and rotate so the dot will be on the right.

15

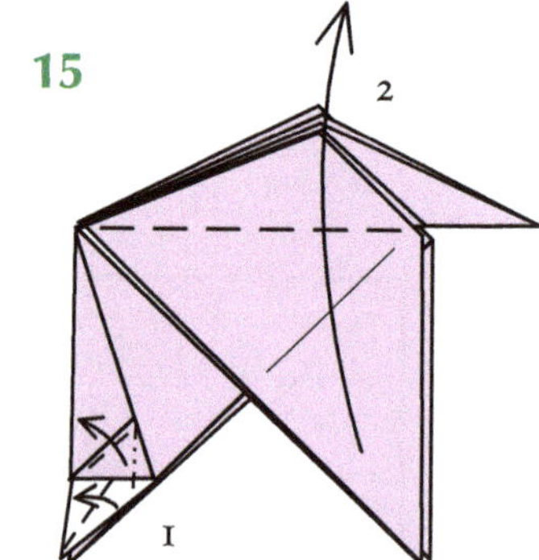

1. Squash-fold.
2. Fold up.
Repeat behind.

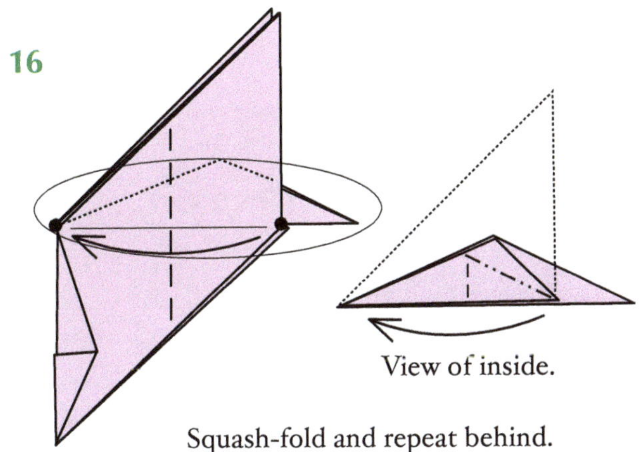

Squash-fold and repeat behind.

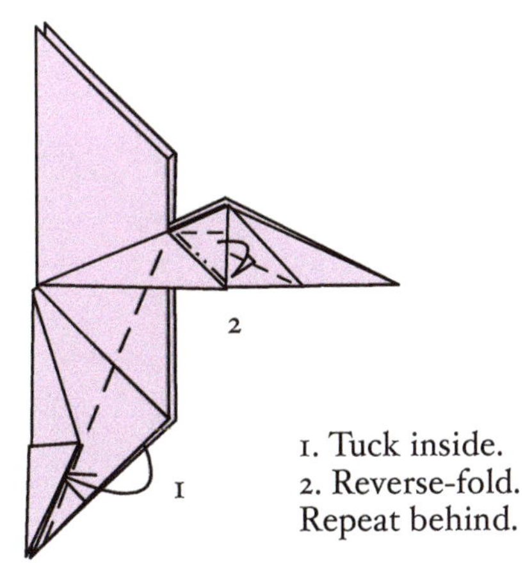

1. Tuck inside.
2. Reverse-fold.
Repeat behind.

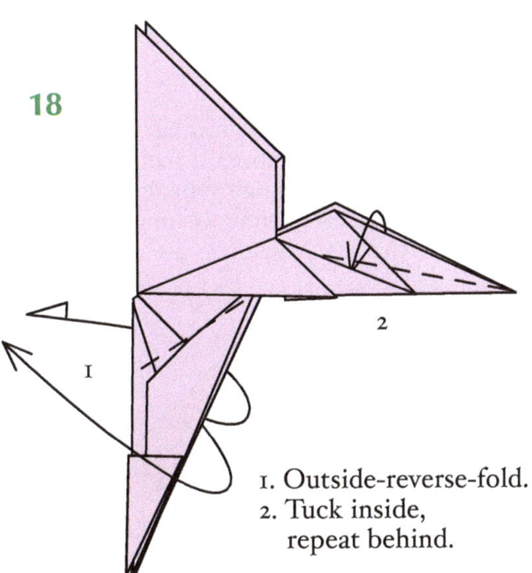

1. Outside-reverse-fold.
2. Tuck inside, repeat behind.

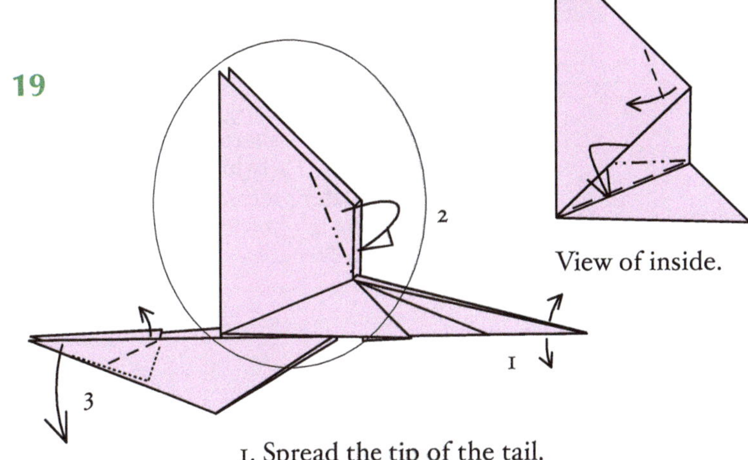

1. Spread the tip of the tail.
2. Squash-fold and tuck inside, repeat behind.
3. Outside-reverse-fold and swing out from inside.

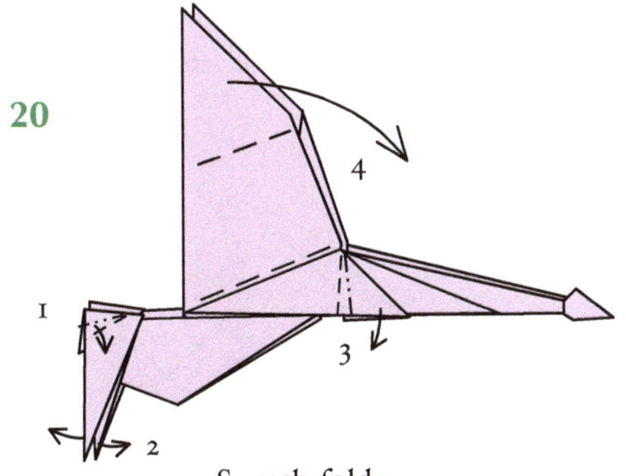

1. Squash-fold.
2. Spread the mouth.
3. Pleat-fold.
4. Spread the wings.
Repeat behind.

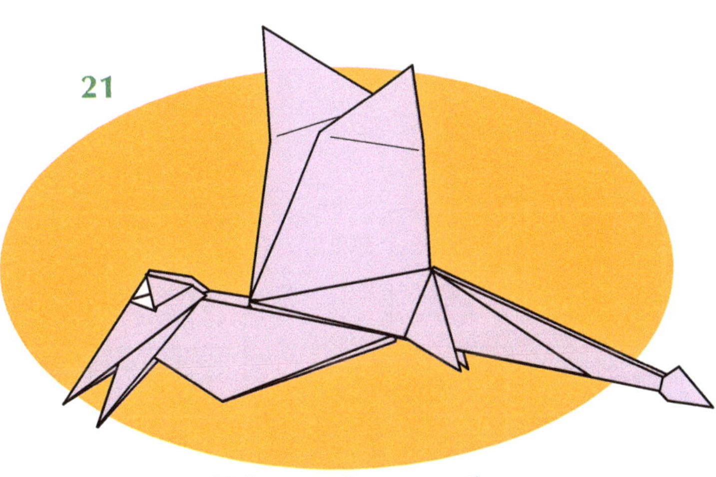

Rhamphorynchus

Dimorphodon

Dimorphodon was an early flying reptile with a large head, short wings, and an unusual mix of tooth shapes—sharp in front and blunt in back. It had a wingspan of about 4 feet and lived during the Early Jurassic Period. This carnivore likely fed on insects, small animals, and fish. Unlike later pterosaurs, Dimorphodon may have spent a good deal of time walking or climbing, showing how early flyers were still experimenting with life in the air.

1

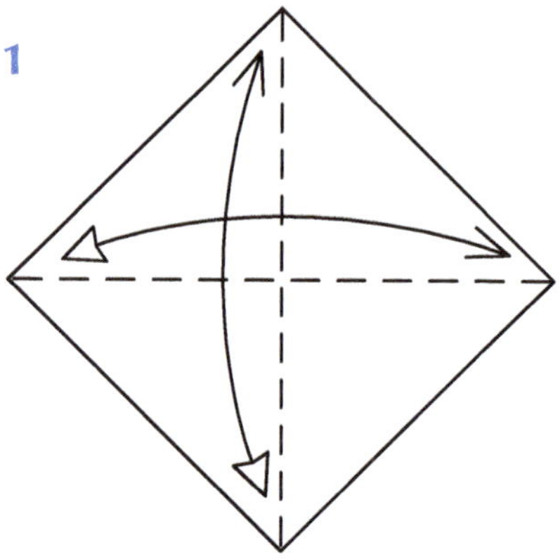

Fold and unfold.

2

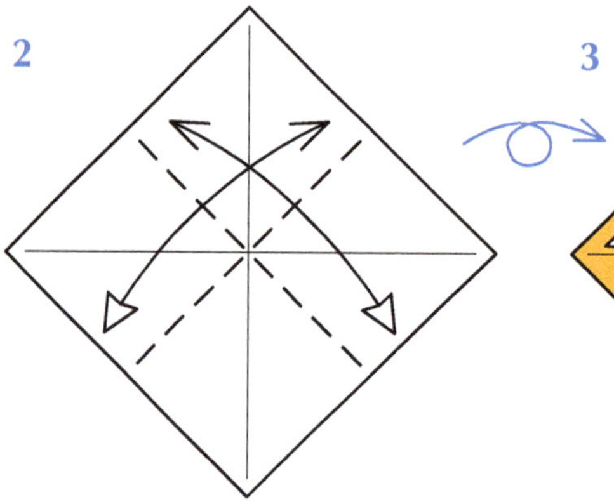

Fold and unfold.

3

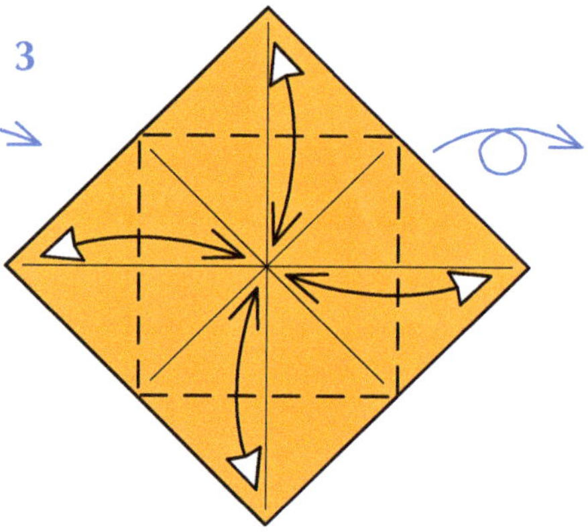

Fold and unfold. Rotate 45°.

4

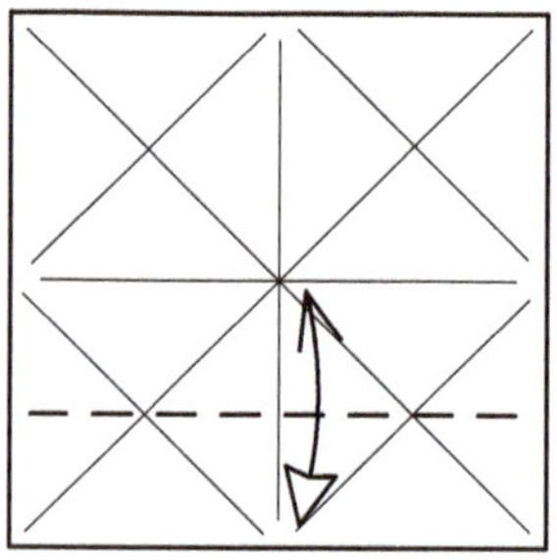

Fold and unfold.
Rotate 90°.

5

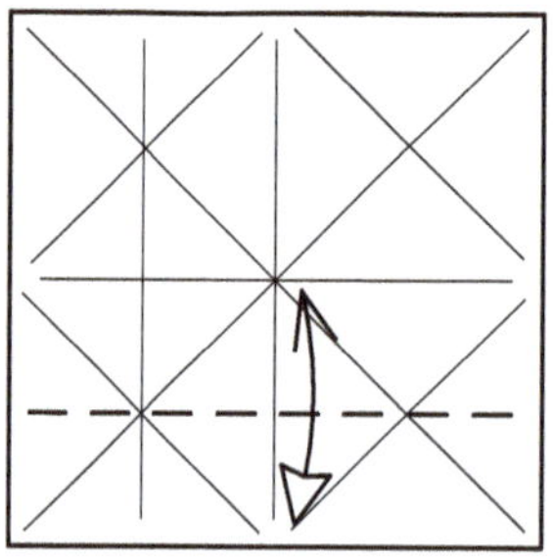

Repeat steps 4 three times. Rotate 45°.

6

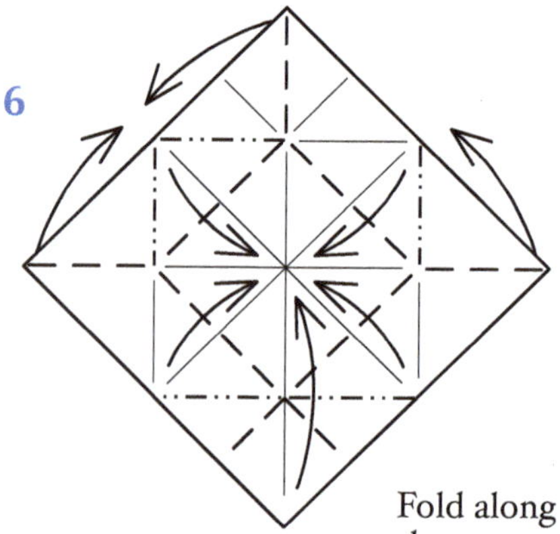

Fold along the creases.

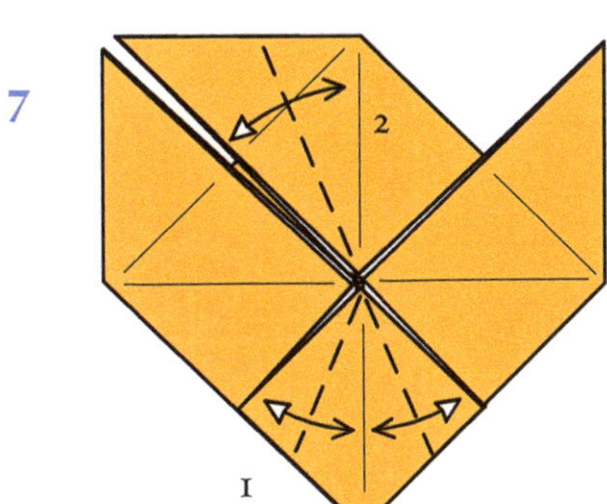

1. Fold and unfold.
2. Fold and unfold.

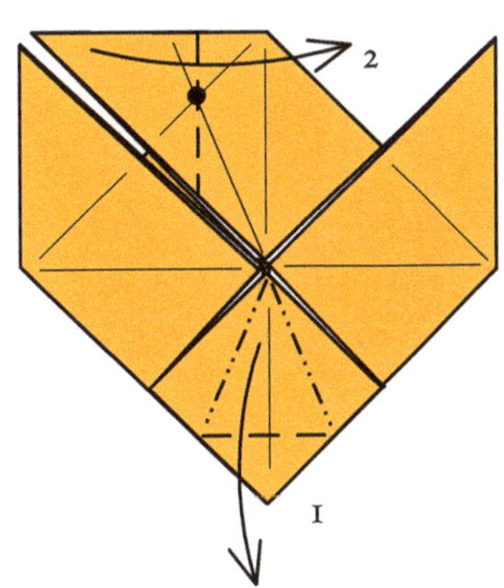

1. Petal-fold.
2. Fold through the dot.

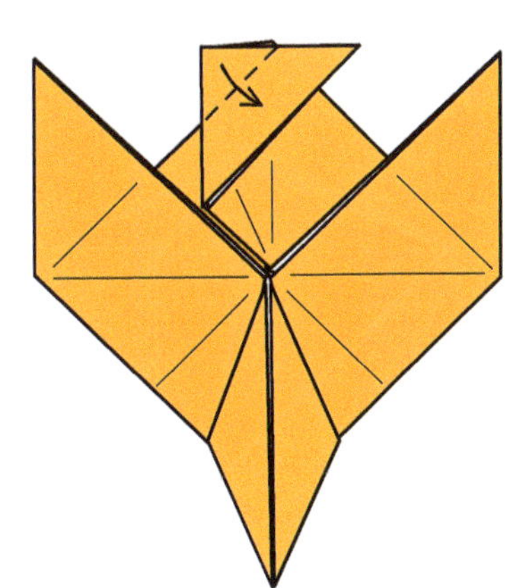

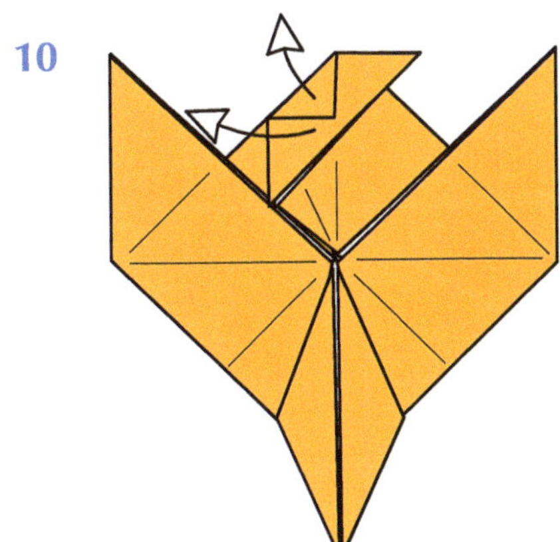

Unfold.

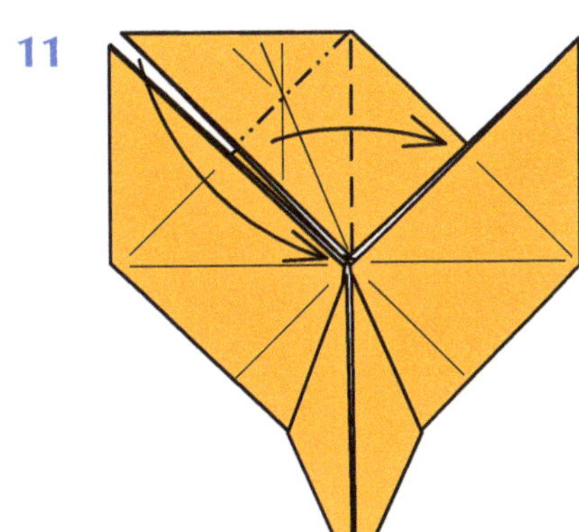

Squash-fold.

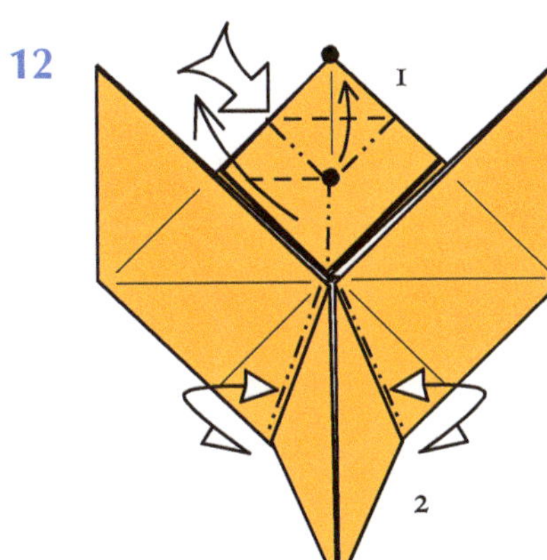

1. This is similar to a petal fold. Push in on the left.
2. Fold and unfold.

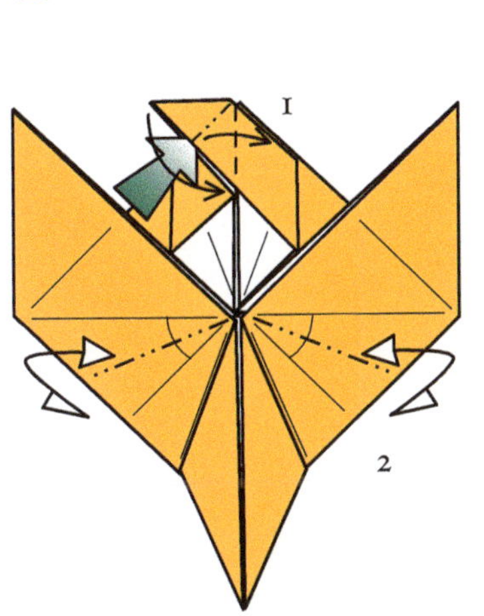

1. Squash-fold.
2. Fold and unfold.

Fold inside at the top.

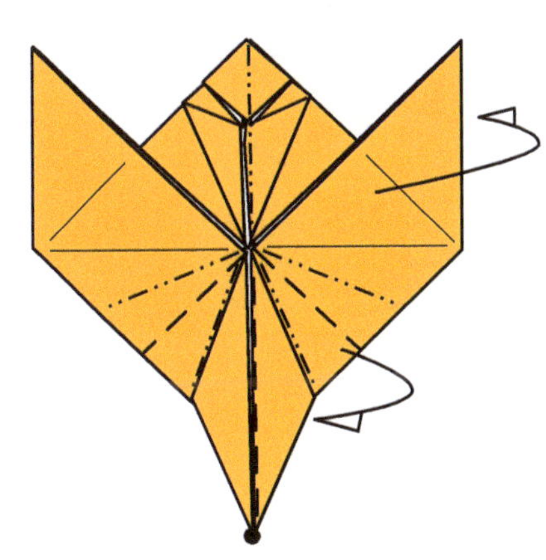

Fold along the creases and rotate so the dot will be on the right.

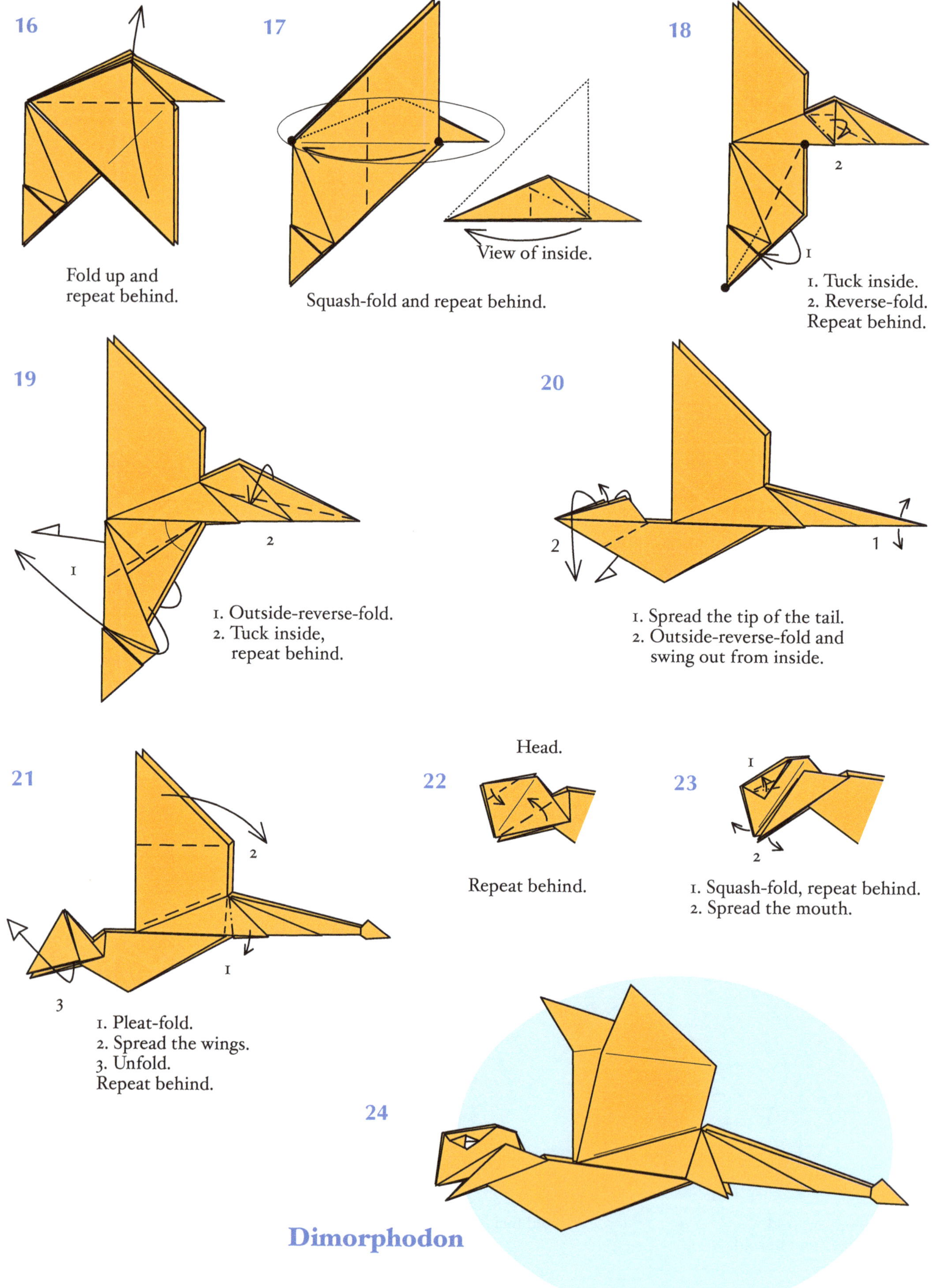
16
Fold up and
repeat behind.
17
View of inside.
Squash-fold and repeat behind.
18
2
1
1. Tuck inside.
2. Reverse-fold.
Repeat behind.
19
1
2
1. Outside-reverse-fold.
2. Tuck inside,
repeat behind.
20
2
1
1. Spread the tip of the tail.
2. Outside-reverse-fold and
swing out from inside.
21
2
1
3
1. Pleat-fold.
2. Spread the wings.
3. Unfold.
Repeat behind.
Head.
22
Repeat behind.
23
1
2
1. Squash-fold, repeat behind.
2. Spread the mouth.
24
Dimorphodon

Pteranodon

Pteranodon is one of the most recognizable flying reptiles, famous for the long crest extending from the back of its head. With a wingspan of up to 25 feet, it soared effortlessly over ancient seas of the Late Cretaceous Period. A fish-eater, Pteranodon used its toothless beak to scoop prey from the water while gliding on ocean winds. Its large crest may have helped with balance or display, making it both a skilled flier and an unmistakable silhouette in the prehistoric sky.

1 Fold and unfold.

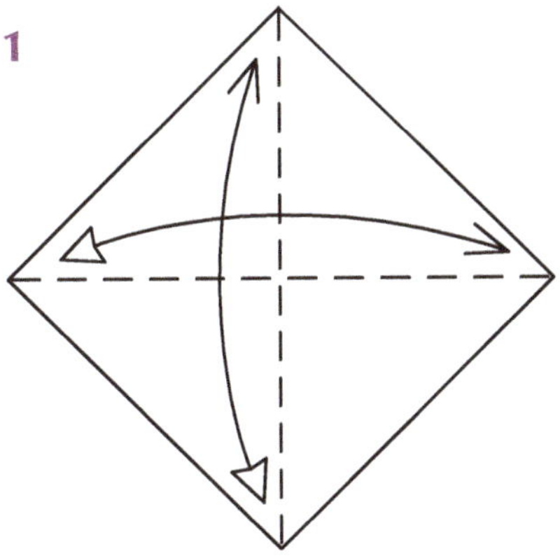

2 Fold to the center and unfold.

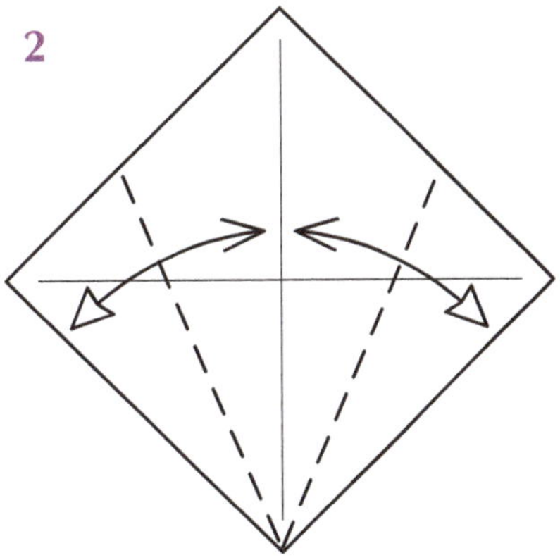

3 Fold and unfold.

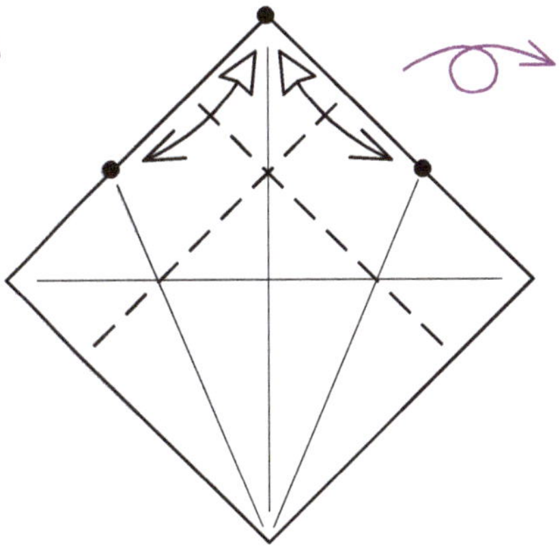

4 Fold and unfold.

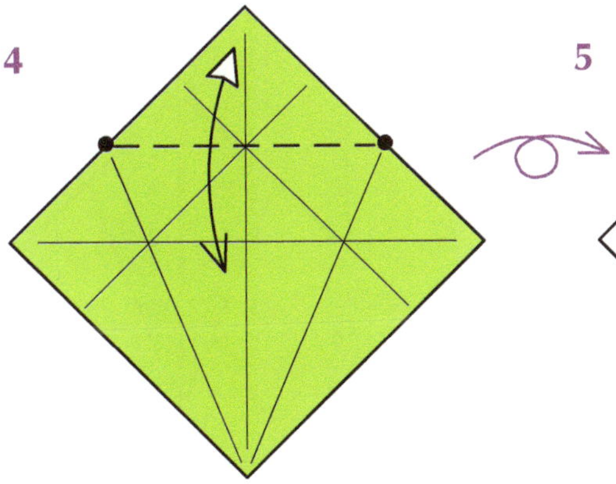

5 Fold along the creases.

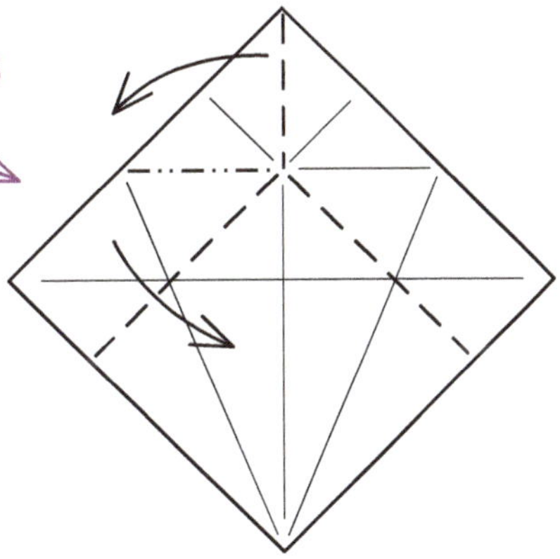

6 Fold and unfold.

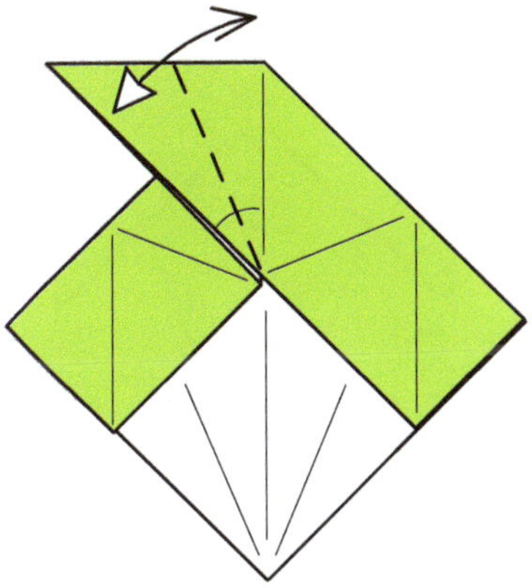

7

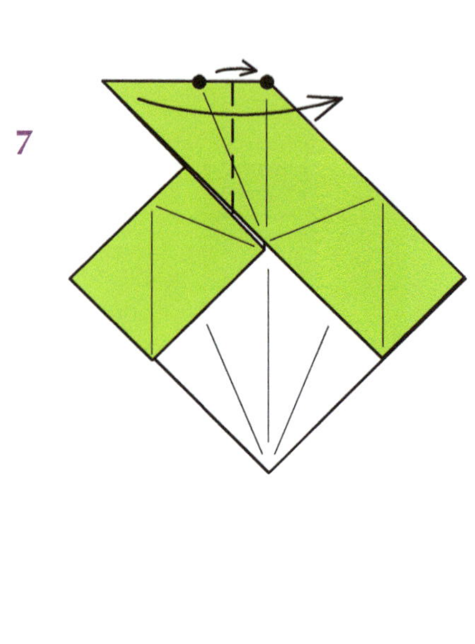

8

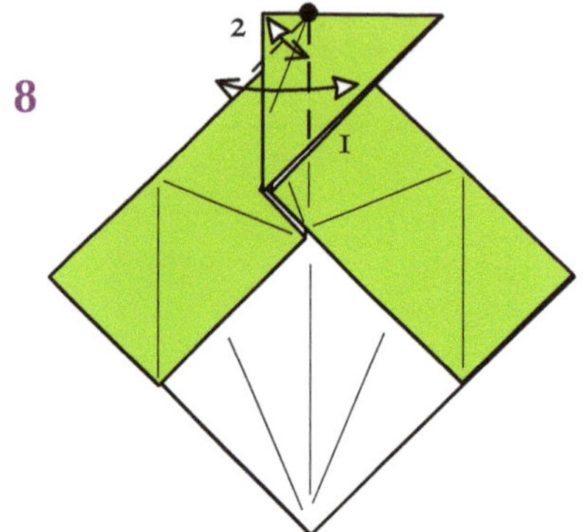

1. Fold and unfold.
2. Fold and unfold.

9

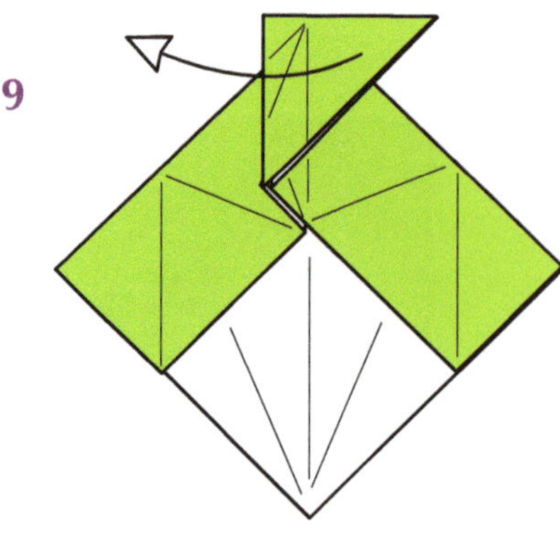

Unfold.

10

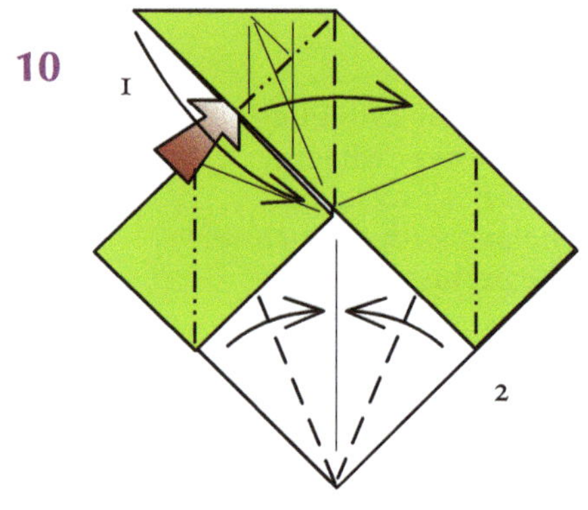

1. Squash-fold.
2. Make reverse folds.

11

This is similar to a petal fold. Push in on the left.

12

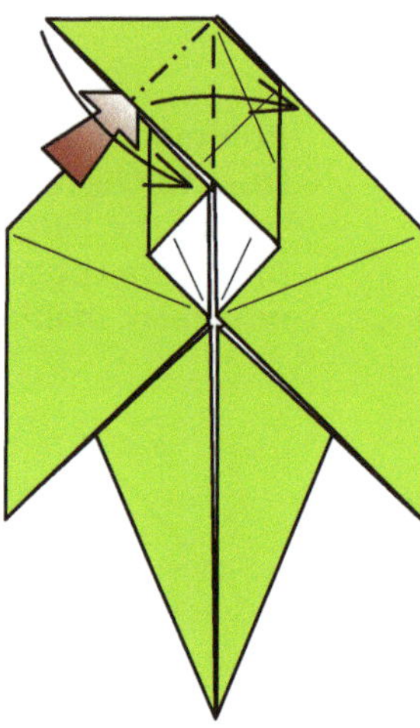

Squash-fold.

13

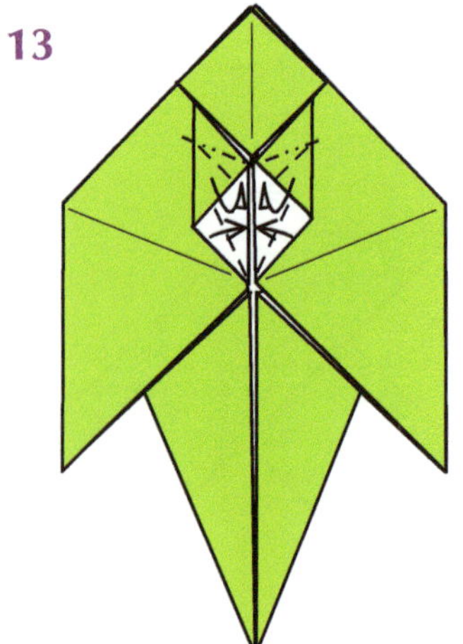

Fold inside on the top.

14

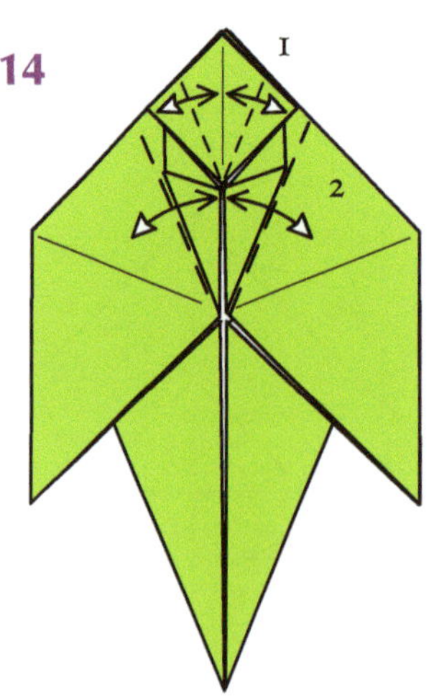

1. Fold and unfold.
2. Fold and unfold.

15

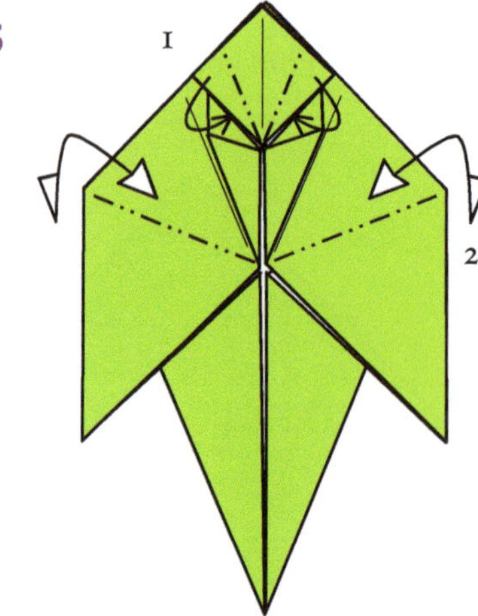

1. Make reverse folds.
2. Fold and unfold all the layers along the creases.

16

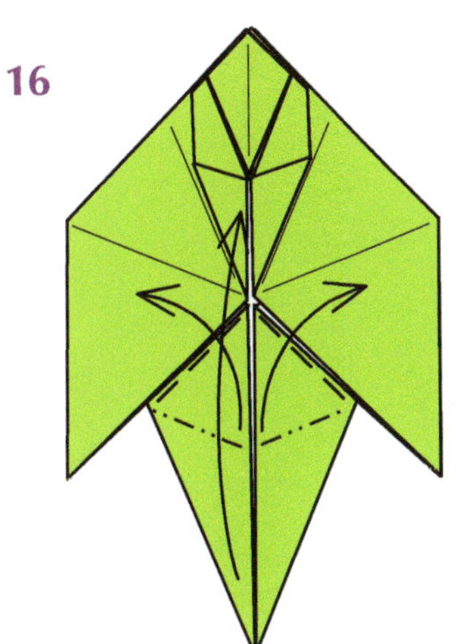

Petal-fold.

17

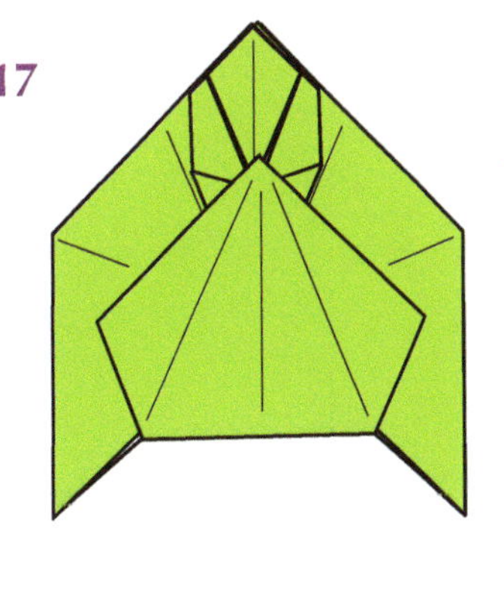

18

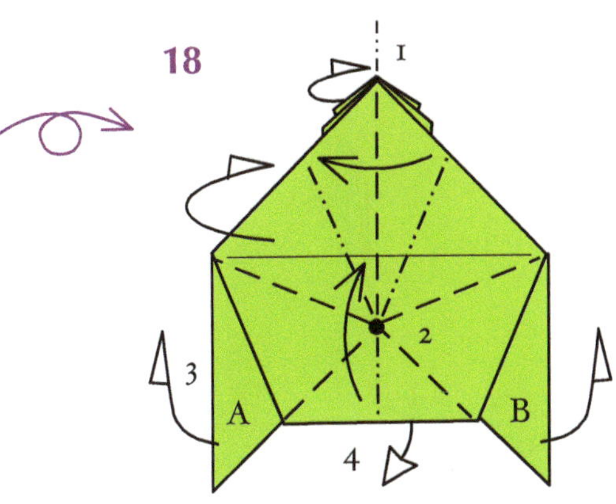

Fold along the creases, most of the creases are there. For this combination:
1. Bring the small flaps together.
2. Push in at the dot.
3. Fold flaps A and B up. These flaps will meet at the top.
4. Fold up and swing out from behind.

19

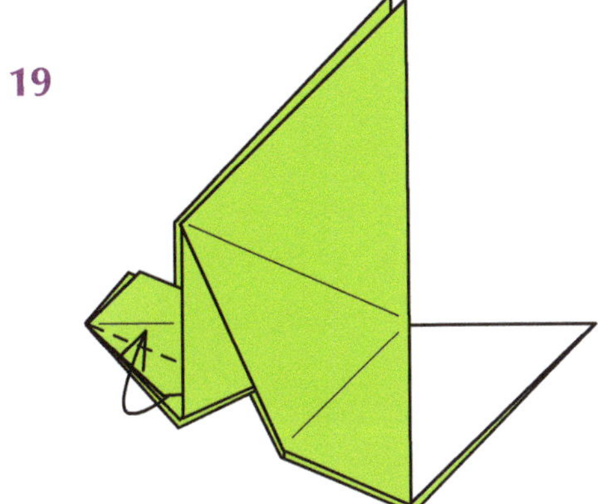

Fold the flap up.
Repeat behind.

20

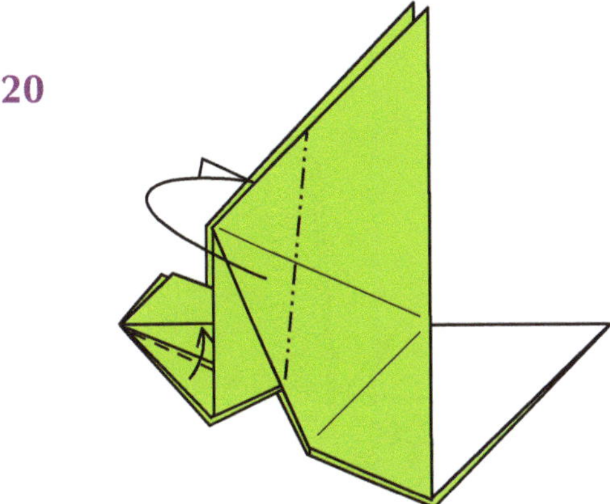

Fold up at the bottom and inside the wings. Repeat behind.

21

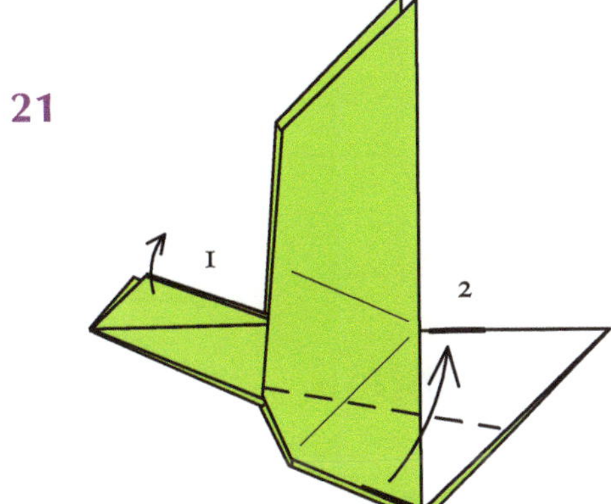

1. Lift up slightly, on both sides, to open the mouth.
2. Fold up so the bold lines meet, repeat behind.

22

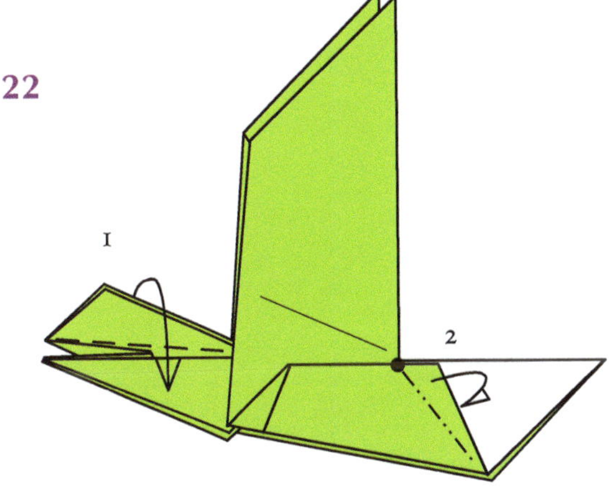

1. Fold down.
2. Fold inside.
Repeat behind.

23

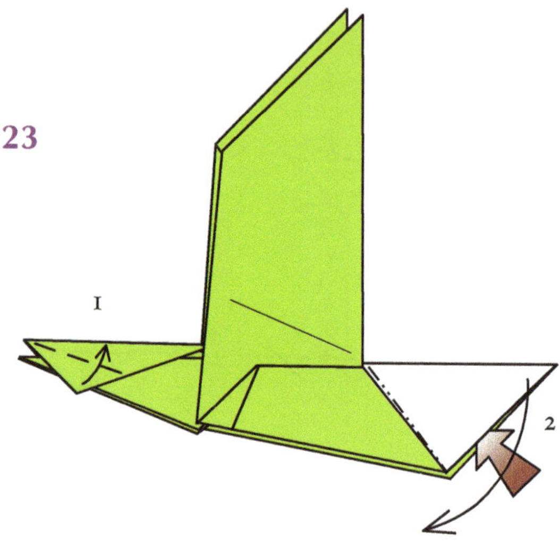

1. Fold up, repeat behind.
2. Reverse-fold.

24

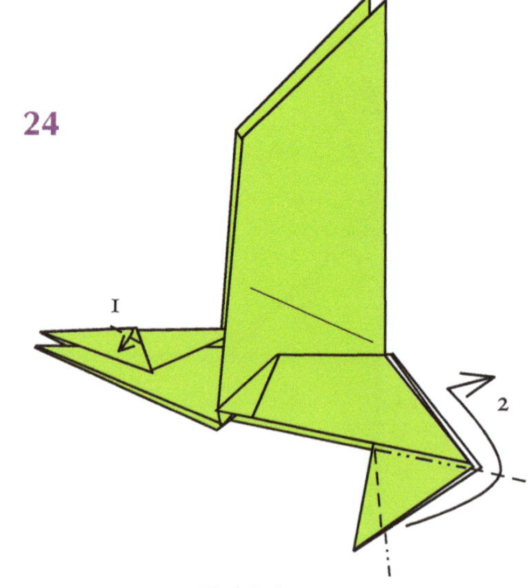

1. Fold the eye, repeat behind.
2. Crimp-fold.

25

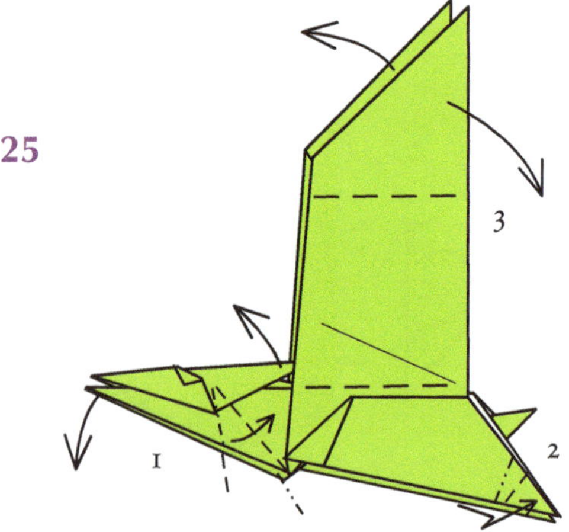

1. Crimp-fold.
2. Crimp-fold, repeat behind.
3. Spread the wings, repeat behind.

26

Pteranodon

Crest, Plates, & Horned Legends

Armored Wonders of the Ancient Earth

In this chapter, dinosaurs wear their stories on their backs and faces. Plates rise like shields, horns curve with confidence, and crests stretch skyward in bold displays of identity. These remarkable dinosaurs were built not for speed or flight, but for protection, presence, and power. Some of these dinosaurs relied on armor for defense, while others used their dramatic crowns to communicate, compete, or simply stand out, making these ancient legends so memorable.

Protoceratops

Protoceratops was a small but sturdy dinosaur with a parrot-like beak and a short frill behind its head. Measuring about 6 feet long, it lived in dry, sandy environments during the Late Cretaceous. A peaceful plant-eater, Protoceratops used its strong beak to clip tough vegetation. Fossils suggest it may have lived in groups, making it one of the most well-known early horned dinosaurs.

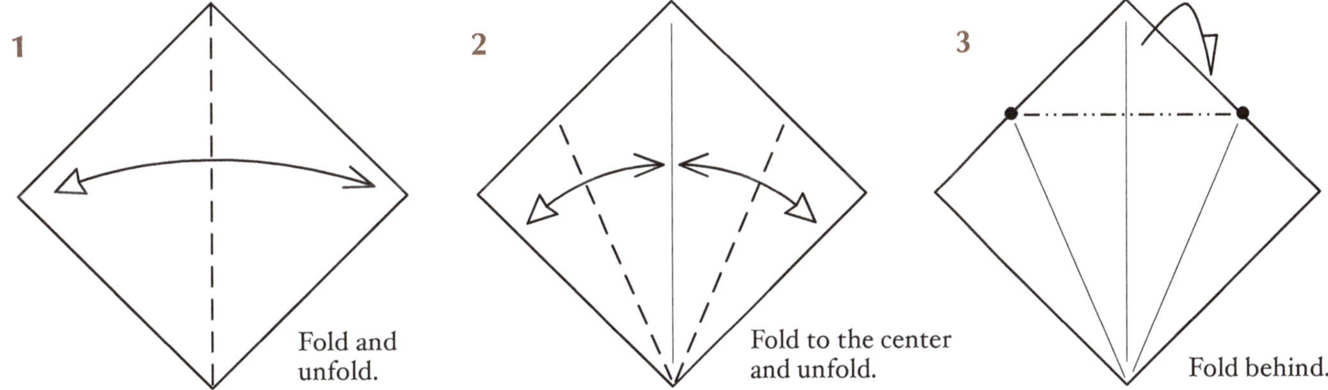

4

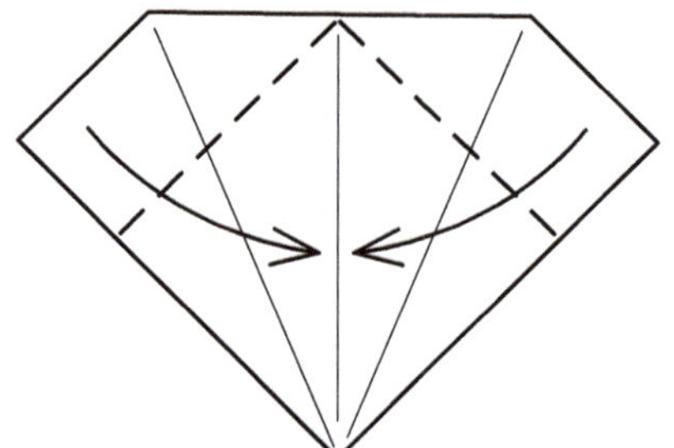

Fold to the center.

5

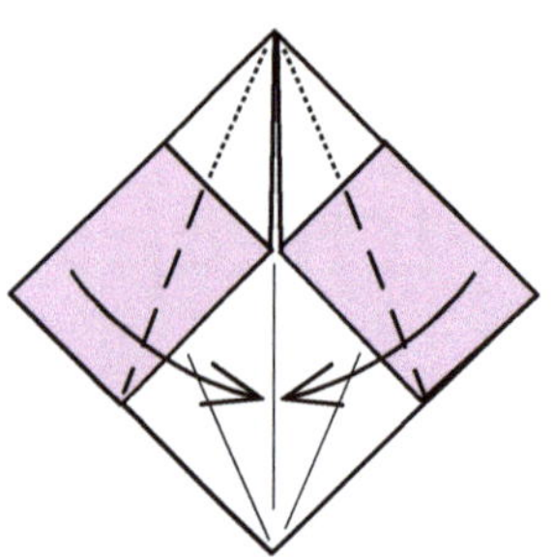

Fold to the center, under the white layers.

6

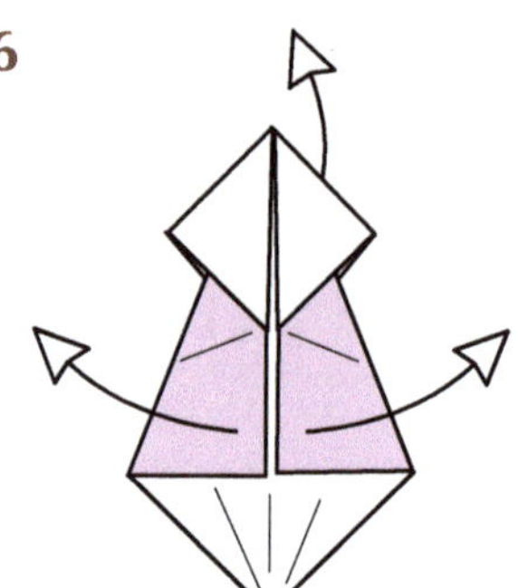

Unfold everything.

7

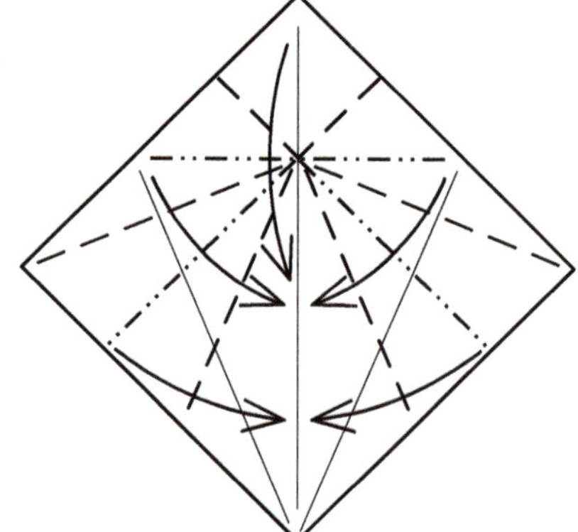

Fold along the creases.

8

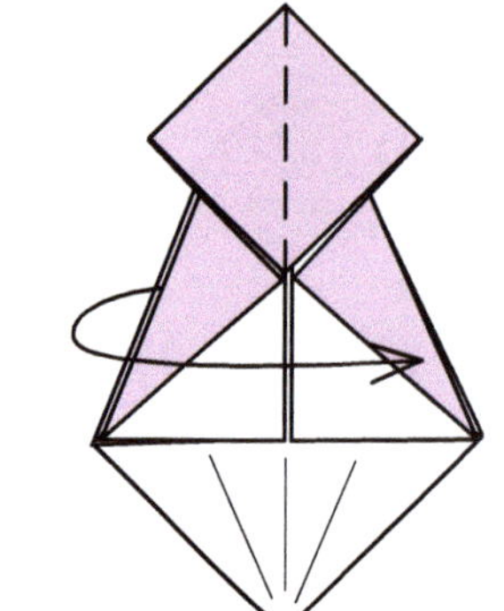

9

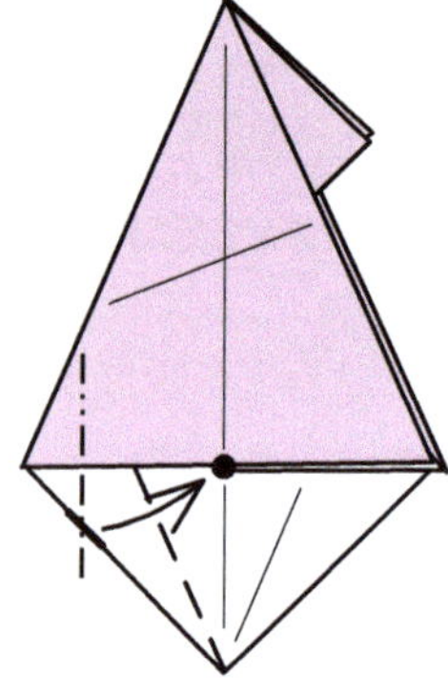

This is similar to a reverse fold. The bold edge will meet the dot.

10

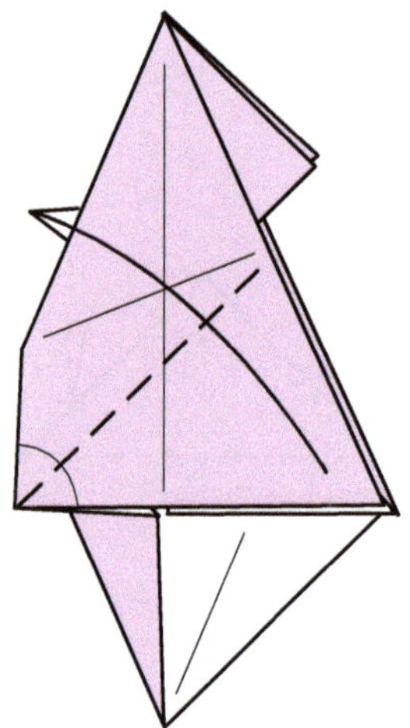

11

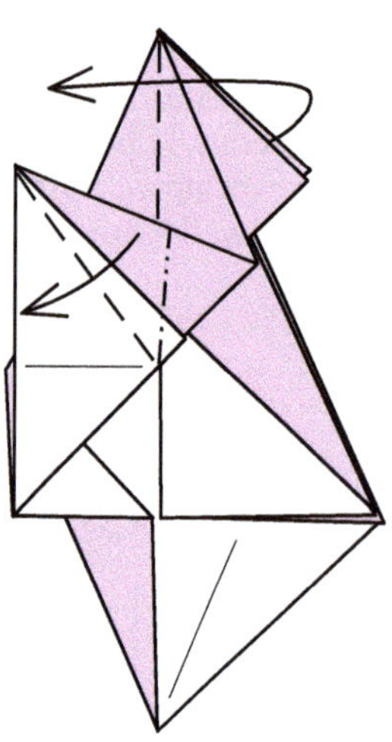

Squash-fold.

12

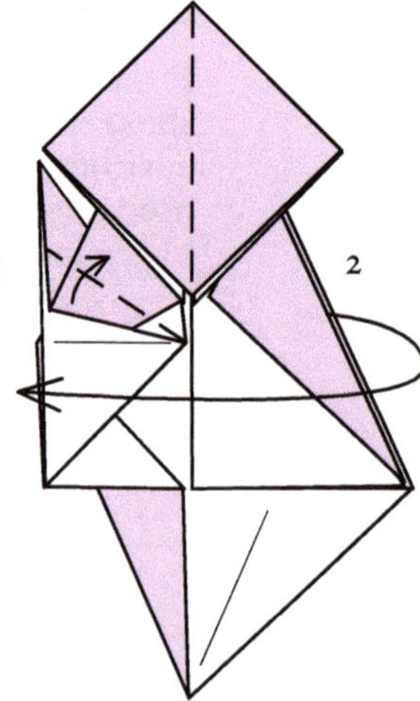

1. Fold up.
2. Repeat steps 8–12 on the right.

13

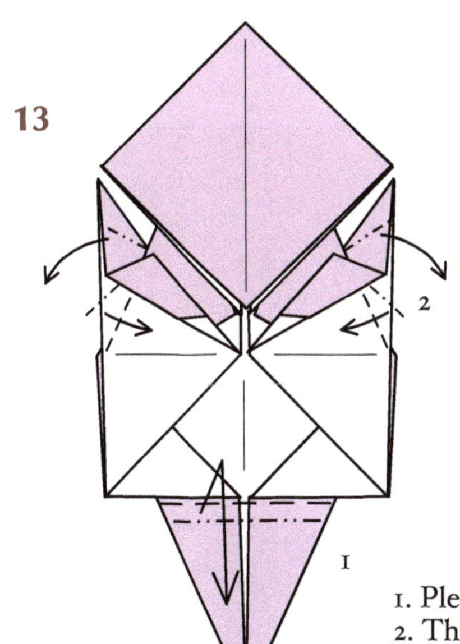

1. Pleat-fold.
2. This is similar to a squash fold. Fold on the left and right.

14

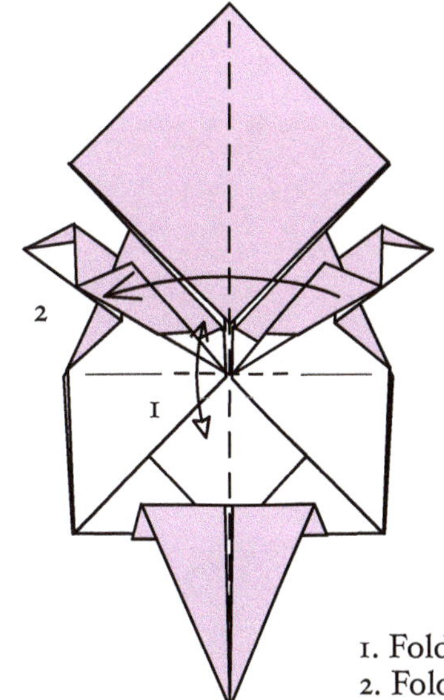

1. Fold and unfold.
2. Fold in half and rotate.

15

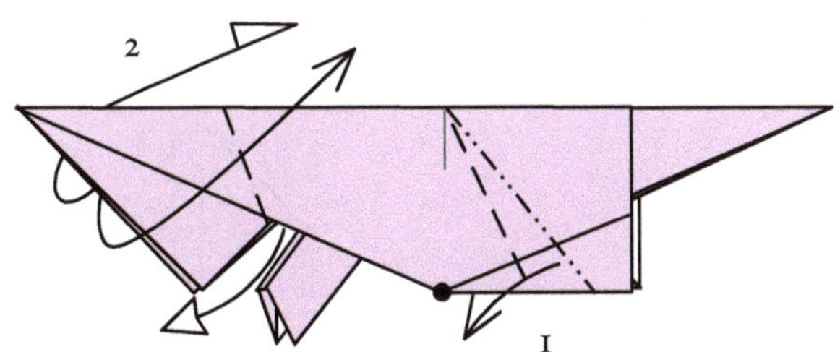

1. Fold close to the dot for this crimp fold.
2. Outside-reverse-fold and swing out from inside.

16

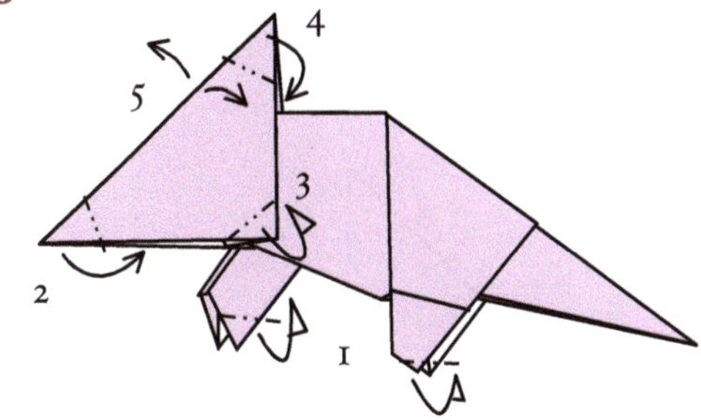

1. Fold inside, repeat behind.
2. Reverse-fold.
3. Fold inside, repeat behind.
4. Reverse-fold.
5. Spread the crown.

Protoceratops

Monoclonius

Monoclonius was a medium-sized horned dinosaur, reaching about 18 feet in length. It featured a large frill and a prominent nose horn, giving it a bold and commanding appearance. This herbivore likely used its horn and frill for display and defense. Living in herds, Monoclonius shows how horned dinosaurs were beginning to grow larger and more elaborate during the Late Cretaceous.

1

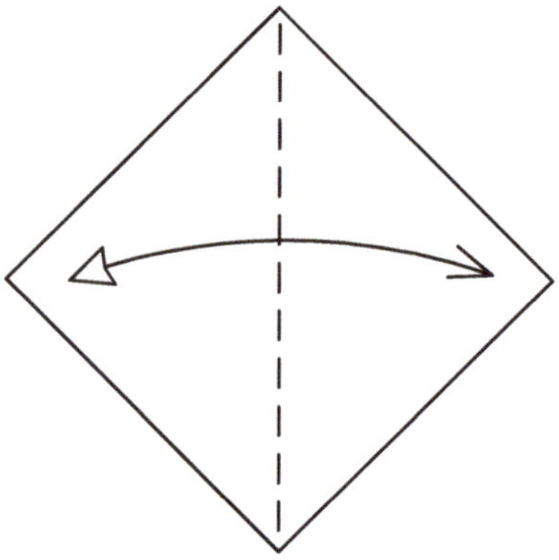

Fold and unfold.

2

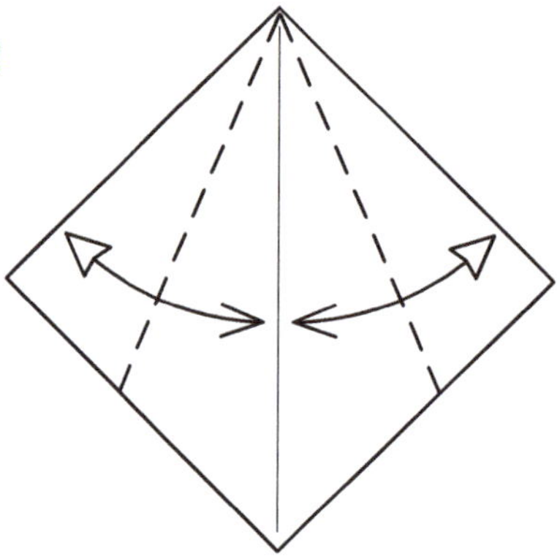

Fold and unfold.

3

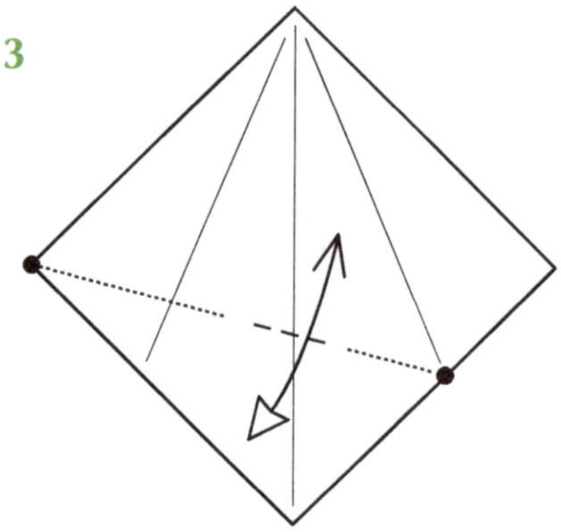

Fold and unfold on the diagonal.

4

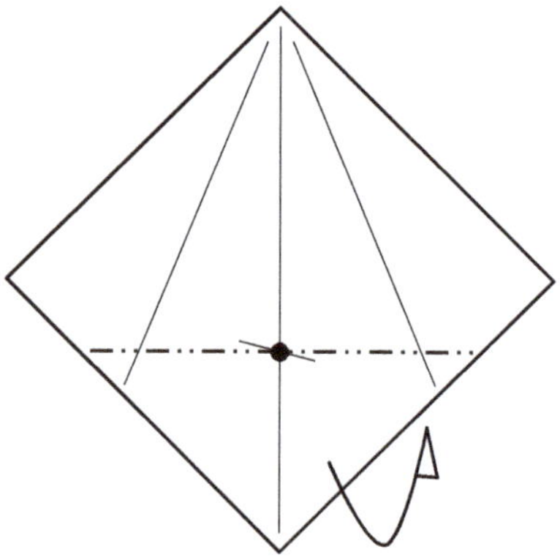

Fold behind and rotate 180°.

5

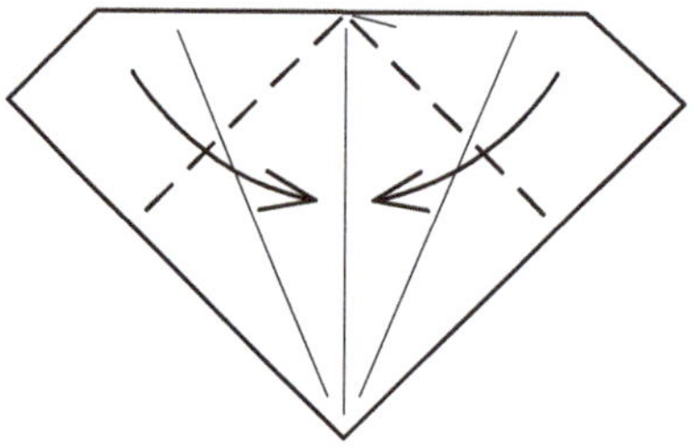

Fold to the center.

6

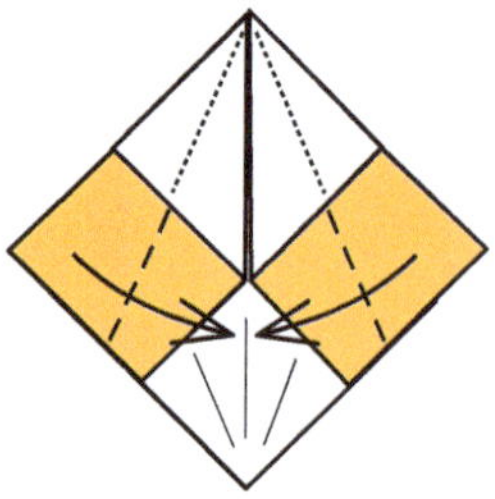

Fold to the center, under the white layers.

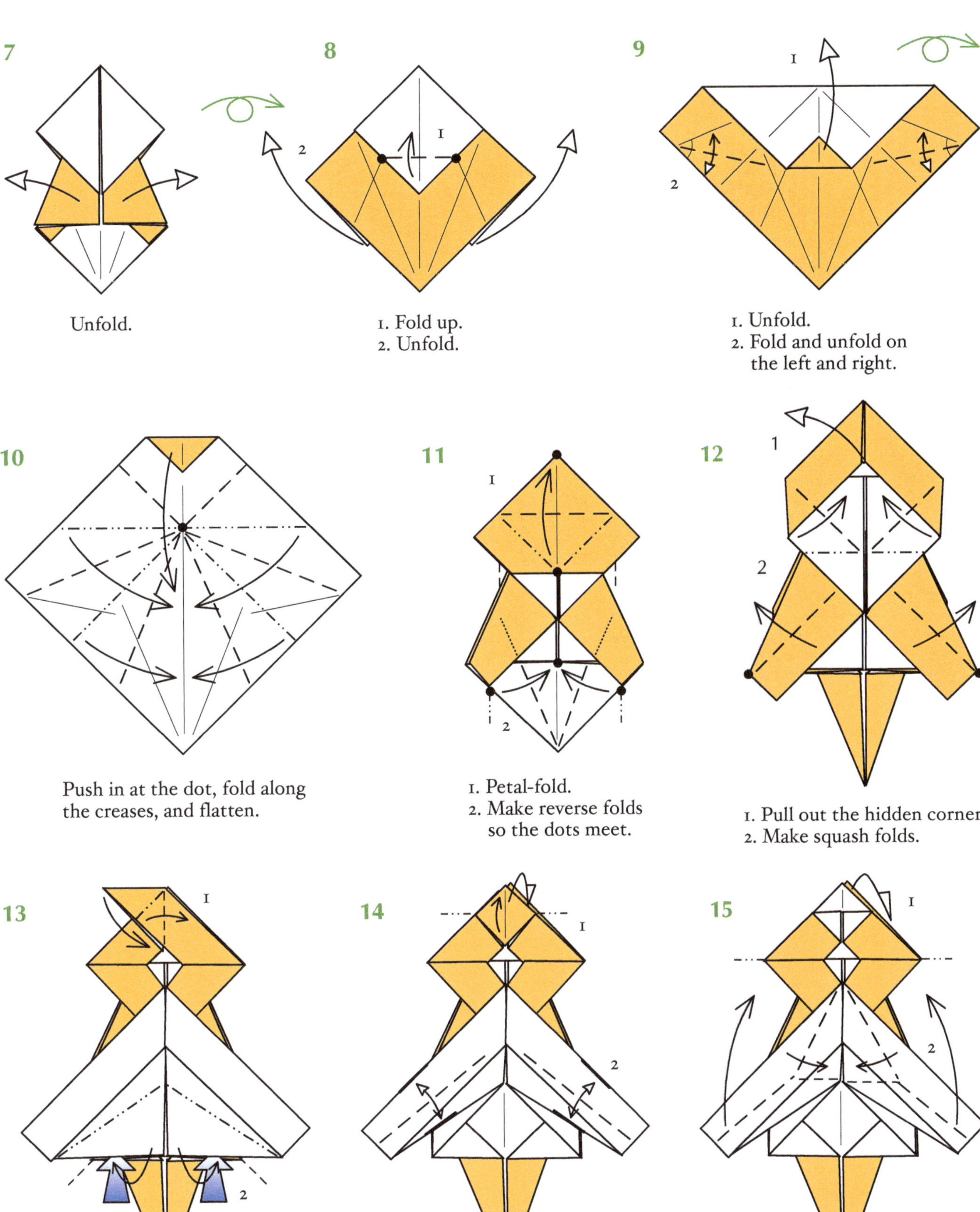

7 Unfold.

8
1. Fold up.
2. Unfold.

9
1. Unfold.
2. Fold and unfold on the left and right.

10 Push in at the dot, fold along the creases, and flatten.

11
1. Petal-fold.
2. Make reverse folds so the dots meet.

12
1. Pull out the hidden corner.
2. Make squash folds.

13
1. Squash-fold.
2. Mountain-fold along the creases for these reverse folds.

14
1. Fold inside and swing out from the front.
2. Fold and unfold the top layers so the bold lines meet.

15
1. Fold behind.
2. Make rabbit ears.

16

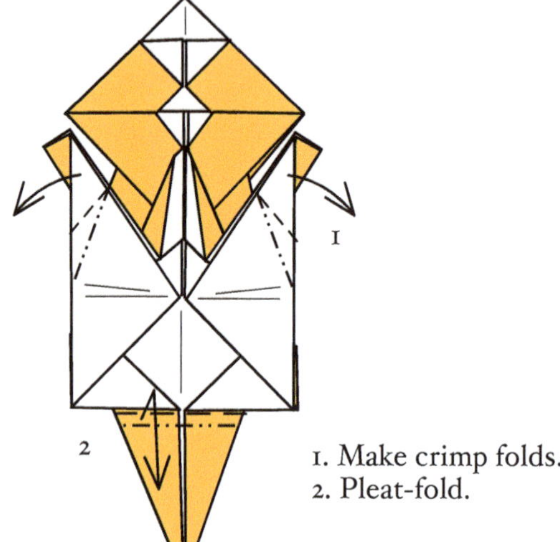

1. Make crimp folds.
2. Pleat-fold.

17

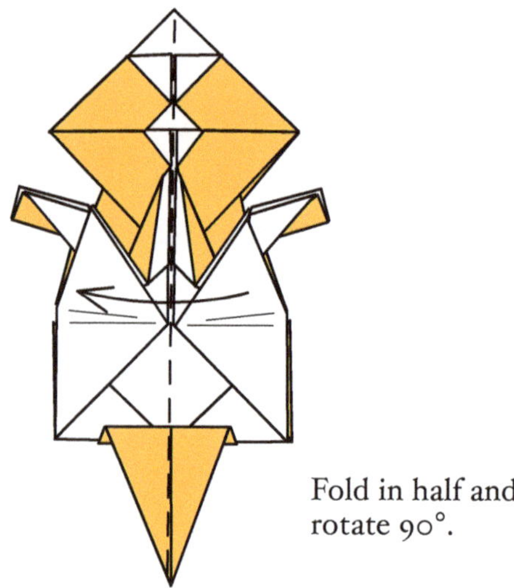

Fold in half and rotate 90°.

18

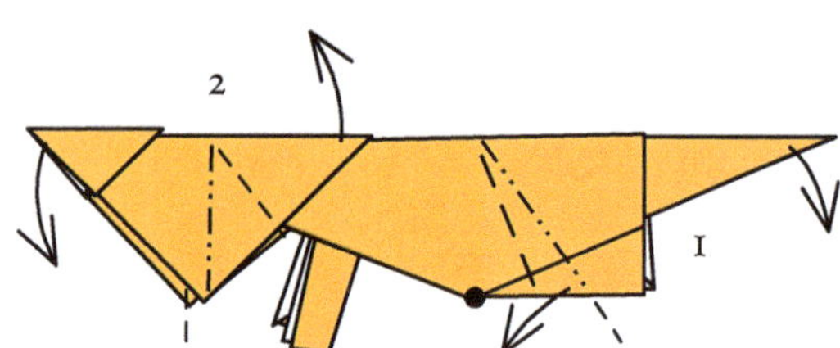

1. Fold close to the dot for this crimp fold.
2. Crimp-fold. Fold on inner layers.

19

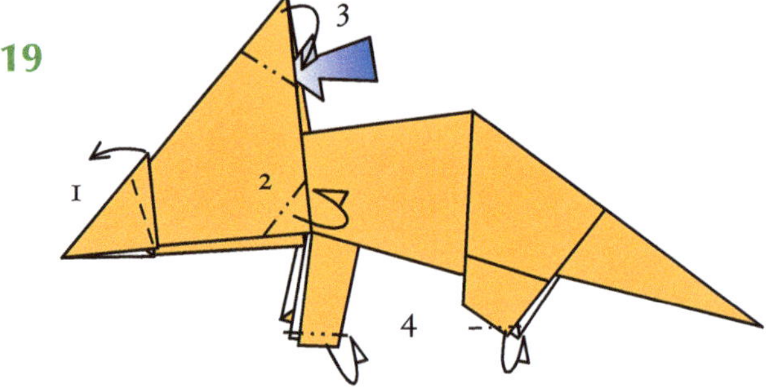

1. Outside-reverse-fold.
2. Fold inside, repeat behind.
3. Reverse-fold.
4. Fold inside, repeat behind.

20

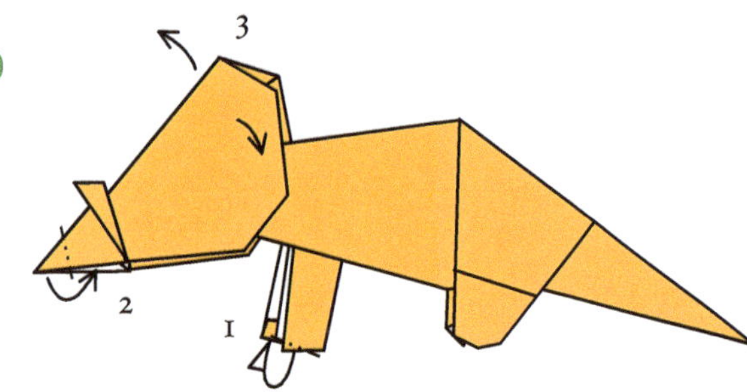

1. Fold inside, repeat behind.
2. Reverse-fold.
3. Spread the crown.

21

Monoclonius

Triceratops

Triceratops is one of the most famous dinosaurs of all time, instantly recognized by its three horns and massive frill. Growing up to 30 feet long, it was one of the largest horned dinosaurs ever to live. From the Late Cretaceous Period, Triceratops was a powerful plant-eater. It used its sharp beak to cut plants and its horns to defend itself from predators. Strong, sturdy, and fearless, it was a true heavyweight of the ancient world.

1

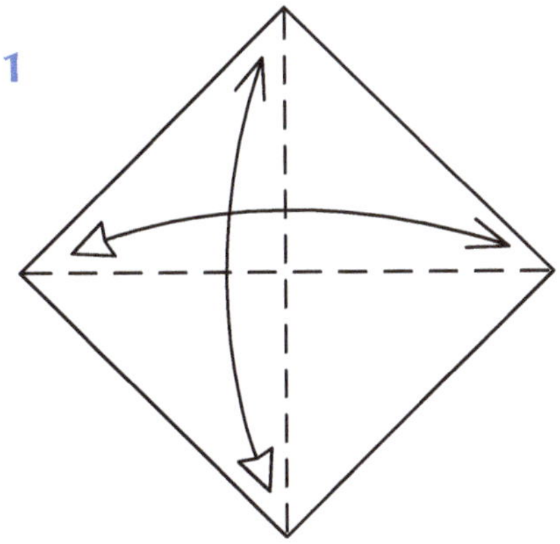

Fold and unfold.

2

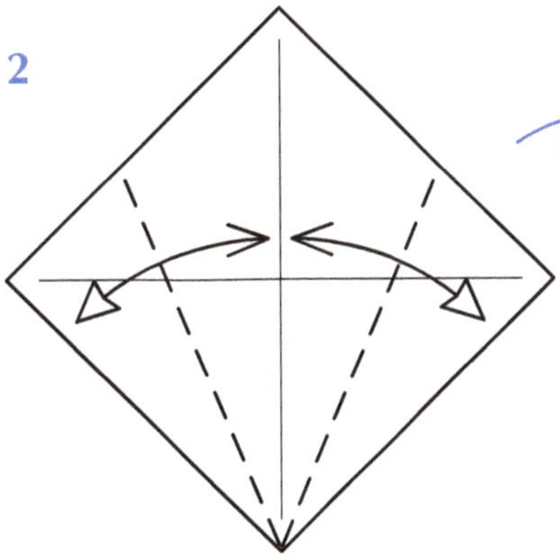

Fold to the center and unfold.

3

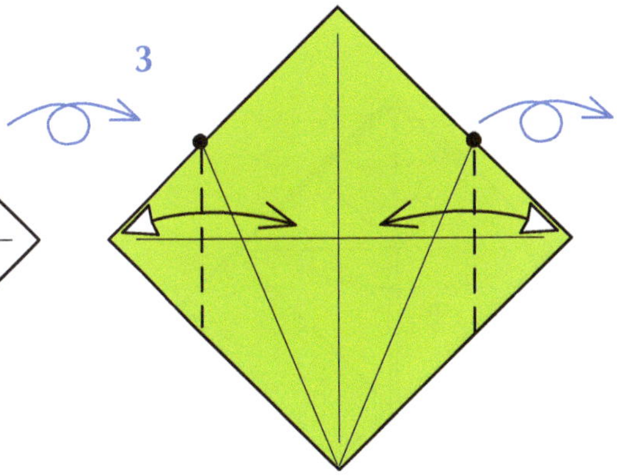

Fold and unfold.

4

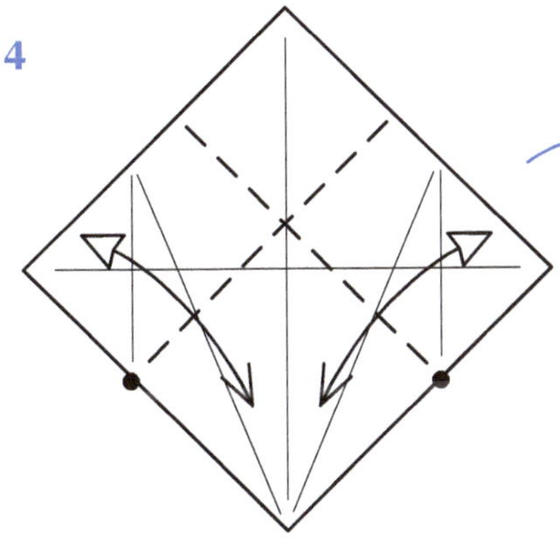

Fold and unfold.

5

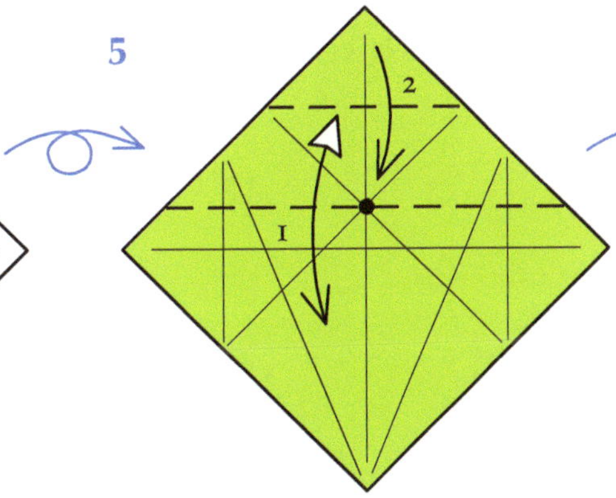

1. Fold and unfold.
2. Fold down.

6

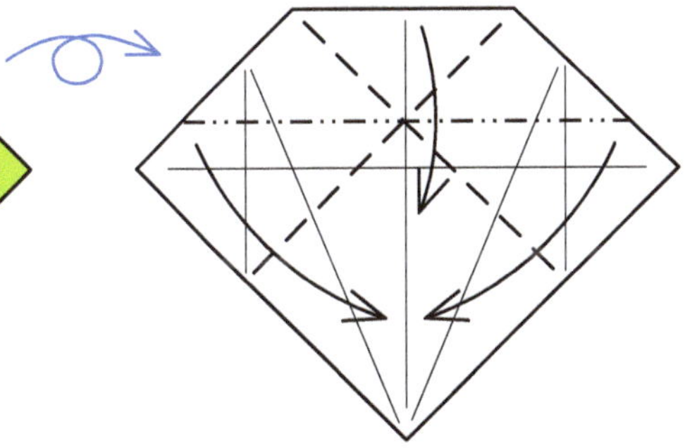

Fold along the creases.

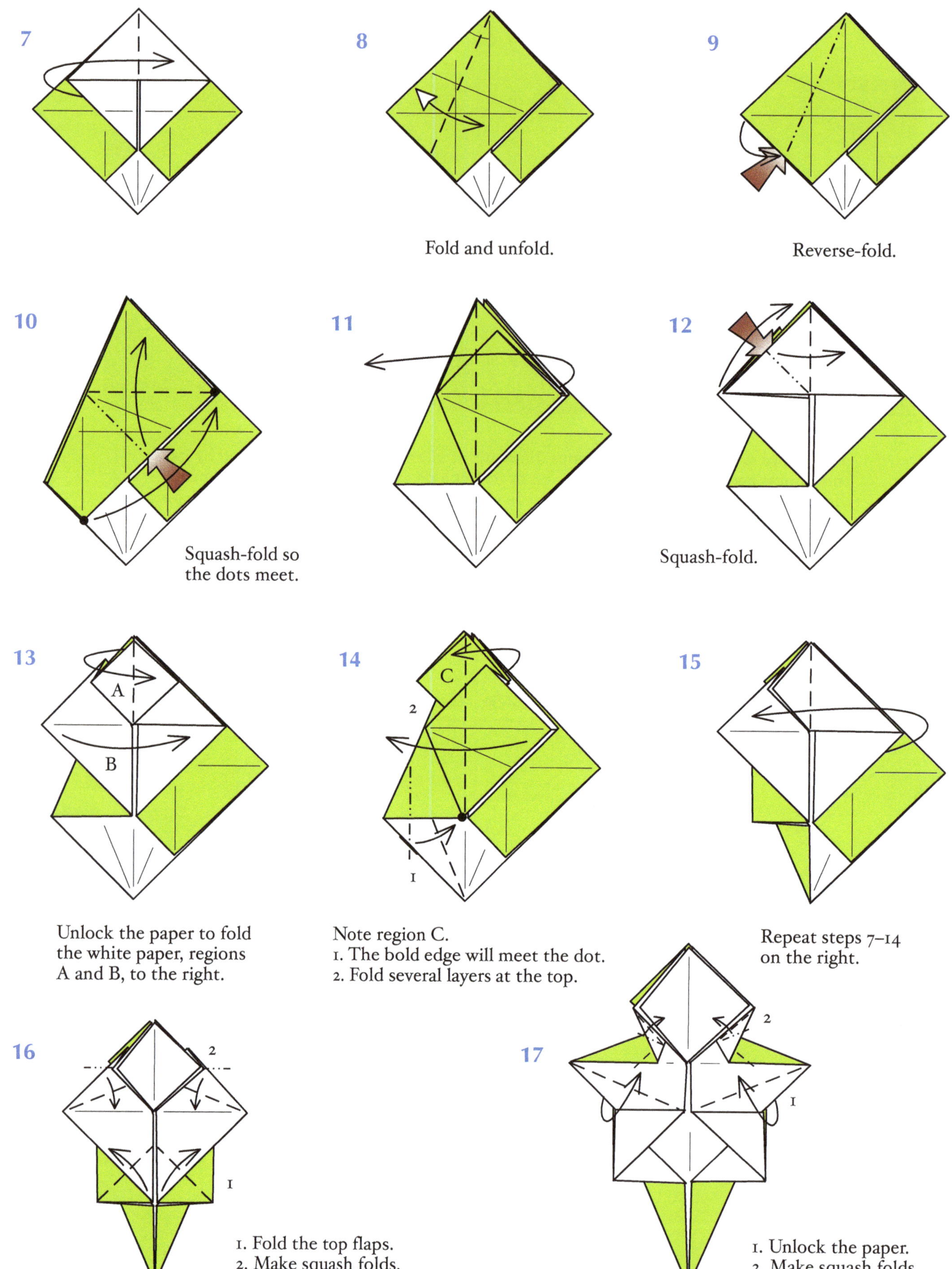

Fold and unfold.

Reverse-fold.

Squash-fold so the dots meet.

Squash-fold.

Unlock the paper to fold the white paper, regions A and B, to the right.

Note region C.
1. The bold edge will meet the dot.
2. Fold several layers at the top.

Repeat steps 7–14 on the right.

1. Fold the top flaps.
2. Make squash folds.

1. Unlock the paper.
2. Make squash folds.

18

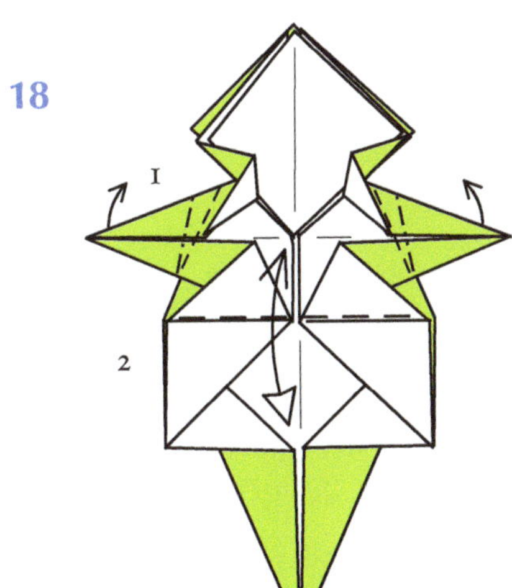

1. Make pleat folds.
2. Fold and unfold.

19

1. Fold a thin strip.
2. Pleat-fold.

20

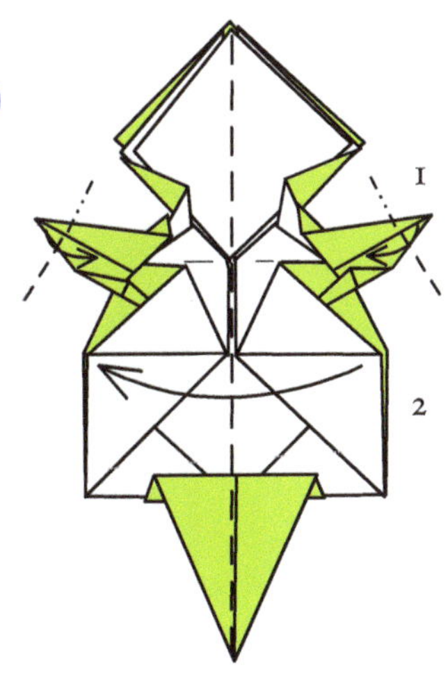

1. Make reverse folds.
2. Fold in half and rotate.

21

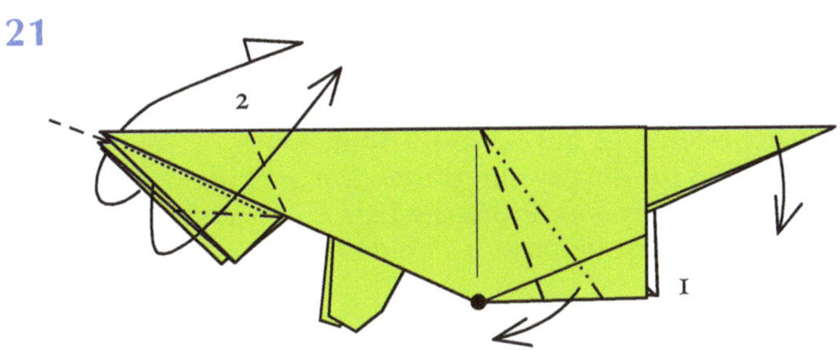

1. Fold close to the dot for this crimp fold.
2. Outside-reverse-fold.

22

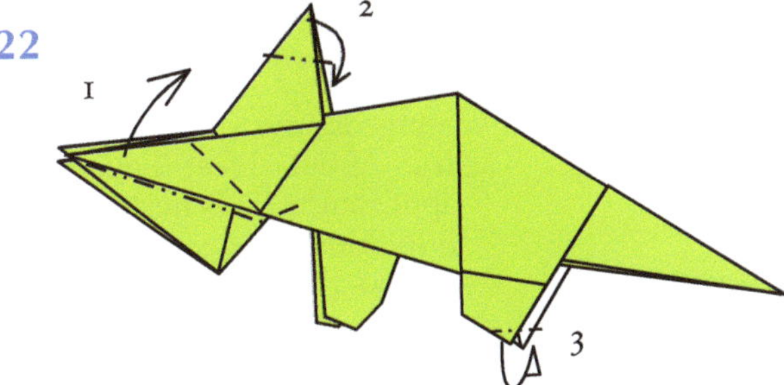

1. Squash-fold, repeat behind.
2. Reverse-fold.
3. Fold inside, repeat behind.

23

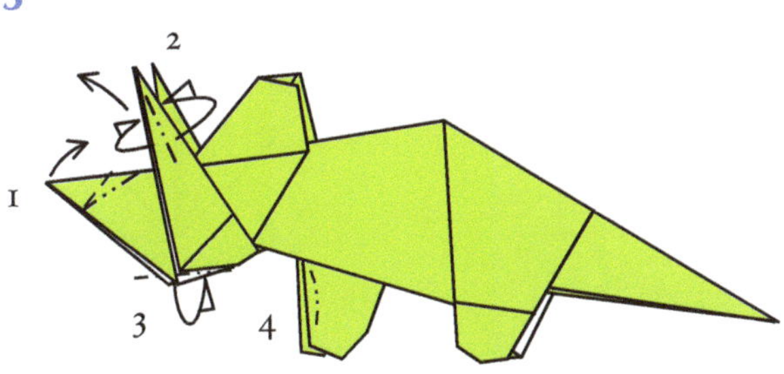

1. Crimp-fold.
2. Thin and shape the horns.
3. Fold inside.
4. Shape the legs.

Repeat behind at 2, 3, and 4.

24

Triceratops

Styracosaurus

Styracosaurus stood out with an impressive crown of long spikes radiating from its frill. About 18 feet long, it was smaller than Triceratops but far more dramatic in appearance. This herbivore likely used its spikes for display and protection, making it look much larger and more dangerous than it really was. From the Late Cretaceous Period, Styracosaurus proves that sometimes the best defense is a bold design.

1

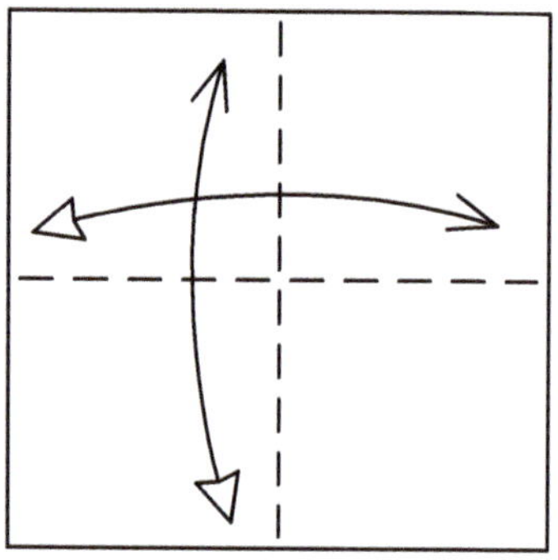

Fold and unfold.

2

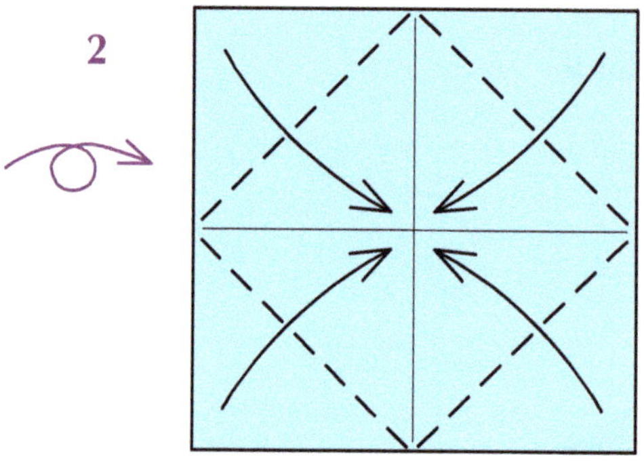

Fold to the center.

3

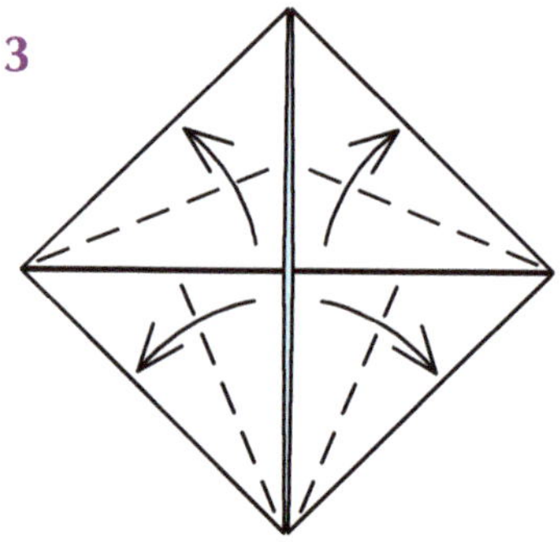

4

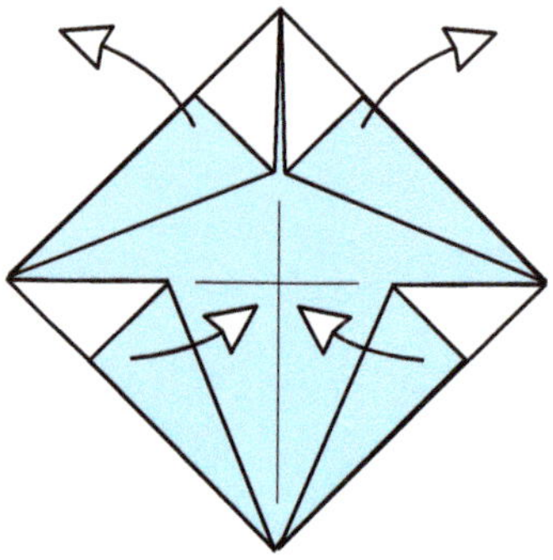

Unfold.

5

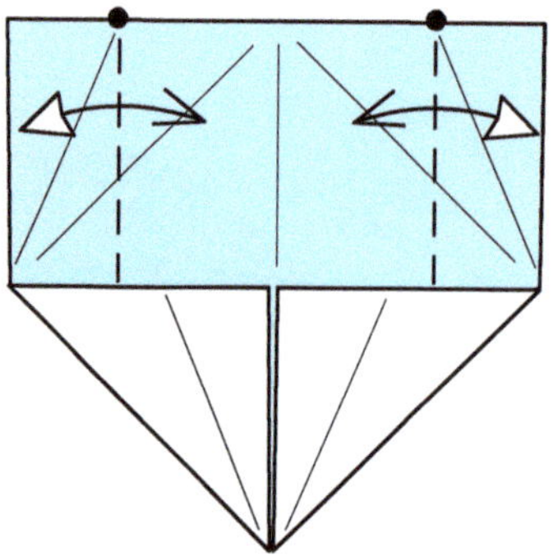

Fold and unfold.

6

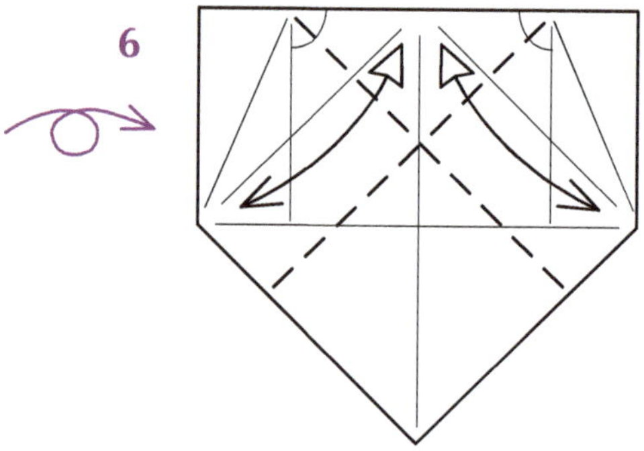

Fold and unfold.

7

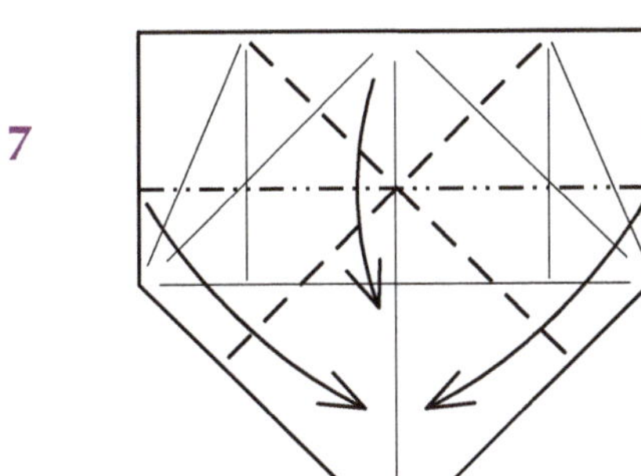

Valley-fold along the creases.

8

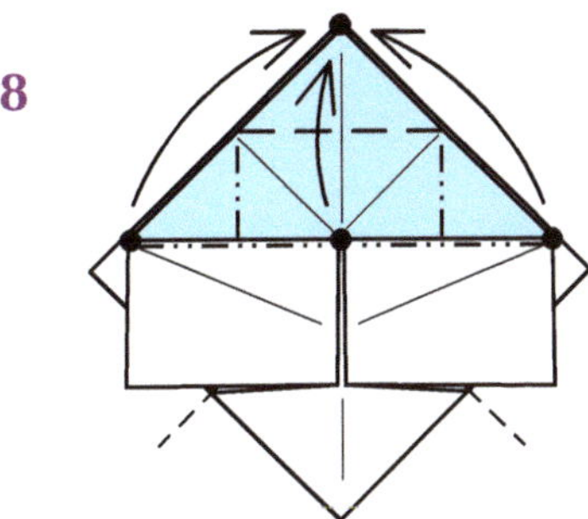

This is a combination of squash folds.

9

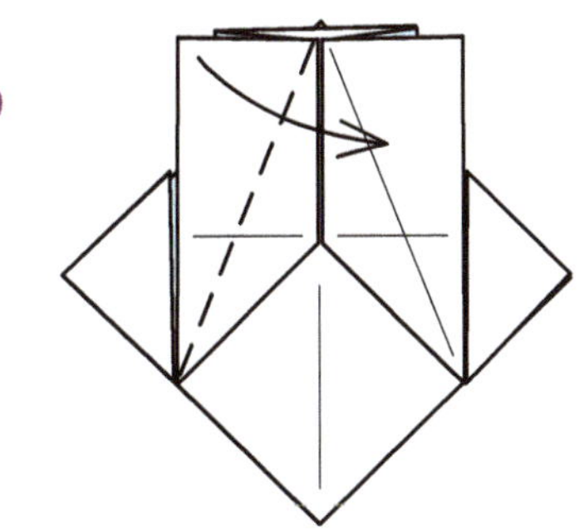

Fold along the crease.

10

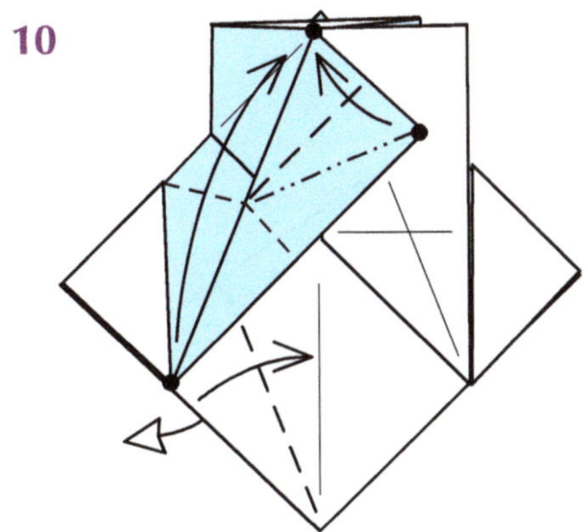

This is a combination of squash folds. The dots will meet and swing out from bhind.

11

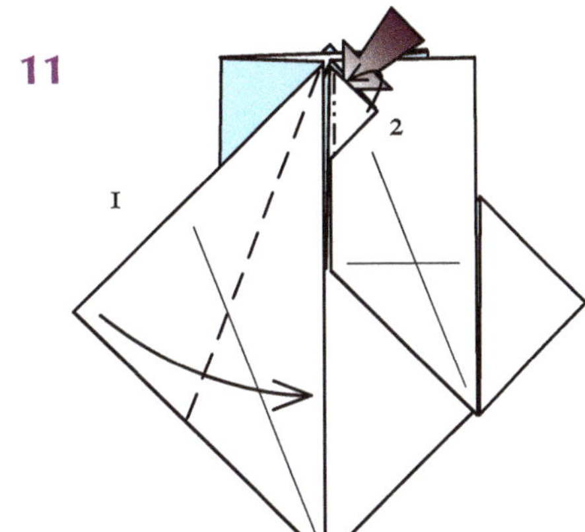

1. Fold to the center.
2. Reverse-fold.

12

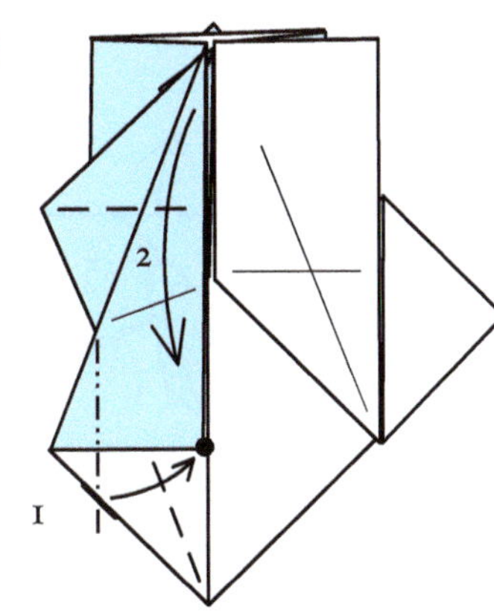

1. The bold edge will meet the dot.
2. Fold down.

13

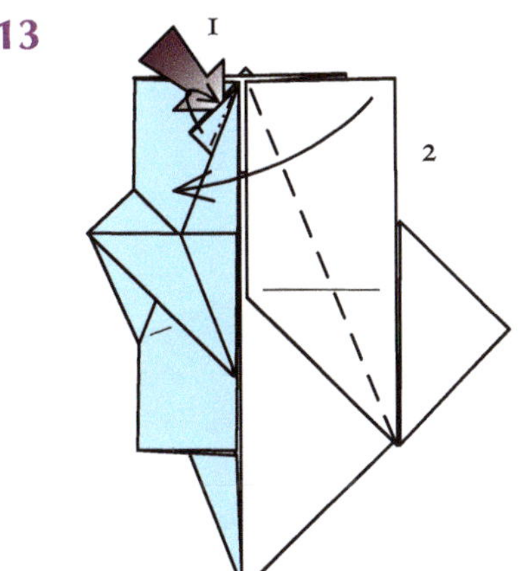

1. Reverse-fold.
2. Repeat steps 9–13 on the right.

14

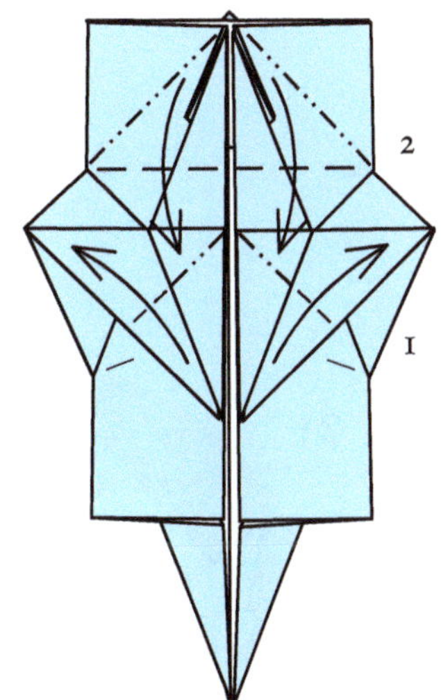

1. Make reverse folds.
2. Make squash folds.

15

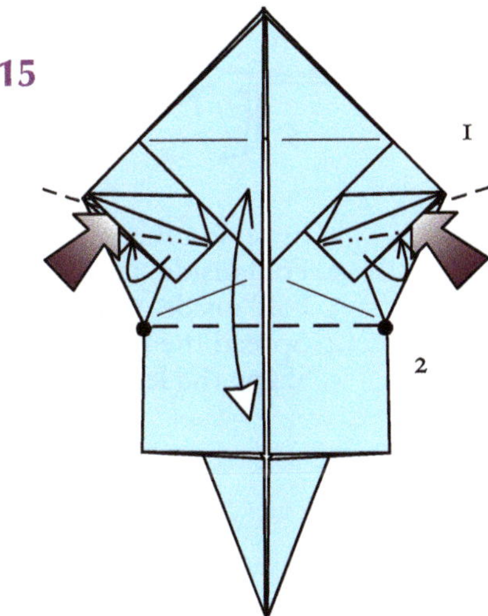

1. Make reverse folds.
2. Fold and unfold.

16

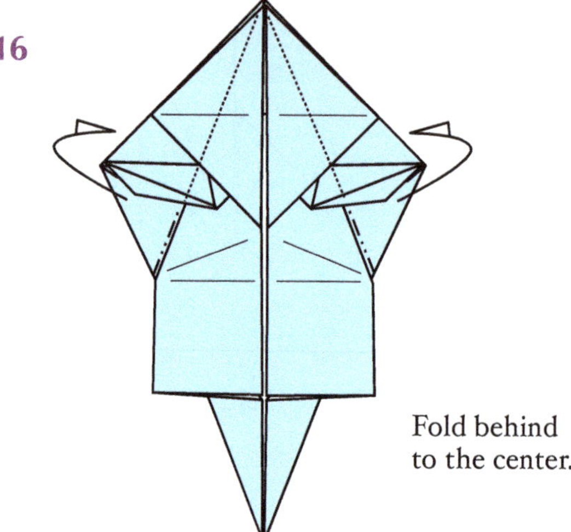

Fold behind
to the center.

17

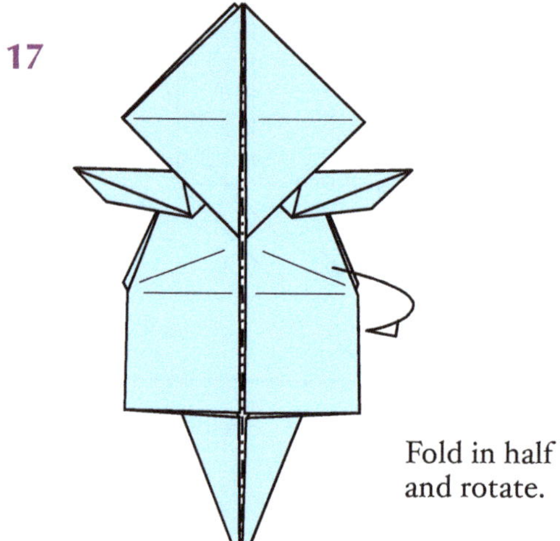

Fold in half
and rotate.

18

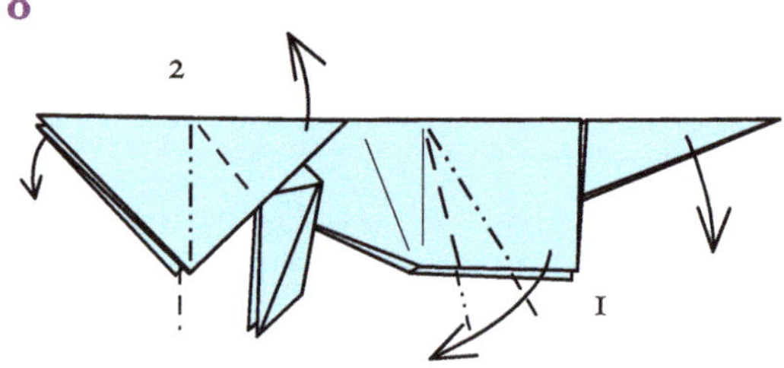

1. Crimp-fold.
2. Crimp-fold. Fold on inner layers.

19

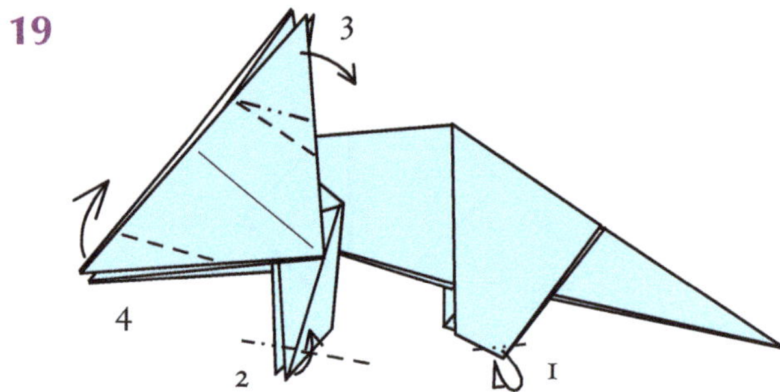

1. Fold inside.
2. Reverse-fold.
3. Pleat-fold.
4. Outside-reverse-fold.

Repeat behind for 1, 2, and 3.

20

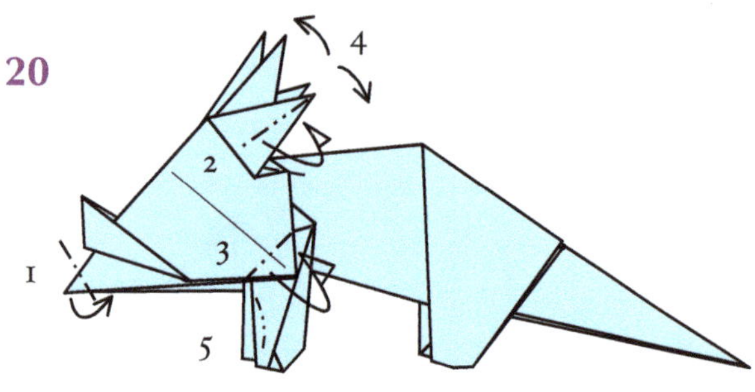

1. Reverse-fold.
2. Fold inside, repeat behind.
3. Fold inside, repeat behind.
4. Spread the horns.
5. Shape the legs, repeat behind.

21

Styracosaurus

Graciliceratops

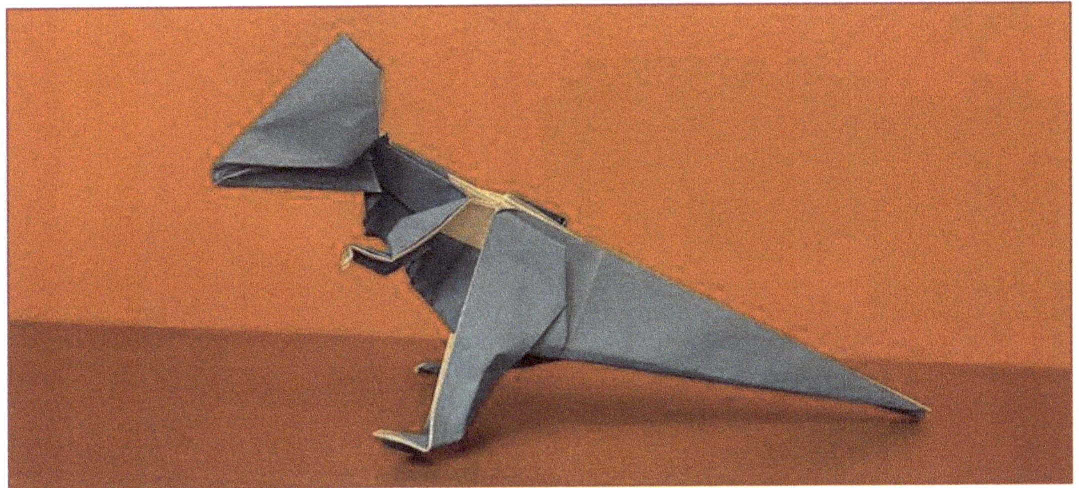

Graciliceratops was a small, lightly built horned dinosaur measuring only about 3 feet long. It lived during the Early Cretaceous, long before the giant ceratopsians appeared. A gentle plant-eater, Graciliceratops fed on low-growing plants and relied on speed rather than armor for safety. It represents an early and elegant stage in the evolution of horned dinosaurs.

1

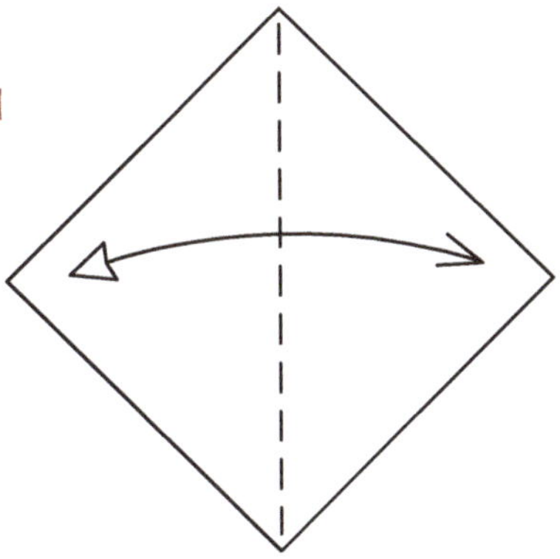

Fold and unfold.

2

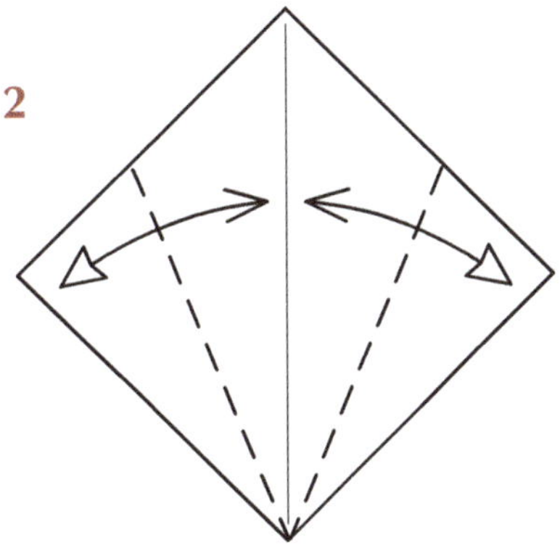

Fold to the center and unfold.

3

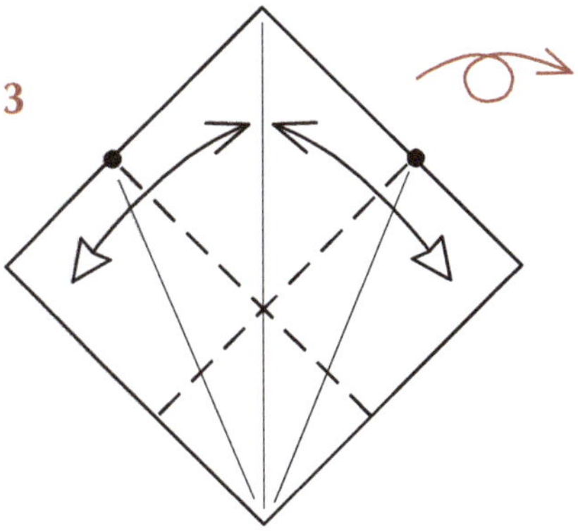

Fold and unfold.

4

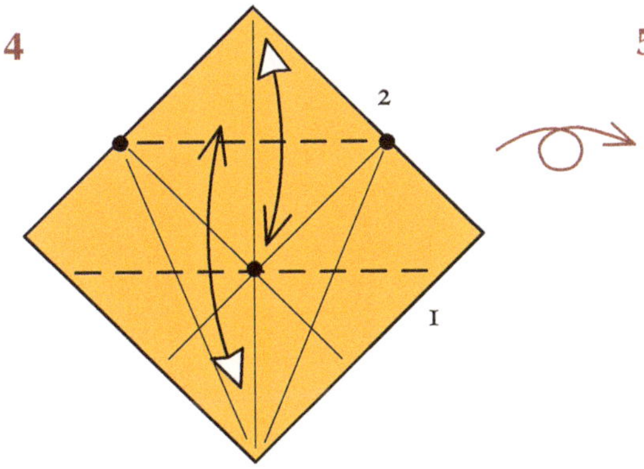

Fold and unfold at 1 and 2.

5

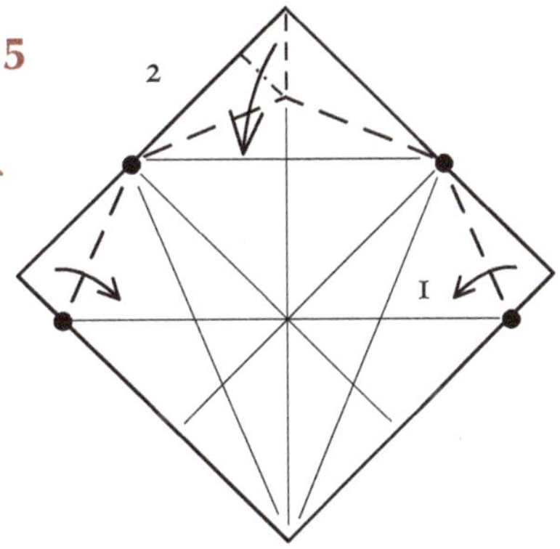

1. Fold on the left and right.
2. Rabbit-ear.

6

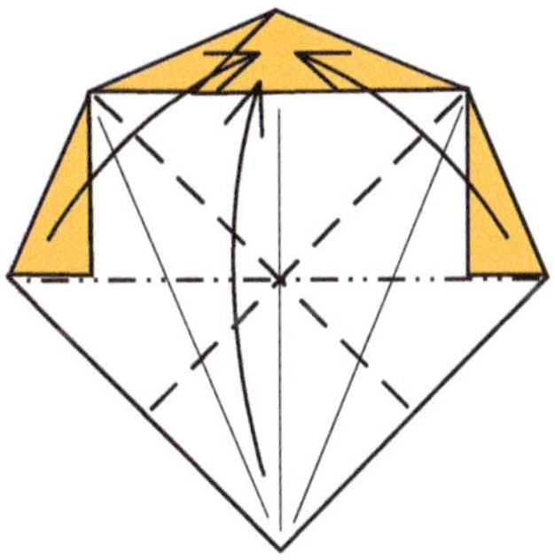

Fold along the creases.

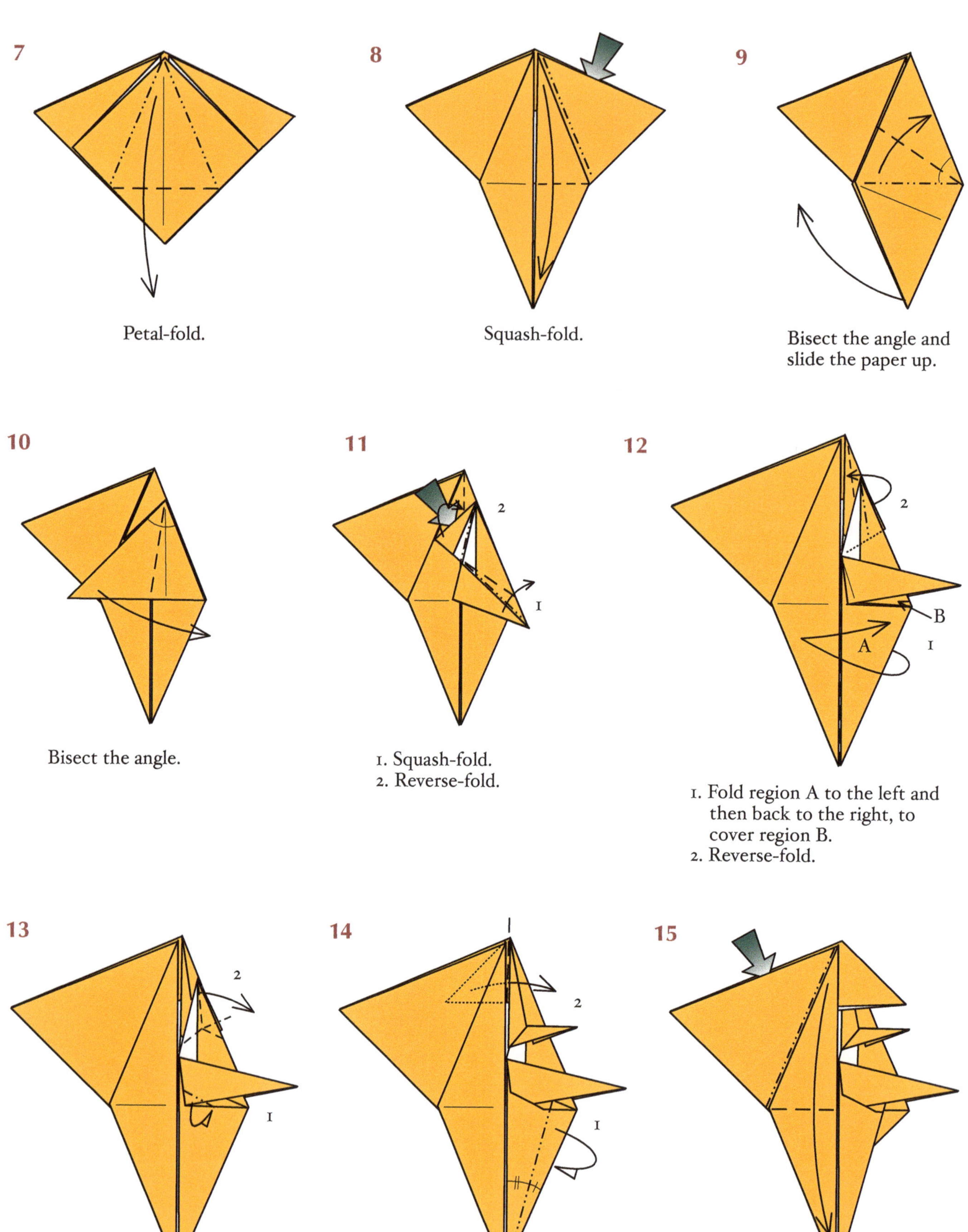

Petal-fold.

Squash-fold.

Bisect the angle and slide the paper up.

Bisect the angle.

1. Squash-fold.
2. Reverse-fold.

1. Fold region A to the left and then back to the right, to cover region B.
2. Reverse-fold.

1. Fold inside.
2. Rabbit-ear.

1. Fold inside at an angle of 1/3.
2. Fold the hidden flap.

Repeat steps 8–14 on the left.

16

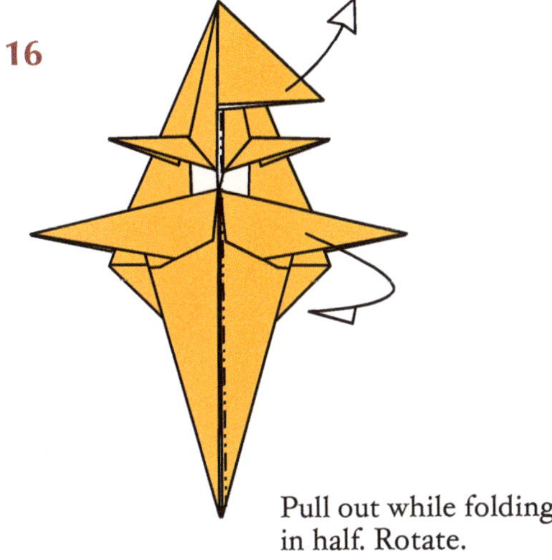

Pull out while folding in half. Rotate.

17

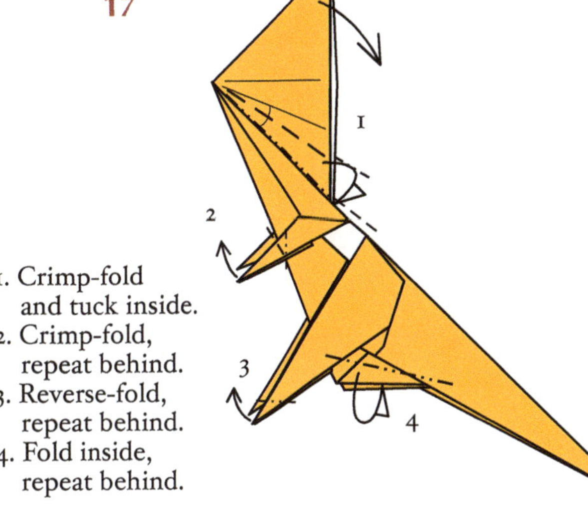

1. Crimp-fold and tuck inside.
2. Crimp-fold, repeat behind.
3. Reverse-fold, repeat behind.
4. Fold inside, repeat behind.

18

1. Reverse-fold, repeat behind.
2. Shape the legs, repeat behind.
3. Crimp-fold.

19

Crimp-fold.

20

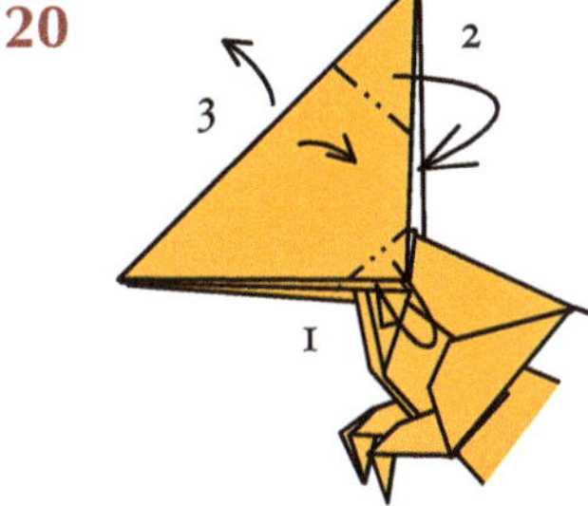

1. Fold inside, repeat behind.
2. Reverse-fold.
3. Spread the crown.

21

Graciliceratops

Tianchisaurus

Tianchisaurus was an early armored dinosaur with small plates and spikes along its back. About 10 feet long, it lived during the Middle Jurassic, making it one of the earliest known armored dinosaurs. This herbivore likely used its armor for protection while feeding on plants close to the ground. Tianchisaurus shows how the idea of defense through armor began long before the most famous plated dinosaurs appeared.

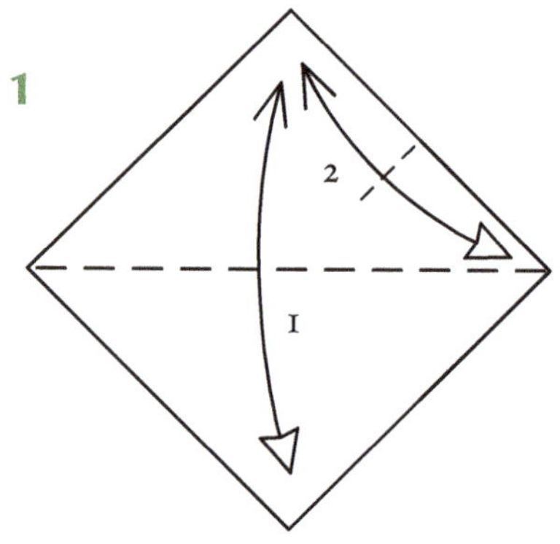

1. Fold and unfold.
2. Fold and unfold on the edge.

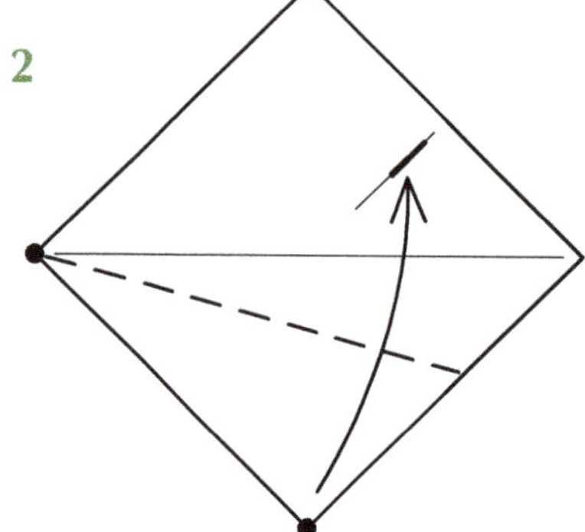

Bring the corner to the line.

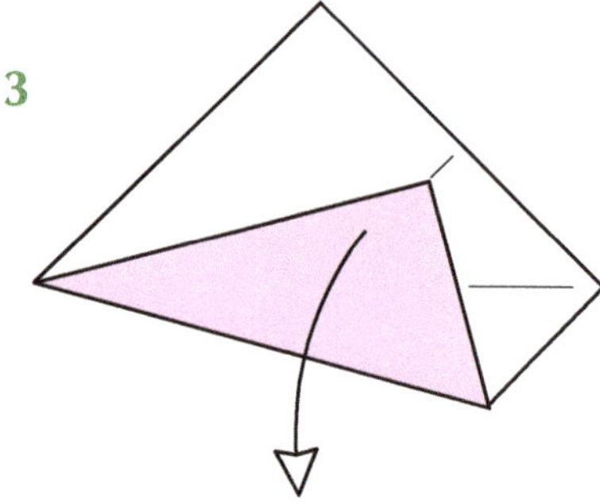

Unfold.

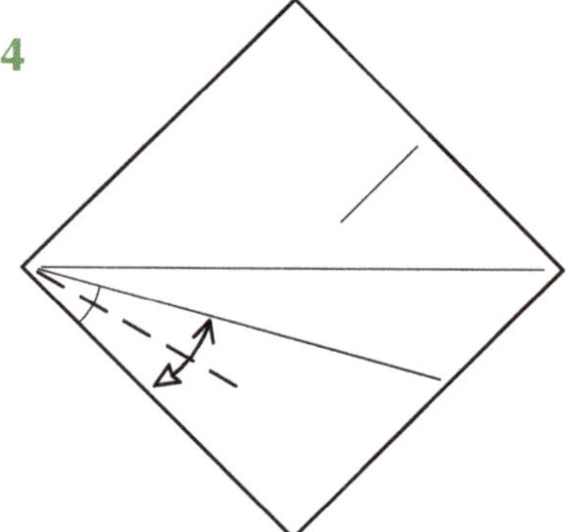

Fold and unfold.

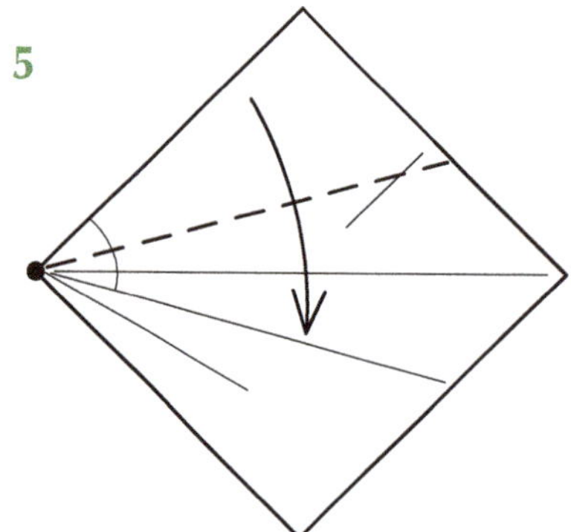

Repeat steps 2–4 on the upper half. Keep the dot on the left.

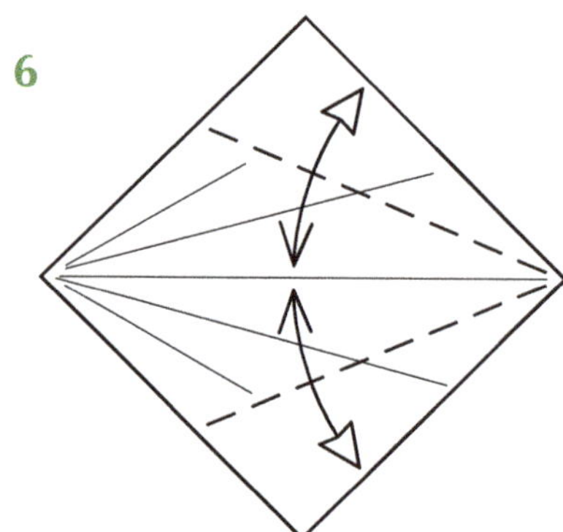

Fold to the center and unfold.

7

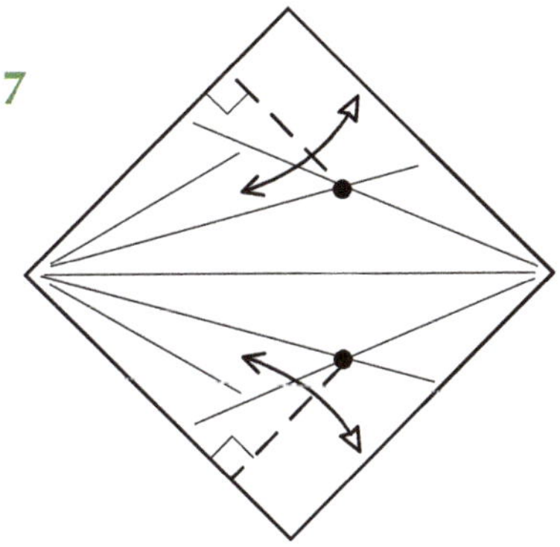

Fold and unfold.

8

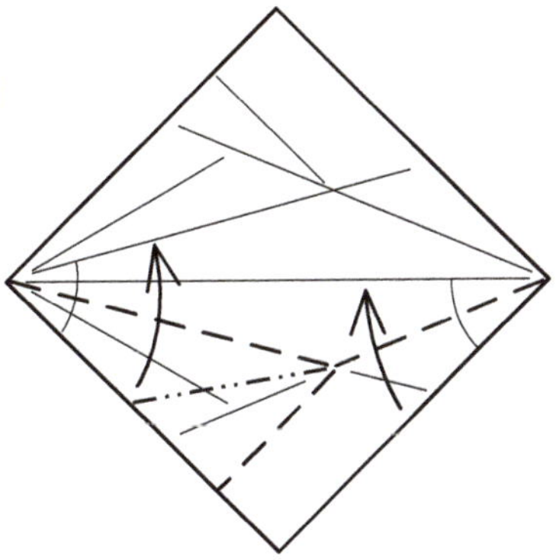

Valley-fold along the creases.

9

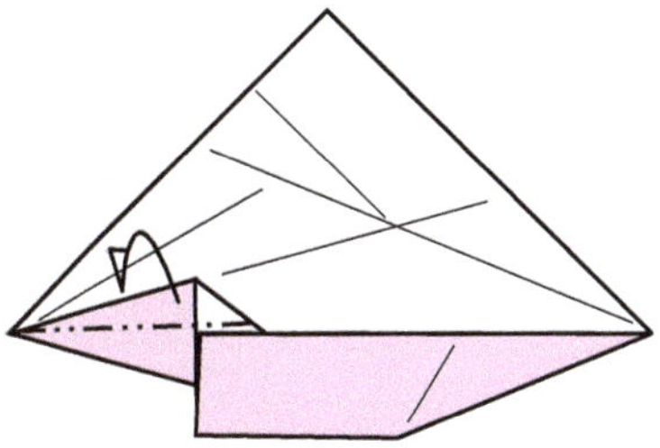

Fold inside.

10

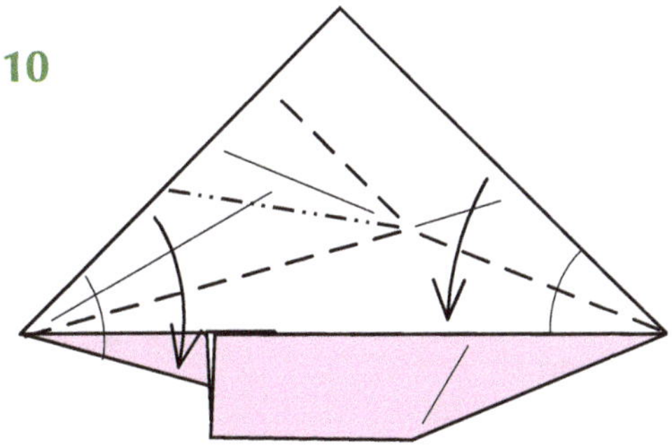

Repeat steps 8–9 on the top.

11

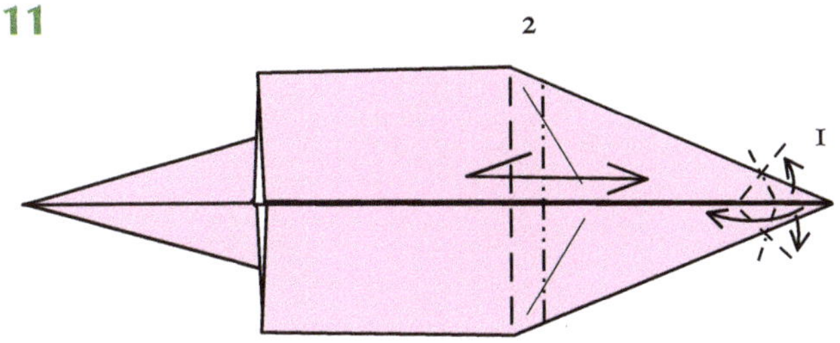

1. Spread.
2. Pleat-fold.

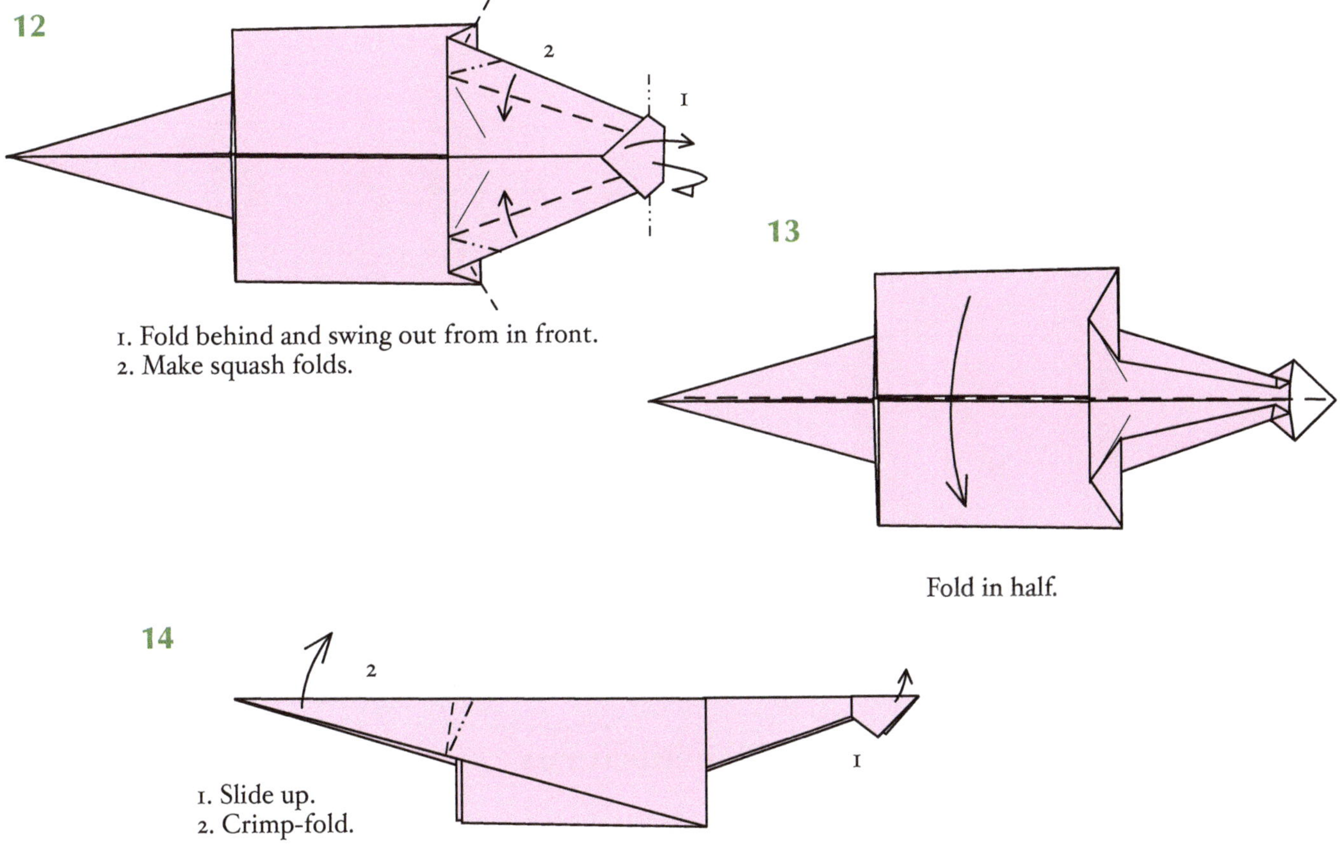

1. Fold behind and swing out from in front.
2. Make squash folds.

Fold in half.

1. Slide up.
2. Crimp-fold.

15

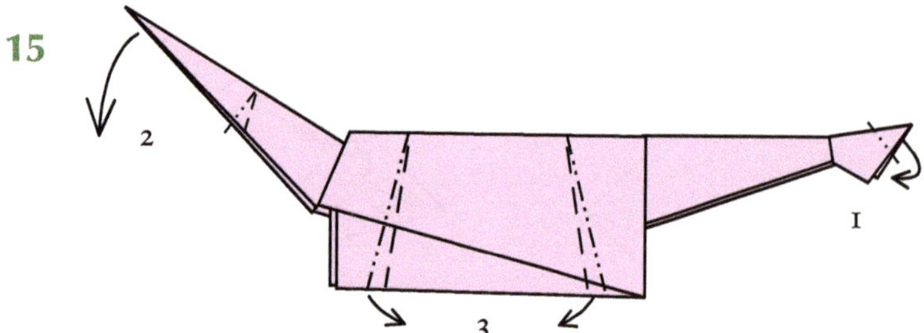

1. Reverse-fold.
2. Crimp-fold.
3. Make crimp folds.

16

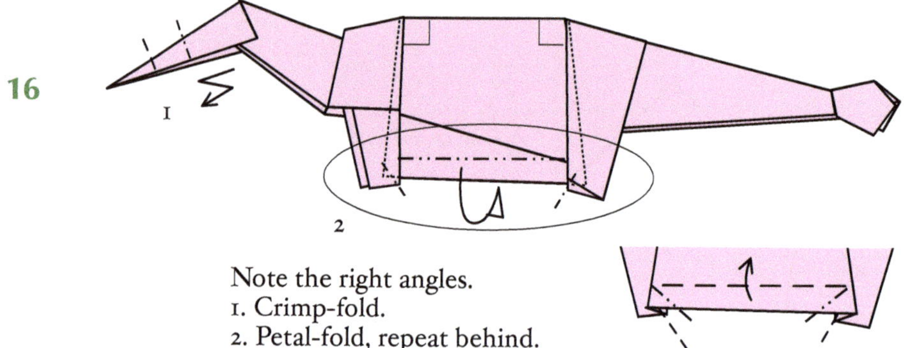

Note the right angles.
1. Crimp-fold.
2. Petal-fold, repeat behind.

View of inside.

17

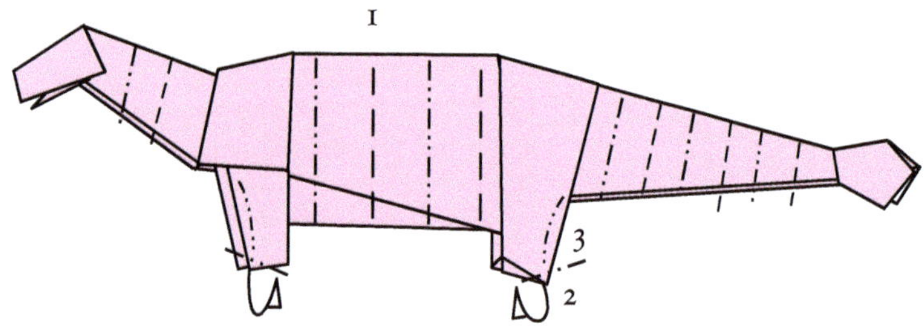

1. Make pleat folds.
2. Fold inside, repeat behind.
3. Shape the legs, repeat behind.

18

Tianchisaurus

Anoplosaurus

Anoplosaurus was a compact, armored dinosaur measuring around 15 feet long. Its body was covered with bony plates that acted like a natural shield. A slow-moving plant-eater, Anoplosaurus relied on its armor rather than speed to stay safe. Its name means "unarmed lizard," though its protective plating made it anything but defenseless. It lived during the Early Cretaceous Period.

1

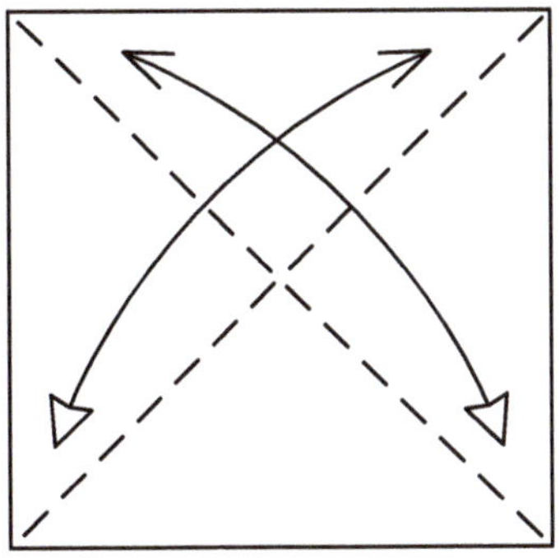

Fold and unfold.

2

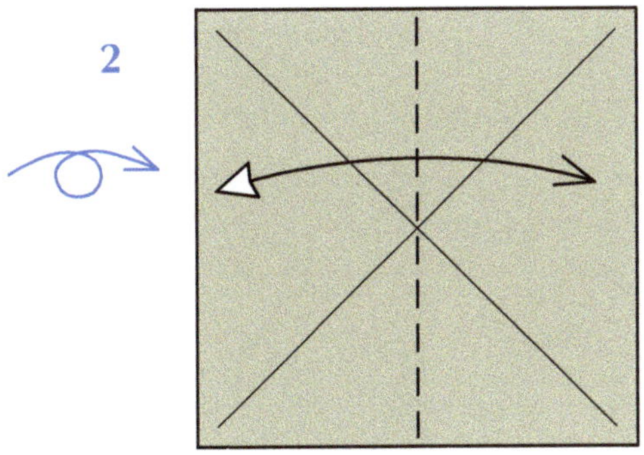

Fold and unfold.

3

Fold to the center.

4

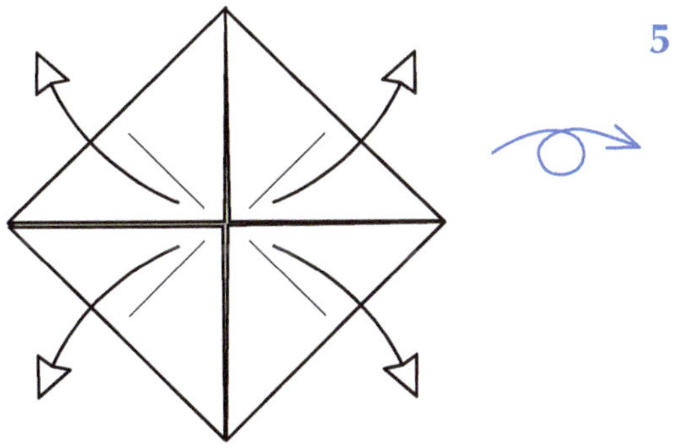

Unfold.

5

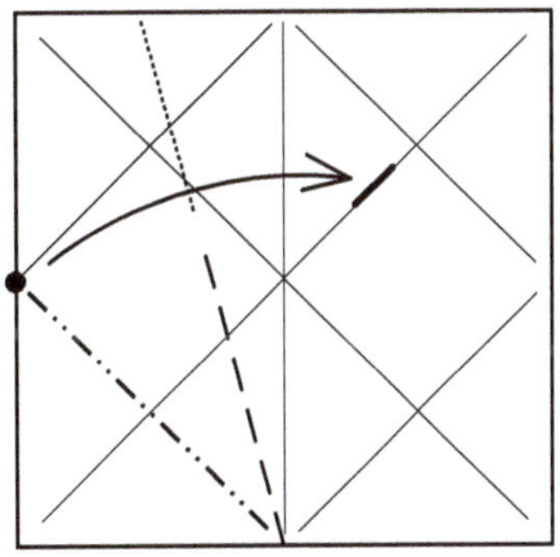

Pleat-fold so the dot meets the bold line. Mountain-fold along the crease.

6

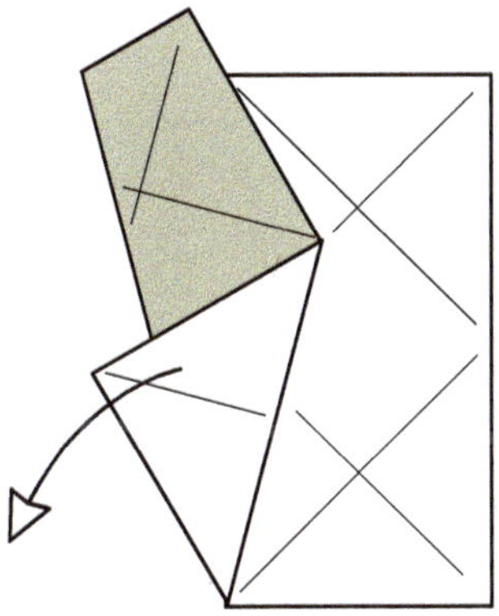

Unfold.

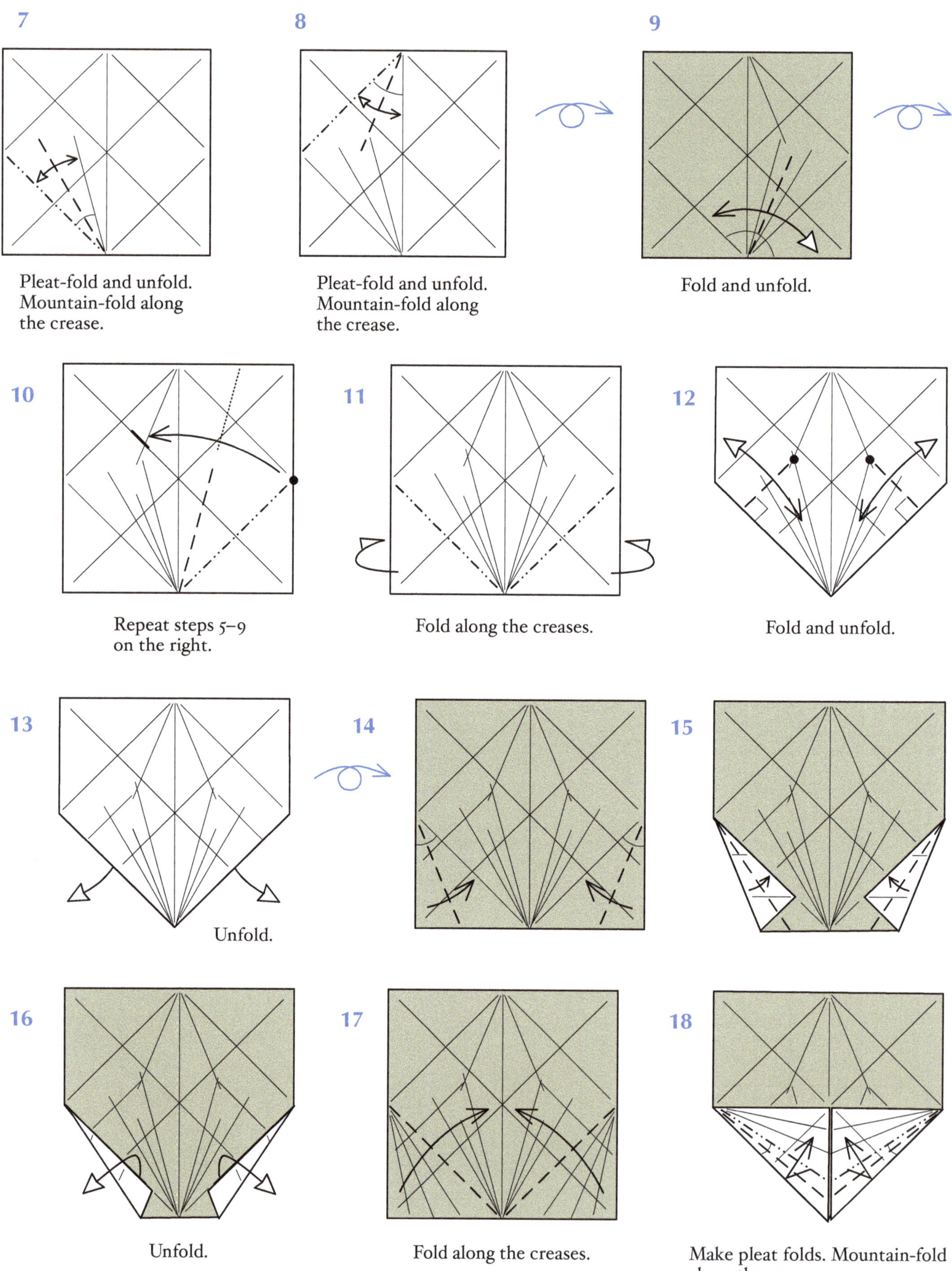
7
Pleat-fold and unfold. Mountain-fold along the crease.
8
Pleat-fold and unfold. Mountain-fold along the crease.
9
Fold and unfold.
10
Repeat steps 5–9 on the right.
11
Fold along the creases.
12
Fold and unfold.
13
Unfold.
14
15
16
Unfold.
17
Fold along the creases.
18
Make pleat folds. Mountain-fold along the creases.

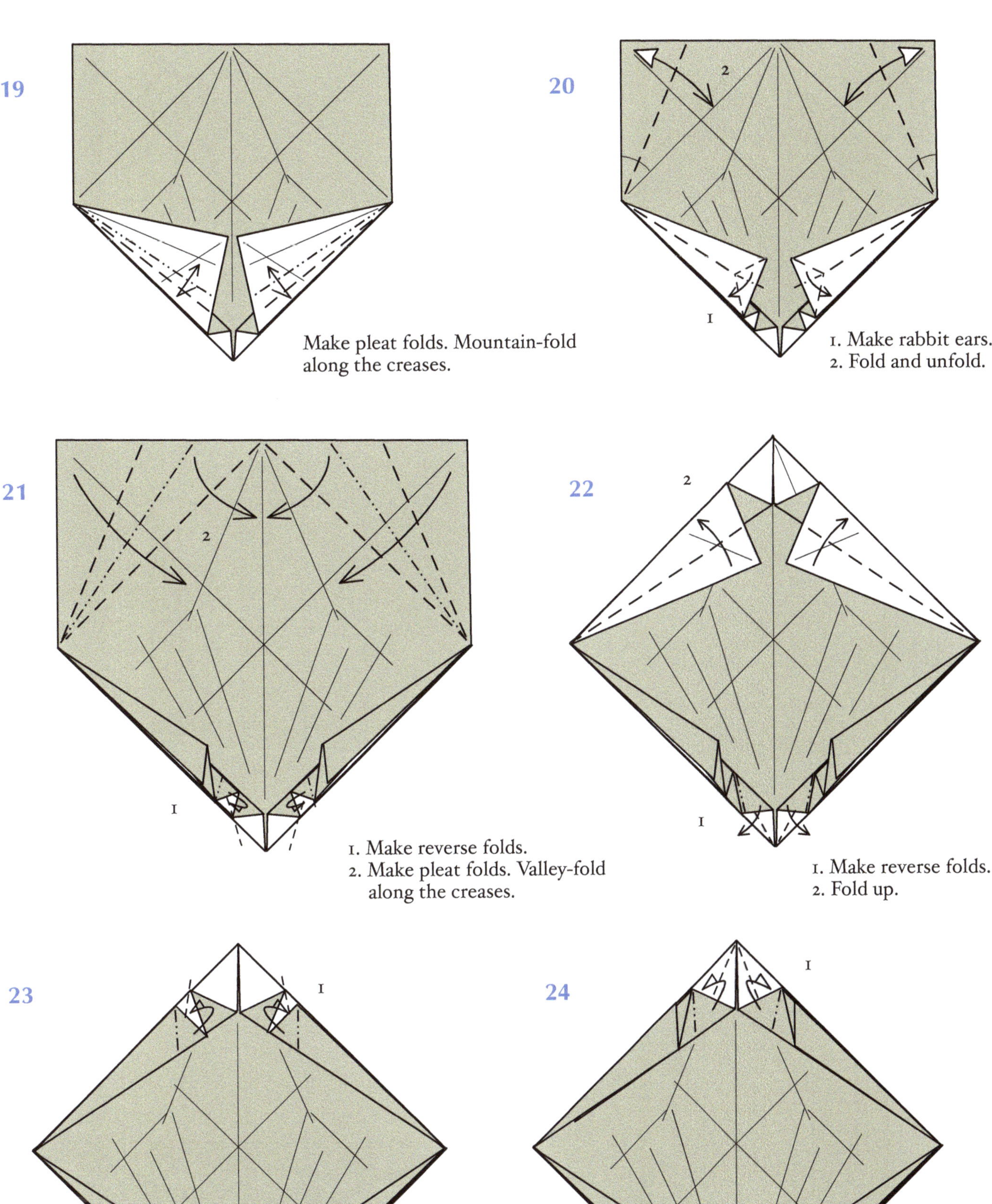

19

Make pleat folds. Mountain-fold along the creases.

20

1. Make rabbit ears.
2. Fold and unfold.

21

1. Make reverse folds.
2. Make pleat folds. Valley-fold along the creases.

22

1. Make reverse folds.
2. Fold up.

23

Make reverse folds at 1 and 2.

24

Make reverse folds at 1 and 2.

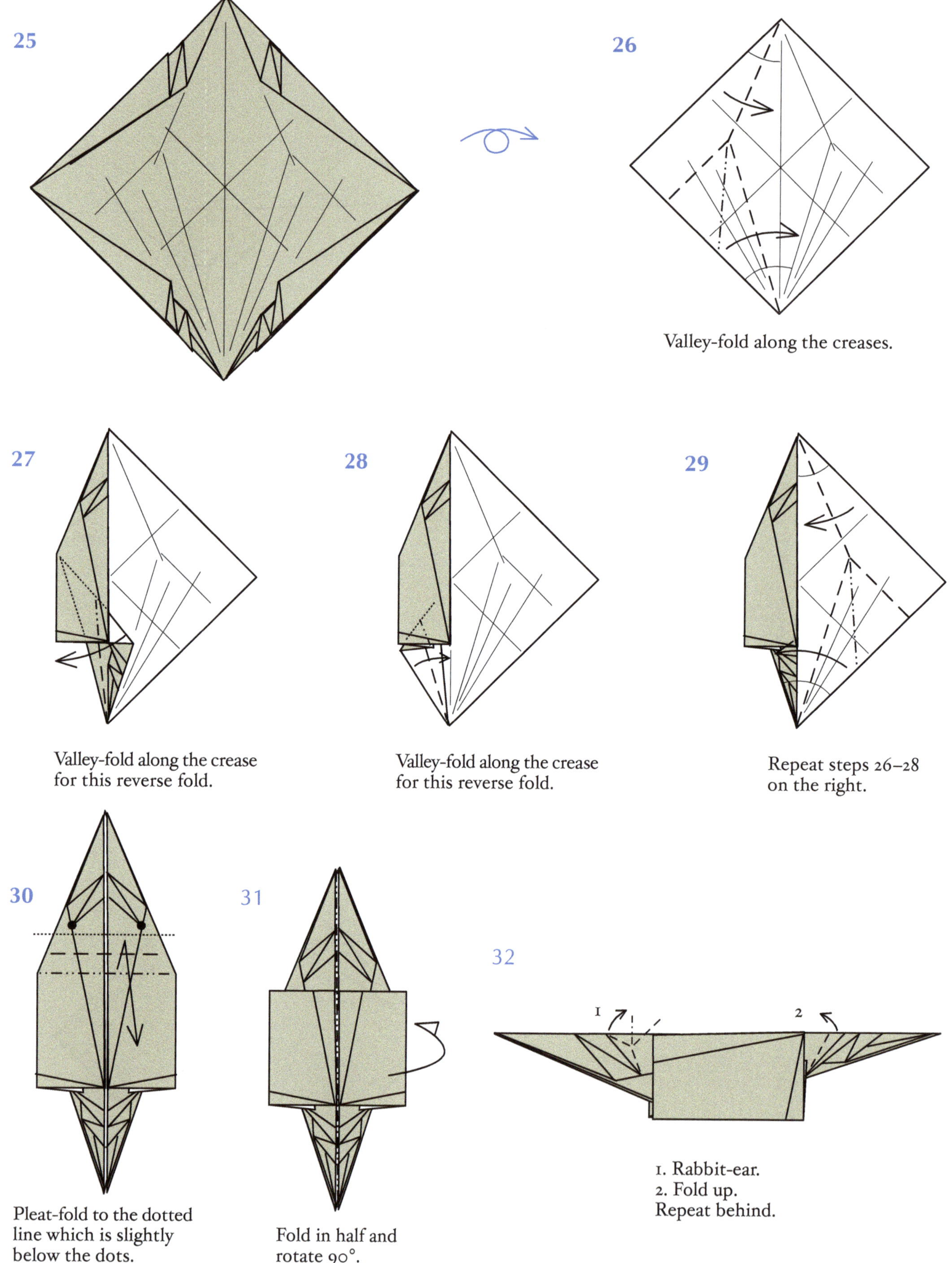

Valley-fold along the creases.

Valley-fold along the crease for this reverse fold.

Valley-fold along the crease for this reverse fold.

Repeat steps 26–28 on the right.

Pleat-fold to the dotted line which is slightly below the dots.

Fold in half and rotate 90°.

1. Rabbit-ear.
2. Fold up.
Repeat behind.

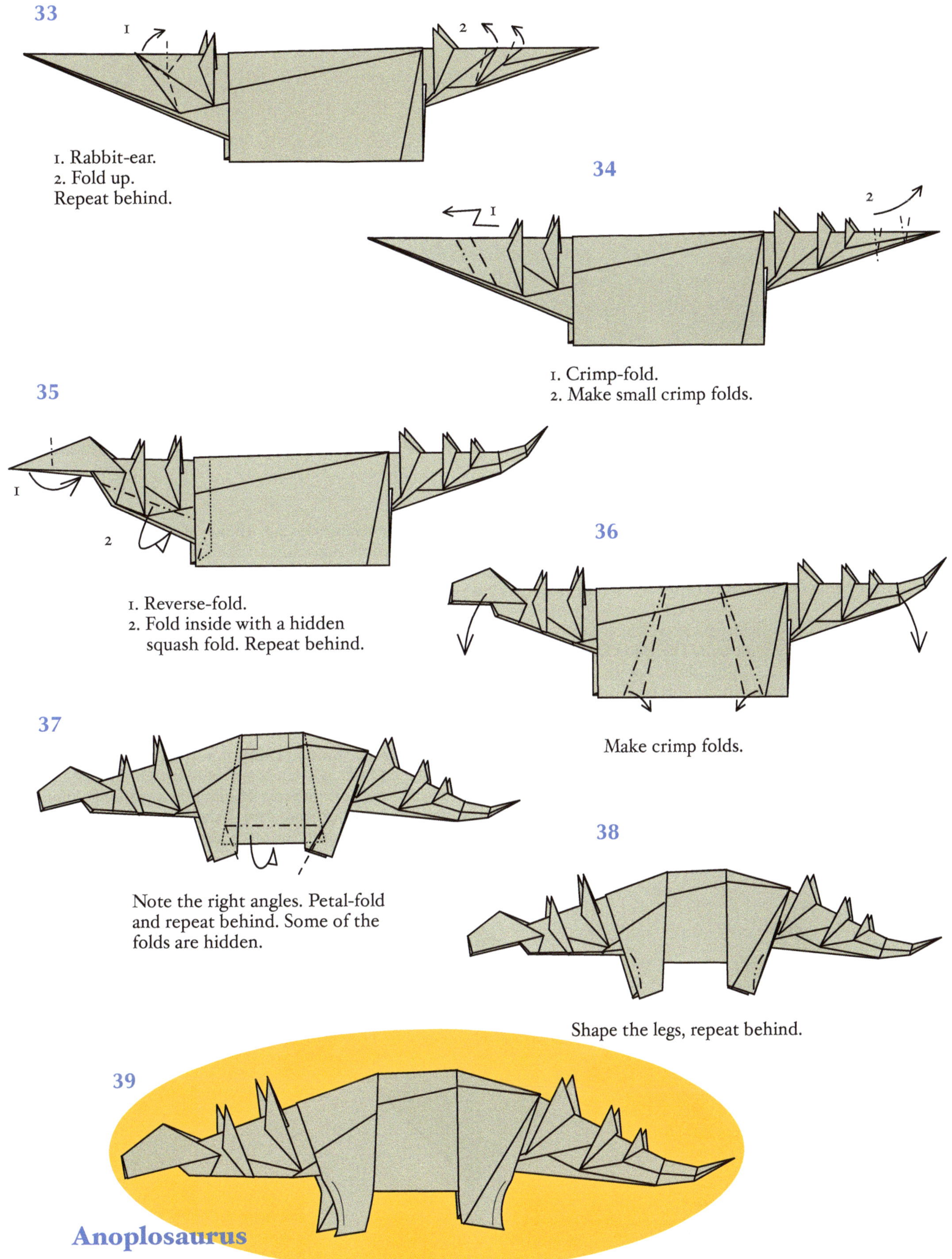
33
1
2
1. Rabbit-ear.
2. Fold up.
Repeat behind.
34
1
2
1. Crimp-fold.
2. Make small crimp folds.
35
1
2
1. Reverse-fold.
2. Fold inside with a hidden squash fold. Repeat behind.
36
Make crimp folds.
37
Note the right angles. Petal-fold and repeat behind. Some of the folds are hidden.
38
Shape the legs, repeat behind.
39
Anoplosaurus

Stegosaurus

Stegosaurus is famous for the large plates lining its back and the spiked tail known as the thagomizer. Growing up to 30 feet long, it was one of the most recognizable dinosaurs of the Late Jurassic. This herbivore fed on low plants and used its tail spikes for defense. The tall plates may have helped regulate body temperature or served as a display, making Stegosaurus both strange and spectacular.

This origami Stegosaurus builds upon the structure of the Young Stegosaurus, which itself evolved from the Baby Dinosaur. The Baby Dinosaur begins with a blintz fish base, the Young Stegosaurus expands this into a double-blintz fish base, and this final model grows from that foundation. Here, the Young Stegosaurus structure is embedded within a larger square, providing extra paper for the four tail spikes and a locking tab system that secures the plates and strengthens the model.

Completing this Stegosaurus is the final fold in a grand journey through deep time and paper. One by one, ancient dinosaurs have risen from simple sheets, shaped by brave hands and bold imagination. Each carries its own spirit—fierce defenders, steadfast giants, and noble wanderers of a long-lost world. Folding them all is a great accomplishment, earned through patience, courage, and care. Now they stand together at the end of the tale, paper heroes at rest, silent and strong, guarding the story they have become.

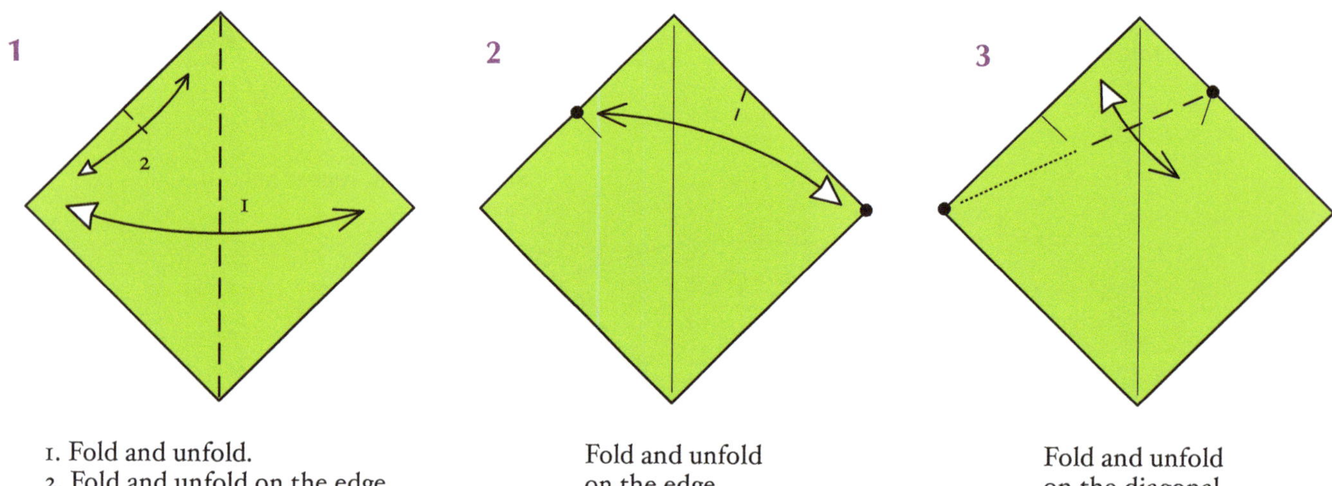

1. Fold and unfold.
2. Fold and unfold on the edge.

2. Fold and unfold on the edge.

3. Fold and unfold on the diagonal.

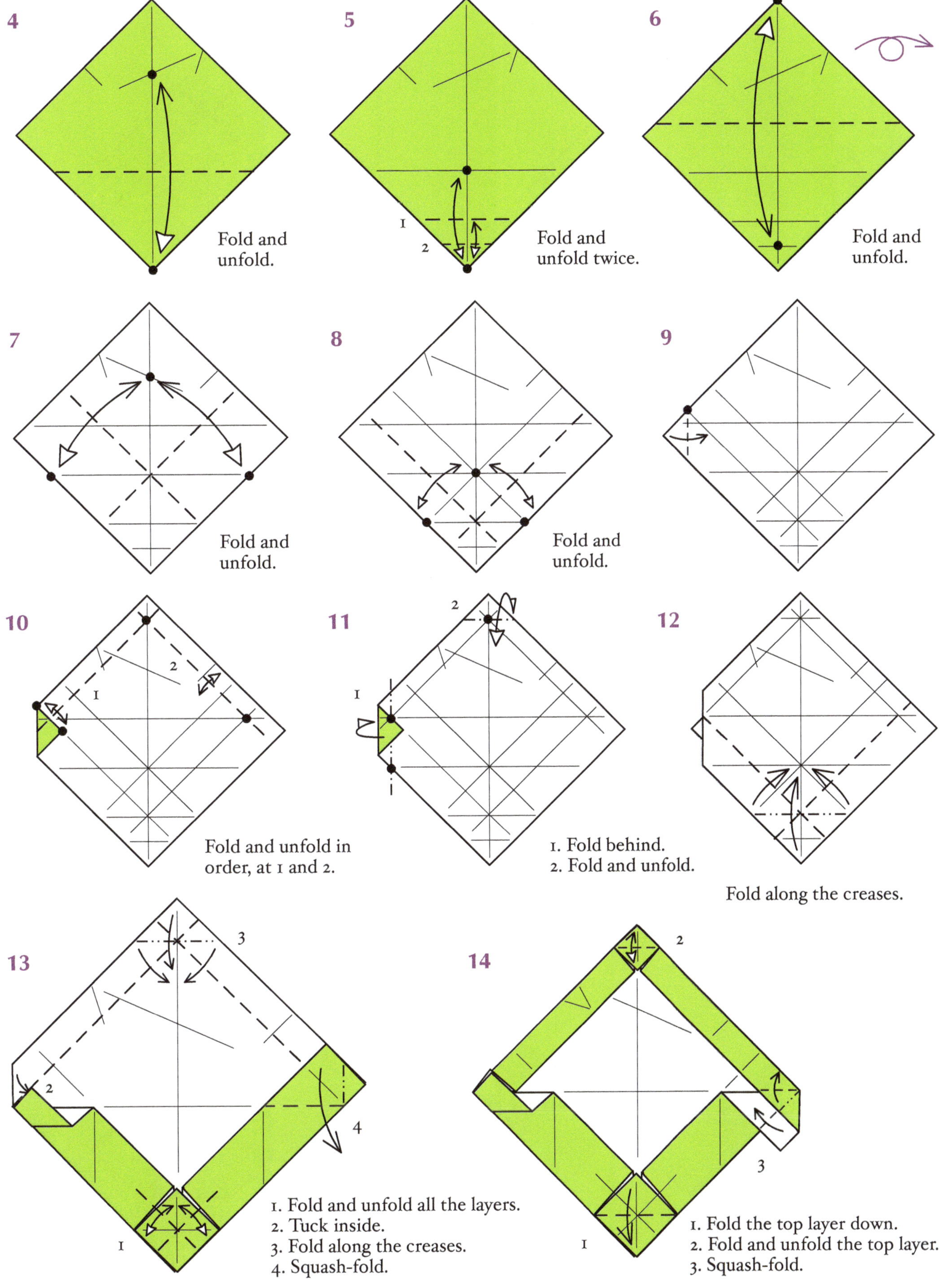
4
Fold and unfold.
5
1
2
Fold and unfold twice.
6
Fold and unfold.
7
Fold and unfold.
8
Fold and unfold.
9
10
1
2
Fold and unfold in order, at 1 and 2.
11
1
2
1. Fold behind.
2. Fold and unfold.
12
Fold along the creases.
13
1
2
3
4
1. Fold and unfold all the layers.
2. Tuck inside.
3. Fold along the creases.
4. Squash-fold.
14
1
2
3
1. Fold the top layer down.
2. Fold and unfold the top layer.
3. Squash-fold.

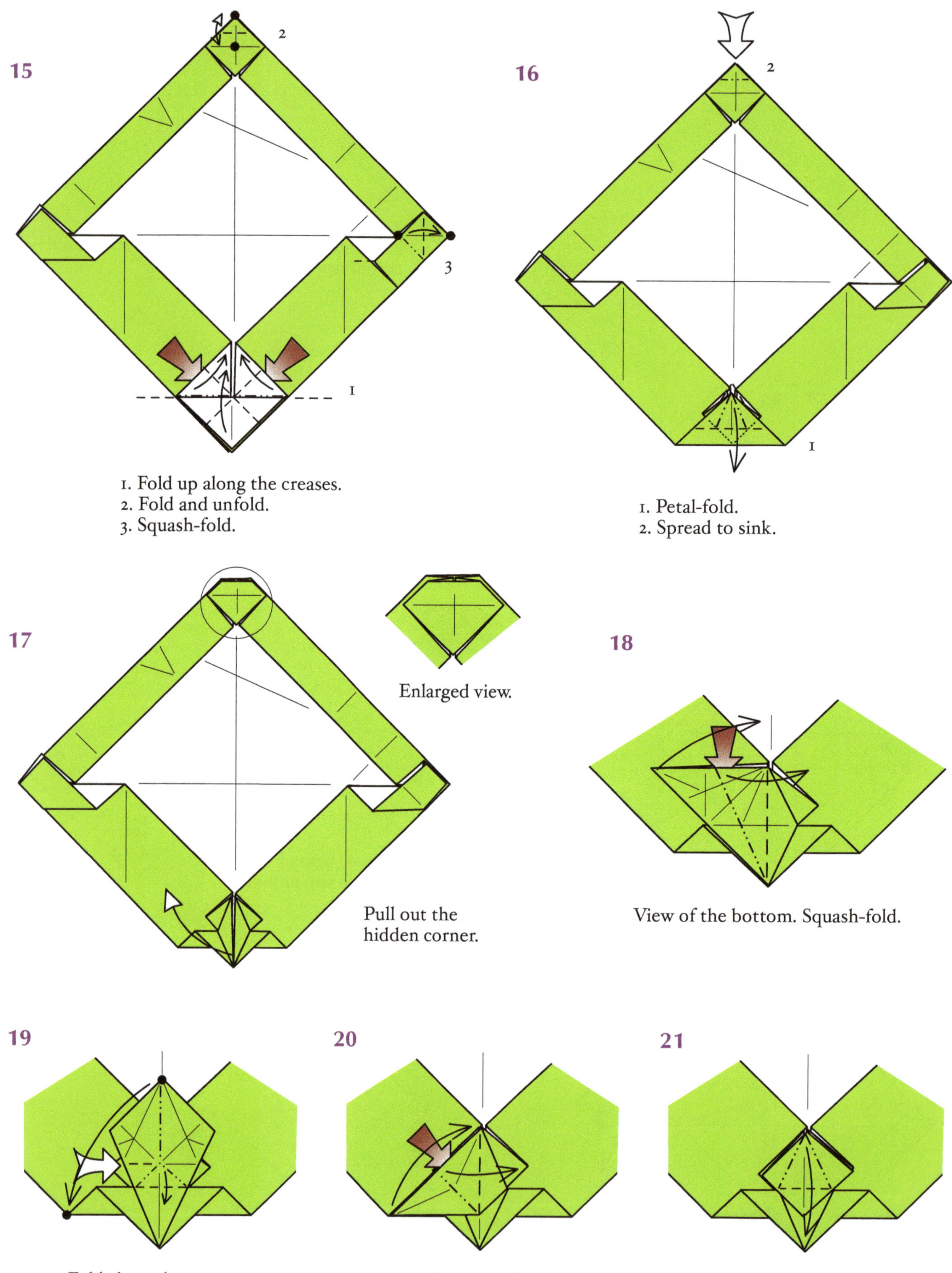

1. Fold up along the creases.
2. Fold and unfold.
3. Squash-fold.

1. Petal-fold.
2. Spread to sink.

Pull out the hidden corner.

View of the bottom. Squash-fold.

Fold along the creases.

Squash-fold.

Petal-fold.

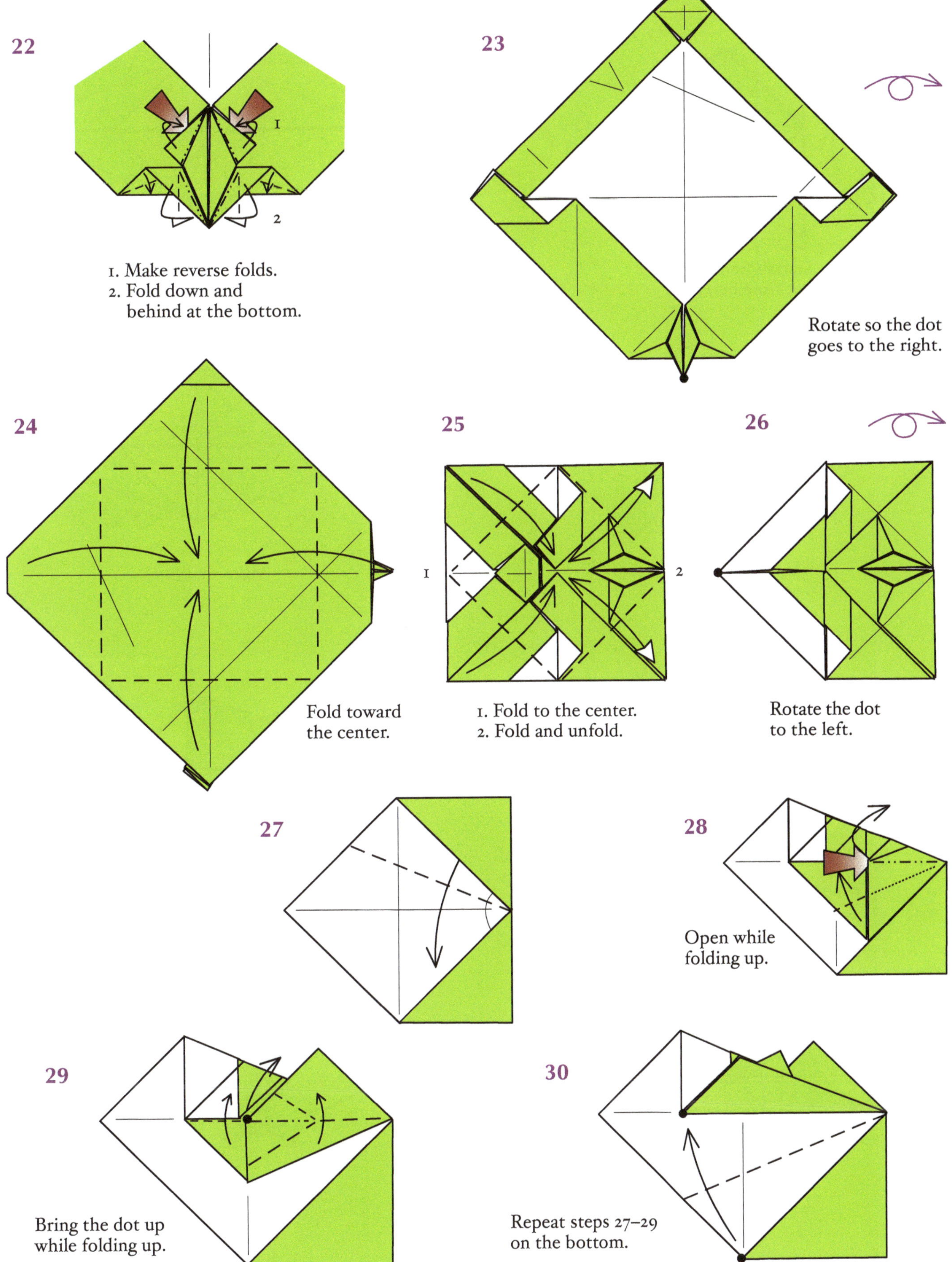
22
1
2
1. Make reverse folds.
2. Fold down and behind at the bottom.
23
Rotate so the dot goes to the right.
24
Fold toward the center.
25
1
2
1. Fold to the center.
2. Fold and unfold.
26
Rotate the dot to the left.
27
28
Open while folding up.
29
Bring the dot up while folding up.
30
Repeat steps 27–29 on the bottom.

31

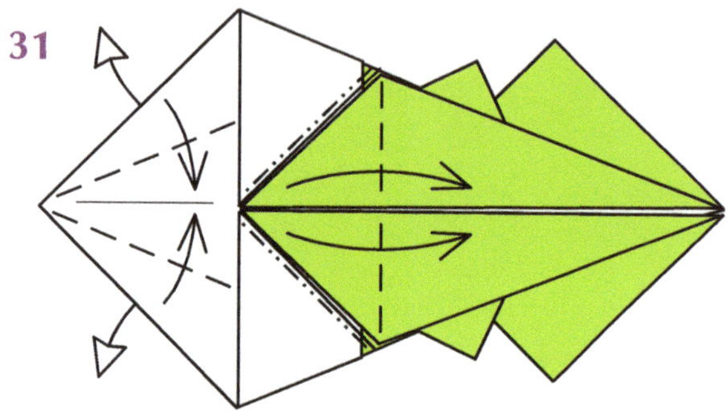

Squash-fold and swing out from behind.

32

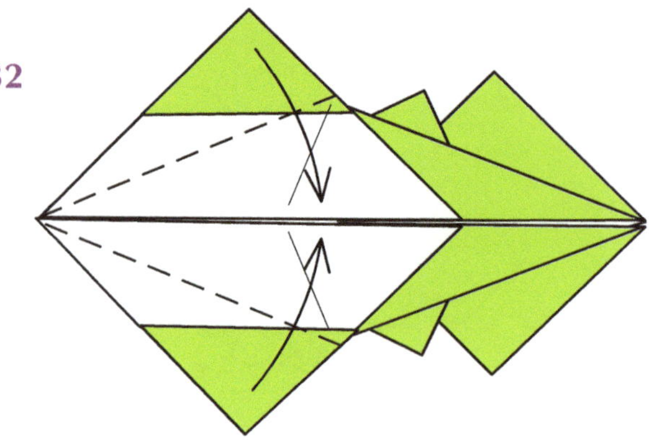

Fold to the center.

33

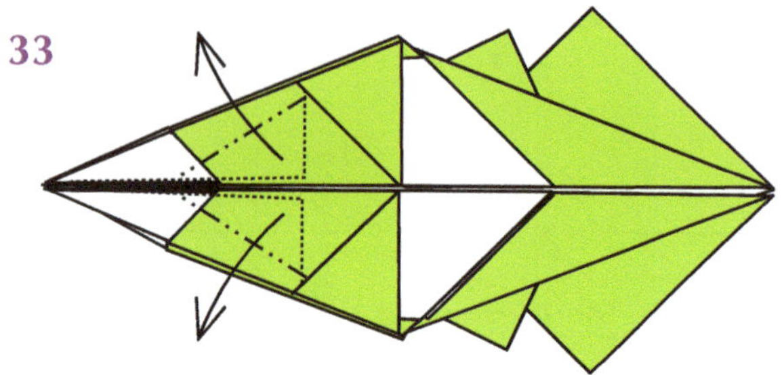

Make reverse folds on the inner layers.

34

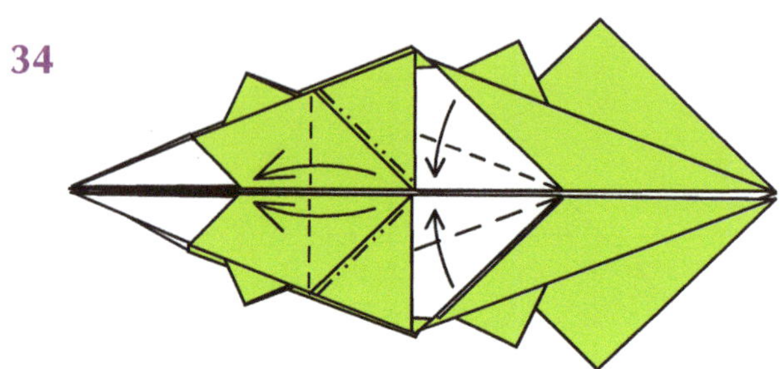

Make squash folds.

35

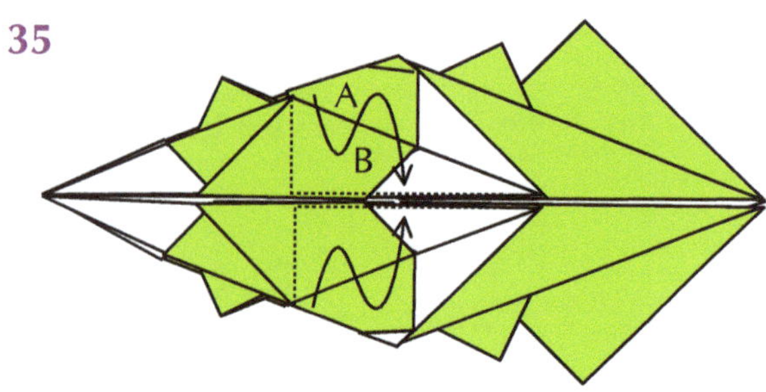

Wrap around so region A covers B.

36

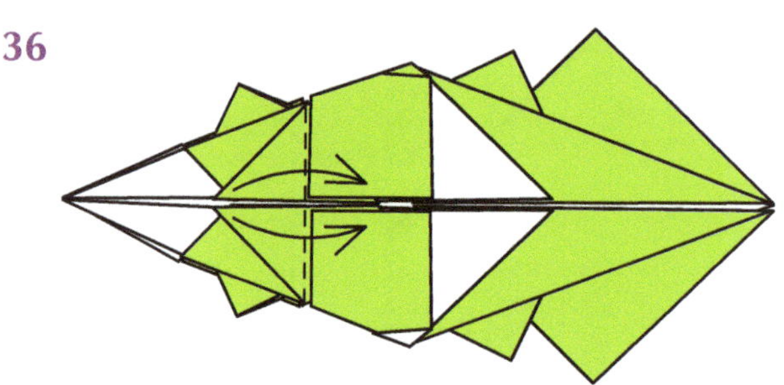

Fold to the right.

37

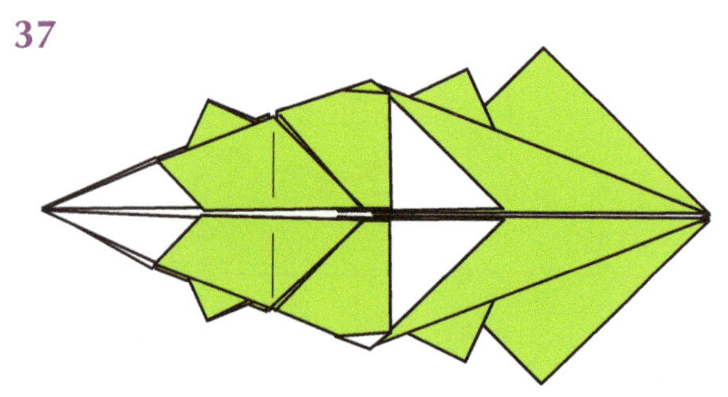

38

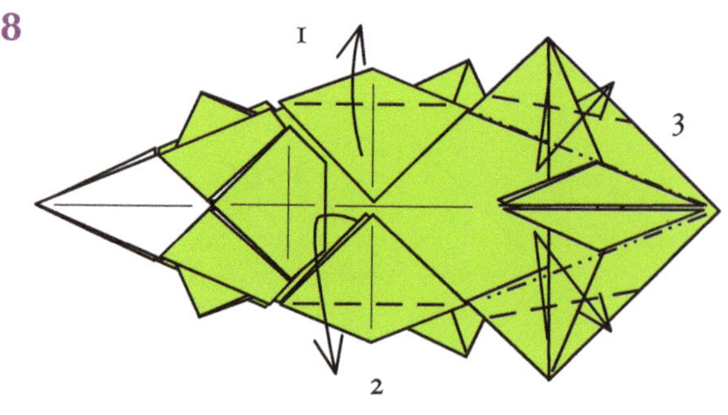

1. Fold the top flap.
2. Fold two flaps.
2. Make crimp folds.

39

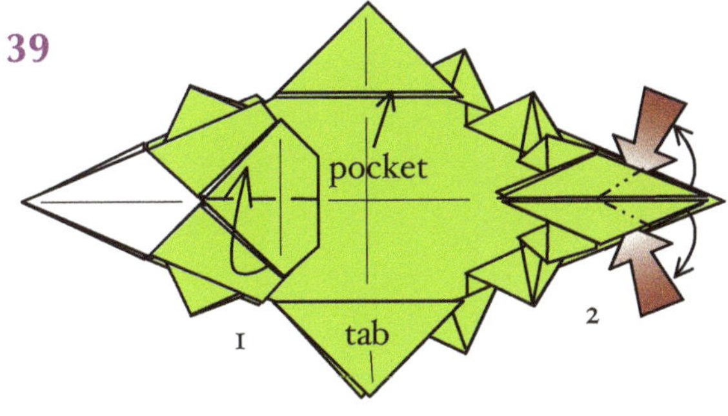

Note the pocket at the top, and the tab at the bottom.
1. Fold up.
2. Make reverse folds.

40

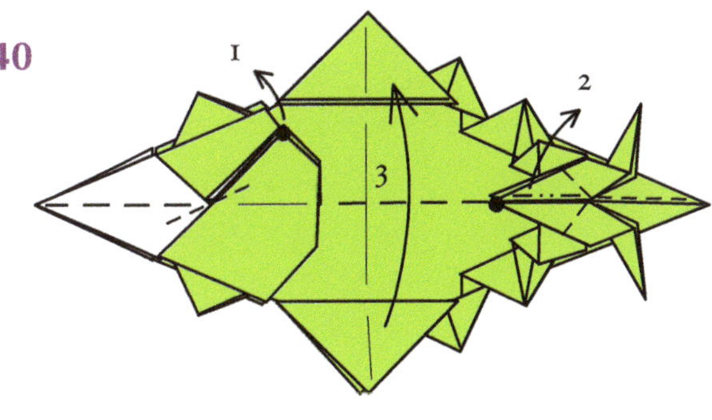

Lift up at the dots while folding in half.
1. Slide the two plates up.
2. Fold the top flap up.
3. Fold in half.

41

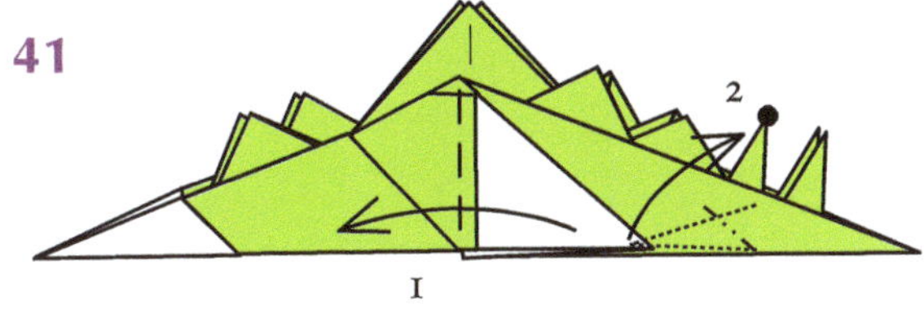

1. Fold the leg, repeat behind.
2. Reverse-fold so the spike will be on top of the one with the dot.

42

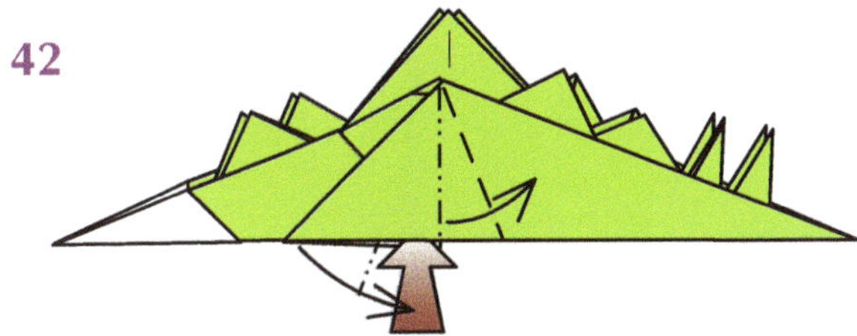

Crimp-fold, repeat behind.

43

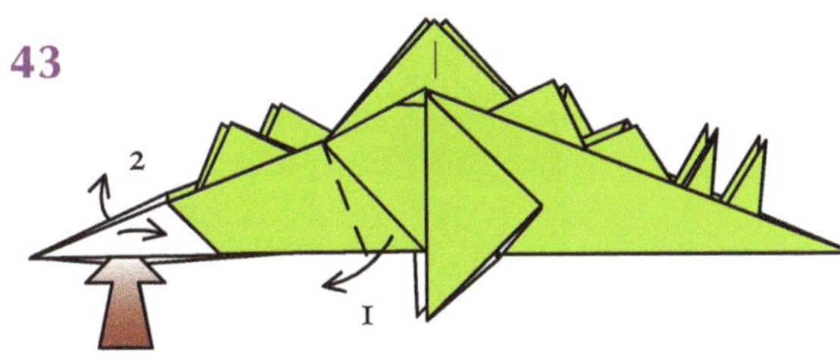

1. Fold the leg, repeat behind.
2. Push up and spread the head.

44

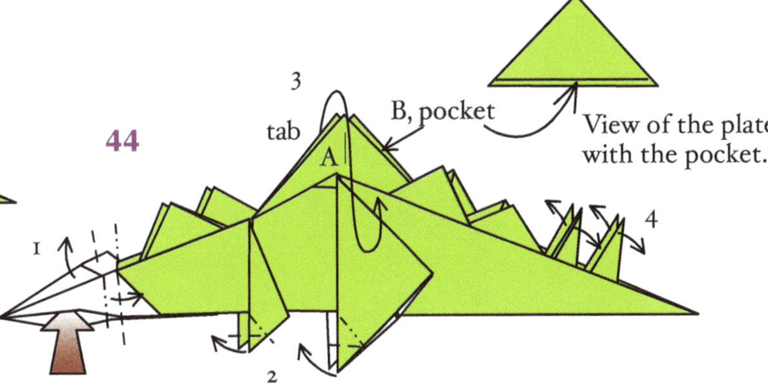

1. The head is 3D. Push in, pull out at the top and flatten with a crimp fold.
2. Make pleat folds, repeat behind.
3. Tuck the tab into the pocket so the model will hold.
4. Slide the four spikes so they make a V in 3D, aiming left and right.

45

Stegosaurus

www.ingramcontent.com/pod-product-compliance
Ingram Content Group UK Ltd.
Pitfield, Milton Keynes, MK11 3LW, UK
UKHW050143280726
14058UKWH00006B/812

9 781877 656774